Julian Hawthorne

Hawthorne's History of the United States

from the landing of Columbus to the signing of the peace protocol with Spain - Vol. 3

Julian Hawthorne

Hawthorne's History of the United States
from the landing of Columbus to the signing of the peace protocol with Spain - Vol. 3

ISBN/EAN: 9783337234904

Printed in Europe, USA, Canada, Australia, Japan

Cover: Foto ©ninafisch / pixelio.de

More available books at **www.hansebooks.com**

ENGAGEMENT OF THE "KEARSARGE" AND "ALABAMA," JUNE 19, 1864

UNITED STATES

*FROM THE LANDING OF COLUMBUS TO
THE SIGNING OF THE PEACE
PROTOCOL WITH SPAIN*

BY

JULIAN HAWTHORNE

IN THREE VOLUMES

ILLUSTRATED

VOL. III

NEW YORK
PETER FENELON COLLIER
MDCCCXCVIII

CONTENTS OF VOLUME THREE

CHAPTER		PAGE
XXVII.	EXTREMES	769
XXVIII.	GREAT MEN AND SMALL DEEDS	798
XXIX.	MEXICO	833
XXX.	THE LAST OF THE WHIGS	864
XXXI.	KANSAS	885
XXXII.	JOHN BROWN	908
XXXIII.	BULL RUN	934
XXXIV.	THE MISSISSIPPI AND THE POTOMAC	964
XXXV.	THROUGH THE VALLEY OF DEATH	997
XXXVI.	PAST AND FUTURE	1029

SUPPLEMENT

WAR WITH SPAIN 1057

LIST OF ILLUSTRATIONS

VOLUME THREE

JEFFERSON DAVIS

LIEUTENANT-GEN. WINFIELD SCOTT, U.S.A.

MAJOR-GEN. JOHN C. FREMONT, U.S.A.

ABRAHAM LINCOLN

MAJOR-GEN. GEORGE B. MCCLELLAN, U.S.A.

ULYSSES S. GRANT

ENGAGEMENT OF UNION AND CONFEDERATE GUNBOATS AT MEMPHIS, 1862

THE BATTLE OF SHILOH, APRIL 7, 1862

FIVE CONFEDERATE COMMANDERS

FIVE UNION GENERALS

FARRAGUT'S FLEET ENGAGING THE BATTERIES AT PORT HUDSON, MARCH, 1863

FARRAGUT'S FLEET ENGAGING THE ENEMY, NEAR NEW ORLEANS, APRIL 26, 1864 . . . .
FARRAGUT'S FLEET ENGAGING FORTS JACKSON AND ST. PHILIP, APRIL 24, 1862 . . . .
ADMIRAL DAVID G. FARRAGUT, U.S.N. . . . .
ENGAGEMENT OF THE "MONITOR" AND "MERRIMAC," MARCH 9, 1862 .
GEN. ROBERT E. LEE. C.S.A. . . . .
THE BATTLE OF ANTIETAM, SEPTEMBER 16 AND 17, 1862 . . . .
MAJOR-GEN. T. J. JACKSON, C.S.A. . . . .
SIEGE OF VICKSBURG—CHARGING THE CONFEDERATE WORKS, MAY 19, 1863 . . . .
UNION ATTACK ON FREDRICKSBURG, VA., NOVEMBER 12, 1862 . .
BATTLE OF CHATTANOOGA—THE UNION ADVANCE, NOVEMBER 25, 1863 .
BATTLE OF GETTYSBURG. JULY 1, 2, AND 3, 1863 . . . . .
GENERAL W. T. SHERMAN . . . .
MAJOR-GEN. JOHN A. LOGAN, U.S.A. . . . .
THE FIGHT AT SPOTTSYLVANIA COURT HOUSE, VA., MAY 10, 1864—THE ATTACK ON THE CONFEDERATE LEFT . . . . . .
"SHERIDAN'S RIDE"—CEDAR CREEK, NEAR WINCHESTER, VA., OCTOBER 19, 1864 . . . .
BATTLE OF MOBILE BAY—FARRAGUT'S FLEET ENGAGING FORT MORGAN, AUGUST 5, 1864 . . . .
ENGAGEMENT OF THE "HARTFORD" AND "TENNESSEE," AUG. 5, 1864 .
BOMBARDMENT OF FORT FISHER, N. C., BY ADMIRAL PORTER'S FLEET, DECEMBER, 1864 . . . .
CAPTURE OF FORT FISHER. N. C.—THE ASSAULT, JANUARY, 1865 . .
BATTLE OF SPOTTSYLVANIA, MAY 12, 1864 . . . .
MAJOR-GEN. PHILIP H. SHERIDAN, U.S.A. . . . .
ENGAGEMENT OF THE "KEARSARGE" AND "ALABAMA," JUNE 19, 1864 .
DESTRUCTION OF THE "MAINE," FEBRUARY 15, 1898 . . . .
SHORTENING SAIL ON U. S. CRUISER "LANCASTER," THE OLDEST VESSEL IN THE SPANISH-AMERICAN WAR . . . .
ROOSEVELT'S "ROUGH RIDERS" IN ACTION, NEAR SANTIAGO, CUBA, JUNE, 1898 . . . .
ADMIRAL SAMPSON'S FLEET SALUTING AT GRANT'S TOMB, AUG. 20, 1898

HAWTHORNE'S
HISTORY OF THE UNITED STATES

VOLUME THREE

with outlawed fugitives from other tribes, prompted a retaliation, by which a boatload of forty persons were surprised and massacred, the women being scalped and the children murdered by having their brains dashed out against the side of the boat. This called for active measures; and Andrew Jackson, the hero of New Orleans, was the man for the work, and more than ready and able to perform it.

The Seminoles—whose name means wanderers—had no fixed abode, but their fastness was in the Florida Everglades; and they claimed that the cession of lands which followed the Creek war was not binding. Of course their position on the borders of American and Spanish territory, and their retreat into the latter when attacked in force, made war against them difficult, if one would avoid all possibility of international complications; but Jackson was the man of all others who would decline to be bound by spider-web scruples of this kind, when his fighting blood was up. It was not for this reason that he had been selected by Monroe for the work; but because Monroe admired and trusted him, and because he was the only soldier in the region able to command an important expedition. Jackson had fretted under the incubus of Spanish treachery, enmity, and intrigue, and saw plainly enough that they had no business, from a common-sensible and humanitarian point of view, to occupy a province which they ruled evilly when they ruled it at all. Before he received his orders from the War Department he wrote a letter to Monroe, in which he proposed that leave should be given him, unofficially if necessary, to not only chastise the Seminoles, but to wrest the Floridas from Spain. This letter reached Monroe when he was ill; he handed it to Calhoun, who reported it to have relation to the proposed campaign; and Monroe, after asking whether Jackson's orders had been transmitted to him, and being told they had, laid the letter aside unread and forgot about it. But Jackson supposed that its contents were known to the President, and tacitly approved by him; and though his instructions were explicit in warning him not to commit any act which could be regarded as hostile to Spain, he concluded that he would be safe in following his own plans. His campaign was brief in the extreme, and very moderate in point of bloodshed; but it came very near to involving us in war with England, not to speak of Spain; and its influence on the politics of the United States was unexpected and curious. The Seminoles, upon Jackson's approach with a relatively large army, fled to the Everglades, and were not seen again; but Jackson marched straight into Spanish territory, and demanded and received the surrender of the Spanish post of St. Marc's, and later of Pensacola, the Spanish commanders protesting in vain, but attempting no forcible resistance. But in addition to these irregularities, the stern general executed a brace of British subjects whom he captured, one of whom was a young English ex-officer named Ambrister, who was convicted by court-martial of having acted as a spy, and the other was an elderly trader of Scotch birth who seemed to have been a plotter with the Seminoles against America. Ambrister was shot, and Arbuthnot, the trader, was hanged; he died declaring that his country would avenge his death; but in this prophecy he was mistaken. The court-martial which condemned Ambrister to be shot afterward modified its verdict to a whipping and imprisonment; but Jackson restored the original penalty, and it was carried out. Jackson then marched his army back again, and disbanded it.

This was the Seminole War. The government, on learning the facts, disavowed the acts of its general, so far as they transgressed international law; yet it protected him so far as was possible; and John Quincy Adams, Secretary of State, who always stood Jackson's friend, in his dispatches to Spain and England, defended him with great skill and ardor; and so successfully that Spain, having her posts returned to her, decided to say no more about the irregularities, and went on with the negotiations for sale; and

England, though Jackson was denounced as a murderer in London, refused to go to war, preferring to disown the acts of Ambrister and Arbuthnot, and to regard them as having forfeited their allegiance before their execution.

But Clay took another view of the matter, and was instrumental in bringing on the Seminole debate in Congress, the object being to pass a resolution condemning the general for his acts—though England and Spain had both professed themselves satisfied. Clay was sincere in his disapproval; nevertheless he was undoubtedly moved to his opinion largely by political considerations; he thought Jackson could easily be suppressed, and quite underrated his popularity in the country. He made a lifelong enemy of Jackson, and he felt the fatal effects of it later, when Jackson, contrary to all calculation, came into power. He made an eloquent speech; Calhoun and Adams spoke for Jackson; and Congress gave its verdict in favor of the latter. The common people made the warrior their hero, and the division of the country into two new parties was foreshadowed by the terms Jacksonites and anti-Jacksonites, or Democrats and Whigs, which began to be heard at this time. The democratic element in America had indeed begun to be conscious of itself; that lower class of the population which resented more or less obviously the pretensions of the wealthier classes to assume the reins of government. Many of them were recent emigrants, who had known only the despotic rule of European governments, and thought that any government must be despotic, and should be resisted and weakened, or if possible destroyed. Allied with them was that great substratum of humble citizens who had hardly thought of taking an active hand in the conduct of affairs, but who saw in Jackson a man like unto themselves, without known parentage or place of birth, who had not the less made himself powerful and conspicuous by his unaided talents and original force. Jackson was of Scotch-Irish blood, and had the Celtic temperament well developed; in temper, principles and habits of thought he was thoroughly of the people; he believed in no friendship that was not personal to himself, without regard to rights or wrongs of policy; he wore his heart upon his sleeve, was easily flattered, was rude and headlong in speech, fiery in temper, and implacable so long as his self-esteem was touched. Yet he was less unable than he seemed to exercise a certain dissimulation and shrewdness, and would enter into any scheme that was not plainly dishonest to undo an opponent. His outward bearing and aspect had however been a good deal modified by success and fame, and he was a much more possible person in polite society than he had originally been. He had the Celtic chivalry toward women, and was a favorite with them; and his unquestionable genius and force of character made him influential with men who were far above him in education and social station. It was right and inevitable that such a man should exist and come to the front in our country; he represented much that is vital in us, and will always have its due weight. The memory of him can never be eradicated from among us; Jacksonian democracy means as much to-day as it did eighty years ago. He was markedly different from Jefferson, the democrat of the aristocracy; he was made of fewer elements, and was of almost infinitely simpler structure; but his effect in the American world was hardly less pronounced. Just such another individual can never appear again; but that which he represented can never die out of our population; it disregards or tramples upon precedent and traditions, sees the essential point, and grasps it, fears nothing, and astonishes all orthodox and conventional folks; while its success, once it sets itself to gain an object, surpasses all anticipation and record. It has many faults, but its virtues are immense; and for a time it is the death of humbug and pretense of all kinds.

After his vindication, during the progress of which he had been a violently interested attendant at Washington, and had nearly got into several duels and affrays, he started on a sort of triumphal tour of the country, and was received with popular enthusiasm of the most unmistakable kind. The patricians might slight him, but he had the masses with him, and perceived no deficiency in his welcome; indeed, those who held themselves aloof were very careful not to do so in an openly offensive manner; for it had become evident that Jackson was not a man to be insulted with impunity. No one at that time, probably, had serious thoughts of him as a presidential possibility; he might even have laughed at the idea himself; for the elegance and austere correctness of the Washingtonian tradition still hung about the chief office of the government; but things were beginning to move fast in America, and opinion was dividing and expanding in a way that already made nothing seem quite impossible.—Meanwhile, in 1819, the treaty ceding Florida to the United States was signed, and the money, five million dollars, paid to Spain; and common opinion connected the transaction with Jackson's campaign, and gave him the credit of it. When a man has once begun to be the popular idol, whatever happens seems to make his pedestal a little higher.

The internal affairs of the country had seemed to be in a most favorable condition; but the appearance was to some extent deceptive, due to ignorance of the real causes which were at work. There was a surplus in the treasury after setting aside a certain amount for paying the interest and an installment of the principal of the public debt. Some taxes were repealed, rather prematurely. Commerce was diminished by the great inrush of foreign commodities; and the policy of protecting infant industries, concerning which we have heard so much ever since, already was under consideration, Clay being prominent among its advocates. The attempt to bring about a reciprocal repeal of discriminating duties with Europe was not very successful. But if commerce was falling off, agriculture was doing well, and manufactures were showing an immense stimulus, especially in

New England, which found here a recompense for the decline of her maritime prosperity. In the absence of strongly marked issues, the Republican party was subsiding as a distinct phenomenon, not because it had been defeated, but because its triumph had been so general. It had brought the nation to a realization of itself and had cut it loose from Europe; and now, almost every one being a Republican, the time was at hand for them to subdivide into other things. But what these were to be was still a secret of destiny.

The most remarkable event of 1817 was the beginning of the Erie Canal, which had long been a pet project of De Witt Clinton, and is due to his persistence and energy; it was the most wonderful enterprise of the kind yet undertaken, and was of immense benefit in opening the country and creating flourishing towns in the interior. Other national improvements were withheld on account of the doubt as to how they were to be carried out with due regard to the Constitution; and discussions on this point led, not to amendments, but to stretching the letter of the Constitution in order to make it cover cases which were assumed to accord with its spirit. This was a dangerous precedent, for there was no line to be drawn; but it prevailed for sixty years.—In Massachusetts and in Connecticut changes of political conditions occurred, tending to emancipate these states from the influence of the old regime. The campaign in Connecticut was especially picturesque, old John Cotton Smith being defeated after a tremendous contest, with all the antiquated ways and opinions which he stood for. In this fight, religious heretics joined the Republicans, and swept the state.

Monroe's first term was remarkable for the increase in colleges which took place during the four years; the greatest novelty among them was a female college founded at Troy, New York, by Mrs. Willard. Missionary and Bible Societies had already been started; Lundy's anti-slavery association had existed since 1815. A new departure of a different kind was the first crossing of the Atlantic by a steam vessel, the

"Savannah," in the year 1819. Four new states were admitted to the Union from 1817 to 1820 inclusive: Mississippi, Illinois, Alabama and Maine: but thereby hangs a tale. In the meanwhile the flush of prosperity had been succeeded by a couple of years of financial panic.

The proximate cause of this was the proceedings of the United States Bank. It was discovered that this institution had been mismanaged to such a degree that no one could tell where the bottom of the defalcation would be found. Many of the branches were joined in the trouble, especially that in Baltimore; a town which for some years had seemed to rise on the top wave of financial success. The rumors were followed by wholesale resignations of bank directors; and a Congressional committee was appointed to make a thorough investigation. Spencer, an able young lawyer, was put at the head of the committee, and he worked with great industry, and without respect of consequences. His report showed a vast mass of iniquities, the result in some cases of ignorance, but mostly of deliberate dishonesty. The evil spread over all the states, except those of New England, which had maintained a specie basis. The question was, whether to stop the bank, or to remodel it; the latter course was taken. Men of tried integrity and knowledge were put at the head of the business, and their efforts presently cleared up the situation, and showed that within a few years the bank would be on its feet again. Langdon Cheves was made president, and the chief director was Nicholas Biddle. The investigation had created many bitter enmities; but it had served as a warning and an enlightenment to the community, and the mania for speculation, encouraged by the paper system, was not likely to be soon repeated.

But the experience had sobered our ideas as to the solidity of the basis of our welfare, and made the men in Congress more solicitous as to the future. When consequently the question as to the balance of power between the free and the slave states began to come to the front, there was evi-

order to minimize risks, and captains did not hesitate to throw the wretched creatures overboard when too closely pursued. The traffic bred a band of scoundrels as black as any that ever existed; and the feeling against slavery among the inhabitants of the states which had no slaves became correspondingly strengthened; while the slaveholders were to some extent driven to defend what they would otherwise have joined in denouncing. Thus there was sure to be much animosity in the struggle which could no longer be deferred: and with a less solid-standing President than Monroe, might have led the country further than it did.

The South had altered greatly, since 1776, in their attitude toward slavery. They had at first regarded it as a lamentable imposition derived from English tyranny, to be got rid of at the first opportunity. But after living with it and by it for forty years, they had insensibly grown to love it. In the first place, it was the condition of their wealth; for it was thought impossible for white men to labor as slaves did under a southern sun. No one, either South or North, would be willing to beggar himself for the sake of a humanitarian sentiment; or if such an individual could be found, certainly a state could not. Suggestions had from time to time been made that there should be emancipation, with national compensation; but it had never borne fruit. It had also been attempted to get the blacks out of the country and settle them in some remote colony by themselves; and it was a partial carrying-out of this scheme which created the African colony of Liberia; but it had no appreciable effect in solving the slave problem. Gradual emancipation had also failed; and the presence of free blacks in slave states was found objectionable, and they were required to go elsewhere under penalties; nor was there lacking opposition to the settling of free blacks from the North in slave states, though, as their freedom made them citizens, and the Constitution allows a citizen to enjoy equal rights in every state, this prohibition could not lawfully be enforced:—but as

dence that it would lead to serious opposition of views. Up to the time of the admission of the twenty-second state, the equilibrium had been preserved; eleven of them were slave, eleven free. But now arose the question of the admission of the vast territory then called Missouri, which covered most of the Louisiana cession. It was proposed to carve out of it a state extending from the meeting point of the Mississippi and Missouri Rivers, southward to the present Arkansas. The representatives from the slave states wished this to be given over to slavery; but the Northern men, through Tallmadge, a New Yorker, as their chief spokesman, opposed it firmly; and when Cobb of Georgia declared that a "fire had been kindled which all the waters of the ocean cannot put out, and which only seas of blood can extinguish," Tallmadge replied, "If civil war, which gentlemen so much threaten, must come, I can only say, let it come. If blood is necessary to extinguish any fire which I have assisted to kindle, while I regret the necessity, I shall not hesitate to contribute my own." The upshot of this first debate on Missouri was, that the bill for admitting it was lost; but the matter of course came up in the next session.

There had been no debate on slavery since 1808, when the law prohibiting further importation of slaves from Africa was put in force. This law had ostensibly been obeyed; but, with the large increase in our population, which now numbered over ten millions, there was room in the South for more slaves than the natural increase of the negroes supplied; and consequently a good deal of surreptitious importation had been going on, much of it under the shelter of the Spanish and Portuguese flags, which readily sold themselves to this disgraceful device. But England had kept up strenuous efforts to put down the traffic, and the American government seconded her; and finally Spain and Portugal themselves had nominally joined with them. The more difficult the trade became, the greater were its horrors, since the cargoes were now crowded into almost impossible space, in

a matter of fact, free blacks had no desire to settle in slave states, so this point was theoretical only. Finally, a plan of Jefferson's to let slavery die out by removing black children from their parents, and taking them, say to San Domingo, was never seriously contemplated.

But the most cogent circumstance that bound the Southerners to slavery was the mode of life and the personal habits and prejudices which it had engendered. The slaves had inflicted slavery on their masters. The latter had insensibly come to confound the idea of labor with that of servitude; and thought it as derogatory for a white man to work with his hands, as to have the overseer's whip laid across his back. They conceived that to be a gentleman one must have slaves; they took pride in them as proofs of gentility; and they acquired those overbearing and despotic manners which are natural to men who exercise irresponsible power over their fellow creatures; nor is it surprising that such men should wear the same haughty bearing in their intercourse with the free white men of the North, in Congress and elsewhere. The fact that this conception of what belongs to a gentleman was based on a preposterous fallacy did not render it less prevalent or emphatic, and on the other hand, it did really create a lordly and charming society, with customs and traditions which endeared it to itself in an extreme and even passionate degree. It was an anachronism, especially in America; and it grew out of a social crime; but, in a sense, no one of the slaveholding community was to blame for it, and its darker side was hidden from Southerners, who either could not or would not discern it. That they knew the weight of civilized opinion condemned them, of course made them cling to their Peculiar Institution more firmly; we all resent a profession of superior virtue in our fellows.

Under these circumstances the second Missouri debate began. Pinckney spoke in support of admitting slavery into Missouri, and Rufus King opposed him. Pinckney—

who might be termed, in respect of artful finish of seemingly extempore oratory, the Pinckney of perfection—spun a glittering web of subtle sophistries; he was the ideal of the elderly exquisite; his eloquence was of the school later made famous by Edward Everett. King was his counterpart; grave, simple, but poignant, and having wholly the best of the argument. The American government had purchased Missouri territory with the nation's money; it had the right to dispose of it as it pleased; and yet the South was denying it the liberty to decide what social institutions it should establish there. If Pinckney's contention were true, then the Missourians might have licensed not slavery only, but free-love, or thuggism. But logic does but seldom decide matters of this kind; circumstances may diminish the weight of the most impenetrable argument. As a matter of fact, Missouri was settled, or to be settled, by a population derived from slave states, and desirous of keeping slaves; and if the government used its Constitutional power to defeat their wishes, there would probably be resistance and revolt. The way to harmony was by compromise. It might have been better, or as well, to have fought the quarrel out then, instead of waiting forty years; but the statesmen of 1820 did not think so.

An attempt was made to get the Missouri bill through by tacking it on the bill for the admission of Maine, which was to be made a state by severing it from Massachusetts; in this way, Missouri would have been admitted without restrictions as to its constitution. But the scheme failed; and the compromise finally accepted was, that slavery, except in Missouri, should be prohibited north of the line 36° 30′. Clay's persuasive powers were ardently exerted for this end, and he may claim such credit as attaches to bringing about its acceptance. The debate became a loadstone to fashion, and the halls of legislature were so filled with women that John Randolph, on one occasion, true to his custom of improving every chance for increasing his humorous notoriety, called attention to their presence, and declared that they would better be at home at their knitting. But women would have their way in this country, both then and since.

The Compromise put off the evil day, but only made its final coming more certain. For to the south and west of us there was a great expanse of territory under the nominal dominion of Spain, which could not fail to be coveted by Southerners as a field for the increase of their possessions and power. The most obvious possible acquisition was the enormous region called Texas, to which we had some shadow of claim as being part of the Louisiana cession. But Monroe perceived that were Texas admitted, either by cession or conquest, it would precipitate the calamity which the Missouri Compromise had postponed; the East could never permit so large a weight to be thrown into the Southern balance. He wished neither party to the controversy to win an overwhelming triumph; as our possessions in the northwest were augmented, it might become safe to enlarge our boundaries in the southwest also; but there was time enough for that. His decision was that of a wise and impartial statesman.

The new population now began to pour into Missouri, in rather a defiant frame of mind. The constitution which they framed contained two objectionable provisions:—That the legislature should be forbidden to interfere with slavery; and that free negroes should be forbidden to settle in the state. The latter article, being against the stipulation of the Constitution of the United States, that a citizen could live in any of the states, was made the ground of attack. The joint resolution admitting Missouri had still to pass, and gave the opening for debate. After much talk, another compromise was devised; the clause excluding free blacks was not to be construed as authorizing any law abridging the rights of citizens. It was little better than a verbal quibble; but it served the purpose of sparing the Missourians' pride; while there was no real prospect that free blacks would ever wish to make Missouri their home. In truth, all concerned were glad to get out of the scrape on any decent or plausible terms; and it was tacitly agreed that slavery should nevermore be mentioned by either party. There was worldly wisdom in the agreement; but such things are never final. If slavery were wrong, it could not be killed by ignoring it. A man might as well expect to get rid of consumption by schooling himself to take no notice of its ravages in his lungs.—Randolph and a few of his followers were irreconcilable; but they were not strong enough to require attention.

National credit was improving; but the need of strict economy was felt, and such projects as coast defense and exploration in the west were suspended. The appropriations for army and navy were reduced. It was generally felt that the administration had done well, and Monroe and Tompkins were re-elected for a second term. Indeed, a safer or more honorable and unselfish Executive it would be hard to find. Monroe was the last of the Revolutionary presidential timber, and with him were to disappear also some of the best qualities of our earlier rulers. His ideal of the true functions of his office had grown higher as time went on, so that he presented the rare spectacle of a politician ending his career on a loftier plane than he began it on. One who knew him well said of him that his soul "might be turned wrong side outward without discovering a blemish." His successor would be chosen on no party issue, for there no longer was one in our politics; but on grounds of personal power and influence; and thus the way was open for underhand intrigue, which the make-up of the Seventeenth Congress favored. There had never yet been a time when the aims of the mass of men in public life had been more petty and personal; and the transactions of Congress were trifling and unimportant.

Nevertheless, there were men of parts among the Presidential aspirants. Of these, John Quincy Adams, Calhoun, Clay and Jackson were the most conspicuous; Crawford, the self-seeking intriguer, was also a strong runner for the goal, but was destined to disappointment, which he well deserved. Another man who made vigorous efforts was De Witt Clinton; but his chances were never equal to his conviction of his political merits. Clay did not at this time make a serious struggle; he believed that his time would surely come later. Calhoun was suddenly attacked by the Presidential ambition, but he was young enough to wait. He was a singular person, of a certain profundity of mind, eloquent, fascinating and weighty; and his aims were, at the outset of his career, broad and generous, and free from local bias. But it is noticeable that though he charmed all, and his most intimate friends spoke highly of his parts, yet he was not deeply trusted; there were hidden depths in him, which he never unveiled. Ambition was his bane; and as time went on, it ate into his heart, and put bitterness and strangeness where there had been gentle and humane feelings. He had a noble intellect, but his nature was less noble, and did not stand the test of political life. He became the supporter of heresies which did great harm to his country. Adams was far from being a lovable man, but he was entirely trustworthy; he had not the great, hot heart of his father, but he was far more impartial and correct in the operations and ideas of his mind. Dry, cold, repellent and pedagogic in manner, he made no friends, though no one would deny him esteem and respect; he loved none, and none loved him. He was not a man to win general popularity, and did not seem therefore a likely candidate for the Presidency; but his honor and firmness, and his great experience of public life in all its higher walks, rendered him practically available, and in the compromise of interests, and with the legislature to decide finally as between him and others, he might (as in fact he did) succeed. Another circumstance in his favor was the fact that he was a Northern man, and the North had a right to be represented in the chair of supreme authority; Virginia had contributed more than her share. As for Jackson, he was, in a curious way, a creature of accident and surprise, as well as a man of strong and salient character. No calculation of probabilities would have designated him as a possible candidate. But in one way or another, he was continually in the public eye, and in a manner that endeared him to the people. When it was necessary to select a governor for the new realm of the Floridas, Monroe, somewhat rashly, fixed upon Jackson. Jackson accepted the appointment, but with some ill-humor; his health was not good, and he had been irritated, though without adequate cause, in the matter of military promotion. Moreover, he was far from friendly toward the Spaniards, and when he found some Spanish officers still holding posts in the country, and indisposed to surrender them except after the unrolling of much red tape, his temper rose, and he acted with the arbitrary severity of an Oriental sultan. He seized the unhappy incumbents, threw them into prison, and appropriated the public documents in their charge; and he also arrested a judge who issued a writ of habeas corpus. This was technically all wrong; yet it was in harmony with the eternal fitness of things, and pleased our people much more than it did the officials who had to straighten the matter out. It is delicious, occasionally, to see a strong, honest, right-feeling man trample upon rules and customs, and going straight to his point like a cannon ball. He soon resigned his appointment, and went back to Tennessee, where his popularity was even greater than before, and whence, in that era of half men and timid measures, it spread over the country, not without artful nursing by the crusty hero's friends. His name was more than once connected with the Presidency, and every one was surprised to see how seriously it was received, and, in many quarters, with what enthusiasm. When the proper moment arrived, he was nominated as a candidate— Andrew Jackson, the Soldier, the Statesman, and the Honest Man. The man of the crowd had got on horseback, and would ride.

The most noticeable change in the aspect of the country at this period was the advance in population and power of the state of New York, and the decline of Virginia. New York had now the largest population in the Union, and her internal improvements, in the way of roads and other means of communication, had developed her back counties to a surprising degree. She was the great maritime center of the country, and would soon be the second greatest in the world, and her political affairs were in competent and energetic hands. In Virginia, on the other hand, there was no brightness in the prospect, or comfort in the present; there was nothing but the glory and pride of the past. Her great men were no more, or were soon to pass away; the men of the day were insignificant and vain. She was weighed down with her slaves, who cost her almost as much as they were worth, even upon a strictly utilitarian basis; her poor whites were a useless encumbrance, and her planters were a whisky-drinking, arrogant, degenerating class, though full of charms and winning traits of a social kind which made their generous hospitality delightful. But Virginia was already a proof of the paralyzing effect upon human development of the slave system, and she was totally lacking in the spirit which prompts men to roll up their sleeves and work for the common good. Her back counties were lapsing into the dark ages, and, compared with New York or the Eastern states, she was still in the last century.

The Erie Canal was not the only public improvement which had been begun; there was, among the most prominent enterprises, the Cumberland Road. This was a highway extending westward through the Alleghanies, and was designed to pass onward to the Mississippi, and finally to reach the Pacific coast. It had been started as a national work; but question had arisen whether such national works were constitutional. The President, after studying the subject, arrived at the conclusion that they were not, and accordingly he vetoed the bill which had been seconded by Clay and Adams, and opposed by Jackson. The veto, however, was directed rather against the principle than against the small appropriation asked for; the road had been begun, constitutionally or not, and should at least be kept in repair, pending further inquiry into constitutional rights, or possible extensions thereof. The sober second thought of the country finally justified the President's course.

The main incident of Monroe's second term was the enunciation of what is called the Monroe doctrine. Europe, alarmed at the unsettled political outlook, caused by the American and French Revolutions, which had shaken every throne, and jolted the crowns on royal brows, cast about to stay the tide of freedom, and three of the great Powers—France, Russia and Prussia—formed what is known as the Holy Alliance. Spain, in a rare burst of impatience with tyranny, had deposed Ferdinand; France assembled an army of a hundred thousand men, and restored him to his throne. It was then determined by the Alliance to extinguish the new South and Central American Republics, and make them appendages of European monarchies. England disapproved this plan, not from any desire to promote republican institutions, but in her own interests; and Canning, the English premier, proposed an Alliance to the United States. Rush, the American minister in London, replied, on the spur of the moment, that all necessary ends would be answered if England would recognize the independence of the South American governments; but this Canning declined to do. On the other hand, he would not interfere with any action which America might take. Monroe approved of Rush's attitude, and consulted with Jefferson and Madison as to what should be done. Jefferson replied, "The question is the most momentous that has been offered to my contemplation since that of Independence. That made us a nation: this sets our compass and points the course which we are to steer. And never could we embark under circumstances more auspicious. Our first and fundamental maxim should be, never to entangle ourselves in the broils of Europe. Our second, never to suffer Europe to meddle in cis-Atlantic affairs. America, north and south, has a set of interests distinct from those of Europe, and peculiarly her own. She should therefore have a system of her own, separate and apart from those of Europe. While the last is laboring to become the domicile of despotism, our endeavor should surely be to make our hemisphere that of freedom." His system contemplated "keeping out of our land all foreign powers, and never permitting those of Europe to intermeddle with the affairs of our nations." And considering that England avowed the principles of freedom, he thought that to accept her moral support in this course would be to maintain, not to depart from, the policy in question, and to make war impossible. Madison agreed with Jefferson, but suspected Canning of some ulterior designs. Monroe, thus supported, wrote his message, which immediately became and has remained one of the most famous of our state papers. It stated that America would consider any attempt on the part of the Holy Alliance to extend their system to any portion of this hemisphere as dangerous to our peace and safety; and that the American continents, by the free and independent condition which they have assumed and maintain, are henceforth not to be considered as subjects for future colonization by any European powers.

This was a momentous announcement. It would be historically foolish to maintain that it was the creation of Monroe's mind, or of that of Jefferson, or of any other individual. It formulated the feeling that had been gradually growing up throughout the Union. It was a statement of our conviction that the Americas had been set apart by Providence as the home of free institutions, in which none of the old, exhausted forms of government could be permitted to remain or to enter. Monroe had the insight and the courage to be the spokesman of this conviction. The warning against entangling alliances which Washington had given was designed as a safeguard against drifting into a position where, as a return for services rendered us by some European power, we would be constrained to allow it privileges which would compromise our political principles; it did not, and could not, prevent us from extending the American system, if opportunity offered, or circumstances demanded, to regions not included within our continental boundaries as at present described. America might incorporate Europe; but Europe must not invade America.

The message caused a sensation in Europe as well as here; and the Holy Alliance relinquished all hope of carrying out its designs on this hemisphere. The doctrine which it embodied has been much discussed since then, but the United States have never receded from their position; and the attempt of Maximilian to occupy the throne of Mexico was the only example of an endeavor to thwart our will. Such an experiment is not likely to be repeated. The message was first read before the Eighteenth Congress, in December, 1823. The power of Spain had then been abolished on the main; after seventy-five years, it is being extirpated from the West India Islands, and even from the remote Pacific.

The Eighteenth Congress contained Hayne, Van Buren, and Webster, as new members, besides Clay and others who had already made their reputation; and it contrasted favorably with the former one. In the debates on internal improvements, Clay and Webster drew toward each other; but upon a protective tariff they were opposed, Clay taking the protective side. Webster was of Federalist stock, but was independent; he as well as Clay supported a strong central power in the government. In the Presidential campaign he was against his fellow New Englander, Adams. He was the head of the Congressional judicial committee, and fathered the new Crimes Bill, which became the basis of our criminal jurisprudence. His greatness was already beginning to be apparent; and he had as yet done nothing to engender enmities. He was a man who can hardly be described save in superlatives, and the estimates of his character ring the changes on terms which sound extravagant, but probably are the only ones fitted to convey a true idea of him. Those who came under his personal influence while he was at his best, exhaust the resources of language to express the impression he produced on them. He was a demigod in the first third of the century; to his opponents, later, he was a fallen archangel. Many called him the greatest man that ever lived. The most recent views of him seem tending to renew the eulogistic vein which prevailed at his prime. He was a man of great intellectual powers, well balanced, and thoroughly trained. His nature was rich and deep, and of a largeness which made him without effort the first man in every company. He was a man on a continental scale, but without diffuseness or waste; every faculty was under the dominion of his will, and responsive to need. He was both synthetic and analytic in the quality of his mind; he grasped the whole, yet saw all the parts. He also had the instinct of sublimity, which gives appreciation of the loftiest and most general relations of things; so that when he turned his head, the world seemed to turn with it; and when he raised his arm, he seemed to signal to the stars. His personal appearance—the fashion of his head and body —were harmonious with this greatness of his mind and soul; so that there was no discordant note in the complete impression he made on the beholder. Mentally, he stood on a plane so high that he could find little company; but he was humane and kind toward others, and willing to enter into friendly relations with any who could meet him. But the trouble with a man like Webster is, that he cannot form ordinary relations with his fellows; and he cannot but be aware that nature, in making him a king of men, has isolated him. Webster could not but know his power—the effect his mere presence wrought; he knew what his voice and look could do; and he must have felt, as regarded the ordinary affairs of life, like a giant in the domain of pigmies; nothing was made to his scale. He could not dwell with his fellows on terms of equality; he was obliged to adapt himself to them in ways which involved some sacrifice of spontaneity. There must be, in other words, a certain histrionic quality in this man: not that he wished to act a part, but that he was forced out of his real character despite himself. The lack of equals with whom to associate drove him, in his fullest moments, to commune with great ideas of government and comprehensive thoughts of human destiny; at other times, he would be indolent, like Hercules, with no labor to perform; or would try to diminish himself, as it were, to the caliber of his companions, because the human strain in him yearned to meet a mate, and would rather have inadequate fellowship than be always lonely. And because that vast organization and intelligence must have some object, some occupation, he accepted ambition, which first perhaps contemplated impersonal issues, but insensibly was directed so as to confound the aimer with the aim: he came to identify himself with that which he pursued; and he sought no less unworthy a goal than the leadership of his country. But to gain that, he must contend with the selfish ends of others, and thus be led to do things which were unworthy of himself. And after all, he was to be disappointed. But he was constant through life to the great idea of a united America, and if, at times, he persuaded himself that means were of less account than the purpose which employed them, it is but to say that he was human.

There is nothing edifying in the story of the Presidential campaign of this year. Crawford, as the regular candidate, was at first the most prominent in the field; but the man in that big carcass was too small to win the prize. He was nominated by a Congressional caucus; but in the midst of the struggle he was stricken with paralysis and threatened with blindness; and though this did not make him withdraw his pretensions, it made the task of his supporters too hard. Adams tried to induce Jackson to accept the second place on his ticket; but this shrewd move failed, for Jackson would be second to no man. Calhoun showed political sagacity in offering to accept the Vice-Presidency with Jackson as chief. Clay tried to get Crawford to retire, and make over his chances to him; but Crawford held on. Each state had some favorite son to recommend; and it soon became evident that there would be no majority among the leaders; the legislature would have to decide between them. A national convention had not yet been thought practicable. Jackson became constantly stronger; the stars in their courses seemed to fight for him; and a letter of his which was published by his enemies, in the hope of discrediting him, redounded to his advantage; it was one of a series which had been written to Monroe eight years before; and Jackson published the whole batch, which happened to contain numerous sentiments singularly pertinent to the present crisis, and he was greatly strengthened in the popular estimation thereby. He received more votes than any of the other candidates; but the House chose Adams, with Calhoun as Vice-President. Jackson acquiesced with ostensible grace, but in private he expressed the belief that he had been betrayed by Clay; he was ever prone to fancy that secret enemies were combining against him.

The most agreeable event of the last year of Monroe's administration—which had been, upon the whole, one of the least faulty ever known—was the visit of Lafayette to America, after an absence of more than forty years. During this interval he had seen many vicissitudes, but had always been the same noble, simple, and devoted man that offered himself to our service in the first flush of his youth. In Europe, as here, he had fought for liberty, and had suffered in the cause. There was no speck on his escutcheon—not one. From first to last he had been brave, honorable, generous, and noble; a Frenchman without guile. He had spent his fortune and his blood for us; now, he was poor, and still limped a little from the wound he had received at Brandywine. He had never received the benefit of a grant of land which had been made to him at the close of the war; and the country wished to show him its gratitude even at so late a day. A national vessel was placed at his disposal, to bring him over here; but he modestly declined such an honor, and sailed on a regular packet ship, reaching New York on the 15th of August. He had expected to take lodgings, and to be the recipient of social courtesies from his old companions-in-arms who still survived; and the reception he met with astonished him.

It is hard for the American nation to be moved to an expression of genuine emotion; they are slow to wear their hearts upon their sleeves; there is a dry humor about them, a touch of good-humored cynicism perhaps, which prevents gushing or heroics of any kind. Possibly they were more easily moved sixty years ago than they are now. But it is as true now as it was then, that when our people are thoroughly convinced of the worth of a given person, they are not afraid to show it. The evidence must be clear; but when the fact is established, our response is as unmeasured as the sunshine. Lafayette's story was writ large before the world, and there was none to impugn it. Moreover, he was in many ways peculiarly endeared to us; he had been the dearest friend of our departed Washington; he had overcome all prejudices of birth and environment to give his heart and sword to our need; he had won the love and respect of all who knew him. He now came to us like an embodiment of a glorious and reverend past returned to assure us that all was true which we had heard of the achievements and grandeur of our fathers. Emerging from so deep and wide an abyss of time, Lafayette was a sort of gracious miracle; and all America rose up to take him to her heart.

It is of little avail to recount what were the specific acts of welcome accorded to him. The words he uttered at New York, when the sincerity and fervor of the popular reception were revealed to him, tell the story both for him and for us. "It will burst!" he cried, with passion, pressing both his hands over his heart, while tears rained down his aged cheeks. We were strong, who had been weak; he was old, who had given us the strength of his youth; and as we, in our crowded thousands, looked upon his beloved figure; and as he beheld the vast array of cheering multitudes, with waving hats, fluttering handkerchiefs, and ardent faces, sending warm to his heart the sympathy and affection of their own, the generous soldier who had never faltered before the enemy, broke down, and had but that pregnant word to reply. The episode is one of the loveliest in all history; and the whole sojourn of Lafayette among us, extending over fourteen months, is forever memorable and honorable. What, in a nation, is so grand as its gratitude?—What gift, to the recipient, is so sweet and glorious? While he was with us, the acerbities of party strife, the malice of rival ambitions, were hushed; in his presence, shame was ashamed to sit. By his side seemed to tower the august shade of Washington, and in his kindly eyes shone the spirit of '76. And he, contemplating the evidences of mighty prosperity which a generation and a half had wrought, was happy in his soul that he had borne a share in creating the conditions from which it sprang.

CHAPTER TWENTY-SEVENTH

EXTREMES

THE Adams family has the unique distinction of having furnished a President from two consecutive generations. On the other hand, neither of them was adapted to the peculiar requirements of that difficult office. Both had ability enough and to spare; both were singularly patriotic and honest; but there their qualifications ended. The elder Adams was too headstrong, vain, and opinionated; the younger was too cock-sure, too chilly, precise and unsympathetic. It might be said of him, paradoxically, that he understood men, but did not fathom human nature; there was no doubt about his familiarity with public affairs; he had been suckled on them. He had no tact, or intuitive insight; he did not know when to bend; he did not understand the feeling and desires of the people. A more correct man could not be found; but, as President, he was as often wrong as right in specific acts. He made enemies by inadvertently wounding men's vanity or prejudices; and his whole administration was a fight and a wrangle; and when he stood for re-election, he found no effective supporters. In the first place, he had been chosen by the House and not by the people; and this made it his duty to proceed with circumspection, and to study to reconcile opposition. He did neither; and the more conscientiously he labored, the more isolated did he become. **Many thwarted** him simply because they did not like him **personally**; many more, because he slighted their projects.

His very first act was crudely injudicious. He appointed Clay his Secretary of State. Clay might or might not have been competent to fill the office; the point was that Clay had, practically, made him President. Everybody knew that Clay coveted the State portfolio; and when he so promptly received it, it was inevitable that there should be accusations of a bargain. Both Clay and Adams denied it, Clay with a lofty air of virtue which was not consonant with his attitude and his letters just before the event; for Clay was really not scrupulous about such things. Adams probably acted from a feeling of gratitude, mingled with a conviction that Clay would make a good Secretary. But this was not enough; he should have avoided the appearance of evil; and in spite of his long and unblemished record, he never recovered from the blow which this gave to his reputation; and in times of such scurrilous political abuse, it was only to be expected that so effective a weapon would be used against him by his enemies. To start wrong is half to lose the battle. The harm suffered by Clay in accepting the office was hardly less; though much more would be forgiven to him than to Adams, because he was so much more likable a person.

Adams's next move was almost equally clumsy; for he offered the Treasury and the War secretaryships to his defeated rivals, Crawford and Jackson respectively. Crawford, who continued to distil venom in his impotence, refused with a snarl. Jackson was the bitter enemy of both Adams and Clay; of the former, because he had obtained the office, through Clay's help, which the electoral votes had put within Jackson's grasp; and Clay, both for this reason, and also because of the part he had taken in the Seminole debate. To make him an offer of a place in the Cabinet was therefore, from his point of view, to insult him; and Adams was warned of this in time to save himself the snubbing which Jackson was prepared to give him. Rush and Barbour accepted the posts in question; and the aged Rufus King, at seventy, consented to go to England as he had done before for Adams's father. But he soon resigned. Adams always meant right, but he blundered. One cannot but respect the firm stand he made, to his loss, against the policy of rotation in office. He would not turn men out except for cause; nor always then. "Change or rotation in office," said he, "would make the government a perpetual and unintermittent scramble for office. A more pernicious expedient could hardly have been devised. I determined to renominate every person against whom there was no complaint which would have warranted his removal; and renominated every person nominated by Monroe and upon whose nomination the Senate had declined acting." This stand was right and brave, and was not receded from. But, as we know, it utterly failed, in our politics, to overcome the principle enunciated by Marcy, that "to the victors belong the spoils."

The coalition against Adams was formed without delay; it combined the forces of Crawford with those of Jackson; and Calhoun, the Vice-President, assisted them; though at the cost of having to eat his own avowed principles in the past. But as Calhoun's purpose was to mold affairs to bring him in as Adams's successor, the alliance between him and Jackson was of course insincere and temporary.

Adams had announced as a settled feature of his policy, disregarding the scruples of Constitutionalists, that internal improvements would be advocated and pushed during his administration; and it seemed likely to be a popular measure. In 1825, the Erie Canal, three hundred and sixty-three miles in length, and forty feet wide, was opened, and a way thus made from Buffalo to New York. Cannon, placed at intervals, signaled the completion of the work, traversing the distance in an hour and a half:—for the electric telegraph was still unthought of. A procession of boats and barges proceeded from Erie to Albany, and thence down the Hudson to Sandy Hook; at which point Clinton, the father of the Canal, in the sight of the multitude, poured the contents of a barrel of Erie water into the salt tide of the Atlantic. The Canal was received with immense interest and enthusiasm, and others were planned in all directions; so that had it not been for the invention of steam coaches, the country would soon have been intersected with waterways. But science, which has made the Nineteenth Century distinguished, was beginning to make its influence felt; and there were steamboats everywhere; the first steamboat explosion on the Mississippi had occurred in 1823. Roads extended over a great part of the country, and before the railroads were established, one could travel speedily enough for ordinary purposes by horse and wagon. But the people were already bitten with the mania for rapid transit; and that disease has by no means run its course yet. It is innate in our blood, and must have its way.

In 1825 took place the inauguration of the granite monument at Bunker Hill, with Webster to make the oration, and Lafayettte to lay the cornerstone. It was a beautiful day, on the 17th of June, and a vast crowd witnessed the ceremonies. Fifty years had passed since that hillside had been the theater of a far different scene; and this imposing function was good evidence that the farmers who fought there had not shed their honest blood in vain. The mighty voice of Webster was the fitting instrument of expression for the deep thoughts and glorious prospects which the occasion must needs call forth.

Meanwhile, there was opposition between the House and the Senate, the latter being hostile to the President. His plans for internal improvements were delayed, defeated, or pronounced fanciful and impracticable. He was also subjected to criticism for advocating our acceptance of an invitation to attend a congress of the Spanish-American republics, to be held on the Isthmus of Panama. Clay had joined with Adams in urging this project; its somewhat sensational and spectacular character seemed in accord with his temperament rather than with the Executive's. Adams proposed to recommend to the members of the Congress liberal maritime laws, religious liberty, an enlargement of the Monroe doctrine, and other things of less moment. He named commissioners to attend in our behalf, asserting his right to do so independently of Congress; but submitted the proposal to them as a matter of courtesy. The Senate hummed and hawed over it, and stated a number of objections, but finally yielded rather than bring on a fight with the House. But the whole scheme collapsed, from the simple fact that its management was in Spanish-American hands. Even Bolivar, the South American popular hero, seen at close quarters, turned out not to be so great as rumor made him. The incident was useful only as indicating the incapacity of the Spanish-Americans to accomplish anything of value, from governing themselves down; but the lesson is one which we seem as yet to have mastered but imperfectly. The connection of the United States with this affair gave the opposition an opportunity of saying that Clay and Adams had taken it up in order to distract public attention from their corrupt bargain with each other. John Randolph, with his squeaky voice, in his stage attire of a dissolute groom, his eyes leering with intoxication, hiccoughed his rambling but occasionally pungent accusations and revilings; in the course of which he happened to remark that the political bond between the President and the Secretary of State was an alliance between a "Puritan and a blackleg." For this Clay challenged him to a duel with pistols; and Clay meant to kill him. Randolph, who had long been accustomed to regard himself as a licensed buffoon, was startled at this check; but had not the moral courage to get out of the scrape, and the men met. Randolph seems to have been badly rattled; his pistol went off before the word was given; he was undecided whether he would fire in the air or at Clay; in the first exchange neither was hit; in the second, after seeing Clay's bullet strike the ground beside him, he let off his own weapon in the air, and then shambled hurriedly forward with outstretched hand and an ingratiating smile. Clay accepted the overture, and the Republic was safe. But Randolph's conduct had become so indecorous and incorrigible, that he could not be re-elected to the Senate; though he was returned to the House some time later. He has been called "the image of a great man stamped on base metal." But there was really nothing incongruous in the man. He was a low-comedy actor of genius, with a native wit and readiness which could sting and amuse. By ill luck, he shambled into politics, instead of on to the stage; his impudence, his irreverence, and his fondness for slashing right and left without regard to principle or person, aided his grotesque personal appearance in making him conspicuous; and his sallies and his faculty of calling names relieved the dullness or the solemnity of debates. His influence, so far as he was able to exercise any, was first in the direction of general criticism; and then in laying the foundation of that defense of slavery which consisted in affirming it to be a private domestic concern of the Southerners, with which the North must not meddle but at its peril. This line was taken up later by the far more able Calhoun; and the two together, with Hayne and some others, supplied the phrases and watchwords which were so often heard afterward in the field days of later times. The doctrine of State rights was made to mean among other things the right of the individual to manage the affairs of his own household. "The moment the United States shall make the unhallowed attempt to interfere with the domestic concerns of Southern States," said Hayne, "those States will consider themselves driven out of the Union." Such adjectives as "unhallowed" and "domestic," used in this connection, were well calculated to stimulate the sensibilities of a race trained to regard themselves as subject to no rule higher than their own will.

Georgia had an opportunity to show her temper in the dispute about the Creek lands in her territory. The government policy was to buy the Indians out, whenever they could be induced to sell; but the Georgians wished to adopt the simpler method of compelling them to vacate. A treaty was negotiated to this end; but it was so corruptly managed that Adams was compelled to interfere. This made the Georgians angry; and in the subsequent rectification of the boundary between Georgia and Alabama, they unconstitutionally insisted upon running the line themselves, and threatened the United States with armed resistance if interfered with. A man named Troup was the leader in this illegality, and he conducted himself with unrestrained insolence, until the news came that United States troops were actually on the march. He then assured the government that he had never contemplated armed resistance; and the affair was suffered to blow over; Adams behaving with much lenience. As for the Indians, they were kept moving toward the west; and it must be admitted that they were fit occupants of no civilized community. Contact with white men's whisky had deprived them of what small claim to tolerance they had ever possessed.

Randolph's successor in the Senate may be mentioned, inasmuch as he accidentally became a national figure afterward; it was John Tyler, a Virginian, who had the misfortune to be always placed in the position of having to explain some past action which seemed inconsistent with his present profession; or of vindicating himself from charges of bad faith.—The year 1826 was signalized by the death, on the Fourth of July, of John Adams and Thomas Jefferson; who had lived, since their retirement, accompanied by honor, love, obedience, troops of friends; who had been cordial personal friends, and who deserved to be associated, in death as they had been in life, with that great act of freedom to which their names are subscribed. Monroe, five years later, had the same distinction. Both he and Jefferson died so poor that they barely fell short of pauperdom; and a subscription was started for Jefferson on the very day of his death. He remained a cheerful philosopher to the end; but Monroe was distressed in mind, and his health suffered from the fact.

In the same year Gallatin, who had exchanged Paris for the dismal quiet of a Pennsylvania village, was sent to England to discuss American relations with Canning. The latter had by this time laid aside his momentary semblance of friendliness toward this country, and now shut us out from commerce with the West Indies, on frivolous grounds. There was also a dispute pending regarding the Canada boundary at Maine and Oregon. Canning's death, unlamented both in England and in America, came opportunely to heal dissension; and did more than Gallatin's efforts to afford prospects of an amicable settlement. But Congress, from a wanton desire to embarrass the President, refused to give him proper assistance in his negotiations. Adams's tendency to centralize power subjected him to suspicion and jealousy, and was of ill augury for the remaining two years of his term.

But the most obvious activity of these two years was the effort of the friends of Jackson to secure his election as the next President. Hitherto, every President, with the exception of Adams's own father, had received the compliment of a second term; but Jackson's energy and Adams's unpopularity were to break the spell once more. He counted upon the support, not of Crawford—for Crawford was incapable of any but selfish thoughts, and though his mind was affected by his disease, he still clung with ludicrous obstinacy to his former hopes—but of Crawford's quondam supporters; and they finally ranged themselves on his side the first to come over being the arch political strategist, Martin Van Buren, who was of great use in importing into the canvass all the tact, suavity, sagacity, and knowledge of ways and means that his principal lacked. Jackson himself could think of no better campaign argument than that of repeating the old cry of Bargain and Corruption against Adams and Clay; and though the proof on which he relied failed him upon trial, he never retracted the charge, and the people accepted it with the heedlessness of democracies. On the other side, Clay rather than Adams appeared as the defender of the administration and Jackson's antagonist. But Clay was rowing against the popular tide, while Jackson was coming with it. Adams refused the most necessary expedients to better his chances, and he early gave up all hope of succeeding himself. Calhoun's defection gave Jackson additional strength in the South, Pennsylvania was for him, and the New York democracy, under the control of Van Buren and Clinton, carried New York. In New England the issue was in some doubt, but the Jackson forces were better disciplined than those of Adams. When the Congressional elections of 1827 were over, the House as well as the Senate was Jacksonian—the first time such a conjunction had occurred. The consequence was, that the national legislature, instead of paying attention to the President's recommendation of measures tending to the public weal, occupied itself almost exclusively with electioneering tactics, and attempts to discredit the Executive for past acts or omissions.

The only measure of public concern at this session was what was known as "the Woolen Bill"; or, otherwise, a bill to reform the tariff. The increased duty on imported woolen goods was from seven to twelve per cent; and iron, hemp and lead were also penalized. Adams signed the bill, though it was not an administration measure; he had always abstained from the question, out of consideration for the prejudices of the South. Neither would Jackson admit supporting it, though it could not have been passed but by the votes of his friends. But it met with great opposition; and Hayne of South Carolina declared it to be partial, unjust and unconstitutional. For the produce of the South had hitherto found its chief market in Europe, and a high duty would diminish this market, by preventing the manufactured product from finding its market here. The question split South and North into two hostile camps at once. The South, except sugar-planting Louisiana, was solid for free trade. She asked to be let alone to form her own policy; she believed she could prosper by making her own terms with Europe; she did not need the North; and the suggestion of secession was scarcely veiled. The North meanwhile from free-trade had become protectionist, being the seat of the manufacturing interest.

Clay resigned his secretaryship on the plea of ill-health. The candidates were named—Adams and Rush on one side, Jackson and Calhoun on the other. The campaign was the most scurrilous thus far in our history; nothing was spared in the way of scandal and abuse. Adams men took the title of National Republicans; Jacksonites, that of Democrats. The former jeered at the illiterate, grog-shop affiliations of the latter; but the latter had the majority in the country. New England alone was true to Adams; and from the first, he never had any real chance against his foes. He gained nothing from the Clay interest. He met defeat coldly and unflinchingly, and the last months of his thoroughly conscientious and patriotic administration were dignified and quiet. He had not succeeded in being a congenial President; but had his recommendations been followed the country would have been the better. He wished to make the United States expand and become richer and more powerful by availing itself of the resources of science and of broadly conceived internal improvements; but he had not sufficiently combined general views with particular applications to carry the people with him. The Tariff Bill alienated the South, under the secret stimulus applied by Calhoun, and the open attacks of Hayne. From being warm in recommending internal improvements and a thorough-going protectionist, Calhoun, for reasons best known to himself, faced square about and supported the opposite principles. Nothing in history is more mysterious than the willingness of men of great parts, in public life, to destroy their reputations before posterity for the sake of gaining a temporary advantage over their immediate opponents. "Honesty is the best policy," said Poor Richard. "It is better to be right than to be President," said another clear-eyed man. But the men who pledge honor for high stakes seem to believe that they can hoodwink history as easily as they can outmaneuver their antagonists on the field.

With feelings somewhat like those with which the patricians of ancient Rome witnessed the irruption of the Goths and Vandals, did the conservative element in the country behold the rough-handed mob swarming into power, with their "Hurrah for Jackson!" Were law and order doomed? —could our institutions survive?—was this America?—The Republic was stancher, and the Union stronger, than anybody suspected; and it was well that they should be tested at every point.

It is easy to be impartial to Jackson now, more than sixty years after he strutted his hour upon the public stage; but during that hour, it must have been well-nigh impossible to be neither his partisan nor his foe. So violent a partisan as he himself was must create, while he occupied the highest place, a like sentiment in all who came in contact with him. There is no defending Jackson's policy as it related to dismissal from office in the internal affairs of the country. He did not care to disguise the fact that he meant to have his friends in, and his opponents out. In order to be his friend, a man did not have to be decent or honorable; all that was required was that he should be an uncompromising Jacksonite. Many of the men whom he appointed to fill places against whose incumbents no charge would stand, were persons more fitted for a cell in a jail than for public trusts. The principle was almost as bad as the practice; it made the conduct of affairs a matter of sale or plunder. A more serious charge against Jackson is, that he constantly and seemingly wantonly lied to men as to his intentions; he would assure them that they would not be disturbed, invite them to take a glass of wine with him in token of cordial friendship, and then, the moment their backs were turned, would chop off their heads. There is much to be said, no doubt, on the plea that an administration is hampered by hostile incumbents of office; but that, or anything, is better than that the civil service should be thrown to the dogs, because the dogs snap and snarl on the side of the Executive.

The fact is that Jackson was one man when his temper was roused, his pride or vanity touched, or his personal feelings in any way engaged, and quite a different man under other circumstances. He was honest except when he was angry; when he was angry it was all chance whether he were honest or not; he did not care. His administration was generally good and sometimes admirable, apart from his private animosities and grudges. His foreign policy was brisk and stiff, and yet not offensive;—"ask nothing that is not right, and submit to nothing that is wrong," was his maxim there. After the reign of terror among office-holders, and the saturnalia among office-seekers, had begun to abate a little, and the main features of his ideas of government were revealed, there turned out to be little to which a well-wisher of his country could not subscribe. He would not tax the people for internal improvements; he wanted the people to have their say and their way in all matters; but on the other hand he, as the representative of the people, insisted upon absolute power in the executive department; so that he was a despot in effect, and a democrat in idea; and the people seemed perfectly satisfied. Get the proletariat to believe that the man on the throne is one of themselves, thinks their thoughts, and shares their aims, and they will back him in any exercise of absolutism. It is not he that is the tyrant, but they; therefore it is not tyranny but freedom. Jackson had a certain luck, or it may have been intuition about the people, which constantly gave him the upper hand in his dealings with opponents in and out of Congress. He relied on the people to back him against Congress, and the success of his vetoes shows he guessed right. His prestige became so formidable that Congress feared him, as schoolboys fear the master. He was much more a man, much franker and more fearless, and much more often right and unselfish in purpose, than the majority of the Senate or House; and therefore they dreaded a contest with him, in which the motives actuating them might be revealed. Besides, Jackson so easily got angry, and when angry, he hit so hard, and was so unrelenting! The man that would openly antagonize him must be desperately in earnest, and unusually strong; and even then, the odds were all with Jackson.

His refusal to advocate improvements did not surprise any one; and what was really needed in that line could be otherwise provided for. But he startled every one when he showed fight to the United States Bank. This institution had become strong and prosperous under Biddle's management, and was a great power: too great, Jackson may have believed; but that was not the reason why he fought it; the reason was personal; Biddle had questioned his authority. A hectoring person named Mason was manager of the Plymouth, New Hampshire, branch of the bank, and complaints were made of him; Biddle investigated, found nothing wrong, and indorsed the man in the face of the suspicions of Ingham, the Secretary of the Treasury; at the same time, in his overweening confidence, writing the following foolish defiance: "I deem it my duty to state to you, in a manner perfectly respectful to your official and personal character, yet so clear as to leave no possibility of misconception, that the board of directors of the Bank of the United States, and the boards of directors of the branches of the Bank of the United States, acknowledge not the slightest responsibility of any description whatsoever to the Secretary of the Treasury touching the political opinions and conduct of their officers." Of course not: but the letter is very amusing, in showing of what abject imbecility a clever financier, who thinks that money is everything, and pulls down his waistcoat with an air, is capable. Biddle wrote as he might have written to a clerk who wanted his salary raised. The idea of a conflict between a Biddle and a Jackson—and that Jackson a President—is almost pathetic. "By the Eternal, I'll take the strut out of this Biddle!" Jackson remarked: and it was not long before floods of light broke upon the unhappy man of money, too late to do him any good. His disgraceful end, many years afterward, doubtless brought a grim smile to Jackson's face, as he reflected that, in striking him, he had not struck amiss.

But before the Bank quarrel could be settled, several other things were to happen. The general aspect of affairs was smiling. Washington Irving was sent as Minister to England; and by way of balancing this excellent appointment, John Randolph was given the mission to Russia. Randolph was a man whose ideas of conduct suited to a gentleman, and to a representative of his country, were peculiar, like all else about him. He had a number of debts, which he had contracted without much hope of paying them; this office would give him the means of doing so. On the other hand, he was averse from the labor which that or any office might entail; so after accepting the appointment, and spending a week or so at his post, he set out for London, where he amused himself for several years, and then drew his salary, amounting to over twenty thousand dollars. It belonged to him no more than it did to the slave overseer on his farm; but he drew it without compunction, liquidated some of his personal liabilities with it, and returned gayly home. It was one of this statesman's practical jokes; and like other jokes, has been often repeated in our politics.—Clay went home and took to farming again, but he was not to remain there long; Webster returned to Congress. Hayne was also there; and Calhoun sat, as before, pale and impenetrable in the chair of the Senate Chamber. The champions of the great debates that were to be were assembled; but as yet unconscious of what they were to do. The country was free and easy, and looked forward to good times. There was some uneasiness regarding the tariff, to be sure; and Jackson's message was slightly ambiguous in respect of it; but it seemed probable that a reasonable course would be pursued. South Carolina, at all events, was quite sure that she knew what she needed better than the official tariff-mongers. A convention, of which much was hoped, met in Virginia under distinguished auspices, and presented an amended constitution; but the result was not considered entirely satisfactory. The opportunity to pass a resolution for the gradual abolition of slavery in the state was not improved; and thus an example which might have been followed by other states was lost. The improved facilities of transport and communication had made it possible for free labor to take the place of slavery, or at least to compete favorably with it; but the Southerners were wedded to their idols. The public debt would soon be paid off, and when that was done, the surplus might be applied in ways that would increase the welfare of the country. In the southwest, there was again trouble with the Indians, this time the Cherokees, who, to the number of fifteen thousand, had a settlement in Georgia, and had made some advances in civilization. They wished to have their settlement made a separate state; the Georgians naturally objected; a test case was made, and appealed to the Supreme Court, which decided favorably to the Indians, but were powerless, without the aid of the President, to enforce their ruling, which Georgia disregarded. The President declined to use the army to secure red men in the rights they claimed, however legally; it was impossible they could live under such conditions. He advised them to cross the Mississippi and avoid trouble; but the dispute was the old original one between white and red men, never to be settled in strict equity. Indians have some rights which white men are bound to respect; but they claim some others which can never be accorded, unless we give up the continent to them.

Jackson began his career as a vetoer with some bills for appropriations for roads. He saw jobbery in them, and that the pickings and stealings of the promoters would exceed the expenditures for the public good. If the states were once encouraged to lay the cost of their internal improvements on the national government, there would ensue a carnival of political thimble-rigging all over the land. Jackson did good work in scotching this boa-constrictor promptly and resolutely.

But though the morning of the administration thus flattered the mountain tops with sovereign eye, there were clouds on the horizon, gathering in an unexpected quarter. Jackson had been indebted to South Carolina for her vote; she had supposed that he would favor her tariff views. Other states had voted for him as a protectionist. Here was a discrepancy which would come to judgment sooner or later. He could not be on both sides of the fence; which would he choose? Calhoun thought the time good to test the matter; and he also thought that Jackson would easily be induced to take South Carolina's view. Being kept from the floor himself, he used Hayne as his mouthpiece. Hayne however was anything but a puppet, moving only when another pulled his strings; he was an able, versatile and charming man, eloquent, winning, graceful, harmonious, nimble in the dance, entertaining at the table, and persuasive and impressive in the Senate. Ordinarily he might have had everything his way; but there was Webster in the field, and one Webster was more than a match for six other champions, be they who they might. The debate was one of the historic ones of Congress. Hayne was the most refined type of the Southern gentleman and man of honor; Webster was Webster.

The discussion began with a suggestion from an Eastern Senator to limit the sale of public lands. This was taken by Southerners as a check to their development; and Hayne attacked New England on that ground. Webster, replying, so demolished his argument as to mortify his self-esteem, and he prepared an elaborate speech, in the course of which he arraigned New England for her disloyalty in the late war with England, denouncing her for the very insistence upon state rights which were the basis of the Southern doctrine of nullification, to which what might be called official expression was now for the first time given. It involved the right of a state to nullify a law which should appear to be clearly unconstitutional, within that state's own borders and for her own protection; the present application being to the tariff. Hayne's speech lasted two days, for he was a verbose as well as a graceful speaker; and it was held by his friends and feared by his opponents to be unmatchable. But it suited Webster well; for he had given thought to the subject long before, and knew what course to take. He needed but an evening to prepare himself for what turned out to be one of the greatest speeches ever made, and perhaps the greatest of his career. "There is Hayne's whole speech," he answered an anxious inquirer, who wished to know whether he had taken full notes; and he showed him a bit of paper as big as an envelope with a few pencil marks on it. A large and excited audience had assembled to hear him. He entered the Chamber with the port of Jove, majestic and composed; obviously able not to conquer only, but to conquer easily. What should graceful panthers like Hayne do when this royal lion came on the arena? Hayne had spoken well, but from a narrow standpoint—the special pleader for local interests, the sophist and skilled manipulator. Webster stood majestic and broad-shouldered, the human embodiment of the nation, the Union and the Constitution. He shaped his ideas in imposing masses, towering with pinnacles of golden eloquence, but based on immutable foundations of granite truth. When he had spoken, there was no voice to answer him; there was nothing to answer. His words went forth to the nation, north and south, and were convincing and final. Even the stout and ambiguous Benton, who had been a Nullifier, was converted thenceforth to Unionism. Hayne had his quietus; his mentor, Calhoun, could find no other shield or sword for him, to replace those which had been that day destroyed. There is no other instance of a single speech having so completely annihilated a political doctrine, and at the same time furnished every requisite defense of a sublime principle against attack. The South, indeed, might nullify, it might declare state rights, it might secede; but it could never refute Webster's arguments, or claim any constitutional sanction for its acts.

As regarded the attack on New England, Webster refused to restrict her defense to the vindication of the knot of malcontents who dallied with England and attended the Hartford Convention. He went beyond and above them to New England herself, who had remonstrated with James, and had resisted George; to the free and unconquerable people who had passed equal laws, stood firm for human rights, and fought at Bunker Hill. The cause of liberty would always be safe with this people, and they were loyal to the Union which they had sacrificed and suffered so much to attain. The Union was a decree of no State legislature, district or clique, but was the realized will of the people at large, who thereby became a nation. Only by means of it could liberty be assured to posterity; it could not be riven asunder by the whim or petulance of selfish minorities, by any state or combination of states; no partial considerations could avail to disrupt it; no plea for liberty without Union could avail; but there must be "liberty *and* Union, now and forever, one and inseparable." The words will never be forgotten; they were the rallying cry that brought the loyal states together under the flag when rebellion was declared; they are the expression of the true America. And the principle which they assert ruled Webster's whole career.

Calhoun made one attempt to draw Jackson over to his side in the controversy; he caused a dinner to be given at Washington by the anti-tariff party, to which he and the

President should be invited. Jackson came; but those reckoned ill who fancied that the old soldier was to be entrapped into any indiscretion; more than that, he utterly turned the tables on them. For when he was asked for a toast, he arose and said with emphasis, "Our Federal Union—it must be preserved!" It was vain, after that, for Calhoun to get up and suavely talk about Union being the next most dear to liberty; the game was up, and it was so understood. Nor did it answer to try to make out Jefferson as having been the father of the nullification idea; he had devised the thing to meet the special occasion of the Alien and Sedition laws, but had never attempted or desired to push it further. It was Calhoun who was responsible for erecting it into a political principle, and making it the cover for designs which Jefferson had during his presidency explicitly and constantly opposed. And Calhoun must bear the credit or the blame of his achievement.

But though Jackson could defeat British regulars at New Orleans, dominate his Cabinet and overpower Congress, there was one thing he was not strong enough to do, and that was, to make fine ladies behave with human charity toward a woman. Their malice is as impalpable as a mephitic vapor, which is nevertheless fatal. There was in Washington an inn-keeper by the name of O'Neil, who had a pretty and lively daughter, Peggy. She was a clever, alert, jolly little personage, who drew company to her father's resort by her wit and lively manners. She would laugh and toss jests back and forth with the gentlemen who came there to drink and smoke their pipes, and who, in the enthusiasm of the moment, would occasionally, perhaps, catch her and give her a kiss, and get a buffet on the ear in return. This was the extent of the indictment against her; all the rest was inference and surmise; and who shall escape calumny? She married a purser in the navy, who died, and afterward became the wife of Major Eaton, who was Jackson's Secretary of War, and had long been an admirer of Peggy's. That he should have made her the guardian of his honor should have been enough to silence scandal; but the white doves of rank and fashion are more bloodthirsty and merciless than harpies when a chance offers to destroy one of their own sex. The manners of the age were free, and its morals none too strict; but it is at least as probable that Peggy was chaste as that her accusers were so. The latter, however, clubbed together to insult and trample on her; they would not attend receptions to which she was invited, or sit at dinner with her, or in any way admit that she was of the same flesh and blood as they. Jackson, who had felt that wrong which rumor does to women, when the good name of his own blameless wife had been assailed in the campaign, was highly indignant, and undertook to be Mrs. Eaton's champion. He issued invitations, he singled out Mrs. Eaton for attentions, he brought the whole pressure that the ruler of the nation and the head of Washington society could exercise, to bear upon recalcitrants: but how are you to compel a woman to attend a given reception, or to forbear to switch her skirt aside when a certain person passes, or to return a salute, or to stay in a room when she chooses to march out? You may manage a man easily enough; you can call him out and shoot him if he is unreasonable; but woman is unassailable, and profits by that fact. Jackson went so far as to threaten to dismiss his whole Cabinet if their wives did not behave themselves; the unhappy gentlemen feared their wives more than they did Jackson, or the destruction of their public careers, and were obliged to tell him that much as they personally liked and believed in Peggy—Bellona, she came to be called, for she was a plucky woman herself, as well as the stirrer-up of war—they dared not encounter curtain-lectures, and were absolutely impotent to convert or constrain the deliverers of them. Well, an impenetrable body had encountered an irresistible impact; and what was to happen? For a time it seemed likely that Washington society would cease to exist; but the futility of the struggle finally became apparent to the old soldier. Nothing was to be gained, even for Mrs. Eaton, by prolonging it. He gradually dropped the matter; but it had the singular effect of bringing his Cabinet councils to an end, and for the present he took counsel only with Martin Van Buren, with whom it was impossible for any one to quarrel, and with certain other henchmen of his own, who identified themselves with him, and were ready to indorse anything he did, or perform any order he might issue. Van Buren was the greatest political manager ever known in American public life up to that time; and under his training, New York was so thoroughly organized as to be a model. Indeed, Van Buren was so busy being a politician that he had no leisure left to be a statesman, though in the fullness of time he did become a President. But he knew how to wait and calculate chances, and was satisfied that Jackson was good for a second term. His own real rival, as he foresaw, was likely to be Calhoun; but by accepting the second place on Jackson's ticket, Van Buren was able to postpone the issue, and avail himself of the aid of time. Meanwhile, Calhoun was fatally injured with Jackson for two reasons: first, because he had been prominent in putting down Bellona; and secondly, because Crawford, languishing in retirement, and wishing to do all the harm he could, communicated the information that Calhoun had recommended the punishment of Jackson for the Seminole affair of 1818. Jackson demanded an explanation from Calhoun, who answered in a long, argumentative, but not conclusive letter; upon which Jackson told him that their friendship was at an end. It had been Calhoun's ambition to succeed Jackson as an ostensible friend of his administration; he had not realized that it was impossible to carry the country on the nullification, or state's rights issue; he knew nothing of the North, and fancied that there was a strong feeling against centralization. In this impression he was encouraged by his Southern supporters. But his quarrel with

Jackson was, in truth, the end of his hopes. Meanwhile it was used by Jackson as a pretext for dissolving his Cabinet and selecting a new one—an unprecedented act in Executive annals. By a shrewd bit of strategy he began the substitution not with Calhoun's friends, but with his own; Eaton being more than ready to leave on account of the embarrassment which the fight for Bellona had brought him; Van Buren from a clear comprehension of the situation and foresight of the future. These two having gone, Jackson intimated to the others that it would be necessary to make a complete change; and they were relieved of their positions without unnecessary violence, as the hotel-bouncers say. Jackson thus prepared to fight Calhoun to a finish, with the advantage on his side; and to fortify himself with the country by dint of his new Cabinet; for his new appointments were popular, and the ensemble was abler than the previous one; while at the same time the President was easily able to control them all. Throughout his whole administration, Jackson profited greatly by his policy of addressing the people through newspapers run in his interests; and the American press thus gained a prominence in politics which led, soon after, to the establishment of journals like the "Sun," "Herald," and "Tribune," which were the foundation of the independent journalism of our day. While thus intrenching himself at home, the old general won victories abroad; obtaining from England, by some harmless concessions of form, the trade with the West Indies which Adams had lost, and securing the payment of the French claims, which had been owing since Napoleon's day. Such a President could not be beaten; and he had the fight with the United States Bank, which was made to appear as a conflict with the moneyed aristocracy and with political jobbery, in reserve. What had Calhoun to bring into action against all this? So far as he personally was concerned, the only thing that was done was to take an opportunity, at a banquet tendered to him in the South, to deliver a philosophic argument in favor of the right of nullification. Should it be denied, he asserted that the federal government would become consolidated, and our liberties would be forfeit. He was put in nomination for the Presidency on this platform; but the country at large perceived dangers from an adoption of his theories greater than those against which he warned; and with Jackson and Webster to vindicate Union, the outlook for the South Carolinian was not bright.

The Twenty-second Congress, which met in December, 1831, was full of men of the first ability, and had an exciting career. Benton was the chief defender of the Executive; there were Webster and Clay, Rufus Choate and Everett, Thomas Corwin of Ohio, and many others of prowess. Clay was chosen to lead the struggle against Jackson. Jackson assumed a composed and peaceful demeanor in his message, waiting for the other side to attack; which, under Clay, they were not slow in doing. The opposition was divided among itself, but united against President Jackson. Clay was himself in nomination for the Presidency, and was now a stronger candidate than Calhoun.

Acting on Clay's advice, the first question brought up was that of the recharter of the Bank. Jackson would perhaps have preferred to have that matter go over until after the next election; but this was the more a reason for Clay to press it now; he hoped to destroy the Executive by a deadly alternative. There was a number of Democrats who favored the recharter; it was most likely that Congress, in both branches, would vote for it; and then it would lie with Jackson either to veto or to accept the measure. If he vetoed it, he would divide his party and be subject to dangerous criticism, even if the bill did not pass over the veto; and if he signed it, he would appear as timorous and weak. In either case, the issue would imperil his re-election. Webster, though siding with Jackson against Calhoun, was with Clay on this question; and McLane, the new Secretary of the

Treasury, had already declared the **Bank to be indispensable.** Moreover, the Bank was apparently in a most prosperous position, and firmly rooted in the scheme of things. Nicholas Biddle did not believe he could be beaten.

The outlook for the Bank was certainly good, on the surface. Its weak points were, first, that Nicholas Biddle was a rascal and secretly guilty of all manner of dishonesty, and that the Bank itself, consequently, which was practically under his exclusive control, was rotten to the core: and secondly, that Jackson was a fighter, that he hated and distrusted the Bank, and would stick at nothing to destroy it. And neither Clay nor Biddle had any adequate conception of Jackson's strength with the country, or the trust it placed in his statements and acts. The battle was long and savagely fought on both sides; but the upshot was never really in doubt.

Biddle bribed right and left, concealed all sinister facts either by direct lying or by covering up traces; and Clay and his followers, many of whom sincerely believed that the Bank was as honest and valuable as Biddle declared it to be, deployed their eloquence in Congress. Benton and the rest of the Jackson men met them with a vast array of charges, some of which were guess-work, but none of which surpassed the facts when the latter came to be known; they hammered everything in sight indiscriminately, and spared nothing and no one; and though they did not prevent the recharter from passing the Senate and House, the conviction aroused in the public mind was, that so much smoke must portend some fire. When, therefore, Jackson, upon receiving the amended bill, sent it back with his veto, the country was prepared for it; and Congress failed to pass it over the veto by the necessary two-thirds vote. The sympathy, after this first round of the fight, was with Jackson, and against the financial octopus which **he affirmed and** believed to be squeezing the independence and **virtue out of the** community. Jackson believed this because he wanted to believe it: because he hated Biddle and had been offended by the Bank's defiance. It was his good luck that the facts happened to justify his suspicions; but it can hardly be doubted that he would have hated the Bank and its manager just as much, had they been as pure as driven snow. To some extent he was fighting in the dark, and might, for aught he knew, have been trying to kill an angel of light instead of a demon of darkness.

The time for the present charter of the Bank to expire was still five years off, and the war was therefore far from being decided yet; but Jackson had the best of it so far. Meanwhile the tariff came up for discussion. This was a problem whose true solution still seems as far off as ever, and it is not to be expected that in the early age of which we are writing it could be handled in a conclusive manner. Too many things had to be considered, and instead of the conclusions of experience, there was little or nothing but theories to go upon. Free trade must always be the theoretical ideal, but protection is the practical necessity, unless all nations are united on the question. In America, at this juncture, various states wanted high duties on some articles and low ones or none at all on others. We had shown that we could be prosperous under a high tariff; but it seemed evident that we must lose by a policy which would open our ports without causing those of Europe to open in return. Clay favored protection—the American system, as he called it—but with the reservation that it should be modified. South Carolina, through Hayne as its spokesman, adopted an independent attitude, defying all the other states, and answering every argument with a threat of secession. Hayne declared, and Calhoun supported him in saying, that protection was unconstitutional. Calhoun had marked the desertion of South Carolina by commerce, and chose to believe that the stagnation of his state was due not to the effects of slavery upon its white inhabitants, but to the tariff. It is probable, too, that South Carolina painted the evils of its plight blacker than they were, in order to urge the remedy of nullification, which had become the pet project of the leaders of the state. Clay was willing to lessen certain duties, but was firm for establishing the principle of protection; and the bill which was submitted to the President in July, 1832, reduced the revenue some eight million dollars, but maintained the right of the government to protect. It was a most moderate measure; yet it was the signal for South Carolina to take a step which was as unjustifiable as it was futile.

Before that could happen, however, Congress adjourned, and the election contest was begun in earnest. Clay and Jackson were the only antagonists to be considered. Clay led the banking people and the aristocracy; Jackson had the rest of the nation. The Bank was the main issue. But Clay obscured this by various charges against Jackson. His corrupt changes in the civil service were denounced, his expensive foreign embassies, his undermining of the authority of the Supreme Bench, and his Indian policy. Clay demanded a firmer bond of union, an extension of internal improvements, and the supremacy of law. His followers were, in turn, accused of being beneficiaries of the Bank. The two armies joined issue as National Republicans, and as Jackson Democrats. It was, in fact, the classes against the masses. A side issue was introduced by a crusade against the Freemasons, brought on by the alleged killing of William Morgan by members of the order, for having revealed Masonic secrets. There was great excitement over this, and the whole principle of secret societies was denounced as un-American; but the charges were never proved, and were probably untrue; though Morgan certainly disappeared, and has never been heard of since. Anti-Masonic candidates took the field, but were overwhelmingly defeated by both the regular tickets.

John Sergeant was Clay's companion on the Republican ticket; Martin Van Buren was the Democratic Vice-President. Van Buren had been sent as minister to London;

but Clay and Calhoun thought it a good diplomatic stroke to get him recalled as if in disgrace, and thus cut short his public career. "It will kill him, sir, kill him dead," Calhoun remarked in Benton's hearing: "He will never kick, sir, never kick." But this was a mistake. The country sympathized with Van Buren, and penetrated the selfish motives which had put this slight upon him; his own behavior in meeting the situation was of course irreproachable; and when Jackson, as a vindication, invited him to stand with him, the people showed their appreciation by giving him a rousing vote. "You have broken a minister and elected a vice-president," remarked Benton to Clay.

Nearly one and a quarter million votes were cast in this election; Jackson's majority over Clay was over one hundred and fifty thousand, a gain of nineteen thousand over the vote for his first term. He had two hundred and nineteen electoral votes; Clay only forty-nine. Van Buren was scarcely less triumphant, though he lost the Pennsylvania vote for special reasons.

South Carolina took no part in this campaign, further than to cast her votes for John Floyd of Virginia for President, and for Henry Lee of Massachusetts for Vice-President, they being the one a states-rights man, the other a free-trader. Calhoun wrote that he believed "that the cause of South Carolina is the cause of the Constitution, of liberty, and of the Union. Our government is tending toward consolidation; and on consolidation corruption, oppression and finally monarchy must closely press." And he announced that "the reserved rights of the states" was the only remedy. This was all the result of pique; the country had modified the grounds of South Carolina's complaints; and she was threatening rebellion, not because of any new grievance, but because an old one, which she had already acquiesced in, was not reduced quite so much as she had desired.

Be that as it way, Nullification dominated in her legislature; a state convention was summoned, which declared the tariff acts of 1828 and 1832 null and void; the legislature called out the militia; and appeal to the Supreme Court was forbidden. To the United States was given the option of withdrawing its own law, or losing South Carolina.

Jackson was ready for the emergency. He ordered Winfield Scott to Charleston, and held troops in readiness; a war vessel was stationed in the harbor, and a proclamation called upon the people of South Carolina to mind what they were about. The country at large warmly approved these steps, and though South Carolina fiercely defied the nation, there was a strong party of her own citizens who declared their national loyalty.

While this matter was still seething in the caldron, the President issued his regular message, in which he recommended still further reduction of duties, the public debt being now nearly paid off. He considered that the election had showed that the people had had enough of protection. This took more ground from under the feet of the Nullifiers; but they were apparently bound to rebel in any case. Hayne, who had been made governor of the state, prepared to resist the Union government by force. Calhoun, elected Senator, took his place in the Chamber. He privately stated that South Carolina merely intended to resist civil process, without bloodshed. But when Jackson asked Congress for enlarged powers to deal with the situation, Calhoun began to feel frightened for his personal safety; it looked as if he might end his career on the gallows. He sent word to his constituents to be more cautious in their treasonable demonstrations, and meanwhile he started a debate on the abstract right of nullification. But here he was met, as Hayne had been, by Webster, and with a similar result. The poison with which he had meant to inoculate the veins of the country was antidoted by the expositions of the great New Englander. South Carolina stood alone among the states as a

Nullifier; only Virginia tried to mediate between her and Jackson, with the result of humiliating herself.

The "Force bill," as it was termed, supported by Webster, passed the Senate, only John Tyler opposing it, while Clay, Benton and Calhoun did not vote. Before it could be decided on by the House, Clay, who being of Southern birth with Northern affiliations, commanded confidence, proposed in the general interest a compromise measure. His plan was to scale down the duties periodically for ten years. Calhoun eagerly welcomed this way out of the serious scrape he had got into. A bill was before the House recommending a reduction of duties; a Congressman rose and moved that Clay's bill be substituted for it. The House agreed, the bill thus doctored was referred back to the Senate, which passed it, together with the Force bill; all being done by a sort of surprise. South Carolina showed her "spirit" by passing an act repealing Nullification, and then another, nullifying the Force bill (which, of course, had been enacted only in order to put down Nullification); as a man might stick his tongue in his cheek after he had been thrashed.

Webster had not been a party to this compromise, and had not approved of it. Jackson had accepted it reluctantly, rather than appear bent on bloodshed. But it was a penny-wise pound-foolish policy at best; it would have been better to crush South Carolina then and there, instead of allowing her, on the pretext of a semi-victory, to disseminate her heresies among the other Southern states. Clay himself practically admitted that the success of his measure could be but temporary; but he was ambitious to appear as a pacificator, and to check Jackson. Calhoun retired into himself; he was distrusted by the majority as a conspirator, but was constantly supported by his own state; and during his long senatorial career he never ceased to plot the destruction of the Union, by his own peculiar methods; cold, quietly argumentative, self-contained, relentless. He was a bloodless intellect; there is no more remarkable figure in our public life. He had missed the supreme place of outward power which he had coveted, but in revenge he exercised a far deeper and wider power over the opinion and policy of the South. To him, more than to any other, is due the Civil War; and the South, who idolized Calhoun, owes to him the disastrous consequences which his doctrines induced her to incur.

CHAPTER TWENTY-EIGHTH

GREAT MEN AND SMALL DEEDS

THE new regime, which was a continuation of the old, began pleasantly, and with strong men in abundance. In addition to Jackson, Clay and Webster — The Preserver of the Union, The Great Pacificator, and the Defender of the Constitution, as they were respectively nicknamed—there were still Chief-justice Marshall, though this was his last appearance at an inauguration, John Quincy Adams, the ex-President, and of future Presidents, Van Buren, Polk, Millard Fillmore, Tyler, Buchanan, and Franklin Pierce; besides such men of mettle as Choate, Everett, Horace Binney, Wise, Corwin, and Dave Crockett. Calhoun, "the weird specter of an idea," as Schouler calls him, was in his place in the Senate, and altogether, so far as ability was concerned, Congress never showed to better advantage. The difficulty was, that the ability was so distributed that it got in its own way; there was a plentiful lack of harmony and co-operation. The debates were sure to be interesting, but the action would be small; the attempt to accomplish anything was likely to have no better success than attended the efforts of the man who tried to lift himself by his own waistband.

Jackson, however, thought he could do something; and now that his policy had received so emphatic an indorsement at the polls, he believed that he could come near dispensing with Congress. He made three changes in his Cabinet, sending Livingstone to France and filling his place in the State secretaryship with McLane, who was succeeded by Duane as Treasury secretary. Duane was the son of a former henchman of Jackson's, and the latter believed that he could use him for his grand, secret purpose of eviscerating the Bank. Duane turned out a disappointment in this regard; but the President, as we shall see, had another card up his sleeve.

Meanwhile, by way of demonstrating the extent of his popularity, he undertook a tour to the Eastern States, which, in spite of certain accidents and mishaps, some of them of a comical character, produced an immense enthusiasm among the masses; but it came to a sudden termination at Concord, New Hampshire, where the President turned short about, and was back in Washington in three days. The reason put forward was that his health would not stand the strain of so much hospitality; but a stronger reason was doubtless his wish to get his campaign against the Bank in working order betimes. Congress being now scattered, he had a free hand; and it presently became known that he meant to withdraw from the Bank the government deposits, amounting to more than half of the whole; and, what was quite as serious for the Bank, he would accompany this act by giving his reasons for it: which were, in brief, that he did not consider the money safe there; he believed it was being used to corrupt the country and Congress; and he would not be a party to nourishing the parasite which was absorbing the vital forces of the nation. Of course, if this were credited, the Bank would be discredited in proportion, and would be obliged to wind up its affairs forthwith.

Jackson took but few into his confidence; but one of these had to be Duane, because only the Secretary of the Treasury had the legal right to withdraw the deposits. After much hesitation and anguish of mind, Duane declined to do it; and Jackson thereupon dismissed him (he refusing to resign) and put in his place a gentleman by the name of Taney, who was a thorough-going advocate of anti-Bank principles. Taney did his duty; not actually drawing out the whole nine millions in one lump, but providing for its removal at a rate altogether too rapid to be comfortable for Mr. Biddle. Biddle, however, had had some warning, which he had utilized to the utmost of his power by contracting his loans; and this of course had an effect on the country; money became dear and wages low. The distress was more in the anticipation of evil than in the actuality of it; for the money taken out of the Bank was deposited in State banks throughout the land, and only time seemed needed to reassure business. Biddle issued a protest which was intended to have a humorous and defiant twang to it; but this was another of Biddle's mistakes; his recognition of the fact that Jackson was not a man to be jested with was strangely delayed.

Clay, who had made himself the champion of the Bank in Congress, was now to make the next move; but he could do little more than move a censure of the President; for it was impossible to return the deposits to the Bank. The Great Pacificator was likewise disgruntled by Jackson's treatment of a land-bill which he had introduced in the last days of the previous session, which proposed to distribute the receipts from the sale of the public lands among the states, pro rata. Benton had a plan to throw the lands open to what was practically free settlement; and to allow those states in which the unoccupied lands were situated to have control of them. Jackson had kept Clay's bill, on the ground that it had come in too late for him to decide upon it; he now sent it to Congress with his veto. The veto was justifiable, though Jackson's grounds for imposing it may have been questionable; it was a job by which Clay had hoped to influence votes, and the gift of so much money to the states could not but have a demoralizing effect. It would encourage speculation, if nothing more. The dispute about this bill was but a preparatory skirmish to the main attack on the President's bank policy, which now began; and the contest lasted long after Jackson had left the White House for good.

The advocates of the Bank in the Senate and House made the most of the business alarm in the country, and did whatever eloquence could to inflame it. Their success was great; monster petitions were sent to Jackson asking him to reverse his policy, and painting the approaching destruction of the financial interests in lurid colors; and the petitions were supplemented by swarms of anxious persons delegated to remonstrate by word of mouth. The friends of Jackson began to fear that the pressure would be too strong; but he himself was immovable; he did not believe there was any real distress; it was only the stock-jobbers and moneyed cormorants who were in trouble, and the more of such trouble the better. The arguments of Webster, the impassioned appeals of Clay, had as little effect. The latter, addressing Van Buren in his place, entreated him to go to the President and bid him "pause and reflect that there is a point beyond which human endurance cannot go; and let him not drive this brave, generous, and patriotic people to despair." Van Buren listened with attention and gravity; but then, as if to indicate that though the heavens fall, there was no reason why sensible men on the inside should not continue to exist and be comfortable, he walked down the aisle and begged the panting orator for a pinch of snuff; after which he walked back and resumed his chair.

At the expense of much breath on both sides, the Senate finally passed a resolution directing the return of the deposits to the Bank. But the House reversed this ruling by a large majority, reporting that the state banks ought to retain the custody of the funds in question. The Senate, however, passed Clay's resolution censuring the President; but Benton rose and moved for its removal from the records, and announced that he should repeat the motion from time to time until it was adopted. There was great dispute over Jackson's nominations, Taney being rejected for the Treasury, and Stevenson for England; upon which Jackson left the latter post vacant for two years; when another Congress confirmed Stevenson. At the end of this "panic session" which had talked so much and done so little, the death of Lafayette was announced, and the members went home with crape on their arms. But in April, the Bank campaign had been continued by a committee appointed to investigate the Bank's books. The Bank squirmed out of this ordeal, and during the following winter obtained the appointment of a Senatorial committee for the same purpose, which, for reasons best known to itself, sent in a very favorable report. But the suspicions of the people were confirmed, and their verdict went the other way.

The foes of the Bank were somewhat embarrassed to find a substitute for it; the swarm of state banks had obstructed the stream of finance with a vast quantity of small paper currency, which was discounted till no one could tell what his money was really worth. Jackson finally attempted to stop the issue of paper below five dollars in face value; at the same time causing gold and silver to be coined; which had a temporary good effect. But he understood little about finance, and had no doubt been rash in tearing down one system before any preparation had been made for a substitute. He was attacked in many quarters; and, on the other hand, the resistance of the poor to the rich which he had seemed to encourage found expression in riots, by which much property was destroyed. In January, 1835, Lawrence, a young English house-painter out of a job, fired two pistols at Jackson as he was leaving the Capitol; both shots missed; Lawrence was knocked down, locked up, and finally put in an insane asylum. This affair had no effect upon Jackson's course; and the fall elections were on the whole favorable to him. The deposits were not returned to the Bank, and for the present the opposition seemed to have no stomach for further fighting. At about this time, moreover, the last installment of the national debt was paid off, and Jackson's administration got the credit of it. His star was still full high advanced.

But his success in defeating the aims of those arrayed against him, had the result of uniting them in a new party, professing to derive from the old Whigs of 1776, and adopting their designation. The idea took over the country, and the Whigs seemed to crystallize almost at once into a homogeneous body. Both South and North contributed to its elements. On the other hand, a socialistic wing of the Jackson Democracy was organized under the nickname of loco-focos, bestowed on account of their having relighted with loco-foco matches the gas which the Tammany Democrats had turned out in the hall where both had assembled. Of the two great parties, the Whigs, as has been remarked, had the better men, though the Democrats had the better principles; but the latter were handicapped, as regarded their personnel, by the system of rotation in office, which made political services instead of merit the condition of tenure. The Whigs resembled the Federalists in their leanings to wealth and education, but had learned to give more consideration to the mass of the people; and they soon showed some measure of success. They gained support in several hitherto Democratic states. But Pennsylvania could not be won over; and the young William H. Seward was defeated for the governorship of New York. This attitude of the two great states finished the Bank, all except the ultimate ceremonies. But the new party felt in itself the promise of future power, and organized for future triumphs. Several Presidential candidates were named by it in different states; Webster in Mas-

was no stronger or braver man in Congress, and none of honesty so unimpeachable. The Southerners feared to bring in a vote of censure against him; though at one time he stood in peril of personal violence. In reply to the dogma that Congress had no right to interfere with slavery in the states, he declared that under the war-power in cases of civil disorder, the government might interfere and control it. And it was upon the basis of this assertion that the government did interfere twenty-five years later.

The debt of the nation being paid, Clay contrived to use the surplus to accomplish the principle of his land-distribution bill already referred to. It was agreed that the surplus remaining in the Treasury should be deposited in the state banks, ostensibly on terms similar to those in which the regular deposits had been transferred to them; but as a matter of fact, the money thus distributed remained the property of the states; another proof that a surplus is not so good a thing as a moderate national debt. Still, this method of disposing of the surplus was better than to yield it to open speculation, which was the growing vice of the time.

Arkansas was admitted as the twenty-fifth state in the Union, open to slavery, and Michigan followed on the free side. The election now coming on, Van Buren was found to have a majority of forty-nine electoral votes; the Vice-President, chosen by the legislature from several competitors, was Richard M. Johnson. Webster got Massachusetts' fourteen votes, and South Carolina again cast her votes for complimentary purposes only. Van Buren was pledged to continue the policy of his predecessor; and, contrary to expectation, the anti-slavery agitation had no influence on this contest. There could be no doubt that, despite its faults, Jackson's administration was approved by the country. He had been successful at home and abroad. The French claims had been paid, not without belligerent demonstrations on both sides; but Louis Philippe was too insecure on his throne to risk a war, especially in defense of a violated promise to pay. Other European nations settled their claims with us, or entered into friendly business relations, and commerce increased. Treaties were made with the Spanish-American republics, though great distrust was felt as to the stability of these little states, and the temptation to extend our boundaries was perceptible. For Jackson, indeed, it had been a temptation and something more. The Texas affair, whose first chapters date back fifteen years or more before this time, affords the first illustration of an annexation policy. The South had wished the region to be incorporated as a slave state; but Monroe had wisely prevented it. It was now a province of Mexico. Mexico herself was too feeble a state to secure respect. But the eastern boundary between Texas and the United States had been fixed at the Sabine River by a treaty negotiated by Clay in 1831. It was Jackson's purpose to keep freedom and slavery balanced. In 1835 he proposed to Mexico to sell not only Texas, but California; but Santa Anna, the Mexican President, refused. Meanwhile a large number of American colonists were settled in Texas, and had intimated their desire for annexation to the United States; this was regarded in the North as a plot to add slaveholding states to the Union. On the other hand, the Mexican government adopted measures which exasperated the American settlers; and under the leadership of Sam Houston, they established a government at Austin, and received material aid from Southern slaveholders. In the battle of San Jacinto, following the massacre of the Alamo, Santa Anna was defeated and taken prisoner. Jackson took a favorable view of all this, and sent United States troops to keep order. To avoid the appearance of forcing an infraction of the treaty, a number of old spoliation claims were revived, in settlement of which Texas might be seized. A rupture with the Mexican government was thus brought about, and all made ready for the next step; which, however, had to be left for Van Buren to make, since Jackson's tenure of power was now at its

sachusetts, McLean in Ohio, White in Georgia, Harrison in
Indiana and Ohio; and in favor of the latter, Webster withdrew his name, Clay also supporting him. The Democrats
nominated Van Buren, who was Jackson's choice. During
the interval before the election, there was a singular outburst of disorder all over the country, expressing itself in
riots, lynchings, strikes, and all manner of riotous disturbances; partly due no doubt to the young country "feeling its
oats," and discovering by experience the difference between
liberty and license; partly to the half-comprehended effect
upon ignorant minds of the Democratic ideas, which seemed
to deny rights to any except the common people. There was
also a hostile feeling against the Papacy, of which many terrible things were prophesied; and finally there was the far
more lasting element of trouble originating in the collisions
between slave sympathizers and their opponents. The new
abolition doctrines, of which William Lloyd Garrison was
the ablest and most unrelenting exponent, were to be a firebrand for more than twenty years to come. The abolitionists demanded instant extinction of slavery because it was
morally wrong; and since the Constitution allowed the system, they would do away with the Constitution, so far as
it commanded union; and were quite as insistent as the
Southerners themselves in their demand for separation. The
weight of opinion at the North was not in sympathy with
the logical extremists; and the negro himself was almost as
much restricted in northern communities as he would have
been in the South. The lines of caste were as sharply
drawn. Garrison's paper, the "Liberator," was as uncompromising and unflattering as he could make it; and his
powers were anything but contemptible. His fierce arraignment of the Constitution set the majority in the North, as
well as the whole South, against him. His importation of a
British anti-slavery speaker to address American audiences
(England having just emancipated the Jamaican negroes)
made things worse; there were furious popular outbreaks

against abolitionists, their meetings and their works; and the slave seemed not to be profiting by his champions. In October, 1835, Garrison was mobbed in Boston, and came near being hanged by the populace; but he only set up his press elsewhere, and continued his attacks. Sentiment was inflamed to a degree hardly credible in these less ardent times. Garrison's friends were quite as passionate as his foes. A negro uprising in Virginia was ascribed to the instigation of emancipation societies; and certainly the pamphlets which were circulated in the South were calculated to inspire negro rebellions. The abolitionists offered no plan for freeing slaves and at the same time compensating their owners; they declared the owners to be criminals who deserved nothing but ruin. All this was very impractical; but it had its good effect; for had it not been for Garrison and his followers, and the rage they aroused on both sides, the collision between South and North might have been indefinitely staved off, and with it our national relief from an incubus from which South and North alike are to-day glad to be free.

But if the abolitionists were extremists, the Southern slaveholders were no less so. Their attitude was haughty in the last degree; they worked the constitutional lash for all it was worth. They cracked their whips and demanded that abolitionists should be sent south to be hanged; and they introduced a gag law into Congress, forbidding any petitions on the subject of slavery to be so much as considered. This stirred up the venerable John Quincy Adams in defense of the right of petition. He had none of the obsequiousness which characterized too many of the public men at the North, in their attitude toward Southern arrogance; he did not favor the abolitionists, but he would countenance no infringement of liberty. "I hold the resolution a direct violation of the Constitution of the United States, of the rules of this House, and of the rights of my constituents"; and thenceforward he fought it until it was repealed. There

end. It is impossible not to admit that the conduct of this affair does not reflect credit upon Jackson's reputation for candor. The instinct for conquest of the soldier overcame the scruples which should have controlled the civil magistrate.

The finances of the country were left in a muddle which Jackson himself could neither comprehend nor control. The state banks were multiplied, and speculation, especially in western lands, was unrestrained. Cities were laid out on paper, and land worth little or nothing per acre was sold at a good price per front foot. Large importations of foreign goods were paid for in bullion, which was thus sent out of the country; and a circular issued by Jackson shortly before the end of his term to pay for public lands in hard money caused the gold and silver remaining to find its way into the Treasury. A panic and failures were inevitable; eight states failed, property lost value, and trade was arrested. Van Buren inherited this legacy of disaster, and bore the brunt of it; for it had not declared itself at the time Jackson withdrew.

Jackson was an extraordinary man; but his fortune was at least as extraordinary as he; no dreamer of romances would have trusted his imagination to invent such a man ruling in such a way over free America. He was as absolute as any despot; yet he was a champion of the Constitution and a true patriot; an illiterate man, in the conventional sense; and yet with as able an intellect, and as keen an insight into many political mill-stones, as men of far higher culture. He never made a mistake with the people; what he did, they liked, and what he liked, they supported. It did not seem to make much difference what views he held; they were certain to be indorsed by the public, if for no better reason, because Jackson held them. His work was often good; but the influence of his example in our politics cannot be commended. He made sycophancy an institution, because his subordinates feared him; he encouraged the lower elements of society, because he hated too narrowly the pretensions of wealth and society. He would not admit that there could be two sides to a question; there was but one side, and he was always on it. He made everything personal; and in this way he stamped his own personality so deeply upon history, that the impression can never be effaced; and yet, so singular was he, that few of his biographers claim fully to understand him. He was frank and blunt, passionate and trenchant; and yet some of the men who were nearest him declare that he was an actor, politic, and crafty. It is certain that he could dissimulate; he would not have been so successful a soldier had he not possessed the faculty of strategy. But like all men of great caliber, he had two men in him, one or the other of which predominated at different times, without any deliberate purpose of duplicity. So strong a man did not need to be a dissimulator, save as it were on the inspiration of the moment, when he might be partly moved by a grim sense of humor. That narrow brain of his was also deep, and he enjoyed outmaneuvering his antagonists as well as crushing them. No one who has looked into the intricacies of public life can have failed to observe how almost impossible it often is for the man in ostensible authority to force his purpose through the myriad obstacles and "pressures" which conflicting and plotting interests supply; but Jackson came as near doing it as any ruler of whom there is record, even though he were a despot in his own right, instead of only the chief magistrate of a free people.

Van Buren inaugurated an epoch of smaller men, not to be broken until Lincoln entered the White House. He was, apparently, a sincere hero-worshiper; and Jackson was the god of his idolatry, and the acknowledged model whose example it was his best ambition humbly to imitate. A more independent or less politic man might have been offended at the pains Jackson took to smooth the way for him; but Van Buren expressed only gratitude; as if a puppet should praise the hand which pulled its strings.

The first thing which Fate brought to pass upon the new President's amiable administration was that panic of 1837 to which we have already alluded. In this calamity every element which could render it complete seemed to combine; there was nothing to redeem the situation far or near; the failure of the crops made it necessary even to purchase grain abroad. The condition of finance was such that the mind shudders to contemplate it; legislatures were forced to pass acts legalizing suspension; not a bank in the country paid bullion. The pet banks which had received the national deposits fared no better than the rest. There seemed to be no money left in the world; notes might be paid for debts, and the next day the bank issuing them might fail. On the other hand, Congress and the President received their salaries in gold; which was not calculated to improve their popularity in the country. Van Buren was compelled to call an extra session to take counsel on the predicament.

To Congress, after reciting the condition of things, he proposed the measure which is his chief title to fame, though its effect upon himself was to defeat his political aspirations. He pointed out the evils inseparable from an alliance of any sort between banks and the government, and advocated abolishing such alliance altogether. In place of it, he would create an independent treasury, or, as it has come to be called, a sub-treasury, where the funds of the government could find a safe and convenient asylum. It was a good plan, as experience has proved; but it was new to those before whom it was laid, and their first instinct was to distrust it. It would give the government too much power, and would lock up in vaults bullion which ought to be circulating in the country. Moreover, the plan seemed incomplete; it was one end of a remedy, with the other left to conjecture. What should be done to secure a sound national currency? Further, it was suspected that the plan might be a disguised attack upon all banks; and that the proposed issue of treasury notes would renew the paper troubles under another form. The real difficulty in this and other affairs of Van Buren's administration, was the lack of confidence in its political integrity—a distrust which was quite as unjustifiable, to say the least, as it would have been if directed toward his predecessor. Van Buren was so artful a manager that it was hard to believe he would draw the line this side of unscrupulousness. The fact was, that Van Buren meant to be Jackson without Jackson's faults; but it would seem that Jackson's faults had been half the secret of his success; and when those were eliminated, the spell of Jacksonian Democracy lost its power.

This sub-treasury scheme, and the necessary retention of the next installment of the surplus promised to the banks, gave the new Whigs a desirable grievance on which to appeal to the people. The party was started with great enthusiasm, though they were obliged to restrict themselves to criticism rather than to suggest remedies. All the nice, clean, respectable folks belonged to it, with monopolies and protection in their train; it had friends in the South, and its advocacy of a national government was agreeable. Besides, it had the benefit of the distaste for the hard-handed Democracy which was beginning to be felt by natural reaction. A good issue was all that was needed to carry the country. On the other hand, Calhoun created a surprise by abandoning his hollow alliance with Clay, and advocating "unbanking the banks"; he called the connection of government with banks an "unholy alliance." Clay and Webster arraigned the sub-treasury plan as a first step toward an Executive Bank, with tyranny as its aim. But the corrupt collapse of Biddle's United States Bank, which was now accomplishing, showed that Jackson and Van Buren were right in the stand they had taken against it, and was a practical reply to the eloquence of the orators on the other side.

But it was the slavery question which, in spite of all efforts to down it, persisted in raising its threatening front in Congress and the country. The Abolitionists had made the conscience of the North uneasy, and divided their councils, while antagonizing the South to an intense degree. The Democrats were controlled by the South; the Whigs were opposed to slavery extension, or to the domination of the slavery cause, but could not go the length of the Abolitionists, who were ready to surrender the Constitution on abstract moral grounds. Abstract right was all very well; but did a man owe nothing to the Constitution, and to the Union which it demanded? Was one man justified in requiring another to conform to his own moral principles or prejudices? The Abolitionists troubled themselves little about arguments; slavery must be abolished, Union or no Union. There was a discrimination to be observed here; we are not yet far enough advanced in human brotherhood to be able to interfere in the affairs of foreign nations, with a view to improving them, unless, as recently in Cuba, we find a decadent and barbarous nation inflicting savage cruelties upon a people struggling for freedom at our very doors. But a nation has a right to regulate, within limits, the conduct of its own citizens, when it plainly outrages morality, and threatens the common weal. For the nation is a homogeneous body, in which the sickness of one part affects all. If slavery was in itself an evil and a menace, the United States had a right to restrain or extirpate it; and it was only because the United States was composed of separate states that this right was obscured. The Southern states took the ground of separate nations, and based their claims thereon. But whatever political hair-splitting might pretend, the effect upon our free states of slavery in our slave states was utterly different from what would be upon us the effect of slavery in a nation really foreign. Our Congress was composed of representatives from all states; and as it was evident that slavery produced radical divergences in points of national policy, either government must be carried on by a system of compromises, with all the dangers and obstructions which that involves; or one party must finally overcome and dominate the other; or the two must part. At present, we were trying the compromise alternative: for the rest, although it was possible for the North to dominate the South, the contrary was not possible, since the physical conditions at the North did not admit of slave labor being used there, all questions of morality aside; whereas in the South free labor might succeed. The alternative of separation remained; but that must be by common agreement of all parties; that agreement wanting, it might be accomplished by force, provided the force available were sufficient for the purpose. It turned out not to be sufficient, when the experiment was tried. But was the South justified in trying the experiment? The answer, on general principles, must be in the affirmative. She had a fair chance of success, and no further justification has ever been deemed necessary, when one body of people wished to divide itself from another. The Constitution could not stand in the way; treaties and paper compacts of all kinds are outgrown and cast aside every day; they are valid so long as they are useful, and no longer. Our Constitution has lasted because its provisions are far-seeing and sensible, and because it admits of remodeling as circumstances may require. But the right of the South to secede—if it could—was confused with a question quite distinct from it: the question whether she had a right to secede in order to continue slavery. Admitting slavery to be wrong, however convenient, is any people justified in bringing on a devastating war for the sake of supporting a wrong? The answer, on moral grounds, must be in the negative. But should the South therefore be condemned? How often, in the history of the world, has a nation molded its national policy against its interests, out of respect for the moral law? Besides, the South had been brought to believe that slavery was not wrong; they quoted Holy Writ in its support, and were furnished by Calhoun and others with many special reasons in addition. The very fact that it was assailed blinded them to its faults. They would fight for it not only as a matter of right, but of affection also—as for a beloved thing which had been attacked. Upon the whole, we may relieve ourselves of the apprehension that several million inhabitants of this country were any worse than the other millions, because they rebelled. They were subjects of human nature and creatures of circumstance, like all other sons of Adam; and Providence used them in its own ways for purposes greater than either they or we could know.

As for the Abolitionists, they cannot be praised for political sagacity; but they did not covet that sort of praise. They deserve the name of martyrs to their moral convictions; some of them, like Lovejoy, were called upon to shed their life-blood literally in defense of their opinions; others, like Jonathan Cilley, were shot on the "field of honor" because they ventured to criticise Southern views—though Cilley was not an Abolitionist in any rabid sense of the term; he was simply not an advocate of slavery. No doubt the Abolitionists exasperated the South exceedingly. But, on the other hand, the Southerners were altogether too haughty and touchy, and too incautious in their expressions of scorn and contempt for the Northerners. They were intolerant to an almost incredible degree; and the patience the Northerners often showed is only less remarkable. They would not permit the subject of slavery to be alluded to or hinted at in their presence. It was something holy, sacred—or perhaps it was a raw sore. This sensitiveness is almost unique in political records, and could be accounted for in various ways. Its origin is probably to be found in the moral question involved; men quarreled about it just as they do about religious creeds; and nobody, not engaged in the discussion, can understand why they so quickly lose their tempers.

Another attempt to annex the free state of Texas (as it now called itself) failed to gain government support; but arrangements were made for a board of arbitration to decide upon the American claims against Mexico. A decision was also wanted regarding the precise location of our Maine boundary line; and quarrels on this point were complicated by a petty rebellion in Canada, which led some hasty spirits to imagine, quite erroneously, that Canada wished to join our Union. In the South, Osceola, after a spirited resistance to our prolonged effort to put down the Seminoles, was captured, and soon after died in prison; but the war lingered along several years more. The war was never popular, and cost more than it was worth; and Van Buren, as usual, got all the blame. The sub-treasury bill finally passed, on the 30th of June, 1840, and was artfully approved by the President on the Fourth of July; but the financial and business condition was still gloomy. But the most important occurrence of the time had been the Whig Convention which assembled in December, 1839, at Harrisburg in Pennsylvania, with Barbour in the chair. Whom would they nominate for the Presidency? Clay was the most prominent candidate; but he had been engaged in so many battles that it seemed doubtful if he could carry the election. Harrison and Winfield Scott were the alternative men; for Webster had no sure following except in his own section. After three days' voting, Harrison was chosen, and Tyler, the friend of Clay, was given the second place, more out of compliment to the latter than on his own account; and also to please Southern delegates. Clay had told his friends to sacrifice him if the good of the party demanded it; but he was bitterly disappointed, nevertheless, to be taken at his word. Seward was accused of having aided in defeating him, in combination with his allies Horace Greeley and Thurlow Weed, who were at the convention; but in truth it was the common sense of the majority of the convention; and there probably never had been a moment in his whole career when Clay could have reasonably counted on the united support of the country. He could see that it was better to be right than to be President; but it was possible to be too brilliant to be President, and, certainly, to be too fertile in compromises.—Large defections from the Democrats increased the strength of the party, till in spite of the advantage of position possessed by the Democrats, and the prestige of past success, the Whigs seemed to have the people.

The Democrats of course nominated Van Buren; they had no one else, and no one could have served their turn better. The campaign had no very sharp issues; the best issue for the Whigs seemed to be that they were new and enthusiastic; but the ardor of the combatants has never been surpassed, and there was hardly a voter in the land who did not cast his vote. The unique spectacle was presented of vast open-air political gatherings where not the voters only, but their wives and children, congregated to see, hear and shout. Enormous processions moved to and fro; they carried emblems of their cause, and mottoes, and they shouted refrains; all the fine young fellows in America seemed to be Whigs, and all confident of victory. They were tired of the autocrat; they wanted a strong but quiet and law-abiding man, who had a good temper and could recognize other elements in the government besides the Executive. The rare assortment of famous orators which the country possessed at this time was turned loose upon the crowds, and made them tenfold more enthusiastic and confident than ever. The nation may be said to have enjoyed this campaign; and for many a year afterward one might hear veterans recalling to one another, with chuckles, the glorious excitement of those days, when their throats were hoarse with shouting "Tippecanoe, and Tyler too!" And what lakes of hard cider were drunk out of pure patriotism, and what cities of log cabins overspread the landscape! What caricatures also, in which the hard-handed Democrats found themselves figured by little Matty Van Buren, in kid gloves and a gilded coach, while the leader of the supposed aristocracy was a plain soldier farmer, who worked with his hands and lived poor and simple. But the fact was that the sentiment of the nation was wholly against aristocracy, and any intimation of an opposite feeling always involved the party betraying it in disaster. The Whigs, so far from suffering for lack of an issue, actually made capital out of their deficiency; they had the more leisure for hooting down their adversaries. The final result of it all was a stupendous victory for the Whigs, who beat the Democrats by two hundred and thirty-four votes against sixty. A third party, called the Liberty Party, also polled a few votes here and there for itself; it was supposed to be constituted of the moral reformers who were becoming singularly numerous about this time; every ism having its followers, from Transcendentalism down. The Liberty Party was to be heard from again later.

Van Buren took his defeat with his usual steadiness, and his next message was the best and boldest he ever wrote. He warned against renewing the public debt, a large part of which would be held by foreign investors; and the state debts were already threatened in some places with repudiation. He renewed the argument against the National Bank; and as if to accent his words, that sinister institution, with Biddle at its head, found in its lowest deep a lower deep to fall into; its final collapse, followed by the revelation of more than its worst enemies had charged of rascality and rottenness, took place in 1841. Biddle lingered three years longer, and then died of mortification rather than shame; for he was too callous in iniquity to feel the latter.

Van Buren began life as the son of a poor farmer, and reached the Presidency. He was not the creature of chance, but of hard work and great sagacity; he had a wonderful brain, and many great virtues; and if he had vices, they were not of such a character as to be known. He had been trained in early life by Aaron Burr, and there were no arts of management with which he was not familiar; he probably designed to lift himself to the top by such arts, and by the help of greater men, such as Jackson; and he succeeded. But if, as was also probable, he meant, on attaining the supreme place, to lay aside all his tricks of fence and in-

trigue, and show himself as a man of independent convictions
and sincere character, he failed; because the reputation of a
lifetime could not be dissipated in four years; and his evil
inheritance from Jackson was too much to carry off. Another handicap from which he suffered was his small stature
and plump figure, which made it impossible to take him
seriously; he may have been no shorter, and no plumper,
than the great Napoleon; but he did not produce the same
effect on beholders. He was too polite, soft-spoken, and too
deft a steersman. Such men are very useful in politics, and
when they are reasonably honest, as Van Buren certainly
was, they may be something more. Van Buren's sub-treasury scheme was sound statesmanship, separating as it did
private from public finance. But he had contrived to avoid
personal quarrels all his life; he had been friendly to everybody; and finally no one believed he was the friend of
anybody, and none stood his friend at the critical hour.
And what good he accomplished was not credited to him,
and was not recognized during his tenure of power. His
defeat on the occasion of this first appeal for re-election was
emphasized by the refusal of the people to reinstate him on
the other two occasions when he was nominated for the
Presidency; their "sober second thought" had no reversal
for him. But he lived to be eighty years old, and doubtless
reconciled himself to a fate which after all was not so bad
for a poor farmer's boy!

Besides the steam-engine and the steamboat, science
added to the breadth of life by the daguerreotype and the
electric telegraph, at this period; for though Morse's first
telegraph line was not opened till 1844, his patent was
granted in 1837. Exploration was carried on chiefly by the
Wilkes expedition, which sailed nearly ninety thousand
miles, and investigated tropic islands and polar snows.
Literature was beginning to be an appreciable quantity
among us, in spite of the competition of pirated books from
England; Emerson had published his earlier essays, which

are still as much read as ever, and better understood; Bryant and Longfellow had proved that Americans could be poets. Irving's reputation was already of long standing; Cooper was our only great novelist so far; though a young man named Nathaniel Hawthorne had become known to a few as showing promise in some short tales and sketches. Bennett had founded his newspaper, and Hoe, the inventor of steam-presses, was led thereto by the wearisomeness of working the press of his little sheet, "The Sun," by hand. Meanwhile honest and doctrinaire Horace Greeley had set the "Tribune" going; and American journalism was an accomplished fact, though little witting of what it was to become. In short, the gate of modern times was swinging ajar.

This is a country of contrasts; but there had been no greater contrast between successive Presidents than that between Harrison and his predecessor. Van Buren had spent his life amid policies, stratagems and intrigues, seeing the seamy side of human nature, and deprived of all possibility of keeping in touch with natural impulses and sincere feelings. He had climbed upward by art and interest, by cunning compromises and concessions; he had regarded men as instruments, and life as a calculation. But Harrison was a countryman; a soldier of proved quality, but only accidentally and incidentally, because circumstance compelled it. He was transparent and honest, with a warm heart and a tender conscience; endowed with manly dignity, and strength of will and self-respect, which could call to order even the impatient audacity of Clay; but approachable by all, kindly, friendly; desirous only to do good to his country, and leave a spotless record behind him. His gray hair and clear dark eyes gave his aspect a certain distinction which was fully carried out by the quality of his mind and character; he had a strength and ability which old politicians like Clay and Webster hardly gave him credit for, finding him below the mark in certain superficial attributes of the public man. But after all we can but surmise what Harrison might have accomplished; he had barely grasped the wand of office, when he fell.

He had lacked but two years of fulfilling the allotted span of man when he came to Washington; nor would he have survived so long, but for his temperate outdoor life in his Ohio home; for his constitution had never been robust. His campaign, as we have seen, had been unusually exciting, and he had several times addressed the people. He made the journey to Washington at an inclement season, with the accompaniments of public demonstrations along the way, to which he responded heartily, as his nature prompted. When he reached the capital, the pressure on his strength was increased instead of being relaxed; the day of inauguration was cold and gloomy, and he spoke in the open air for an hour. His address was friendly and conciliating in tone, and gave promise of purity and independence in administration; he would abate abuse of patronage, would not invade Southern susceptibilities, would not advocate a currency exclusively metallic. In the manner and general tone, rather than in special phrases, he made it evident that he intended to do good and dispense justice to all. Even his opponents trusted him and honored him.

Immediately began the scramble for place, in which the Whigs showed themselves full as active as the Democrats had been, though during the campaign they had been noisy in denouncing the spoils system. But it might be argued that after a spoils system has been once begun, it can never end; for if a man gets an office, not for merit but for service done, he should be ousted at the first opportunity—which would of course be when the next change of party occurred. But inasmuch as his successor is no better than he, the vicious routine can never end. As a matter of fact, it is a constant surprise, not that our civil service is so bad, but that it is no worse; the men who clamor for office (and no others get it) being uniformly the least fitted to receive it

There must be a great deal of latent virtue in the body corporate.

Harrison offered the portfolio of State to Clay, who declined it, but recommended two of his friends for places in the Cabinet. Harrison then gave Webster the option of being either State or Treasury secretary, and he took the former. Webster and Clay were already rivals for that which neither would ever attain. But they had combined to put Harrison in the saddle, and he, perhaps in acknowledgment of their service, pledged himself in his inaugural not to seek a second nomination. He might have spared himself that trouble.—The other men in the Cabinet, though respectable, possessed no marked ability; they were fairly competent to their duties.

From sunrise till midnight the President was kept busy tossing the morsels of patronage to the roaring pack of wild animals who surged round him. There were more offices than ever before, and more applicants for each office; and every Congressman had his group of friends to recommend. Harrison worked along systematically and intelligently, doing the best he could. On the 17th of March he convened an extra session for the last of May; but about the first of April he caught a chill from careless exposure, which his frame lacked vitality to resist. It developed into pneumonia, and he died on the 4th of the month. "Sir," said he, addressing some imaginary interlocutor as he lay on the brink of the next world, "I wish you to understand the true principles of the government; I wish them carried out; I ask no more."

His death startled and saddened the nation. He was the first President who had died with his term uncompleted; and he was the object of a more widespread personal affection than most public men. All that could be done was to give him a great funeral; thousands followed in the train; there was complaining of bugles and trample of muffled drums, and a black, open car, with white horses and heaps of mounded flowers. In the hearse lay the body of a poor country gentleman, whom a nation had trusted, whom they had lifted to the highest place in their gift, and for whom they heartily grieved. He was buried in the cemetery of Congress; but afterward, at his friends' request, his body was removed to his home at North Bend on the Ohio, a more fitting resting place for a President who was so little of a politician.

Among those who followed the procession was John Tyler, the former Vice-President, now President by the grace of God. He had come post-haste from Virginia on learning the news which elevated him to the unhoped-for dignity. He continued the Cabinet in their places, and his address seemed to pledge him to carry out the dead man's policy. He promised that there should be no further war between the government and the currency. In short, his attitude was just what it ought to have been, and the nation felt relieved from a momentary anxiety. Tyler was Harrison over again, mutato nomine. But gentlemen in Congress, who knew him better, may have suspended their full confidence until further developments.

In fact, however, no one at this time knew Tyler; he did not know himself. He found himself suddenly in the place of power, and was at first subdued by the shock; his nature was susceptible of fine impressions, and he may have told himself that this was a great opportunity vouchsafed by Providence, of which he would make the highest use he could. His record showed him to be a man who had taken no decided or irrevocable line on prominent questions; either from caution or from lack of conviction, he had kept a middle course, though not without occasional reproach of bad faith, which he had zealously sought to repel. But he was now called upon to fill one of the most conspicuous positions in the world, where he must avouch himself one thing or the other; a position to which he had not been elected, and which he entered under unique circumstances. His first instinct, natural to one of his temperament, was to deprecate criticism, and conciliate public opinion; afterward he would review his situation more coolly, and map out his plans.

Tyler was a tall, slight, fair man, with delicate brown hair, which he wore rather long; he was of good family, and always showed high breeding in his manners, which were also affable and attractive, especially to women. He thought well of himself, physically, mentally and morally; and believed that he had a very sensitive conscience. His mind ran to fine discriminations, to hair-splitting; and this quality he found useful in accounting to himself for his own conduct, and squaring it with his rule of right and honor. He could, so to say, argue one thing into another, and thus establish an apparent consistency between acts which a more straightforward moralist would have called irreconcilable. Thus far in life he had been free from grave responsibilities, and his views of public matters had been colored by circumstances, and by his own chance predilections; he saw some things in Democracy that he liked, and accepted other things which belonged to the Whig policy. He was independent; there was no reason why he should not be so—until the time should come when his further political career depended upon his allying himself finally with one side or the other. When that time should come, he would still have the option of remaining independent and keeping out of responsibilities; or of accepting responsibilities and respecting allegiance to party.

In accepting the office of Vice-President, he had not felt that this epoch of final choice had arrived. He belonged to that wing of the Whig party which was nearest to the moderate wing of the Democratic party; it was of no consequence, because the office itself carried no weight. He might have been a Democratic Vice-President almost as well as a Whig one. But he was now President, and there could be no half measures. If he felt that he could not be a true Whig, it was his duty to resign. If he was not willing to carry out the policy of Harrison, and to act in harmony with the Whig majority in the legislature, he had no business in the White House.

But it was easy for a hair-splitter like Tyler to persuade himself that the alternative was not so sharp as this; and if he hesitated himself, there was no lack of advisers to strengthen his resolution. A little knot of Virginians, to whom Clay gave the name of the corporal's guard, soon attached itself to him, and helped him to make up his mind, and to gloss over his scruples. Of this group, Wise and Beverly Tucker were the ablest. Under their ministrations, his first timidity gradually gave way. He was after all a Southerner and a slaveholder; that was in his nature; and when a conflict between the nature and the mental conclusion occurs, nature prevails, and the mind proceeds to confirm its action. Nature, in this case, was also on the side of self-interest, and of personal feeling. Tyler suddenly realized that he was in a position of supreme power, if he chose to make the most of it; and he at the same time conceived the ambition to be re-elected at the end of his term, on his own merits, and thus do away with the stigma of having been only an accidental President. The ambition was in itself legitimate; although he had vehemently declared against the principle of a second term, before it occurred to him that he might get it.

Tyler could also reflect that there was nothing wrong in being moderate; and between moderation and treason, in a party man, the line is not always easily drawn. But a still stronger temptation to abandon the Whigs was found in the rivalry between Tyler and Henry Clay, who arrogated to himself, not without good reason, the real leadership of the party, and who obviously expected Tyler to carry out his commands. Tyler and Clay had been friends for twenty years; but when Clay called upon Tyler, a month after Harrison's death, and refused to support Tyler's scheme of a district bank, they quarreled, and were thenceforth enemies. Tyler knew that Clay was the next candidate for President in 1844; and he resolved that he would defeat him for the prize. He was sure that he could count upon the support of the South, and he believed that he could win more in the North than Clay could. He could harmonize the parties; or he could make a party of his own and lead it to victory. Thus, partly by accident, partly by selfish ambition and private pique, and partly by the urgency of others, Tyler was forced into an attitude which history has failed to approve. He betrayed the party by which he had been placed in power, and his administration was a continual battle between Congress and himself, in which neither achieved any decisive victory.

As a dramatic episode, this administration is full of human interest; for on either side of Tyler were contending Clay and Webster. Webster's course is not readily reconciled with unselfish desire for the public welfare; and his behavior was less frank than Clay's, who never disguised that the Presidency was his goal. Webster was Tyler's Secretary of State, and he defended his financial policy, and took his part against Clay; after all the rest of the Cabinet had resigned, he remained, ostensibly in order to conclude delicate negotiations with England, with whom we were on the brink of war over the questions of the northeast boundary, and the right of search in the slave-trade. Edward Everett was our representative in England, and Lord Ashburton, son of Baring the banker, came to Washington with full powers to settle the difficulty or to declare a settlement impossible. It was finally arranged, creditably to both sides, but Webster still lingered in the Cabinet. He hoped to improve opportunities to defeat Clay; but events were not to be controlled. Tyler's main fight with Congress was over the financial problem; expedients to supply the place of the defunct United States Bank were suggested and defeated. Clay had one plan, Tyler another; Congress went far toward meeting Tyler's views, on the promise, given by him, that he would immediately sign the amended bill; but he broke his pledge, and vetoed it. His vetoes were numerous, and the necessary two-thirds majority to pass bills over his veto could not be secured, in the peculiar state of parties. At length he was formally read out of his party; he tried to form another by inviting men from both sides; but neither the Democrats nor the Whigs would accept his overtures. In March, 1842, Clay bade farewell to Congress in a farewell speech, it being his intention never again to sit in the body; though in fact he returned seven years later under Fillmore. He was deeply moved, and he moved others; the Senate adjourned till the next day, and Calhoun, Clay's former friend, who had been estranged from him for five years, met him as he left the Chamber, with outstretched hands, and the two great men embraced each other with a common impulse. It is seldom, in public affairs, that the great men of the country are on the same side; they oppose one another, and thus defeat one another's power for good. In the Colonial and Revolutionary days, the hostility of England banded our leaders all together in one cause, and we have seen the results, even against the greatest odds; but now, when the Republic was established, and the country developed and capable of the highest prosperity, we see its possibilities hampered by the feuds of those who were most highly endowed to benefit it. Their mutual jealousies and personal ambitions made them forget their duty. History must take note of these men, and ignore to a great extent the mass of the population, who knew little of their disputes, successes and failures, and lived from day to day busied with their private concerns. Attempts have indeed been made to write the history of the people, and of other peoples besides the American; but it is found impossible to make the story clear without the annals of the Presidents and the monarchs, their doings and vicissitudes. For through them alone does the story advance, and the sequence of cause and effect appear. The people, for whose sake the rulers exist, and by whom they are created, serve but as the side scenes and background of the tale. We can depict them in broad lines; we can note the changes of costume and manners from generation to generation; we can brighten the scene with anecdotes and apologues; but these do but serve, in the end, to give substance and firmness to our understanding of the dominant and guiding few. To however great a degree we extend our canvas and multiply our figures, the result is the same. We cannot but feel some resentment at the restriction, remembering how much more agreeable or not less inthralling would be many a tale of private experience which never can reach history's page. But in truth, history must body forth the state and make of it the semblance of a living entity; and discipline her pen to mark only those features which concern the state's character and acts. The novelist holds the other field, and the future student of mankind will perhaps not assign him the second place.

Tyler was misunderstood even by his corporal's guard; they thought him easier to manage than he was. His facile manner did not prevent him from manifesting a stubborn fiber of determination; upon his own plane, and in his own depth, he would do as he pleased. He had an emotional but shallow nature; tending to the use of strong adjectives in public and private utterances, but his tears and smiles came from no great depth, and were soon forgotten. His heart may have amused him, but it never troubled him, and it never controlled his policy. But it is the heart which gives insight; and this is what Tyler lacked. He saw reasons and distinctions in abundance; but he did not understand the temper or desires of the nation, nor comprehend their opinion of him. He was most disposed to believe what pleased his self-esteem most, he was active, skillful, resourceful, and airily cheerful, and became constantly less scrupulous about the means he employed to prevail. He thought to use Webster to help him crush Clay; but he meant to get rid of Webster himself as soon as he had served his turn. What precisely was his relation to Calhoun cannot be certainly known; but it is probable that the great South Carolinian furnished him with whatever distinct policy he had. The true character of his designs was not fully fathomed until the Texas question reappeared; it then became evident that Tyler intended to back its admission as a slave territory, and the North finally turned its back on him. It was a curious result after the generous enthusiasm of the Tippecanoe-and-Tyler-too campaign.

The revision of the tariff was one of the measures which were dear to the Whigs, but Tyler vetoed two of their bills, and the compromise bill which received his signature favored the Nullification party. The compromise tariff bill which Clay had devised years before had been of benefit to manufacturers and to the whole country; and in the South the value of the cotton crop had so increased that the saying "Cotton is King" passed into a proverb. But Clay's bill had provided that the scaling down of duties should be suddenly accelerated at the end of the term; which of course cut off the revenue abruptly. In order to secure our credit, it was necessary to change the law. The Whigs wanted to make revenue the end and protection only incidental to it. Such an act was passed for the emergency, but when its time limit expired there were difficulties again. Fresh action had to be taken. After Tyler had vetoed a provisional and a regular tariff bill, Congress emitted a protest charging him with misusing the veto power; and debated whether to adjourn and leave him without a revenue. But it was finally agreed to omit from the bill the features to which Tyler had objected, and the latter had his triumph over Clay once more. Another cause of mortification to us was the state debts, which were due to the speculation which preceded the panic of 1837; they were owing chiefly in Europe, which desired to make the national government responsible for them. Mississippi threatened to repudiate her debt in 1841; but the other states, led by Pennsylvania, refused to follow her example. It was at this time that Dickens visited America, and his criticisms stung the more for the basis of truth that was in them. But slavery, even more than finance, gave point to his pen; for Tyler was bringing this trouble toward its climax. The South was growing constantly more arrogant, and the North was to some degree intimidated. Adams and the younger but not less valiant Giddings of Ohio alone defied them in Congress, and issue was joined for the present on the fugitive slave law. Finally, in 1842, the Supreme Court handed down a decision making the slaveholder independent of extradition laws which might hinder him in recapturing his runaways; but the free states often disobeyed this ruling.

The mid-term elections distracted public attention from other things. Clay's retirement from Congress had not, of course, prejudiced his claim to the Presidency; he was nominated, and it seemed hardly possible he could be defeated. Webster's position was now peculiar. He was still a member of the Cabinet, and he made a speech in Faneuil Hall commending Tyler, though not in very hearty terms. He had hoped to rally the Northern Whigs, believing that they would nominate him instead of Tyler; but the only effect of his speech was to discourage them; and the open attitude of Clay won him the Whig preference over both Tyler and Webster. But Webster could not yet reach such a pitch of magnanimity as to support Clay; he preferred to get out of the country and forget politics for a time. An attempt was made to get the English mission for him by inducing Everett to go to China; but it failed; and Webster, without cause assigned, resigned his place in the Cabinet, Tyler promptly though politely accepting his resignation. There was danger of Webster's final extinction at this juncture; but it happened that Bunker Hill Monument had just been completed, and he was asked to deliver the oration, as he had done at the laying of the cornerstone. His speech on this occasion was so impressive that it revived his popularity, and the Whigs opened their arms to him once more, though it was too late for any question of the Presidency. It was now that the reconciliation with Clay, perfunctory or not, was effected; but meanwhile the mid-term elections had favored the Democrats, and Clay was not so sure of success as he had been. Moreover, in the Texas annexation question Tyler had the means of dividing Whig councils.

Texas, after the defeat of the Spanish at San Jacinto, had posed as an independent republic, and had been acknowledged as such by America and also in Europe. But Mexico, with the blind stubbornness which marks the Spanish character, and resembles that of their own cattle, would acknowledge nothing, and kept up a dribbling warfare on the borders. Sam Houston, President of the republic, wished it to be annexed to this country; but Tyler had feared hitherto to consent, lest he be deserted by the Northern states. But now he was no longer withheld by this consideration, and he made overtures, which Houston, after some hesitation on his side, due to doubts whether the country would support the President, accepted. Mexico meantime had announced that she would consider annexation an act of war. Her attitude was more foolish than wrong; and she had begun paying our claims against her in hard money, though she stripped her people to do it. Texas, at this time, meant the whole southwest country which now includes the states of New Mexico, Arizona, California, and the Lone Star State itself. With slavery and the cotton crop established there, the South would gain a decisive preponderance in the Union.

Houston had stipulated that he should be protected by United States troops against invasion by Mexico. Tyler accordingly stationed troops on the border; Commodore Jones had before been dispatched with a squadron to the Pacific, where he took temporary possession of Monterey. All this time, the country, Congress, and even Webster, had been kept in ignorance at what was going forward.

Upshur and Gilmer, members of the Cabinet, were Tyler's confederates. While the negotiations were at an interesting stage, they were both killed, together with other distinguished persons, while witnessing experiments with a new big gun, which exploded, Tyler himself narrowly escaping. Calhoun was selected to fill Upshur's place. He afterward claimed that Texas annexation was his work; but Tyler never conceded it. Rumors of the plot now got abroad, and South divided against North upon Texan admission. At the national conventions, both Clay and Van Buren, who was the leading Democratic candidate, declared against annexation. The Tyler convention, which was not regarded as regular, made immediate annexation the leading plank in its platform. But the Van Buren Democrats were divided on the question, and Cass was advocated by the Virginia delegates as their candidate. After some balloting, James K. Polk of Tennessee was unexpectedly nominated, and was pledged to annexation. Reoccupation of Oregon was also a leading principle with the Democrats; the whole Pacific slope had gradually been settled by streams of emigrants from the East. Meanwhile the Senate voted against admitting Texas, except with the concurrence of Mexico. Each branch of the government was obstructing the other.

The campaign of 1844 seemed bound to terminate in favor of Clay; he was certainly one of the best known and most popular men in the country. Polk was hardly known at all, and had always taken subordinate positions; but he was "safe and simple." Jackson advocated him; and finally Tyler, perceiving the hopelessness of his canvass, retired in his favor. "The Democracy of the North are the natural allies of the South," said a Richmond paper. Both Clay and Polk being slave-holders, it was suggested that the best man to win with would be the least risky one, who was Polk. There were outside complications: no-popery riots, and the appearance of the Liberty Party with Birney as their nominee. The anti-slavery society agitated, under the lead of Garrison and Wendell Phillips, for the dissolution of the Union. Adams, Seward and Giddings backed Clay as an anti-annexationist. But Clay was being denounced as an abolitionist in the South, while in the North he was arraigned as slavery's friend. His instinct to run with the hare and hunt with the hounds was doing him an ill turn at this crisis of his destiny. He even allowed an expression to escape him which was quoted as making him favor Texas annexation. In the end, it was New York which decided the election, as it has done more than once since. It went for Polk by only five thousand majority; but for the Liberty Party, it would have given twice as many for Clay. Massachusetts did not vote till after the result was assured; then, under the stimulus of Webster at Faneuil Hall, it gave its whole vote to the defeated candidate. It was pleasant to see a great man thus true to the cause of his rival; though it may have been that Webster was not wholly cast down by Clay's defeat.

The Texas annexation bill now came before Congress with the current in its favor; a pretext of British intervention was set up, which would make it an independent and non-slave-holding state; after an intricate debate, the bill passed both Houses, under the lead of Benton. Yet the act might have been still longer delayed had not a revolution in Mexico overthrown Santa Anna, its President, and put Herrera in his place. On the first of March, 1845, Tyler signed the bill. Texas was a part of the Union; four states might be formed out of her; in those below the Missouri Compromise line, slavery would be optional; those above it should be free. The matter of the war with Mexico was left for Polk to deal with.

The annexation of Texas is the only noteworthy incident of Tyler's administration; for the Patroon war in New York, and Dorr's rebellion in Rhode Island, had no special significance, except as showing the growth, irregular but inevitable, of the freedom of the individual in the state.

But Texas must have become incorporate with us sooner or later; the rights of the question were complicated with the slavery dispute, and the claims of Mexico; but there could be only one issue, and those who have condemned our conduct are hypercritical. Passion and accident combined with manifest destiny to bring about the result; but men are human, and in blood and money we paid a fair price for our acquisition. Whatever obloquy attaches to the transaction we may safely ascribe to the "renegade President."

CHAPTER TWENTY-NINTH

MEXICO

POLK was not a great man; he might be called a small one, if the comparison is to be with such figures as those of Clay, Calhoun and Webster. He was elected by an unforeseen contingency, and seemed even less likely than Tyler to accomplish anything of importance. He was a disciple of Jackson, who still lived and talked at his Hermitage in Tennessee; he was a strict party man, and never entertained a thought of transcending the obligations which his election had imposed upon him. There was nothing striking in his character or physical appearance; he was a sober-looking individual in the neighborhood of fifty years of age, with plain manners and guileless habits—which included the national habit of tobacco chewing—and he was the husband of a lady who had strict ideas of religion and behavior. Such people might have been postmaster and postmistress of a small country town; blameless in their private lives, keeping up with current politics, observant of their routine civic and social duties. They were commonplace Americans. Polk was born in North Carolina and brought up on a Tennessee farm; he had been a member of Congress, and was industrious and trustworthy; he had tenacity of purpose, and could see clearly within his limited range; he had plenty of courage, and believed in his country, especially in the Democratic aspect of it. In short he was a good, honest business man, whose business was politics; and his unlooked-for elevation neither frightened him, nor made him vain. He looked upon it as a business contract, which he would proceed to carry out, on party lines, without fear or favor. He chose an able Cabinet, but was the master of it, and commanded its respect. Such a man is a proof, if anything can be, that any ordinary American of good character and political training can make a good President of the United States. And it may happen that, like Polk, the ordinary American will be the agent of events no less momentous than those which marked Polk's presidential career. We have just seen how great men may produce small results; we now see a small man produce great results—so far as an Executive can be said to produce anything.

But Polk was not only methodical: the plans that he made he carried out. Up to this time all the Presidents, from Washington down, had planned things which they did not execute; but Polk proposed to himself four special things, and he did them all during his four years of power. They were, reduction of the tariff, an independent treasury, the settlement of the Oregon boundary, and the Texan or Californian acquisition. That was a large contract for four years; but he carried it out. The changes he made in the civil service of course occasioned some dissensions; he alienated Calhoun and Tyler; but he could afford to do that; for Tyler was now nobody, and Calhoun was South Carolina only. Upon the whole, his appointments were judicious. In June, 1845, Jackson died, nearly eighty years old, pursued almost to the last by swarms of office-seekers who thought his word with the President would be conclusive. Polk, assuredly, had been his faithful disciple; but times were changing, and it is probable that Polk did quite as well without that autocratic power in the background.

The most pressing matter at the beginning of his term was the Oregon boundary. The United States had been the first, through Captain Grey, many years before, to discover the Columbia River; and with its discovery went the lands which it drained. But the British Fur Company had been collecting furs in the northwest region for generations, and the British government laid claim to everything in its usual high-handed and insolent manner. Our claim extended north to latitude 54° 40'; the English would concede nothing above 49°. They wished to keep the country wild and uninhabited, in order to preserve their game; we wished to settle in it, and had been doing so for years; and meanwhile a "joint occupation" had been agreed to, which was inconvenient, and admittedly temporary. Polk's inaugural address asserted our right to all Oregon; and the country took up the claim with the cry of "Fifty-Four Forty or Fight!" Considering that we were on the brink of war with Mexico, this recalled our belligerent attitude at the time of the war of 1812, when we had debated whether we ought not to take on France as well as England. But though it was thought that England might fight for Oregon, it was not believed that Mexico would fight for Texas and California; an offer of money would satisfy her. If Congress had properly echoed the feeling of the country at this juncture, it is likely that war with England would have taken place. But Congress, the more it deliberated, grew the more moderate; and the messages of Polk were gradually toned down, till the final Congressional report became a practical basis for diplomatic negotiation. During the discussion, the influx of emigrants had been greatly increased, whereas the British only held fortified posts, and instead of making bona-fide settlements of their own, did all they could to put difficulties in the way of our emigrants, and did not hesitate to incite the Indians against them. But Buchanan was our Secretary of State; and he finally agreed to accept from Pakenham, the British minister, the boundary of 49°, with navigation of the Columbia for the Fur Company. It was less than our right, but for practical purposes it was quite as much as we could make use of.

After passing a new tariff bill, which reduced duties and assessed ad valorem, which was criticised by both Whigs and Democrats, but did not interrupt the prosperity of the country, the Mexican business came to the fore.

The war with Mexico was violently denounced at the time, and has often been condemned since; it gave James Russell Lowell a memorable opportunity to display his talent for satire and his command of Yankee dialect, in the Biglow Papers. The majority of New England people were never reconciled to it. The objectors make out a plausible case on paper, but the facts do not sustain them. The Mexicans were a semi-barbarous people, with whom no civilized association was possible; they conducted negotiations by massacre and murder, and in war mutilated the bodies of the slain. They were a cross between Spaniards and Aztec Indians, combining the least attractive features of both. Because a man is offensive, however, it does not follow that he has no rights; but the rights of Mexico in this affair are very dubious at best. When Texas revolted, she claimed the Rio Grande River as her Mexican boundary; and it is the natural geographical one. Mexico thereupon insisted on the river Nueces as their limit, a small stream about a hundred and fifty miles further east. It was this claim of theirs which was their only pretext for war. When Texas was annexed to us, her boundaries became ours; and General Taylor, who with a few thousand men had been for several months on the Nueces, crossed the disputed strip of ground, and took up his station on the Rio Grande, close to its mouth, on the American side. This was the extent of the provocation we offered to Mexico; we were on what we claimed as our own soil; and our reason for being there was that the Mexicans were continually making border raids and murdering persons who were now American citizens.

Mexico, like all Spanish-American states, was continually subject to revolutions; and at this juncture Herrera, the President, was deposed in favor of a soldier, Paredes. Meanwhile Polk had endeavored to open negotiations with Mexico, with a view to settling the matter without bloodshed if possible; but Slidell, our envoy, was insulted, and returned.

Taylor occupied a fort twenty miles from Point Isabel, opposite the Mexican town of Matamoras on the Rio Grande. A large Mexican force was on the other side. General Ampudia, in command of the Mexicans, ordered him to retire within twenty-four hours. Taylor of course held his ground; but a few days later the Mexicans waylaid Colonel Cross outside the American lines, killed him, pounding out his brains, and stripped him of his uniform and arms. When he was missed from the American camp, Captain Thornton with a few horsemen was sent in search of him; he also was ambushed and killed. This first blood of the war was shed on what could be reasonably claimed as American soil; and in a manner characteristically Mexican. "War exists," said Polk in his message, "and notwithstanding all our efforts to avoid it, exists by the act of Mexico herself."

After the killing of Captain Thornton, Taylor, leaving three hundred men in the little fort, went with the rest of his force to Point Isabel, where his supplies were stored. Having secured them, he set out on the return march the same evening, bringing ten cannon with him. At Palo Alto, the following noon, he was confronted by six thousand Mexican troops. Taylor had but two thousand; but he engaged his enemy, and by sunset had defeated him, with a loss of but nine men killed and less than fifty wounded; for the Mexicans, like the Spaniards, are poor marksmen on the field of battle, and cannot withstand civilized troops. Advancing the next day, Taylor found the enemy strongly re-enforced and advantageously posted in a ravine flanked by chaparral. The fate of this battle hung on the Mexican artillery, which was well served; but Captain May, at Taylor's order, charged with his cavalry on the gunners and sabered them at their guns, but at the cost of half his men. General La Vega was captured in this charge, and, the infantry following it up, the Mexicans fled in haste. Taylor reached the fort and found it safe, though Brown had been killed in one of the assaults upon it. In all these contests, the dead and wounded who had fallen into Mexican hands had been uniformly stripped and mutilated.

It was in May, 1846, that these actions took place; before invading Mexico, General Taylor waited for orders from Washington. But the government were taking a comprehensive view of the situation, and were moving both north and south of Taylor's position. Indeed, the expeditions of John C. Fremont to Oregon and California had begun in 1842, when there was no thought of doing more than investigating the nature of the great western country, with the intention, should it prove desirable, of making offers to Mexico for its purchase. This vast region belonged to Mexico by courtesy only; the Indians had better claim to it than she. She had never occupied it, in the sense of governing or protecting it; and the scattered inhabitants who dwelt isolated in its picturesque expanses could not by the most licensed imagination be regarded as a population. They were the feeble dregs of a decaying race, which at its best was ever hostile to progress and civilization; they were sunk in sloth and religious bigotry, and the mixture of ignorance, stupidity and obstinacy which they called pride was not more pathetic than absurd. Mexico was so weak and unstable that even within her own proper domain she was unable to insure any government a month's lease of power; and that she should pretend to control the stupendous realm lying west of the

Rocky Mountains was preposterous. Nevertheless our government, anxious to keep far within the limits of reasonable obligations, aimed to make every concession which the most fastidious scruple could require. The American people were forcing the government's hand; they were pouring across the mountains in ever-increasing numbers, and had already made the land American in all but name. It was necessary to provide against disorders arising from this source; for a free and enterprising body of emigrants cannot accommodate their ways and thoughts to the lifeless and obstructive usages of semi-barbarous degenerates, such as were these mongrel descendants of the red men and Spanish. That the "Greasers" should be overwhelmed was inevitable; but it was our wish to afford them all possible compensation. Another element in the situation was the apparent intention of England to seize California for herself; to check this policy, with its sinister consequences, was the part of prudent and beneficent statesmanship. The impulse and the policy were national and non-partisan; conquest, in the ordinary sense, was not contemplated; at most, only a recognition of the fact that the horse is his who rides it. Fremont's surveys and his picturesque and stirring adventures were of great value, and made him personally popular; his romantic disposition gave color and character to what he did; and though, on one or two occasions, he was compelled by unforeseen circumstances to act up to the limit of his responsibility, no step that he took was other than honorable and sagacious.

But Fremont's third expedition was in 1846, when war between Mexico and the United States was imminent. He found the Mexican governor, Castro, exercising tyrannical powers over the American emigrants, and admonished him to beware. Meanwhile Commodore Sloat, who at this time was too old for command, had been instructed to take possession of the port of San Francisco and other points during the continuance of the war. Sloat was timid about carrying out these instructions, fearing to involve himself in political complications; but upon their being reiterated, and in order to forestall the English Admiral Seymour, he finally received the surrender, without bloodshed, of San Francisco, Monterey, and the other ports on the coast. He sailed for home a few weeks later, and was succeeded by Stockton, a younger man, of more energy and resource, with whom Fremont could co-operate.

History sometimes imitates, if it do not repeat itself; and we can find in this Mexican war many similarities to that with which we engaged with Spain fifty years later. Polk, like McKinley, was a man of peace, and his Cabinet were of the like complexion; but war forced itself upon them. The Mexicans were never successful in any engagement, and never had a chance of success in the objects for which they fought; we continually offered them the opportunity of negotiation with a view to peace, and never struck a blow until after it was certain that nothing short of a blow would suffice; but the Mexicans, with the mulish and unreasoning obstinacy which took the place in them of patriotism and courage, insisted upon continuing the contest in the face of inevitable disaster. Thousands of their soldiers were killed to flatter the blind vanity or greed of their commanders; and thousands of square miles of territory were lost to Mexico, which might have remained hers had her leaders been truly patriotic. But the terms of peace we finally allowed her were ridiculously lenient, and she owes it to our clemency, and not to herself, that she exists as a distinct people to-day. The case has been the same with Spain; though her power of resistance has proved even less than that of Mexico. But the Spanish nature is a kind of disease, which has long afflicted the human race, and is now happily on the verge of final extinction.

As a means of averting the conflict, the government entered into negotiations with Santa Anna, who was a refugee in Cuba, offering him safe conduct to Mexico, where the brief **government of Paredes was already** tottering, on **the understanding that he use his influence** with **the nation for peace. He came accordingly; but once he was in the** saddle, he **abjured his promise and became a more aggressive leader of the war. Upon learning this, in October, the government was fain to issue orders for the raising of volunteer** troops; and **the response was enthusiastic: six times as** many offering themselves **as were required. So far as** the people were concerned, **the war was popular; though it** is to be observed **that the majority of the volunteers, as** might have **been expected, were from the Southern states.**

General Kearney now set out from Fort Leavenworth, on the Missouri border, and led a thousand men southwestward along the Arkansas River to Santa Fe, a march of nine hundred miles; it was the outpost of New Mexico, and submitted without resistance. After taking measures for the organization of a government here, Kearney continued his march southward, along the western slopes of the mountains, till he was met by the famous scout, Kit Carson, who had been with Fremont, and who informed him that the latter had brought California to subjection. He sent the greater part of his troops back, but himself kept on with a small force on horseback to the Pacific, his goal being San Diego, on the coast. The main body, under Doniphan, marched south to Chihuahua, on the other side of the Rio Grande, fighting their way against largely superior numbers, and capturing the town, with forty thousand inhabitants. Doniphan effected a junction with Wool, who had brought a force of three thousand undisciplined troops from San Antonio, drilling them by the way, until at the end of the march they were seasoned veterans. The union of the two forces was effected at Saltillo, south of Chihuahua, near which place Taylor had by that time penetrated. Doniphan's men, on the expiration of their term, marched to New Orleans, and were disbanded, having traversed in all five thousand miles within twelve months.

Though there was no lack of men anxious to fight Mexico, there was a strong opposition to the war on the part of many politicians and theorists. The same causes which had operated against the admission of Texas—fears of the extension of slavery—were active now; and there is no doubt that the slave states would willingly have seen their institution established in the new country. In consequence, the elections showed a tendency to the return of Whig influence; and when money was asked for by the government for the purchase of Mexican claims, a proviso was tacked to the bill stipulating that all land bought with such money should be closed to slavery. The proviso, called after Wilmot, who introduced it, met with angry opposition; but it was popular in the North, and was heard of later. Slavery or no, the war must be carried on, and Congress passed the necessary measures. The government, which desired to get all the credit for the war that was possible, from political motives, were embarrassed by the fact that no Democratic generals were available; both Taylor and Winfield Scott were Whigs. Benton might have been used, for he had seen service before becoming a statesman; but there were technical difficulties in the way of his appointment, even had he been certainly competent to discharge his military duties. The President had to make the best of it; and after all, if the war were Democratic, it was perhaps to his advantage that it should be carried on by Whig officers. But the rivalry of parties was very keen; and the admission of Iowa and Wisconsin as free states did not lull the apprehensions of the anti-slavery section.

The majority of our population probably regarded the war as an outward incident of the spontaneous expansion of the nation over the continent. There could be no question of the spontaneity of that expansion, and there was no means of checking it. It was in 1846 that the Mormon emigration, which had started from Missouri under its prophet, Joseph Smith, in 1842, and had tarried for some years in Illinois, building the city of Nauvoo, came under the guidance of the new prophet, Brigham Young, to Utah, where they founded their present abode. Smith had been arrested in Illinois for breaking the laws of the state, and had been taken from jail and shot by the mob. This singular sect, known to the world chiefly as advocates of polygamy, made many converts, and exercised great influence; and their settlement in the far west undoubtedly helped the general tendency in that direction. They were fortunate in their leaders; Smith was as sure he was right as was Mohammed centuries before, and his belief in himself, and the odd circumstances which he imported into his propaganda, won him disciples; while Young was a man of great ability, and a master of discipline and organization. He made the desert into an Eden, and the great city which he built is now, since its peculiar shadow of polygamy has been removed, the center of a growing civilization.

Scott and Taylor were both Virginians, and, as has been said, both Whigs; but here all likeness between them ceased. Scott was a martinet, a pompous and irritable man, vain as a peacock, fond of dress and display, arrogant and domineering; a man who could never win the personal affection of his officers and men, though they might respect him as an able and far-seeing general, which he certainly was. Physically he was a striking figure, towering a head and shoulders above the rest of the army; and in his plumed hat and showy uniform, mounted on his charger, he was the type of Mars come to earth. He was jealous and ambitious, finding great difficulty in conceding merit to any other soldier in the army; and his ambition had long aimed at the Presidency. Taylor, on the contrary, was of medium height, and in all respects as homely as Scott was handsome. His sobriquet was "Rough-and-Ready," and it suited him well. He had no graces of culture; his speech was rude and ungrammatical; he abhorred conspicuousness in attire or anything else; his manners were kindly and democratic, he was fond of his soldiers and looked personally after their welfare; and their devotion to him was confirmed by the fact that he was a great fighter, and absolutely free from fear; he would loll in his saddle, and crack jokes, in the midst of a rain of bullets and cannon balls that would have stiffened and sobered any other man whom they did not frighten. Scott was brave enough, as had often been proved in the past, though he had once avoided a duel; but his ideas of military propriety kept him from needlessly exposing himself; he remained grandly in reserve, and sent his subordinates to the front. In his conduct of this war, he never made an error, and his exploits were almost as brilliant as Taylor's; but he could not gain the love of his soldiers, nor was the impression he produced at home comparable to his rival's, who was immediately understood and liked as a true American type of the good old simple sort: unpretending, sagacious, humorous, and grit all the way through. It was not long, as we shall see, before this feeling for Taylor declared itself in a very practical manner.

Scott was commander-in-chief of the army. But the outbreak of the war had found Taylor at the front; and the first news from him indicated that his little force was in some danger. Scott expected to be sent with a large army to take the lead in the campaign, his idea being to make a magnificent tour down the Mississippi, with the admiration of the world upon him, and then to cross the Rio Grande and shrivel up the Mexicans. But as soon as Democratic politicians perceived the significance of this intention, and realized that Scott was playing for other stakes than mere victory in war, they remonstrated with the President, and Polk was obliged to intimate that he contemplated making other arrangements. To clinch the matter, news was now received that Taylor was safe, having, beyond all expectation, beaten his enemy without assistance. Scott was very angry, and allowed his irritation to appear in letters which made the people laugh, but not on his side. Taylor was promoted to be major-general, and the conduct of the campaign was intrusted to him. He was gratified, so far as this favor showed that the people appreciated his efforts; but he was not disposed to rely very far upon the smile of the Democratic government, and felt that were he to fail their support of him would be withdrawn. In fact, the men and supplies of which they were lavish on paper were not always forthcoming in real life, and he had to do the best he could with what he had.

His proceedings on the Rio Grande have already been outlined. The general first in command of the Spanish forces, Ampudia, had quickly been superseded by Arista, but with no favorable results so far as the Mexican army was concerned; the Americans were better disciplined and commanded, and their morale was perfect; while man for man they were of course immensely superior; their only deficiency was in numbers.

At odds of nearly three to one the battle of Palo Alto was fought and won; but Arista, though retreating, seems to have shared the delusion which we have lately observed in the Spanish in Cuba, that the Americans would not pursue. But Taylor, anxious for the safety of his fort, kept steadily on, and overtook the enemy at Reseca de Palma, in a formidable position. But as before, the charge of our troops was irresistible, and once in retreat, and their fear of their own officers forgotten, the flight of the Mexicans was headlong. Spanish courage is like the spurt of a match; it comes and is gone again in a moment, and if that moment does not decide the contest, all is over for them. The Mexican government, still following the Spanish fashion, court-martialed Arista, whom it never should have appointed to such a command.

These brilliant little victories sent Taylor's name all over the Union, and he was already spoken of for the Presidency. He, however, thought of nothing but attending to the work in hand; and was soon advancing upon Matamoras. Arista fled without attempting a battle; and Taylor took possession and treated the inhabitants well. For a time he paused, while re-enforcements were on the way, and the political squabbles in Washington, which always occur on such occasions, and which appear so contemptible in the retrospect, were being fought out. The line on which Taylor was now advancing could not reach the City of Mexico; the attack on that should be made by way of Vera Cruz, as Taylor himself pointed out; his duty, meanwhile, would be to push on to Saltillo via Monterey, cutting the Mexicans' line of communications. But in carrying out this programme he was hampered in various ways: the inhabitants had few supplies, and sold them dear; transport was difficult in the rough country, and the short term volunteers would be ready to go home just when they were most wanted. However, by the end of July he was joined by General Worth, their united army numbering between six and seven thousand, three thousand of whom were regulars. Taylor reached a small town twenty miles from Monterey on the 15th of September. Monterey was occupied by ten thousand Mexicans under Ampudia, who had again superseded Arista, but who was almost equally cowardly and incompetent. The defenses of the town were very strong, and so was its natural position along a river, with heights behind. Taylor decided to make his main attack on the west; but he began by a strong feint on the east under Garland, which was only partially successful, and was accompanied by severe loss from the enemy's well-posted artillery. But Worth had had better fortune on the west, carrying with small loss the heights on that end of the town, and cutting off the enemy's supplies and re-enforcements on the Saltillo road. During the next two days, it was to Worth that the laboring oar was necessarily given, and in a series of magnificent attacks, he won position after position, and finally swept down the heights, driving the foe before him into the town. Ampudia, terrified by this advance, shrunk within his inmost defenses. Taylor had not yet established communication with his victorious subordinate, with a view to combining an attack; but it was not necessary; for Worth kept advancing, fighting his way from street to street, until he planted his guns in a position whence he could throw shells into the central square in which the Mexicans were huddled in stupid consternation. Fortunately for them, night put a stop to the attack; and before it could be resumed the next day, Ampudia sent a flag of truce. The Mexicans, in treating for surrender, showed precisely the same imbecility which we see displayed by the beaten Spanish commanders in the Cuban war; they would sooner perish with the city, they declared, than evacuate as paroled prisoners of war. And Taylor, like our contemporary generals, was perhaps overindulgent; he loved not slaughter for its own sake; and finally agreed to let them march out with small arms, a battery, and twenty-one rounds of ammunition. Mexican "honor" was satisfied, and Monterey, with its guns, munitions and stores, passed into our possession.

There were no eager newspapers with their daily bulletins and their army of war correspondents, in those days; but there seems to have been present at this battle a gentleman connected with the "Louisville Courier," who was moved to write to that newspaper in the following terms, which we may compare with the style of half a century later. "In the midst of the conflict," he writes, "a Mexican woman was busily engaged in carrying bread and water to the wounded men of both armies. I saw the ministering angel raise the head of a wounded man, give him water and food, and then bind up the ghastly head with a handkerchief she took from her own head. After having exhausted her supplies, she went back to her house to get more bread and water for others. As she was returning on her errand of mercy, to comfort other wounded persons, I heard the report of a gun, and the poor innocent creature fell dead. I think it was an accidental shot that killed her. I would not be willing to believe otherwise. It made me sick at heart; and, turning from the scene, I involuntarily raised my eyes toward heaven, and thought, Great God! is this war? Passing the spot the next day, I saw her body still lying there, with the bread by her side, and the broken gourd, with a few drops of water in it—emblems of her errand! We buried her; and while we were digging her grave, the cannon-balls flew around us like hail."—It seems as if fifty years were scarce enough to mark the abyss which stretches between whipsyllabub of this kind, and the terse, stern telegrams which tell us of war nowadays. One can imagine the sweep of the blue pencil in a modern newspaper office upon receipt of such a communication.

The victory of Monterey had a somewhat illogical result—from the strictly military point of view. Taylor was deprived of a large part of his command, and left to face the enemy with a remnant, at a moment when the latter was re-enforced to the amount of twenty thousand men, and was commanded by the ablest of the Mexican generals, Santa Anna. Owing, moreover, to what must be supposed to have been an accident, a duplicate of the communication from General Scott, informing Taylor of this depletion, was allowed to fall into Santa Anna's hands; so that the Mexicans were encouraged to attack a foe whom they already heavily outnumbered.

What was the explanation of this change of commanders and of the plan of campaign? As regards the latter point, the attack on Mexico City by the Vera Cruz route was judicious; the city could not have been reached from Taylor's position, as he had himself pointed out. For the rest, we must seek the reason in the intrigues of politics, and in the professional jealousy and selfishness of Scott. The Democrats in Congress saw in Taylor's successes a menace to their own continuance in power, and feared that a continuance of them would make the old general Polk's successor.

Their only defense against this danger was so to weaken him in the field that he would either be obliged to retreat, or, if he engaged, would be defeated. Scott, ordinarily a man of honor, was seduced by his ambition into aiding this unsavory plot. But all parties to it were ashamed of their own work, and also fearful lest the country, getting wind of it, should condemn them; so instead of ordering Taylor, frankly, to put himself under the orders of his ranking superior, they tried to hoodwink him and obscure their true purposes; and Scott, rather than brave a personal interview with Taylor, which the etiquette and courtesy of the service demanded, put him off with letters and excuses, and committed the gross breach of decorum of giving orders directly to one of Taylor's subordinates. Taylor saw through the whole ignoble transaction, and was bitterly mortified and indignant. Almost any other commander—certainly, Scott—would have resigned his place; but Taylor showed a greatness of soul worthy of Washington himself. He held his peace, went ahead with his duty, and, with a force which after his junction with Worth amounted to less than a quarter of that under Santa Anna, prepared to meet the latter at Buena Vista. Such patriotism and magnanimity sometimes meet reward even in this world.

In a gorge of the mountains a high plateau was protected front and rear by ravines, while a connecting ridge joined it to higher ground commanding the roads. On this plain Taylor drew up his force. Santa Anna sent him a grandiloquent summons to surrender on pain of annihilation. Taylor curtly declined. It was the anniversary of the birthday of Washington, February 22, 1847.

Santa Anna thought it best to defer the annihilation of the Americans until the next day; and meanwhile Taylor rode back to Saltillo, in his rear, to provide for its safety. Before he could get back in the morning the battle had begun. Ampudia was attacking our left with strong support, and an Indiana regiment of volunteers was giving way in disorder. Taylor brought two regiments and Braxton Bragg's artillery to their support, turned back the enemy, charged, and reoccupied most of the ground which had been given up. Santa Anna, with his superabundance of men, attacked in front and on either flank; but his soldiers, as soon as the bubble of their audacity, blown up by their own boastings, had been pricked by American resistance, betrayed the cowardice which is deep in the heart of all men of Spanish race, and could not be led to the attack again. A strong detachment made a detour to capture our baggage; but were hurled back with heavy loss by the volunteers of Kentucky and Arkansas, assisted by May's cavalry charge. At the end of the day, the enemy's attack had failed at all points; our troops bivouacked where they were, and the next morning Santa Anna with the remains of his vainglorious army had disappeared. Our total loss was about seven hundred; but not more than half of Santa Anna's force reassembled at San Louis Potosi, whence he had set forth. Those who were not killed, wounded or prisoners had deserted.

This victory ranks with the great battles of history; and none of the combatants comes out of it with quite so much credit as Taylor himself; he was in the thick of it all the time, saw everything, provided against everything, placed the troops where they would do the most good, sent supports at the moment they were needed, and inspired the men to fight like heroes under every trial. A strategy board, sitting at home, would have decided that Taylor must be beaten; but the homely old warrior was willing to do his best first; and his best proved more than good enough for four times his number of Mexicans, led by their best generals. There were many brilliant exploits during the war, but none to equal this; and when Taylor fired his last gun he had—though he was far from being aware of it at the time—burst open the doors of the **White House** at Washington. Zack Taylor, betrayed by his government and wronged by his **fellow commander,** was the coming President of the

United States. The news of his wonderful victory reached home just at the right moment, when all were expecting to hear of his defeat. The country knew that he had been foully dealt with, and its joy at his success was doubled on that account. His most malignant enemies at Washington dared not attempt to check the torrent of enthusiasm; and Taylor was and he remained the popular hero from that hour until his death. The detachment taken from his army, by which our Secretary of War, Marcy, had hoped to cripple him, accomplished nothing; its ostensible purpose had been to besiege Tampico on the coast; but Perry had taken it before Patterson, with the detachment, arrived, and the latter was able only to garrison it. But meanwhile Scott, in pursuit of glory for personal ends, was making a gallant record along the road to Mexico City.

Distrusting the sincerity of the favor which had put him forward, but resolved to take advantage of it to the utmost, and profiting by the revelation of the incompetence of the enemy which Taylor's campaign had afforded, Scott sailed from New Orleans and landed at Vera Cruz with twelve thousand men. His regulars were led by Worth and Twiggs, his volunteers by Patterson; and a host of smaller fry, mostly Democratic political generals anxious to forward their fortunes, made up the list. On the 9th of March, after the most anxious preparations for a strong resistance from Santa Anna, who had just been annihilated by Taylor, though Scott did not know it, the latter got his men ashore on a smooth sea without the loss of a life, and was ready to begin the siege of the castle and fortifications.

From Vera Cruz to the City of Mexico is a distance of about two hundred miles in an air line, and the capital is raised above the sea about a mile and a half. The road to it, defended by brave and intelligent troops, could be held against the world in arms. But these wretched people were divided among themselves, and were bewildered and terrified by the sight of an invading army. Juan Morales, com-

manding at **Vera Cruz, had** forty-five hundred men under
him; but he could get no re-enforcements, **and** depended
on holding out till that favorite ally of Spanish Americans,
the yellow **fever, should** fight on his side. **His** position was
of immense **strength; but his artillery** was poor, and what
was more to the purpose, his soldiers were Mexicans. Scott
had one **eye on politics and the other on his** army; but the
result was good; he determined **to risk nothing** by assault,
but to proceed **by the regular operations of a siege.** Commodore Perry deployed his ships so **as to assist him, and the bombardment** began on the 23d of March, after Scott had offered
to allow the non-combatants to withdraw—an offer which
Morales **had characteristically refused. But** the next day
this proud commander caused the foreign consuls to make a
request for a truce, while the withdrawal might take place;
**but Scott would now entertain the proposal only in case
Morales himself should proffer it, with a view** to surrender;
**and meanwhile he opened another battery. This was too
much for** Morales, **who,** too cowardly (or **as** Spanish ethics
interpret it, **too proud) himself to sue for terms,** handed the
command over **to a subordinate to do it for him.** We have
seen precisely the same subterfuge adopted of late at Santiago de Cuba. Scott was not particular on that point; the
city **and fort were surrendered, the garrison** being allowed
to march **out** with the honors **of war.**

After waiting for **transport, the advance was** made in
April, and no resistance **was met with until** our army
reached Cerro Gordo, in the mountains. Here Santa Anna,
who had recovered his volatile spirits after Taylor's chastisement, **was arrayed with ten thousand men.** His proclamation to **the Mexicans** announced that triumph or death
was the alternative he **proposed** to himself. Three days later
he was in headlong flight, leaving even his wooden leg behind him. **But in** Spanish philosophy, **a word is** as good as
a blow, and they take as much credit for **saying they will
be** heroes, as others do for being so.

Santa Anna's position, indeed, was theoretically impregnable, and was defended with elaborate works and ample artillery. His main force was in the pass of Cerro Gordo, a steep mountain ascending from the river's bank; the road passes through the ravine to Jalapa above. The hilltops had been fortified; Santa Anna's right was protected by a precipice; but his extreme left could be turned by the almost impossible feat of scaling Cerro Gordo itself. Twiggs, however, succeeded in accomplishing this, thereby gaining the rear of the enemy's main force, between the latter and Jalapa. Resting behind the shelter of the peak during that night, while heavy guns were brought up, Twiggs then joined in a general assault, which Scott had planned in detail, and which was carried out just as he had designed. Pillow kept the enemy busy on the right, Riley engaged the center, and Shields took the left in front; and Colonel Harney, of Twiggs's division, clambered up an ascent which hardly afforded foothold, in the face of a heavy fire, and carried the intrenchments on the summit with the bayonet. The enemy gave way everywhere, and when the cavalry started in pursuit, the rout was complete. Several thousand Mexicans escaped with Santa Anna and Ampudia by the Jalapa road just before Twiggs was able to get down to intercept them; but their losses were very heavy; our own was four hundred and fifty men.

Santa Anna arrived with his shattered army in Mexico City; but although he knew that further resistance was vain, his desire to hold the reins of government prompted him to deceive his countrymen with audacious falsehoods, and stimulate them to defend the City. The approaches were accordingly well fortified; and the arrival of a clerk of the War Department at this juncture, with ambiguous messages to Scott, and a sealed packet of unknown contents for the Mexican government, irritated the American general with the idea that the fruits of his victory were to be stolen from him The packet turned out to contain the offer of a treaty on a money basis; Santa Anna made it the pretext of delays, and finally told the clerk that he could not venture to appoint peace commissioners until the American army had carried one of his defenses at Mexico City. By the time this conclusion was reached, Santa Anna's preparations were complete, and Brigadier-general Franklin Pierce, a New Hampshire Democrat, just appointed, arrived to re-enforce Scott with twenty-five hundred men. It was August, and four months had been frittered away, to the profit of the enemy.

Proceeding from Pueblo, Scott, marching in four divisions, came in sight of the plain on which the city stands about the middle of the month. After reconnoitering the fortifications, Scott decided to attack on the left, which Santa Anna fancied to be impregnable. Fighting began at the suburb of Contreras, where Santa Anna himself was driven back and the works captured, with the road on that side to the city. At Cherubesco, another outlying hamlet, with a stone convent by way of citadel, a severe engagement took place; Twiggs was finally assisted by Worth and Pillow, who had been successful at the village of San Antonio; the outworks were carried, and the convent surrendered. In this action, General Pierce, who had been wounded in the foot the day before, had his horse shot under him: the wounded foot was caught beneath the horse; the general fainted from pain, and was carried from the field. The total losses of the enemy were seven thousand killed, wounded and prisoners, with three times as many cannon as the invaders had brought with them. The total number of Mexicans engaged was twenty-seven thousand, while Scott had less than half as many; he lost a thousand killed and wounded.

In compliance with orders from Washington not to conquer the enemy too much, Scott forbore to enter the city at once as he might have done, and offered to receive tenders of surrender. Santa Anna, however, had resources of ruscality and duplicity which Scott had not fathomed; and was ready to ruin his country, or to accept the bribes which he hoped to secure from our government, as circumstances might dictate. After the American commissioners had stated our terms of peace—a sum of money, and the cession of Texas, New Mexico, and Upper California—Santa Anna replied by offering to sell Texas east of the Nueces, and to cede so much of California as was above the latitude of San Francisco; requiring of us, in return for these favors, the payment of all Mexico's expenses in the war, the restoration of all forts which we had captured, and a solemn promise never hereafter to attempt to annex a foot of Mexican territory. Such was our reward for treating men of Spanish blood with consideration. While the negotiations were in progress, the Mexicans had violated the terms of the truce, and were repairing and strengthening their fortifications.

But this tricky and profligate adventurer had overestimated the power of mere politics in America; he had left the American people out of account. His impudent proposal had been a bid for more money; but Scott admonished him that hostilities would be resumed at once. On the 8th of September Worth destroyed a powder magazine at the base of the fortified hill of Chapultepec; but as no attempt was made on this occasion to capture Chapultepec itself, the Mexicans hailed it as a victory, and gave medals to the heroes who had crouched behind the castle walls while Worth was carrying off the powder. On the following days Scott attacked the defenses of the city, which were strong enough to have defied any assault had they been defended by men of courage. On the 12th of the month Chapultepec was bombarded; on the 13th it was carried by assault; the terrified Mexicans actually leaping down precipices in their mad rush to escape. In a roaring mass of confusion the huge throngs of the flying enemy crowded into the city, of which at the end of the day Scott occupied

two gates; but during the night Santa Anna stole out on
the other side, and was personally safe. He had played for
a large stake, trusting that others were as base and corrupt
as himself; it was almost his last appearance in history.
For although, years after, he succeeded for a moment in
snatching once more the reins of power, he was almost immediately overthrown; and, after long exile, he died at last,
a neglected and despised outcast, at the age of eighty-one, in
the city he had betrayed and abandoned. He was a typical
Mexican; but one of the worst, as well as one of the clever-
est, of his type.

After he had been ousted from the government which he
had unlawfully seized—if law could have any application to
the Mexico of that era—denounced by his own late subjects
as a traitor and robber of the public treasury, the treaty of
peace was concluded by Scott, with terms which showed
every desire to be just and tolerant to the vanquished. In
consideration of the large amount of territory taken, we
agreed to pay Mexico fifteen million dollars, a fifth of this
upon signature of the instrument. The boundary line agreed
upon was as specified in our earlier proposals, and as it now
appears on our maps; and time to remove, and protection,
were accorded to the inhabitants of the ceded provinces. So
far as Mexico was concerned, the proceedings were over, and
we had shown ourselves more lenient than the customs of
war would have warranted; though of course no American
desired the annexation of Mexico itself, with its undesirable
population. But Scott had still other battles to fight with
his own Democratic subordinates; which resulted in his
ordering Worth and other officers under arrest, pending
charges brought against them; but the War Department
directed these charges to be preferred at home, and they
resulted in a virtual acquittal. Before this time there had
been an immense quantity of Whig and Democratic talk in
Congress anent the war, little of which was sincere; but the
critics of the war were upon the whole less sincere than were

its defenders. The moral issues which they sought to raise were absurd; the real point of dispute, more or less cunningly disguised, was as to the admission into the conquered district of slavery. Should the Missouri Compromise line be run to the Pacific, or should the entire new region be open to slaves? This was a pregnant question; it was compromised for a time by Clay, as we shall see; but meanwhile the Wilmot Proviso served to formulate the issue before the country. The slavery dispute was rushing fiercely to its issue, and men were divided between the passions which it excited, and their wish to avoid a fatal rupture. The greatest statesmen of the country were to lavish their best thoughts and energies upon the problem, and after all the knot was to be severed by the sword.

At present, it became evident that the Democrats were losing. The Whigs had been helped by the fact that after the Mexicans had been proved unable to effectually resist us, the war lost most of its interest for the people; the result seemed known beforehand, and the details were monotonous if not tedious. The Mexicans were called patriotic because they so prolonged the peace arrangements, when in truth the delay was due partly to the selfish designs of their officials, and partly to the latter's fear to take the responsibility of negotiating at all. When the peace was established, the Whigs charged that the Democrats had waged the whole war in the interests of slavery; and in the inflamed state of men's minds, even so extravagant an accusation as this was allowed to pass. But the strongest argument for the return of the Whigs to power was the prospect of electing Zachary Taylor to the Presidency; he could unite both parties as no one else could, since his own party predilections were anything but bigoted, and he was the hero of the war, whether the war were right or wrong. "I beat 'em at Buena Vista" was all the politics he needed for his election. Yet his victories were not his only qualifications for the Presidency by any means; and the American people had divined that the man who had won such battles over not only the enemy, but himself, was able to make the office of Executive respected.

There was a dwindling Whiggish minority, however, who clung to their ancient idol Henry Clay, who had become a farmer since his retirement, and had experienced religion. Horace Greeley, through his "Tribune," represented these patterns of constancy; and the famous old leader, now seventy years old, was induced to make a speech at Lexington, Kentucky, denouncing the war, abusing the Democrats, and advocating "the virtues of moderation and magnanimity." The veteran's eloquence was almost as bright as ever, but he could no longer move the people by exhortations and attacks of this kind. It was observable that though the Whigs had constantly abused the war while it lasted, they had not ventured to stop supplies. They wanted both the moral advantage of having opposed it, and the concrete benefits it would secure. Webster himself would commit himself to nothing further than general disapproval. In the House, a new member, Abraham Lincoln, made an able speech analyzing the Democratic professions; but it had no serious effect. The remonstrances of the aged but still fiery John Quincy Adams had more weight; but just before the news of peace came, Adams, in his place in the House, was stricken by death; he lingered from the 21st to the 23d of February, but his last conscious words were uttered within a few minutes of the attack: "This is the last of earth," he said; "I am content." He might well be content; he had lived eighty years, had served his country all his life, and had never done an ignoble deed. From his funeral the House returned to give its approval to the treaty of peace; and now the question must be decided, How was this new world to be divided, as between the slaveholders and the free? Peace with Mexico was the beginning of civil war in the United States.

Pending that decision, Oregon was admitted as a territory, under the Wilmot Proviso, though, as Polk remarked, the Missouri Compromise was a sufficient protection in itself. Clayton of Delaware proposed that new territory should be slave or free according to the decisions of the Supreme Court; but this "Clayton Compromise" was not approved, though Jefferson Davis, among others, advocated it. It was thought that the platforms of the national conventions would shed light upon the problem; but the Whig convention, after nominating Taylor and Fillmore in preference to either Clay or Webster, adjourned without a mention of the Wilmot Proviso, or any other platform plank; and the Democrats, who chose Cass and Butler for their standard-bearers (Polk having declined to run), were almost equally reticent. The desperate eagerness of the Whigs for power, at any cost, was demonstrated in their choice of a slave-holding candidate, and their silence as to the Proviso. Indeed, an extreme wing, comprising Henry Wilson of Massachusetts, Charles Sumner and Samuel Hoar, combined with the corresponding subdivision of the Democrats known as Barnburners, and set up a Free-soil Party; the old Liberty Party joining them. They met in convention at Utica, and nominated Martin Van Buren, on a platform which, while abstaining from interfering with established slave states, forbade the creation of any more. Charles Francis Adams, son of John Quincy, was nominated for the Vice-Presidency.

Clay and Webster had been much mortified by the preference given to Taylor; for what is the use of being a leading statesman all one's life, if a rude soldier who knows nothing of statesmanship is to be chosen over one's head at last? Webster had been offered the Vice-Presidency, but had declined it from pride; yet had he accepted it he would have been President after a year. Clay accepted his defeat as final; he would not help Taylor's canvass, but refrained from opposing it, as Webster—not explicitly, but by implication—certainly did. For the rest, little could be gathered as to Webster's real attitude till toward the latter part of the summer, when he made that powerful declaration: "I shall oppose all slavery extension and all increase of slave representation," he said, speaking on the Oregon bill, "in all places, at all times, under all circumstances, even against all inducemnets, against all supposed limitation of great interests, against all combinations, against all compromise." This seems sweeping enough; yet Webster remains open to the imputation of having regarded the Union and the Constitution as superior to the simple law of right and wrong.

Calhoun and his followers took the bolder and franker course of declaring that any citizen of the United States had the right to reside in any state of the Union he pleased, and to take his slaves, if he had any, with him; and Calhoun added that the time was come to arm against the North. Mexico had been conquered chiefly by Southern soldiers, and Southerners should have the privilege of occupying the territory upon their own terms. The Missouri Compromise no longer satisfied these men; they demanded not only to be "let alone" where they were, but to have liberty to carry their institutions elsewhere. After taking such a stand, the alternative of mere secession might seem almost like conceding a favor. They did not succeed in enforcing their opinions upon Congress, for the Southern Whigs would not go so far; but they managed to block decisive legislation as regarded California, and postpone the issue to the next session at least.

Polk's administration accomplished solid and valuable results; in this respect it is entitled to far more credit than were several which had preceded it—not to speak of its immediate followers. But Polk personally had not been a success, in the popular sense; he was too reticent; he never spoke with the people as man to man; he took his course, and vindicated it in his long and dry messages; but he sought no means of getting into closer touch with the country; he was totally devoid of what is called magnetism. His enemies abused him without stint; but what he accomplished is a sufficient answer to most of their charges and denunciations. He was faithful in his work and devoted to his country; in his silent way, he suffered keenly from the wanton abuse which was directed against him; his four years in the White House made him prematurely old; and he died in June, 1849, a few months after his successor had been inaugurated. He received no public funeral; no national monument commemorates him; but Texas and California, and the vast region between, are his contribution to our greatness; and Oregon, with the northern boundary of the Republic. Again, his tariff bill, with its tendency to free trade, was of immense benefit to our commerce, and proved anything but a check to our manufactures—thus falsifying the predictions of its eminent opponents. The financial situation had also greatly improved. The only really serious charge brought against him—that he provoked the Mexican War for party ends, and for the sake of illicit conquest—will not stand the test of dispassionate scrutiny. It was a war forced upon us, partly by the natural westward movement of our population, partly by the outrages perpetrated by Mexico, whose cruelty and anarchy made all political association with her impossible. It was a thoroughly justifiable war, and was carried on with as much humanity as brilliance.

To turn aside for a moment from these political matters, let us remember that it was during Polk's administration that a discovery was made which, more than any other single fact in medical annals, has proved of lasting benefit to mankind. Pain is the great evil that afflicts mortal man; and the inseparable connection of pain with surgical operations had been, since earliest history, one of the darkest shadows of human life. It had moreover rendered practically impossible all those extraordinary surgical triumphs which the latter half of this century has won; for they are dependent for success not only on the entire immobility of the patient during the operation, but upon his ability to survive the shock of the often long and exquisite agony inflicted by the knife. The discovery of anæsthesia by Dr. W. T. G.

Morton, in 1846, has saved thousands of lives, and has spared millions of men and women incalculable suffering. The world owes this young New England physician a debt which can never be repaid, save by acknowledging its indebtedness.

W. T. G. Morton was born in Massachusetts in 1820; he had a good academy education, but was largely dependent upon his own ability, courage and resolution for a livelihood. He studied medicine first with a private physician in Boston, afterward entering the Harvard Medical School, and following a course of lectures there; and it was while still a student, and engaged in the practice of dentistry, that he became impressed with the anæsthetic properties of sulphuric ether. On the 16th of October, 1846, in the operating room of the Massachusetts General Hospital, Morton demonstrated to an assembly of distinguished physicians the value of his discovery. In so doing he not only went against the opinions and warning of some of the best medical minds of the age, but he risked an indictment for manslaughter, should his experiment terminate unfavorably. It is not easy to overestimate the heroism which, in the face of such discouragement, went steadily forward to establish what he knew was a truth, and what has proved so vast a blessing to the world.

A patient was to be treated for tumor. Morton had his ether in a little glass globe; he put the rubber mouthpiece of the globe between the patient's lips, and caused him to inhale the contents. The man speedily became insensible; the removal of the tumor was successfully accomplished by Dr. John C. Warren, the patient appearing all the while as if in profound slumber, except some slight movements toward the end of the operation; and upon recovering consciousness he declared that he had felt no pain. Such were the simple circumstances which ushered in this stupendous revolution.

We can well imagine that though the patient felt nothing, the feelings of the young experimenter during that critical half hour must have been poignant enough; and any one might envy the glad thrill of generous emotion with which he welcomed the recognition of his success. He was destined, like so many other benefactors of their species, to subsequent misrepresentation, and to suffer, in ways which ether could not avert, from the efforts of conscienceless pretenders to rob him of the credit of his intelligence and bravery. But time has done Dr. Morton justice; and thirty years after his untimely death, the Semi-Centennial Anniversary of anæsthesia was celebrated by a gathering of the leaders of the profession in America, and Morton's sole right to the honor of the discovery and its application was finally vindicated and celebrated. Fulton and Morse had already won our gratitude for their immense contributions to the material wealth and progress of the race; but the service rendered by Morton is more tender and intimate than theirs, and a warmer sentiment than gratitude must always mingle with our memories of him.

CHAPTER THIRTIETH

THE LAST OF THE WHIGS

AS the time of which we write draws nearer to the present, the difficulty of comprehending the meaning of events increases; we see wrongs, and marvel why they were permitted, and how they shall be made right;—for we must believe in the good purpose of an almighty God, or else history becomes a meaningless juggle of accidents, which it would be worth no man's while to recount or disentangle. But the wrong of slavery has now passed away from us, and the steps which led to its passing are known, if not always in their innermost secrets, yet broadly enough to enable us to draw inferences and deductions. We can begin, at least, to understand how events were overruled for our ultimate benefit; though doubtless the great account is not yet fully settled; there are other kinds of slavery than that of the negro, and this country is not yet free. During the struggle between North and South before the outbreak of actual war, many of the greatest minds that America has produced were bent upon the problem of the slave; and some of them lost their bearings entirely; some chose the wrong deliberately in preference to the good; some doubted and hesitated, wishing to do right, but fearing to admit to themselves what the right truly was, until the golden moment, for them, was forever gone; and some few saw the right and clave to it through good and evil report, and will not fail of their meed of honor, when

(864)

all is done, and men are weighed as to their motives and their acts.

That human slavery was an evil, there are none now to deny; not because those who were moved to support it by the sword were conquered in the battle: for conquest does not prove right: but because, now that the burden has fallen from us, we discover that it was never necessary to our best development, and that though, for a time, it seemed as if much of our material prosperity was to be ascribed to it, we have learned that without it we should have been a better and happier people, and that wealth also would not have been denied us, though it came through other channels. Slave labor was never a necessity to the prosperity of this Union; and that it was a detriment on other grounds is clear. But it had come upon us without our consent, and, once established, there were many practical obstacles to getting rid of it. At first all parties had loyally wished to accomplish emancipation; but gradually, as slavery bred a race of slave-holders, different in training and ideas from the rest of their countrymen, these came to approve the institution for itself; they defended it, and the moral outcry against it of the rest of civilization only confirmed them in their defiant attitude. They even declared it to be a holy institution; it became almost a point of religion with them, as well as of honor, to uphold it. Southern honor was a local phenomenon; it was, indeed, derived from medieval sources, and was an anachronism in the Nineteenth Century; but it existed in the South because there men had become used to holding opinions as they held a wife, and allowing no question thereupon. A Southerner's opinion, his word, his institution, all were sacred; he would not argue about them, or if he did it was with no intention of admitting arguments on the other side. Calhoun argued in behalf of slavery; but he did not the less adhere to his conclusions after they had been shown, as they often were, to be untenable. An argument—a syllogism—is something to fight with, even though it be unsound; and in any argument it will generally happen that nine-tenths of the words spoken are vain words, having no true relevance to the matter in hand, and serving only to make the outward show of resistance. Southerners, then, had deliberately shut the avenues of the mind through which they might be approached on the subject of the abstract right or wrong of slavery; and in Congress, as we have seen, they so far imposed their will that for many years the subject was taboo, and to refer to it was to risk a quarrel.

To this, the North, or a major part of it, submitted; they were resigned to letting slavery continue to exist where it had always been; and with this concession, the only opening for quarrel was when a slave escaped into a free state, and, according to the law of the land relating to property, must be given back to the owner upon demand. Such a law was odious to the North, not because negroes were property, but because they were human beings. But, save in sporadic instances, the odious law was obeyed, because it was the law; and the way to protest against it was not to break it, but to obtain its repeal. The Abolitionists would break the law, and sever the Union; but that was to cure one wrong by another; and their course was wrong, because other means had not been exhausted. When the time came that a majority of the people wished slavery to cease, it would cease, though the will of the majority were enforced by the sword; but until it was the will of the majority, nothing but agitation within lawful and constitutional limits was justifiable. Let the Abolitionists hold up the torch of truth before the people, and bid them bow to it; but let them not use it to set fire to the foundations of the state.

The Southerners, however, would not let the matter rest here, where it might have rested indefinitely. And we may note that all evil is like a fire, which must be extinguished, or it will extend its bounds; it cannot be shut up in a given compass, and there be content. The evil of slavery could not rest within its historic limits, but must needs come forth and spread over the whole continent. The general pretext given was that unless the equilibrium of free and slave states was preserved, the free would obtain preponderance, and would use it to destroy the institution on its own ground. Slavery must spread, on pain of being altogether extirpated. This was the Southern plea, and it was not without plausibility. Yet it is probable that the North would never have interfered with the slave states; they had their own affairs to attend to, and were willing to let the South attend to hers —if only she would. It would presently have become obvious, too, that the slave states, occupying a limited area, would gradually have declined, and expired of internal disease, if not by the revolt of their human cattle, as in San Domingo. If they would have agreed to keep themselves to themselves, the North need have done nothing more than leave them thus isolated, and the end would have been a question of time only. But to this the South would not agree; and indeed it would have been a practical impossibility, under the geographical and political conditions of the Republic.

The South, then, must extend the area of slavery: and how should it be done? Clay had said, Let it be done by drawing an east and west line, and assigning all south thereof to slavery, the northern division to freedom. This compromise served until the movement of emigration to the far west, and the Mexican war, raised the question whether the east and west line should be continued across the Continent to the Pacific. The Southerners assumed that it should, as a matter of right; but the North demurred. But the South had here the stronger logical position. What right had the North to limit the extension of that east and west line? If they allowed it to rule to the Mississippi, why ought it not to rule to the Pacific? In this was the mischief of the Missouri Compromise, as of any compromise between right and wrong, apparent. The North had forfeited the privilege of logical consistency.

Of course, the true answer was, that consistency itself is sometimes the worst of evils. But many of the North did not declare this; and they were at this disadvantage with the South, that whereas the latter had, in slavery, a positive point to urge and to fight for, the North had only an abstract and practically a negative one—that slavery ought not to extend. It was too late for them to assert that a country originally free ought never to become the seat of slaveholding; they should have made that objection at the time the Compromise was first urged. And the majority of them feared to be inconsistent; and they also feared the Constitution; and they also feared to shoulder the responsibility of severing the Union, which, in case they took the opposite course, the South threatened. For a threat it was, though disguised as an inevitable necessity. In short, the North hesitated and was weak.

The other contention of the South—that any slaveholder had the right to take his slaves with him and settle in any Northern state—though it was not carried out, was not relinquished, but was held in terrorem. It was useful as indicating how moderate, after all, was the Southern attitude—how much more troublesome they might be if they chose; and it lent color to their assertion that it was the North who was the aggressor. Upon the whole, therefore, it seemed, at the end of the Mexican war, as if the whole southwest was dedicated to slavery, and no help for it. Rather than break the Union, let it go at that!

But in the midst of these very human squabbles, through which no way appeared to peace with honor, there occurred one of those events which are termed, by way of distinction, Providential; because the hand of God is manifest in them, instead of being hidden, as usual. Far on the west of the continent, its fertile hills and valleys spreading broad between the Rocky Mountains and the Pacific, and extending far to the north and the south of the Missouri Compromise line, lay the mighty and as yet scarce known domain of

California. Under ordinary circumstances it would have taken a generation at least to settle this territory; and in the ordinary course it would have been divided, at best, between slavery and freedom. But at this moment a New Jersey man who was digging the channel of a mill race for a sawmill, happened to notice, in the gravel washed down by the stream, some grains of a yellow substance, heavy and metallic; which he picked up, tested, and found to be pure gold. Those grains had lurked there since the beginning of things, waiting the time to appear, and change the course of human history. One might moralize over the fact that mortal greed should be the means of preventing a great social catastrophe; but such speculations are vain, because the arc we can survey is so small compared with the whole sweep of the Divine round. Men are governed by their passions; a low age by low stimuli, a higher, by lofty ones. In 1849 the passion for gold, and what gold means, was sufficient to cause a shifting of the population, hitherto without parallel for its rapidity and extent. A half-built mill became a great city; a town of two thousand inhabitants became a city of twenty thousand; and all within a year. Loose atoms of humanity from every country of the earth gathered in California during little more than the lapse of a summer vacation, and those vast solitudes suddenly became peopled with the tumultuous and lawless crowd of gold-seekers. Lawless they were, at first, for there was none to enforce law; and the visions, and the reality, of sudden and great wealth dazzled out of view all other considerations. Here was a splendid wilderness, a nearly perfect climate, no conventions, no traditions, no restraints, no women at the outset, and when women came, they were generally but another lure to disorder. Many of these gold-seekers were men of no education, of no moral perceptions, wholly unused to the idea of riches; and when such men became rich by the stroke of a pick, they knew not what to do with wealth, and in their ignorance they used it only to minister to their physical lusts. At the end of each week, at the end of each day, they were ready to spend what they had found in drunkenness and gambling; if they lost what they had gained, they had but to dig up enough to replace it; if they won, there must be more debauch. The only safeguard, for a while, against a reign of universal confusion and mutual destruction, was the seemingly inexhaustible amount of the treasure; it was believed that the whole extent of California was gold thinly veiled by vegetation. Robbery was rare, and, when discovered, was terribly punished; fights were common, but they were almost always the outcome of drink, and if they did not result fatally, were forgotten the next day. The common causes of enmity between man and man were here absent; there was enough for all so far as gold was concerned; and there were no materials for social or political feuds. Yet such a good-humored and dissolute anarchy could not indefinitely continue; because, for one thing, the continuous rush of emigration would finally occasion personal collisions; and because a life without law is sooner or later self-destructive. Even savages have their laws, or their superstitions, the organization of which takes law's place. But an aggregation of savages who have become so by degradation can only issue in mutual annihilation.

This, however, was not to be the destiny of California; and the reason was that the majority of the gold-seekers were Americans, or men of Anglo-Saxon lineage and instincts. That race cannot exist long without law; the sentiments of justice, equity and order are in their marrow, and must manifest themselves. They do not need kings or prophets to rouse them from anarchy; they rally and marshal themselves by a spontaneous impulse, and therefore they are the inevitable rulers of the earth. Many of the new Californians were men of some education; and the majority were marked by that strength of character and depth of vitality which is essential to the successful pioneer or adventurer. These soon found one another out, and were united to one another by common thoughts and views. They became dominant over the chaotic mass; order cannot help dominating chaos, for it knows what it wants, and it always wants the same thing; whereas chaos knows and aims at nothing. In a surprisingly brief time therefore the Anglo-Saxon minority established laws and regulations in the midst of this roaring, seething, aimless multitude: such things might be done, such might not; this penalty waited upon this crime, that upon that. The Vigilance Committee took the place of Congress and President; the laws were liberal enough, but they were strict within their bounds. Men were hanged, flogged or banished, as the case might be; there was no appeal, and the community perceived that the laws observed a rough impartiality, securing to each man his own, and permitting no infringements. And while the diggers thus protected themselves, the opportunity of profit which trade afforded caused an immense influx of dealers of all sorts; and trade is necessarily orderly. Houses took the place of tents; streets replaced wandering foot paths; fixed property asserted itself on all sides, and was respected. There arose a pure democracy from the whirlpool of mobocracy; and it was rigid, in spite of its breadth, because mobocracy was its twin sister and might else be mistaken for it. It was an American community, and of course it was free; there could be no foothold for human slavery among such men. There were among them many who had been Southern slaveholders; but they never ventured to air their opinions there, far less to attempt to introduce their institutions. There would have been short shrift for them, had they done so. Each man must work for himself, or go, or starve. The Missouri Compromise line would serve only to hang its advocate with, in California.

This vital result could, so far as we can judge, have been attained in no other way, and at no other time. Had gold been discovered before the Mexican war, and the cession of territory that involved, it is hardly possible that Americans would have gained control; England and other nations would have seized what they could; conflicting claims would have stirred up wars, California would have become a shambles, and would have been lost to freedom even had it not become wedded to slavery. Had gold been discovered later than it was, the Missouri line would probably have been drawn, with all that it implied. But as it was, gold saved California to America and to freedom in 1849; and incidentally it bred a race of men fitted by nature and temper to occupy that outpost of our nation, and make it rich and respected; for the solid residue of merit which stands after the flotsam and jetsam of weakness and disorder have been dispersed, comprises the very pith of mankind, which nothing can uproot. The Forty-Niners and their descendants came in good season to remind America what she contained of simple strength; and to renew on the Pacific the valiant traditions which had won the Atlantic coast from Europe.

The roads by which California could be reached were three; one across the breadth of the Continent, with peril of wild beasts, wild men, and wild and desolate nature; another by sea to Panama and across and up the coast to San Francisco; the third, round Cape Horn. All these routes were thronged, and all of them had their varying adventures and vicissitudes; the overland was perhaps the most picturesque and striking, and the strain and suffering were the longest drawn-out. But that story cannot be even outlined here; and it has been painted again and again in unforgettable colors by masters. Indeed, nothing in our history is stranger, more stirring, or better known than this so-called episode of the Argonauts. Bret Harte has told it all, perhaps with too bizarre a mingling of cynicism and optimism; but after making allowances his pictures will stand.

General Taylor, President of the United States, had the eye of a soldier for the significance of the California emigration, and the sagacity of a statesman in dealing with it. He took immediate measures to assist in the formation of a stable government, and recommended that California be admitted as a state at the earliest moment. Though a Virginian and a slaveholder, he had no wish to see California ceded to slavery, and he knew that only violence could effect such a result. Let her come in on her own terms, said he; and he would have New Mexico also determine to which side she would adhere. This liberality offended the South and surprised them; they had not thought that a President of their own section, though a Whig, would thus oppose their policy; but they feared to denounce him, for his position, and the firmness which began to appear through his friendly straightforwardness, made him formidable. He was the President of the whole nation, not of any part of it only; and he did not fear the South, as many eminent Northerners did. When a delegation of Southern Whigs called on him to ask him to pledge himself to sign no bill with the Wilmot Proviso in it, he replied that any constitutional bill should have his signature. "If you send troops to coerce Texas, Southern officers will not obey your orders," they rejoined. This made the soldier indignant. "Then I will command the army in person," thundered he; "and if any man is taken in treason against the Union, I will hang him as I did the deserters and spies at Monterey." Plainly, this law-abiding, impartial, fearless President was not to be led by the nose by any one.

California had voted itself an anti-slave constitution; and with that constitution she should come in, if Taylor had his way. Nothing did he say about the Wilmot Proviso in his recommendation; there was no need for it, and he would not tread on his Southern fellow countrymen's susceptibilities wantonly. But the mass of the Southerners were against California's admission as a free state; Quitman, a New Yorker who had become a slaveholder, was especially virulent against it; he wanted both New Mexico and California for slavery; and hinted at designs against Cuba and the country further south—that shadowy southern empire which so many Southerners dreamed of at this time, after the secession which they contemplated should have been accomplished. The two causes began to count up their several champions in Congress, and to listen to what counsels they might give.

There was not much debating power of a high order in the House; but in the Senate there was more than enough. Besides the great discordant triumvirate of Webster, Clay and Calhoun, now making their last appearances in the arena, there were Seward, who was looming larger and clearer every day, Salmon P. Chase, Sam Houston of Texas, Benton, and Bell. Clay had meant to retire from Congress; he was overpersuaded to return; and though he came, as he thought, merely to look on, he remained to offer one more great compromise. He had his own ideas as to how the impending collision might be averted; it was not the President's idea, for Clay would take suggestions from no one; and his divergence from Taylor divided the Whigs and prepared their defeat. He brought in his proposal a week or so after the President's suggestions, and showed it previously to Webster, whose attitude was still in doubt. The plan, on the whole, greatly favored the South; but it contained measures intended to sweeten it to the Northern palate. California was to be admitted; but only on condition that she carried New Mexico and Utah on her back, and took her chances with them, which were not states but territories. The buying and selling of slaves in the District of Columbia was to be discontinued; but the fugitive slave law was to be enforced strictly. Texas, which had made an untenable claim to a large part of the soil of New Mexico, was to be bought off on terms favorable to her. The Wilmot Proviso was ignored, and the option of slavery or freedom was to be given to states applying for admission. It was manifestly unjust that California, which stood alone, should be saddled with territories concerning whose status as regarded slavery nothing definite was promised. The right of Congress to decide such matters was abnegated. Both South and North had objections against the bill; and Jefferson Davis demanded that the slaveholders be permitted to bring their slaves into New Mexico without reference to legislation in that territory. The extension of the Compromise line was not demanded in Clay's bill; and this opened the whole question.

Three great speeches were made on the question, besides that great one of Clay's in which he introduced his measure. Calhoun's was written out, and was delivered for him by Mason, Calhoun listening to its delivery. He wished California to return to her territorial condition; he supported neither Taylor nor Clay, but hinted at secession as the probable solution of the problem. Unless South and North were given equal rights in the new territory, agitation of the slavery question stopped, and the Constitution amended to favor the South, then the South must leave the Union. The speech was able, but it was not creative, and it determined nothing. It was followed on the 7th of March by the famous speech of Webster, in which he took the course that brought upon him the hostility of the North, while failing to secure for him the full measure of Southern confidence. The true significance of Webster's attitude has been a bone of contention ever since; but it is certain that it destroyed his influence during the short remainder of his life. He never retracted the views he then expressed; and whether in his heart he believed that he had been mistaken cannot be known. He tried to achieve the impossible, and failed.

He professed to speak for the cause of the Union and of the Constitution; and as an American without party, and without reference to sections. He gave Clay's bill his support; he granted all the demands of the South, while denouncing as visionary Calhoun's idea of a peaceable secession. He would give no countenance to free-soil doctrines, and scoffed at the Wilmot Proviso. He left slavery where it was, though with indications that he had no objection to its extension. For him, the Union and the Constitution were paramount; no law of morality or of right and wrong could take precedence of them. In speaking, his eloquence was as great as ever; but the substance of what he said was profoundly disappointing. Upon a review of all the circumstances and conditions it does not appear likely that Webster intended any wrong; rather did he aim at a mark which seemed to be above mortal limitations, only because in truth it did not exist at all. Shooting his arrow in the air, he wounded his own friend. He wished to be an American; he would stand on equal ground between South and North, recognizing only his fellow-countrymen. He thought that by owning no leaning to partisan rancors on either side, he was asserting impartiality and independence. But what he really did was to confound morality with geography. A man's country is not its topographical particulars, but its highest spirit: its approximation to the ideal good and true. If the South were wrong, it made no difference that they were Southerners; if the North were right, it was no narrow partiality that should declare them so to be. If wrong seemed to be buttressed by the Constitution, that only proved that the Constitution was not infallible; if to champion the right imperiled the Union, that could only imply that the terms of our Union should be purified. Webster sought to be national; but he succeeded only in declaring a cynicism profounder even than Calhoun's. The powers of his great brain had been too strong for his moral integrity; for the sake of an outward good, he had refined away the barriers which divide between good and evil in the soul.

This error was not committed by the young Seward, who followed him in the debate, and introduced that consideration for "the higher law" which has made the phrase famous. Beginning with symptoms of embarrassment, he warmed to his theme and became eloquent, and announced doctrines which one would wish to have heard in Webster's organ tones. They were novel doctrines in that chamber; sublime

JEFFERSON DAVIS

and seemingly impracticable, though time has shown them to be as practicable as they were true. Seward would have no dealings with unrighteousness; he would not believe that this people needed for their safety to compromise with evil; rather did he have faith that their only real safety lay in doing right and trusting to God for the consequence. There is a higher law, he affirmed, than that of worldly prudence; and to that law he summoned us to be loyal. But he was heard with ears which for the most part were unbelieving. Calhoun, who made his last appearance in the Senate on this occasion, left it anathematizing this new man with his Promethean sword; and died within the month.

The immediate upshot of the debate was, that no one except Benton stood by the President; Clay and Webster, standing together against Taylor, divided the Whigs; it seemed an opportunity for the Democrats. A committee was got together to discuss the subject, Clay being chairman; it consisted of thirteen members, six Northerners and six Southerners besides Clay himself. Webster, though appointed, did not serve. While the committee was discussing, the treaty was signed which Clayton and Sir Henry Bulwer negotiated, regarding a proposed Nicaragua canal; the terms of which were that neither England nor the United States were to have exclusive control of it, and that no colonizing should take place; but it later transpired that England was secretly holding in reserve her alleged protectorate rights. The Canal, however, still remains in the limbo of projects unachieved.

Clay's committee reported in May; it inspired no enthusiasm, and the President was against it, though not demonstratively so. Congress showed a disposition to disentangle the California matter from the rest, and pass it independently. Southern extremists wished Texas to accomplish her designs on New Mexico by force; but the sturdy President was standing square in the way. The boundary must be settled, he said, not by Texas nor by New Mexico, but by the United States, which was New Mexico's guardian during her minority as a territory. He sent Colonel Monroe with troops to oppose the attempt at invasion of the Texans. When Crawford, the son of the Crawford of Jackson's era, refused to sign the order as Secretary of War, "Then I'll sign it myself," said the old soldier. And events were drawing to an interesting climax, when Taylor, stricken by cholera, suddenly died. Never did an American President, so far as one can humanly judge, die at a moment apparently so inopportune. "I've tried to do my duty," was his last utterance, on that 9th of July which was his last of earth. He had surely done his duty, with a purity and firmness never surpassed. He had done it well, as well as faithfully, and he was daily learning how to do it better. He loved the Union as much as Clay and Webster professed to do, but he would defend it not by compromises, but by putting down treason with the strong hand. He saw things in the large and the mass, and understood the right course to steer. Had he lived another year, either the war of secession would have taken place with him in the saddle for the Union, or it would never have taken place at all. But he died, because his time was come; and so made way for the immortal career of Lincoln.

Millard Fillmore, a good Whig, took the oath as President the same day that Taylor died. He was under the Webster-Clay influence, and Seward found his weight with the administration correspondingly decreased. The entire Cabinet resigned, and were replaced by Clay men. They were good men, and Webster was Secretary of State; but they made a cipher of the President. They favored compromise and conciliation; and the fate of Clay's bill, which had lately seemed so precarious, now bloomed with promise. But an unlooked-for spasm of virility in the Senate upset the "Omnibus" and from the disjected members framed new bills. It was found easier to pass the several parts when thus separated, than the whole in a **lump; but** of course the separation also modified the effect of the parts. To the outside mind, the difference might seem like that historic one 'twixt Tweedledum and Tweedledee; but the Congressional mind is on the inside always. The Clay Omnibus was set up, and patched together, and set a-going on its appointed course, looking quite the same as before the accident. Texas was bought off with a good slice of New Mexico and ten million dollars (of which Congress got its share); New Mexico and Utah were admitted territories, with option as to slavery; California was admitted on her own basis; and so on. Fillmore signed the bills as fast as they came in, the fugitive slave bill along with the rest. Clay retired, satisfied that he had saved the Union. Fillmore countermanded Taylor's military orders regarding the Texan revolt; and Webster was busy arguing down plain morality. But all his cringing under the Southern whip seemed to leave the South still unsatisfied; a convention of slave states to agree upon secession was called for; but either because they had no obvious leader to unite under, or because they began to think that they could get all they wanted without secession, no overt act of disloyalty was carried out. Give us back our runaway slaves, and never mention the word slavery in our hearing, and we may condescend to live with you—was the gist of the Southern dictum to the North. Still if a Northerner but ventured to look hard at a Southern gentleman, the threat of secession rang in his ears. Clay alone was superior to this petulance; "Never," he declared before the Kentucky legislature, "would I consent to a dissolution of the Union. If Congress ever usurps the power to abolish slavery in the states where it exists—but I am sure it will never do so—I will yield." This was manly on Clay's part, and all very well; but the fugitive slave act could not fail to breed serious trouble at once; and the law giving new states the option of slavery or freedom would do so later on. By the fugitive slave law, federal officers became slave hunters throughout the free states; they could arrest any negro without recourse or need of identification, and under any circumstances. That their action was legal, and that the South could get back its fugitives in no other way, were facts which had no effect in reconciling the North to the edict; there were many cases of resistance and rescue in Boston and elsewhere; and Webster was sedulous in prosecuting them, while the Attorney-General, Crittenden, declared the act to be constitutional. There is no question that the South and the administration were in the right in enforcing the law, since it existed; and if it ought not to have existed, why did not the North prevent it in Congress? If slavery were to be tolerated at all, then fugitive slaves were like runaway cattle, and honest folk were bound to return them to their owners. One of the plainest lessons of the situation was, that the people were no longer represented by Congress. But that was the people's fault. Webster arraigned Seward for venturing to set private conscience above law; a New York Whig convention split, some adhering to Fillmore and Webster, with the title of "silver-grays," the others to Seward. Fusions with Democrats began. Boutwell was elected governor of Massachusetts by a coalition of Democrats and Free-soilers. Hamilton Fish, a Seward Whig, was elected to the House in New York. In Ohio, a free-soil state, Ben Wade, strongly anti-slavery, took the place of the veteran Ewing. Charles Sumner beat Winthrop for the Senate. Sumner was a big, good-looking, voluble Boston Brahmin, with high pretensions to culture. and hyperion hair; but he was a good offset to the arrogance of the Southern slaveholders in the Senate, being able, so far as words went, to give them quite as good as they brought. No one could exasperate them as he could; no one heeded their sensibilities so little as he; until the memorable time when they succeeded in getting rid of him, for a while, by other arguments than those of reason. But in fact, reason's rule was over in America for the present. There were party fighting and transformation scenes all over the country. At this juncture, Fillmore's message cried "Peace—Peace!" when there was no peace; and Congress did nothing, nor was anything intelligible heard, except the tones of Clay's voice, preaching mutual forbearance.

But the people were tired of contention on the one monotonous point of slavery, and were also bewildered by the spectacle of men in whose integrity they could hardly help confiding, exhorting them to submission to the law, whether or not it conformed to what had vulgarly been considered morality. They needed a rest; and if persons more intellectual and better informed than they assured them that rest was not only compatible with honor, but essential to the preservation thereof, why should they not believe it? Secessionists at the South and Abolitionists at the North were alike reproved, not too violently; and the government sought to interest the nation in matters of commonplace business. The irreconcilables in the South amused themselves with plans of Central American and Cuban acquisitions, which took form in numerous filibustering expeditions, which met with uniform disaster; the final attempt on the part of the adventurer Lopez to stampede Cuba being extinguished by the killing or shooting of the entire band of five hundred men, and the "garotting" of the leader. Meanwhile the work of the country went on; railways were vigorously developed; the Collins Line of American steamers rivaled the Cunarders as an Atlantic ferry; the telegraph was extended, and the hum of industry was everywhere heard. Webster toured about the land making "compromise" speeches, and extolling the sanctity of the Constitution and the Union; meeting with applause everywhere save in stern Massachusetts, where the Boston aldermen voted to close Faneuil Hall against him. Jenny Lind came to add her matchless voice to the chorus of harmony; and Louis Kossuth, picturesque and heroic, and charmingly eloquent even in the English tongue, tried to woo us to come across the ocean and fight for Hungarian independence against Austria. We cheered him, caressed him, passed resolutions and made speeches supporting his plea; but in the end, of course, were fain to let him depart with his mission unaccomplished. The gift that he lacked was the sense of humor which should have prevented him from expecting aid to freedom from a country which had just given its indorsement to slavery. But we could console ourselves, if not him, by celebrating the victory of our yacht "America" over the Queen's fleet at Cowes Regatta—the race in which there "was no second." We could build fast ships, at any rate!

All this while, the Democrats, in one way or another, had been pushing to the front, or toward it; and the apparent disposition at the South to let a Northern man have the Presidency gave them a better outlook than the Whigs. It was this campaign which first identified the Democratic party with the South; although the Whigs were the party of wealth and aristocracy, the South trusted more in the loyalty of the Democrats to those principles which they deemed vital. The Whigs omitted no act or profession of subservience which might ingratiate them with the South in the premises, and men like Cass and Buchanan tried to out-Herod Herod in their protestations; but that sort of thing may be overdone. The conventions of the two parties met in June, 1852, the fatal last year of Whigism. They had had the greatest statesmen in their ranks that America had produced; they had every opportunity to leave a record commensurate with their ability; but they had been timid and time-serving, and full of misfortunes. Now they were to suffer a crushing defeat, and their two chief champions were to die within five months of each other. Such were the contents of the immediate future; but the party went on hoping and scheming, if not rejoicing; and the coming event did not cast its shadow before. They had three chief candidates—Fillmore, Webster, and Winfield Scott. It was Webster's final effort, and as such he recognized it; and he would certainly not have entered the race had he not hoped to win. He could not but believe that the invaluable support he had given the South would earn their gratitude; and he had omitted no means of persuading the North that the Compromise was their salvation as well. If he was not the representative American, who was?—and should not the representative American be the Americans' leader? Certainly Webster had one of the greatest brains of his century; and we may believe that he had at heart almost solely the welfare of his country, vitiated in a degree though that may have been with a deep-seated, life-long, passionate desire for his own personal triumph. But nothing is better established than that brains do not win the suffrages for the highest office of the brainiest people in the world—if we indeed are that. What exactly is sure to win their suffrages is another and far more abstruse question, into the intricacies of which we will not enter; but a predominating brain is not trusted; its possessor is too clever for common people to be sure what he may do. Had Lincoln's great brain not been balanced by a heart even greater, he would never have led this country through the Civil War; nor, of course, would he have been Lincoln.

The Democratic convention met first, on the 1st of June, and after five days' warm work, gave up the attempt to win with either Cass, Buchanan, Douglas or Marcy, and under the Jacksonian two-thirds rule, unexpectedly united upon the comparatively unknown Franklin Pierce of New Hampshire and of the Mexican War. He was a man who, without having committed himself one way or the other, had made no enemies, but was liked by all. A fortnight later the Whigs came together. Their platform was substantially the same as the Democrats'—support of the Compromise of 1850; but with the delicate modification, which they tried to refine to its least substantiality, that should time and experience demand further legislation—why, it might be effected. Gentle though the hint was, the South caught it up at once, and grew savagely suspicious. Nevertheless, their array of candidates was so imposing, that one could hardly believe that they could all fail. The first votes showed Fillmore leading with 133 votes, Scott second with 131, and Webster almost out of sight in the rear with 29 only. But Webster believed that Fillmore would retire in his favor; he had also hoped that Clay, whose word was still potent in the party, would have declared for him; but in both expectations he was disappointed. Fillmore would not retire, and Clay had given his preference for Scott; and in the end, the vote stood, Scott 159, Fillmore 112, and Webster 21. That vote broke Webster's heart. Yet he survived Clay, who died soon after the Whig convention adjourned. There is deep pathos, if not tragedy, in the story of these two great men, who lost the crown for which they strove for the very reason that they strove for it so hard. Theirs was a noble ambition, but it sometimes stooped to means that were not noble to win. Of the two, Clay, perhaps, has the purer fame; but when we look for the benefits which Clay and Webster actually accomplished, we cannot but be amazed to find them so small. They concentrated the gaze of their contemporaries; they reached the topmost heights of oratory; they advocated and opposed many measures; but after all, we cannot deny that the country might have been better off politically if neither of them had entered public life.

At the polls, Pierce defeated Scott by a vote of 254 to 42. The Free-soilers showed no strength. The great Whig party disappeared from history, and left behind it no lasting or valuable achievement. It had tried to do things impossible, and had shrunk from doing what it might have done. But it sowed the seeds of a successor which was to win the greatest glory that had ever fallen to an American party.

CHAPTER THIRTY-FIRST

KANSAS

YOU may see a ship slipping smoothly through the blue ripples of a summer sea, with the sunshine broad on her sails and deck, and musical breezes whispering through her shrouds: and right across her path, dark, and lurid with strange hues, the awful menace of an approaching hurricane. Here is peace and well-being; yonder, war and destruction. Is the helmsman asleep? If not, let him furl those white sails betimes and batten down his hatches, or his ship will be crushed and sunk.

Fillmore, the amiable nonentity, firm only in his docility to the great men about him, had left the helm of State with warm prosperity all around him. He passed smiling over the side, and was carried safe ashore. He gave no warning order; he himself saw nothing to fear. Yet the tempest was all but on us; you might hear the moan of its rage from afar. And mainsail and foresail, stun'sail and topsail, were spread abroad, and the Stars and Stripes, emblem of freedom and power, floated aloft.

Meanwhile, upon the quarter-deck, appears the new commander, cheerful, hopeful and resolute; honest and faithful too, and a sailor born. He marshals his crew and issues his orders; he explains to his officers the course he will steer and what port he means to make. There is no apprehension in his bearing; he is proud of his ship; he has confidence in his men, and they in him. He has a good brain, a brave heart, and a firm will. All is well; hear the shouting of the multitude from the wharf! And yet captain, crew, and shouting multitude, all are blind. The hurricane will smite the Ship of State, and she will lie on her beam ends, with the seas breaking heavily across her, her flag rent, her masts gone by the board. It shall be by the mercy of God only that she does not founder and go down.

Optimism and self-confidence are good qualities in a man or in a nation; but they should be molded by foresight and reason. It seems incredible, now, that we could have headed into the Kansas troubles, and through them into the Civil War, without realizing it. Yet so it was. It is useless to assert that we were shipwrecked deliberately. South Carolina had prattled of secession, no doubt, as a pretty woman threatens her husband with leaving him if he does not buy her a new bonnet; but nothing serious was meant. Abolitionists clamored for virtue or non-intercourse, and a million people read Harriet Beecher Stowe's new book; but the great common-sensible populace took it all with allowances, and said to themselves that the worst was probably over. Folks might chop at the Union with their little hatchets, but it would stand a great deal of such attack; and they might criticise the Constitution, but it was a very wise old document after all, and could be made wiser if necessary. That fugitive-slave law was a nuisance, of course; a man doesn't like to have his house entered by a sheriff, and the attic and cellar ransacked for stray niggers; but, if he harbored the nigger, he knew what he was risking. As to the menace of slaveholding invading free states, that was all talk; what would they do there if they came? Besides, had not the Missouri Compromise settled all that? The South had all she wanted, with Cuba and the Isthmus in the background, perhaps; she did not want to interfere with the North, any more than the North wanted to meddle with her. Some of us like one thing, and some another; this is a big country; but we are all Americans, and we can live and let live, and make money hand over fist.

Such was the general attitude of the country; if there were nervous persons here and there who mouthed disaster, such we have always with us. Franklin Pierce was a New Hampshire boy; he had showed the stuff he was made of in the Mexican War; he was clean-handed and incorruptible; he would be certain to do the North justice, and if he was fair to the South too, that is only what a President ought to be. He was a young man, too: barely fifty: and youth, with its courage, and its freedom from hampering entanglements, is a good ingredient in politics. He meant to do right, and so did we all; so how could things go wrong?

The fact is that a man or a nation may do right, while going all the while in a wrong direction; and it is the direction that tells. We were started on a wrong course; we were setting logical consistency against human nature; and the more correct and logical our consistency, the more certain were we to meet disaster. The Constitution had been so interpreted by the leaders of opinion as to sanction the Missouri Compromise and the fugitive slave law; the Constitution also permitted citizens of one state to reside in any other; the domestic concerns of individuals were of course sacred; and the extent of state rights was still undetermined, but the tendency of late had been to enlarge them. The existence of all these ingredients of gunpowder was conceded; there seemed to be no harm in any of them; and the fact that their combination would produce an explosion was not considered till too late.

On the journey to Washington a tragic accident befell the party of the President-elect. There was a railway collision; the car in which Pierce, his wife, and their son were sitting was shattered, and the little boy was crushed where he sat by a beam. Mrs. Pierce did not see the horror; and her husband, in the midst of his anguish, thought first of her, and quickly threw his cloak over the dreadful spectacle.

This act was characteristic of Pierce, who ever thought of others before himself. Many years afterward, when he was standing beside the grave of his wife, to whom he had been devotedly attached, listening to the words of the burial service, a life-long friend stood beside him. The winter wind blew cold across the grave; and Pierce, solicitous even in that moment for his friend, passed a hand over his shoulder to turn up the collar of his coat against the blast. The fiber of the man was intensely masculine, and his physical strength was exceptional: deep chest, lean flanks, wiry and tireless limbs: but with this masculine strength went an exquisite natural tenderness and courtesy, coming from the heart, and enriched with human sympathy. Once, when the daughter of a friend was lying ill of a disease which was likely to end fatally, Pierce used to come to the house day after day, and sit for an hour or so in the room with the anxious family; saying little, making no demonstration; but permeating and strengthening all with his deep, loving sympathy. Children loved him, and men and women acknowledged his sway. He was a conscientious man, with a high ideal of rectitude and duty. Like other public men of his time, he was accustomed to drink, occasionally to excess, and his strong social qualities aided this tendency; but when he entered the Presidential office, he wholly abstained from wine or liquor during his entire term. He was a striking figure to look at, erect and soldierly to the end of his life, with a step full of power; his hair was black and wiry, bushing at the ends. Such was the man who, because he steadily pursued the course that he believed to be right, made himself during his term, from one of the most popular, the most unpopular man who had held the office of President. Like Clay and Webster, he loved and cherished the Union; on assuming the reins of authority, he accepted things as he found them, and resolutely carried out the policy which his party authorized, and which he deemed best for the country. But Pierce's penetrating gray eyes could see only straight ahead; the path of what he thought his duty was narrow; and it led to calamity.

At first, however, all promised well, and the energy of the country was shown in the variety and energy of its activities. Traffic increased; the scandals of the municipal government of New York under Fernando Wood were already notorious; San Francisco was growing great under the stern rule of its Vigilance Committee; Oregon was becoming steadily populous; Lucretia Mott was setting in motion that movement for women's rights which claimed for the sex all masculine things, from trousers to the suffrage; and which is only now beginning to realize that women's privileges go further and fare better; and Neal Dow, the best exemplar of the value of his own opinions, was founding the Temperance Society. In short, our people were entering into the detail of life on all sides, trying experiments, laughing at failures, profiting by both failures and successes. Meanwhile Pierce, under agreeable auspices, was selecting his Cabinet, whose most prominent members were Jefferson Davis, Secretary of War, William Marcy, Secretary of State, and Caleb Cushing, Attorney-General. Davis and Cushing seemed most near to the President; Marcy was older than the others, and less pronounced in his views. James Buchanan was sent to England. The President's address foreshadowed a reasonable home policy, and a firm foreign one; he pledged himself to carry out the Compromise of 1850; and throughout expressed a hearty confidence in the country's future. It was noticed that the Cabinet had rather a Southern look to it, as a whole; but since Pierce himself was Northern, that was good policy.

The first salient event of the administration confirmed the current good opinion of it. A Hungarian named Koszta, of revolutionary proclivities, was arrested in Smyrna by the Austrians, and was on the point of being carried into captivity, when our Captain Ingraham, who commanded a sloop of war, interfered, on the ground that Koszta was an embryo American citizen; and threatened to bombard the Austrian brig if he were not given up. Marcy backed Ingraham up, and declared the rights all over the world of American citizens: much to the delight of our citizens at home, who have not always been so well vindicated since then. But it was plain that Pierce had not done all his fighting in Mexico; and the intimation from a member of his Cabinet that the annexation of further outlying territory would not necessarily meet with the opposition of the government was also taken in good part. The World's Fair opened in New York, in emulation of that in England, and was regarded as a good sign, though its financial success was not what might have been wished; but, upon the whole, we appeared to be getting on, and to be a great nation already. In this way we had covered the space between the inauguration and 1854. Then, all of a sudden, Stephen A. Douglas, a Vermont politician, at this time about forty-two years old, introduced what was known as the Kansas-Nebraska bill. Not much notice of Douglas had hitherto been taken by the country, though in Congress he was known as an effective speaker of the coarsely vigorous kind. He was small in stature, but with the voice of a stentor, and an uproarious manner of speaking, waving his arms, bellowing manfully in the ardent passages, and tearing off his stock in the heat of action to give himself breathing room. These intimations of the pressure of a great soul upon a small body caused him to get the nickname of the Little Giant. He was a Democrat, sprung from the ranks, but allied in sentiment with the South, and in favor of annexing territory in their behalf. That he was ambitious is certain; and he had brains above the average; nor was he incapable of making his brains serve his ambition at the expense of what are ordinarily termed scruples. He perceived his advantage in ingratiating himself with the South, which seemed likely to hold the reins of power for some time to come; and he was young enough to afford to wait some years for the Presidency, though not

too young to begin to play for those great stakes. The
Kansas-Nebraska bill seemed to him a good way of beginning.

The essence of his political idea in the bill was to develop
the discrepancy between the Missouri Compromise and the
Compromise of 1850. The first forbade slavery above 36° 30':
the latter made slavery optional in all new territories.
Douglas conceived—as the conditions gave him the right
to do—that the Compromise of 1850 annulled the other.
For if new territories could admit slaves if they liked, then
by what authority could the restriction of 36° 30' be applied
to them? If they happened to be south of the line, of course
whatever force the restriction might have would be in favor
of slavery; but if they were above the line, then they were
justified in declaring that the later bill annulled the earlier
one. For a hard and fast line, which was sure to do injustice to some one, was substituted the free choice of the
settlers in the region; the wishes of the majority should rule
them, as the Constitution declared and intended should be
the case. Furthermore, the measure was rigidly impartial as
between North and South; because, if a community south
of the old line should prefer to dispense with slaves, they
would be just as free to do so as would be the settlers in a
northern district to introduce them. It was in accordance
with the spirit of all American institutions that the people
should live as they chose within the due limits of the law.
This bill was not a slave measure any more than it was a
free-soil measure; it was a national measure, and was in the
line of true progress and development.

By what arguments should the position taken by this bill
be overthrown? It could not be overthrown by any argument of principle; could it have been, this would of course
have been done. It was vindicated by the Compromise of
1850, which had been passed by Congress and acquiesced in
by the whole nation; which says that whenever Nebraska
(or other territory) applied for admission, it should be at

liberty to do so "with or without slavery." And this was a knife that cut both ways; for what was to prevent the inhabitants of some southern region, applying for admission, from stipulating that slavery should not exist within their limits, and thus introducing free soil into the heart of slavedom? The Southerners, in accepting the 1850 Compromise, had accepted this contingency; and it would be unjust of the North not to do as much. In fact, there, already, was California, part of which extended below 36° 30', which had come in as a free state, because the majority of its populace so desired. Turn and turn about is fair play.

The most obvious method of attack upon the bill was to maintain that the Missouri Compromise was not annulled by that of 1850. By way of testing this point, Dixon of Kentucky moved to amend the bill by repealing the Missouri Compromise. This prompted Douglas so to modify his bill as to pronounce the Missouri Compromise explicitly void; and it divided Nebraska into two territories, one called Nebraska, the other Kansas; in which popular or "squatter" sovereignty should obtain. "The object is not to admit or exclude slavery," said Douglas, "but to remove whatever obstacles Congress has placed in the way of it, and to apply to all our territories the doctrine of non-intervention." Should Congress, after debate, admit that the Missouri Compromise was void, what other objection could the opponents of the bill urge against it?

Before submitting it to debate, Douglas caused its provisions to be laid before Pierce by a committee of which Jefferson Davis, who approved the bill, was a member. Pierce listened to the reading of the bill, and then said, according to the report, "I consider the bill based upon a sound principle which the Compromise of 1820 infringed upon, and to which we have now returned." This was the first that Pierce had heard of the bill, and that was his opinion upon it. Davis himself, it may be observed, had violently opposed the 1850 Compromise; he wished the 36°

30' line to be carried to the Pacific. Manifestly he had undergone a change of heart, since the Douglas bill was built out of the materials furnished by the 1850 act. As a matter of fact, he had opposed the latter without due consideration; now that he realized what could be done with it, his opposition vanished. As to the President, he could have no choice, as a Constitutional Executive, but to declare that the bill was in his opinion strictly Constitutional. He was there not to make laws, nor to find fault with them after they had been made; but simply to see that they were enforced. He could see no Constitutional flaw in Douglas's bill, and he so declared. Whether he personally liked it or not is another question, having no bearing upon his course. The President has great power, and is able in a degree to influence legislation; and Pierce, had he disliked this bill, and been able to give sound reasons against it, might have vetoed it when it came officially before him. But Pierce was a Democrat; he did not believe in antagonizing slaveholders or in abolishing slavery; and if the whole nation should express a desire for the extension of slavery, he would not have hindered them, any more than he would have hindered free soil extension, had that been the national preference. Obviously he could not foresee the disturbance and disorder which the squatter-sovereignty bill would make; neither could Douglas. The commencement of the mischief ante-dated all of them; it lay in allowing slavery to overstep its original boundaries at the time the Constitution was adopted. Had an amendment to that effect been carried then, as it probably might have been, all would have been well now; but what had been done since was all in the nature of a corollary; and all we can say against the South's conduct, up to the time they seceded, is, that if they had shown less arrogance and been more forbearing, the only harm done by slavery would have been confined to the original slave states.

The attitude of Davis, however, is significant, and typifies that of the whole South. He and the South knew that, apart from abstractions, the Douglas bill would benefit them and not the North. No Southern communities would arise desiring the abolition of slavery within their boundaries; there was no propaganda in that direction; the only propaganda was that of slavery toward the North. Their assertion that the bill was impartial as between South and North was therefore lacking in candor; it was impartial in theory, but not in fact. Had the bill been equally favorable to both sections, it would have met with no opposition from the North; had it been equally hostile to both, it would never have been passed. It is to be observed, moreover, that although the interpretation of the 1850 Compromise was legally correct, the present outcome of it had not been realized by the people at the time; and it took them by surprise. We may say it was their fault; eternal vigilance is the price of liberty, and a free people are bound to foresee all contingencies of any act which their representatives pass. But in practice, the people commonly attend to their private business, and let politicians manage their politics; and though it is the duty of the politicians to protect the people against their own heedlessness, the counsel is one of perfection, and is not observed in practice.

The debate on the bill began in January and lasted nearly till June. Clay and Webster being no more, the debate lacked the eloquence it would otherwise have had; but Seward, Salmon P. Chase and Sumner were arrayed against the bill, and it made their reputations. They had not much logical material to work with, but they made a stubborn fight. The bill discharged Congress of responsibility for the doings of the territories; and it did not specify at what period the exclusion or adoption of slavery in a territory should be determined. This was a fault of detail, however—not of principle. The North as a whole took the ground, instinctively, of protesting against the repeal of the Missouri Compromise. Popular speakers declared the bill to be a slaveholder's plot to spread slavery over the Union. But to ascribe sinister motives to a given action is not the same thing as proving the action itself to be unlawful. Be that as it might, the indignation aroused by the bill at the North was vehement; the friendly feeling toward the South, which had been growing up, was dispersed at once. The battle was fought in the Senate with no mincing of phrases; but the majority was in its favor, and the vote which sent it to the House on the 3d of March was a majority of twenty-three. The House resorted to all manner of parliamentary tactics, in addition to mere argument, to support or defeat the measure; but on the 22d of May tactics came to an end, and the bill was passed, with unimportant amendments, by 113 to 100. The Senate now reconsidered it, and passed it on May 26th without a division. On the 30th it went to the President, who signed his name to it, and it became the law of the land. The peculiar feature of this lamentable affair is, that the bill was an entirely gratuitous one. The settlers in Nebraska had never asked for it; they had assumed that the 36° 30' line settled their status. Had it not been for Mr. Douglas, reasoning in vacuo, the bill might never have been born. That it was born, therefore, lends color to the suspicion that Douglas may have conspired with certain Southern leaders to take this means of advancing slavery. That is an inference, and a strong one; but of positive proof there is none. Douglas must bear the odium of the doubt. But the plot, if there were one, was very limited in its membership; the South at large, in and out of Congress, however much the bill may have gratified them, had no more to do with it than to take it when it was offered them. Whoever else was in the plot, Pierce certainly was not; he had nothing to gain by the bill, and it cost him his political future. He acted from conscience solely; and he accepted the consequences without flinching.

After Congress had had its say, the people began to be heard; and their first demonstration was at Boston. Owing to an indiscretion, the presence in the house of a Boston citizen of a fugitive slave, Anthony Burns by name, was revealed; and a sheriff came to Boston and tried in vain to persuade the man to return with him peaceably. He then brought a writ of arrest. When this became known, there was a riot, which could barely be put down by military force. A meeting convened in Faneuil Hall, and Wendell Phillips and Theodore Parker fanned its flames. The excitement continued for a week; a rescue was tried and failed. Another week was consumed in the trial of the case before Commissioner Loring. The only possible result occurred; Burns was decided to be a fugitive slave, and it was decreed that he return to slavery. The law must be obeyed; but the Boston people were very angry, and their anger generally had meant something. They draped their houses in black, and hissed the procession that took Burns to the ship; and he was the last fugitive slave to be taken out of Boston.

The fugitive slave law had no ostensible connection with the Squatter Rights bill; but the inflammation caused by the latter affected the Northern sensitiveness regarding the former. The judge who tried the case was dismissed, for deciding it according to law; inventions were elaborated to defeat the law by delays, if it could not be broken; and as for Anthony Burns, he was bought back from his Southern master by subscriptions and enabled to become a free Bostonian. Possibly the South would have been willing to accept an extension of the same idea, and sell all its slaves to the North at a fair price; but the proposition was not made.

Whatever happened now was interpreted as a new symptom of Southern plots against the peace and liberty of the realm. General Quitman, an inextinguishable disquietist, made fantastic efforts to capture Cuba; the Cuban government had seized our ship, "Black Warrior," in a high-handed way, calling forth a stern message from Pierce; and our relations with Spain were temporarily clouded; Quitman had few followers in the South, but he was regarded in the North as the would-be founder of an independent Southern empire. Walker of Nicaragua (as he was later called) sailed with a picturesque band of adventurers for La Paz, in Southern California, and appropriated the place, issuing a picturesque proclamation to the inhabitants; but the support he had counted on failed him, and he had to come back. Gadsden made an official treaty with Mexico, fixing our boundary line a little further south, in order to get space for a projected railway. The North regarded all these movements with the same suspicion; though only the latter had the support of the administration; Pierce rigidly suppressed the filibustering tendency, to the disappointment of Southern agitators; but he was as alert to enforce the Constitution against them as he had been to declare the validity of the Kansas-Nebraska bill. Both sides called him sectional, because he was impartial.

But it was impossible for him, or for any man, to please both sides in this quarrel. If he kept his oath to preserve the Constitution and the Union, he must inevitably anger first one party and then the other, or both at once. The people and the Constitution—or the several interpretations of it—were at odds; Sumner touched the point when he replied to Butler, "I swore to support the Constitution as I understood it—not as it was understood by others." The divergence between the two sides was of sentiment and morality, and the attempt of either to support it on legal grounds was natural, but futile. It would have to be accommodated, if at all, in other ways.

The fear of slavery extension, the danger of which was real, but immensely exaggerated, drove the discordant parties of the North to make common cause; free Democrats, old Whigs, Free-soilers, rallied under a common impulse, and assumed the collective title of Republicans: a title which the Civil War made glorious, and which retained the confidence of the people for the better part of a generation. Their

manifesto in Congress was issued by George W. Julian and
other reformers, and it affirmed that the free states had no
longer any guarantee for the freedom in territories which
former compromises had promised, and that with this guarantee had vanished all assurance of harmony and union between all the states. It charged that the South contemplated conquering or buying Cuba and parts of Mexico, and
seeking an alliance with Russia against the other European
powers, taking advantage of the Crimean war. Brazil, according to these memorialists, was to be made a center of
Southern slavery, and when all was prepared, the South
proposed to dissolve her connection with the rest of the
United States, and set up an empire of her own. Southern
leaders replied to the manifesto by remarking that they had
never seen a production which "contained in so few words
so much fiction and pure imagination." It is difficult, as
Burke had observed many years before, to draw an indictment against a whole people; there were men in the South
who aimed at all that Julian charged, and more; but there
were innumerable more who projected or desired nothing of
the kind. These reachings-out into the unknown were a
natural manifestation of an active and restless race, avid of
new experiences; but there was nothing awful or wicked in
them. And most of the people wished chiefly to stay at
home and mind their own business.

The movement to unite at the North was steady but not
so rapid as the extremists would have wished. State conventions were called, and some progress was made. It was at
this time that the Know-Nothings became prominent; they
wished to "put none but Americans on guard":—a sentiment
which was sure to find expression in a new nation which had
begun to feel the pressure of unassimilated material from the
old world, much of it of an aspect by no means attractive, or
even safe. There was a great deal of apparent justification
for it; but it was impossible that it could long endure; for
Americans are the world—the old world in the new. Roman

Catholicism came under the ban of the new society, which was strictly secret in its operations; but a war against a religious faith could never succeed in a land devoted to religious freedom. The Know-Nothings were strong for a while, though never so strong as was imagined; they got into politics, and nominated candidates; Gardner was elected governor of Massachusetts by their ballots; but the attitude of neutrality which they were obliged to assume between slavery and its opponents was sure, at a time like this, to bring them between the two stools to the ground, as soon as they aimed at the Presidency. Only while the elements of opinion were still in solution, before finally crystallizing, could they, or any new combination, obtain a hearing.

Abroad, meanwhile, some minor treaties, looking to improvements of commercial relations, and of the fisheries, were concluded; and at a conference of our ministers held in Ostend in October, 1854, the purchase of Cuba from Spain for a maximum sum of one hundred and twenty million dollars was advocated. If Spain declined the transaction, the suggestion was thrown out that we might compel her to give it by force; Russia acting as our ally and co-beneficiary in the enterprise. But Pierce would not support any such scheme; Russia had enough to do with England and France in the Crimea; and Spain made reparation for the "Black Warrior" outrage. Soule, who had been our minister to Spain, and the chief agent in the affair, resigned in discouragement and returned home. On the other hand, Perry succeeded in establishing commercial relations with the hitherto hermit empire of Japan, and curiosities and utilities from that fascinating corner of the world began to be seen in the homes of the American people. But there was as yet nothing cordial in the attitude of the shy and supercilious antipodeans.

All this was by-play; the real business before the country was the working out of the consequences of the Kansas Nebraska bill. The South was somewhat puzzled by the attitude of the North; many Southerners believed what the President had long before affirmed—that the bill favored freedom, and that its passage would prevent the addition of any more slave states to the Union. It was not likely, on the face of it, that a territory north of 36° 30' would be settled by more Southern than Northern men. But a panic had been started at the North, and there is no reasoning with panic. And again, the sight of this panic aroused the South to its opportunity of rescuing the region in question from the free soilers; and so the fight began. If the South could not get Kansas, it could hope for nothing else above 36° 30'. Oregon, Minnesota, and the other northern territories were beyond Southern reach; if the South could not expand northward, they were certain to be in a minority ere long. And if, as they believed, Northern supremacy meant abolition of slavery everywhere, evidently this was their death-struggle as members of the Union. The only alternative was secession; and that meant a death-struggle too.

But Missouri, a slave state, bordered upon Kansas, and the South had a chance there. Living or roaming along the border were numbers of rough characters, with a whisky bottle in one pocket and a revolver in the other, who were ripe for any enterprise. There was no real colonizing ability in the South; they were lacking in the business faculty which prevailed in the North—and assumed to be proud of the fact; but by means of this class of men they could seize the land. There were already slaves in Kansas; and the movement to take possession for slavery was led by Atchinson of Kentucky, president of the Senate, a strong slavery sympathizer and a man of defiant energy. The borderers were ferried over the river in droves, and spread over the country, founding pro-slavery towns, and making a great noise for their side. They were not bona-fide settlers in most cases; or they had residences on both sides of the border, as political and other considerations might demand. As no stipulation had been **made by Douglas's** bill as to the time or manner in which the choice for or against slavery in a territory should be made, there seemed every likelihood that Kansas was lost to freedom.

But there were in the North also men of energy, not restrained by scruples too fine-spun. Eli Thayer was one of these; and he suggested a plan for Northern colonization of the disputed land. There was plenty of material in the North; free laborers and lusty emigrants, who were qualified to take hold of a new country and reduce it to fruitfulness and civilization. Thayer, after some tentative agitation, dubbed his plan the New England Emigration Aid Society, and in July, 1854, it began operations. Other similar Kansas Leagues were formed, and large bodies of free soilers, with their wives and children, when they had any, were transported to the point of interest. Hereupon Stringfellow, a supporter of Atchison, tried to get Congress to help arrange a Southern colonization scheme to counteract the Northern one; but though Southern members approved the plan, they could not provide it with practical support; so Atchison and Stringfellow were forced to rely on maneuvers at the polls to effect what they could not do by more legitimate means. They dumped hundreds of fraudulent voters into the territory, who remained there only long enough to flourish their revolvers, drink their whisky, and cast as many votes as they pleased for slavery; and then went home again. The Northern colonists had not provided themselves with any other tools than those of peaceful agriculture, and were somewhat overawed by these demonstrations; so that the total pro-slavery vote, when counted, was a good deal more than the total number of genuine settlers in the territory. A gentleman named Reeder, inclined to anti-slavery, was sent out by Pierce as territorial governor; and he remonstrated against a legislature elected in a manner so transparently irregular. But the pro-slavery party had judges as well as law-makers in their possession; and the Chief-justice, Lecompte, a man unqualified for any position of trust, decided all questions in their favor. The legislature, meeting at Shawnee Mission, instead of at Pawnee, as the governor had directed, unseated all but a fraction of the free-soil minority, and that fraction retired voluntarily in dismay. Reeder still protesting, the now unanimous legislature charged him with being corruptly interested in real estate in Pawnee; and this accusation being supported in other quarters, was laid before Pierce, who, as in duty bound, suspended Reeder from his office. Pro-slavery measures of the most radical and menacing sort were now passed by the legislature, and there was none to say them nay.

But however corrupt might have been the means by which this legislature got elected, and however violent might be its behavior and measures, it was all done in the form of law, and had legal sanction until, by Constitutional means, it should be discredited. Any attempt to ignore or supplant it otherwise would be revolutionary. It was the misfortune of the Free-soil party to put themselves in a revolutionary attitude; and the circumstances went far to justify them, since time was of importance in a struggle of this kind, and unless something were done without waiting for the slow processes of judicial examination, Kansas would be lost forever. The pro-slavery party had committed a crime, but under the screen of the law; the anti-slavery people were doing right, but the law pronounced them wrong. This state of things is always difficult to manage, and those who engage in it must be prepared to take the consequences.

The unauthorized convention of the Free-soilers met at Lawrence, provided with that necessary adjunct of legislation in these times, a consignment of Sharpe's rifles, and led by Robinson, an ex-Argonaut, familiar with bold proceedings, but a man of pith and gravity. They repudiated the Shawnee Mission assembly and its works, and summoned two other conventions, at Big Springs, and finally at Topeka. Reeder was chosen delegate to Congress, and election day was appointed on October 9, 1855, a week or so later than the election day of the "regular" legislature. But the pro-slavery voters still distanced their rivals in the fertility of their repeaters. Each party, of course, ignored the other. In October the Free-soilers sent delegates to Topeka to frame a constitution and apply for admission as a state. At this juncture arrived on the scene the new governor sent by Pierce to supply the place of Reeder; his name was Shannon, and he was of a hasty temperament; without waiting to inquire into the merits of the case, he denounced the Free-soilers as revolutionists, traitors, and breeders of insurrection; all of which things they were, technically; but in the condition that Kansas was, one should modify one's expressions. As a matter of fact, they were honest men, as this world goes, who were trying to remedy a crying abuse. There could be no possible agreement between slaveholders and free-soilers living side by side in the same territory or state; and civil war really existed in posse, if not in actuality.

The President's regular annual message was not strongly accented as regarded Kansas; but soon after he sent another message to Congress which denounced the irregularity of the late proceedings, and called for the repression of Reeder, who had not yet purged himself of the charges which had compelled his retirement. The message also called attention to the unconstitutional character of the laws lately passed by Massachusetts, forbidding any aid of State troops, officials or buildings in executing the fugitive slave acts, and penalizing slave-hunters as kidnapers. This bill had been passed over the governor's veto, and had been followed by the public burning of a copy of the Constitution by Garrison, who had solemnly decreed that "the Union must be dissolved." Such grotesque absurdities were perhaps not worth noticing; but if they were noticed by the Executive, it could not be done in terms more moderate than those he used. The situation was inevitably bad, and the less attention was called to it, the better, for the present.

But hard words were common at this epoch; and Senator Sumner paid dear for his contribution to the supply of them in Congress. Sumner was a very egotistic and supercilious personage, with a fine command of invective, and a scholarly touch which was not always at the command of his Southern opponents. In reply to their "arrogant, old-plantation strain" he brought shafts bitterly barbed, which exasperated his adversaries none the less for the truth which winged many of them. The custom in the South, among gentlemen, was to resent an affront by some physical remonstrance, such as a slap on the face, and then to await the demand of the smitten party for the "satisfaction usual among gentlemen." Sumner, a broad-shouldered, athletic man, in the prime of his age and strength, had been particularly rasping to the personal sensibilities of Butler of South Carolina, a man in the decline of life. The latter made no demonstration; but he had a nephew, a young ass by the name of Preston Brooks; and Brooks, taking unto himself a friend of the same kind and caliber named Keitt, went to the Senate Chamber two days after Sumner's speech, and found the latter writing quietly at his desk, and looking for anything but violence. Brooks and Keitt had canes—that of Brooks being of black rubber, not very formidable to look at, but capable of giving a sharp and painful blow. Advancing abruptly upon the seated Senator, "You have libeled the State of South Carolina and my aged relative!" shouted the gentlemanly ruffian, at the same time fetching the object of his rage a violent blow on the head, which bewildered him and brought blood, and following it up with many more blows on the back and shoulders, until the cane was broken to pieces: the chivalric Keitt, meanwhile, keeping off would-be rescuers by flourishing his cane in their faces. Sumner could have annihilated Brooks if only he could have got hold of him; but his long legs were hampered by the desk, which was clamped to the floor with iron screws, and he was unable to rise. The effort he made to do so was so vigorous that it partly tore the desk from its moorings, and strained his own back so severely that for years he was a partial cripple. Having accomplished this dastardly "vindication" of South Carolina and his aged relative, Brooks was removed; and public sentiment would have supported Sumner had he called him out and shot him. Men who use words as Sumner used them should be prepared to make them good in any manner the aggrieved may propose. But Sumner was conscientiously opposed to dueling, and he went to Europe to recover his health, and posed as the first martyr of the anti-slavery cause; while Brooks, having made his one bid for immortality, expired by natural processes not long after. History will probably decide that too much sympathy was lavished upon Sumner; but one can hardly be too unrelenting in one's condemnation of Brooks, and of the type he stood for.

In Kansas things continued to go from bad to worse. Shannon, the new governor, demanded and got United States troops to restore what he was pleased to call order; and a pro-slavery mob marched on Lawrence and sacked and wrecked it. A Congressional committee, of which John Sherman, then a young man, was a member, was appointed to go to Kansas and find out what really was the matter. After examining and reducing to writing the testimony of over three hundred witnesses of all shades of opinion, they made a report declaring that the pro-slavery people were in the wrong, and that Kansas ought by right to be a free state. A bill to admit it accordingly under its Topeka constitution was passed in the House, but could not get through the Senate. Civil war of a desultory but very disturbing kind continued in the unhappy country for some years longer; Governor Shannon resigned his difficult functions in 1856, and was succeeded by a son of Anak called Geary, who did the best he could with a hopeless job, pending a final settlement.

The year before this, the filibuster Walker had under-the United States. This negro, Dred Scott by name, had so long ago as 1838 brought suit to recover his freedom on the plea that his master had taken him into a free state; he had been ever since used by lawyers on both sides of the question as an anvil on which to hammer out their views and arguments. After having won and lost several times, the moment for the final decision had arrived. Not only was the Supreme Court about to pronounce its verdict, but it had already arrived at it; and it is not to be supposed that the President, with whose politics the majority of the Court was in sympathy, could have been ignorant of the direction in which their opinions would incline. Nevertheless, in his inaugural, he deprecated excitement on the matter, remarking that the judgment of the Court was about to be given, and that whichever way it went, he should loyally uphold it, and trusted the country would do the same. A few days later, the judgment was pronounced, and it consigned Dred Scott to slavery. Had this conclusion been reached before the elections, it is nearly certain that Fremont instead of Buchanan would have been President; for, coming as it did on the top of the Kansas troubles, it would have warned the people against admitting a slave sympathizer to the highest office. Of the whole Bench, two judges only, McLean and Curtis, dissented. The verdict had this peculiarity, that it first disposed of the case by declaring that no negro of African descent could be entitled to be plaintiff before a court. This ended the matter; but after this the Court went on to give a gratuitous opinion as to the merits of the situation. Having denied the man's citizenship, they said that the Missouri Compromise was illegal; that a slave could be carried into any territory without thereby gaining immunity from his status as a slave; and that, in short, as the Chief-justice, Taney, expressed it (the same man who, as Secretary of the Treasury under Jackson, drew out the funds from the United States Bank), the slave had no rights which white men were bound to respect. The decision was founded on special reasoning, and ignored the true merits of the question, as well as the views of such giants of Constitutional law and the principles of human rights as Jefferson and the English Mansfield. Dred Scott, the individual, was afterward freed by the voluntary act of his master; but the precedent thus established remained as a menace to peace and freedom in America.

Governor Geary of Kansas came up to Washington after the inauguration to discover the drift of things, and perceiving that it was hostile to him, he resigned his office. R. J. Walker, an honest man, was sent out as his successor, his avowed aim being to support the will of the majority. The indictments against the political defendants were quashed, and Robinson was set at liberty; and as a means of arriving at a satisfactory settlement, Walker advised the free state men to abandon the Topeka principles and submit their cause to the polls under the legally established regime. Not without misgivings, this was agreed to; and the result showed a large preponderance of free state votes. But the pro-slavery men were not going to yield so easily; and under the lead of a political scoundrel named Calhoun—no relation of the great statesman—the plan was evolved of foisting a slave constitution upon the country without submitting it to the people; thereby annulling the value of the late vote for freedom. Not all of the legislature would agree to this, however; and a compromise finally was made by which the question should be submitted to the people whether they would have the constitution with slavery or without slavery: leaving all the rest of the articles of the constitution to be accepted in any event: —and they were so framed as practically to make slavery inevitable. Walker protested against this swindle, and went to Washington to remonstrate; but Buchanan informed him that the government would support Calhoun. When the voting day came, the free state men declined to go to the polls, and the pro-slavery party won by a ten to one vote. But when it came to electing state officers under this constitution, the free state supporters came out, and reversed the verdict; and the final result of the whole Kansas struggle was, that the pro-slavery men were utterly defeated, though the result of the trial was kept as long as possible from being made known, and the admission of Kansas as a free state was postponed until there should be a census of 93,000 inhabitants. Meanwhile Walker had resigned.

The Dred Scott decision and the Kansas muddle had created much indignation and uneasiness in the North; but during the autumn and winter of 1857 there was another period of financial and business disaster, due to too reckless borrowing of money on all sides, relying on an impossible standard of prosperity to make money good. Banks again suspended payment, towns went bankrupt, there were widespread mercantile failures, and all looked pinched and gloomy. In this state of things, the people were disinclined to go to dangerous lengths in politics, and the election showed no very decided condemnation of the administration. But upon the whole, the Democrats appeared to be losing their cohesion, while in Congress there was a compact minority in opposition. Buchanan however was imprudent enough to urge the admission of Kansas as a slave territory, in defiance of the patent preferences of its inhabitants; and at this juncture Douglas himself, who was responsible for the whole Kansas imbroglio, came out with an unexpected protest against the conduct of the administration. Whether or not his new attitude was sincere may be questioned; it had the appearance of being a courageous act, alienating many Southern adherents; and it was undoubtedly a step in the direction of justice. But Douglas was far from lacking in political insight, and one is disposed to ask whether he might not have thought this a good way of bringing himself again into prominence, and conciliating Northern support. But, again, it may have been a genuine impulse, which he turned to political advantage. He was an ingrained demagogue, and loved conspicuousness, and the clamor of audiences;

and later on he showed symptoms of wishing to hedge somewhat on his valiant attitude; but the secret heart of a politician is an obscure place to grope in, nor does what one finds there often reward the pain of search. The House voted for an investigation of the Kansas proceedings; but Orr, the Speaker of the House, by appointing a committee of pro-slavery men, succeeded in stifling the matter. There were prolonged and disorderly debates, in which drunken members from Southern states called Northerners bad names, and denounced Northerners in general as the "mudsills of society." This had no special bearing on the merits of the topic under discussion; but Jefferson Davis spoke to the point when he recommended keeping United States troops in Kansas, to keep down "disorder." He had perceived, before the end of Pierce's administration, as Secretary of War, that war was likely to occur in these States, and had conducted the affairs under his supervision with an eye to preparing the South for that contingency.

Kansas did not monopolize the disorders of the country; far away on the further side of the Continent the new community of Utah came into collision with the government. Brigham Young had been the governor chosen by the people, and accepted under the Pierce administration; and he was not only the temporal ruler of the people, but their religious head as well. Buchanan, not appreciating this peculiarity, thought to supplant him by an appointee of his own; and sent out a gentleman of good character named Cumming; and apprehending that in so remote a wilderness contingencies might arise, he caused a detachment of regulars to accompany him. His only mistake was in not having sent regulars enough; Young and his Mormons defied him and the minions of oppression, and managed so to interrupt their supplies that the situation became awkward. The Mormons, indeed, in spite of their many saints, were capable of great fierceness; and terrible tales were told of the exploits of their sect of thugs known as Danites, who made away with the unfaithful. Buchanan was equal to this emergency, however, inasmuch as politics were not concerned in it; and he sent out more troops, until the Mormons succumbed. But whatever might be their external aspect as to allegiance to the United States, their true head would always be Brigham Young, so long as life remained in his stalwart and defiant body.

As time went on, the administration lost more and more its hold upon the country. For the first time in twenty years Pennsylvania ceased to support the South. A contest which aroused general interest was that between Douglas and Lincoln in Illinois. They were both of them picturesque men on the stump, though of very opposite styles, principles, and appearance: Lincoln being six feet four inches in height, and of comparatively rustic bearing, and homely speech; while Douglas was a manikin in height, though big enough in brain and energy. Lincoln was a humorous, but straightforward and logical reasoner; Douglas had all the tricks of the demagogue, and a great gift of becoming hail-fellow-well-met with "the boys." His principles were of the *laisser aller* order as regarded slavery; he professed to care nothing about it one way or the other on sentimental or moral grounds; he would have it let alone where it was, but would not advocate its being violently forced upon a free majority; let it expand toward Mexico and Cuba, if it would. Lincoln finally cornered him with a question growing from the Dred Scott decision: What had he to say about the right to hold slaves in a territory by virtue of the federal compact? Douglas replied that without prejudice to the Supreme Court view, if a people or a territory wished to exclude slavery from it, they would always be able to do so. Unfriendly legislation by the local legislature could settle it. This answered Douglas's immediate purpose of carrying his Illinois audiences; but Lincoln, in eliciting the statement from him, had had in view the far more important contest of 1860; for Douglas, by his answer, had definitely alienated Southern support for his

Presidential aspirations. The South would demand perfect explicitness in the support of slavery, in their candidate. Although, therefore, Lincoln lost the immediate prize of the senatorship, he prepared the way for defeating Douglas for the Presidency. But he, also, had uttered a sentiment which was remembered against him by the South—"A house divided against itself cannot stand: I believe this government cannot endure permanently half slave and half free. . . . It will become all one thing or all the other." The idea here expressed was the same as that of Seward: "the irrepressible conflict." These two men were already the most eminent in the Republican party; Seward had the best chance of being chosen the standard-bearer; but the bridge is not crossed until one comes to it.

The manifest defeat of Buchanan's effort to win Kansas for the South prompted him to seek compensation for them elsewhere; and in his message at the opening of the year 1859 he recommended expansion in Mexico and the South American countries. There were always disturbances there sufficient to form a pretext for military interference, if the United States were set upon it; but his suggestions were not taken up. Cuba could not be got by purchase, and there was no likelihood that the Cubans would co-operate in an attempt to shake off Spain. Moreover, England and France were opposed to our annexing any more territory, and took such measures to prevent it as might be effective without being too obvious. But England was led into the mistake of rousing our susceptibilities as to the right of search, which they were always claiming, in season and out, and which they now sought to practice on the plea of checking the violation of the slave trade law. The government at once sent an American fleet to the scene, and the English made explanations; but it was a pity that the only occasion on which Buchanan had an opportunity to show spirit in foreign policy should have been in a cause so discreditable as this. Beggars cannot be choosers.

The previous year had not gone by without further advance in the line of scientific improvement; an Atlantic cable was laid, and messages exchanged; but the cable soon broke, and was not permanently re-established till after the war. More important, for the moment, was the discovery of coal oil in Pennsylvania, by which great fortunes were made in record time, and a beautiful region was, incidentally, transformed into a lurid wilderness. Horse railroads were running in most of the great eastern towns; Arctic exploration continued; rowing regattas were held between Yale and Harvard; Heenan and Morrisey fought in the prize-ring, and Thackeray, greatest of English novelists, read his lectures on the Four Georges to the descendants of those who had thrown off their yoke and forgotten it. Music and the drama were developed, and literature had now achieved an importance which compelled recognition outside of this country. It was a larger and richer life, though much of it assumed trifling and frivolous forms. The people wished to be instructed in the lore of the world, and the lyceum bureaus brought information to them through the mouths of eminent lecturers. But most of this quasi-intellectual activity was at the North; the South, like the English aristocracy, affected to look down upon such things with good-natured scorn. They stuck to politics as the proper pursuit for gentlemen. Three eminent Southerners, Rhett, Davis and Alexander Stephens, made speeches advocating the enactment by Congress of a slave code directly protective of the institution; and also demanding that the slave trade be permitted to such states as chose to practice it. They continued to seek southern enlargement of boundaries, and founded the order of the Knights of the Golden Circle to that end, of which Walker, in his final and fatal expedition, was one of the most distinguished members. But these movements and propositions did not attract general attention; and it was not until October, 1859, that an event occurred which at once aroused the most intense feelings both North and

South, and the echoes of which lasted through the war, and after it.

In the year 1800 there was born at the little town of Torrington, Connecticut, of a family which claimed Pilgrim origin, a child named John Brown. When he was six years old, his family removed to Ohio, where the boy learned the tanner's and currier's trade; and when he was a man grown, he became a wool merchant. But misfortune pursued him in all his efforts to make a living; while on the other hand he bred a family of patriarchal dimensions. But he was an earnest though narrow thinker, and one who wished to carry his thought into act; he had been deeply impressed by the anti-slavery lucubrations of Garrison's "Liberator," and emigrating to Kansas in 1855, he became active against the pro-slavery part of the community. Sorrow, disappointment and hardship, as well as the old Pilgrim strain in his blood, had made him a fanatic; and the good and bad qualities of the type were strongly accented in him. In his conflicts with the slaveholders he was helped by his sons, and saw more than one of them die; on his part, he slew without compunction, and would drag inoffensive persons out of their beds and kill them, for no other crime than holding opinions which he deemed damnable. At Ossawatomie he defeated with a small band a greatly superior force of Missouri invaders; and the exploits of this action gained him the title of Ossawatomie Brown, by which he was afterward known. He was a very formidable personage, inconvenient to those who were in general sympathy with his anti-slavery ideas, as well as terrible to his avowed enemies. He was prepared for anything; and the arts of diplomacy were beneath his contempt. Perhaps he was at this time hardly in his right mind; there was abundant reason why he should not have been. Death by violence had struck down those nearest to him, and long brooding over the wrongs of the slave had made him implacable to those whom he held responsible for them. He was a tall, shaggy, impressive figure; a great

heap of disordered hair piled up on his tall, narrow head;
a long tangled beard, and a bony, athletic frame. His eyes
gazed out sternly from beneath his rugged brows, and his
manner was grave and harsh. But there was in him indomitable courage, and the iron fiber of the old Covenanters.
His almost savage manhood, however, was not destitute of
its tender side, which was noted and marked by his intimates
and biographers; but it may be said of him, as of others,
that nothing in old John Brown's troubled life so well
became him as did the closing scenes of it.

In 1858 he had already conceived his grotesque plan of
emancipating the blacks single-handed, and by force. It is
needless to say that he despised politics and politicians. He
had seen slavery talked against for many years, and it was
now more strongly established than ever. He understood
that the moral reprobation with which the North professed
to regard slavery was not strong enough to induce them to
lift a hand to crush it; they would prate of the Union and
the Constitution, and let "I dare not" wait upon "I would."
But John was withheld by no constitutional scruples: he had
seen those he loved die, and he had slain men in cold blood
with his own hand; and he pictured to himself the slaves
rising at his call, and massacring their masters wholesale,
while he himself led them to the slaughter and gloried in it.
The slaves, he imagined, were ready to spring up like tigers
at the signal, and he would be at the head of a million
fighters who, should the United States government side with
the South against them, would fight the government too, and
conquer them, with the aid of the white abolitionists who
would also join him; and a new republic would be established
on the ashes of the present one, in which whites and blacks
would be equal, man for man, and before the law. In planning thus, Brown must have imagined that all negroes and
all other white abolitionists were monomaniacs like himself,
who would hold their lives at a pin's fee, and fight to the
death. And if one can picture an army of John Browns, it

is not difficult to surmise that all the resources of the mighty States might have been insufficient to put it down. Fanatics—monomaniacs—men who will literally die rather than yield—are more formidable than many times their number of ordinary brave soldiers, no matter how well disciplined and armed. Ordinary human courage has its well-defined limits; and after ten men have been killed out of a hundred, the ninety will generally retreat; if twenty have been killed, the retreat becomes a flight. But what should be done with a hundred men who would fight till ninety of them were slain, and then still fight till not one was left alive? With a million men of this stamp, it was not unreasonable to believe that Brown might have conquered any army or armies in the world; and were he to lose half his million, or nine-tenths of it, or all of it, that would make no difference to him; he would have put an end to slavery.

The error Brown made, then, was not in theory, wild and almost incredible though that was, but in the belief that his army, if he could raise it, would resemble him. There happened not to be a million John Browns available in the United States; indeed, so far as we know, there never was or would be but one. But even that one was enough to shake the whole nation to its center; and had he not lived and died, it is possible that slaves would still be slaves to-day. In this world, no power equal to the one man power has yet been found.

Brown was a practical man in ordinary respects, and he could reason out the details of his plan logically. The slaves must have arms. It would not be possible to arm them all at once; but that was not necessary; if he could put guns in the hands of a few thousand of them, that would do for a beginning; when the army got to its work, it could obtain arms from its enemies. There was an arsenal at Harper's Ferry, a small village on the Virginia side of the Potomac, at the point where the river breaks asunder the barriers of the Alleghanies. There was a little Virginia farmhouse near the village, which Brown rented, ostensibly for farming purposes; but little work was done upon it; only his farm wagon made frequent visits to the railway station, and returned loaded with heavy cases, which might have contained books, or farming tools, but which really were full of rifles. With the aid of these rifles, in the hands of himself, his sons, and a few more, he meant to capture the arsenal; and the rest would be easy. Messengers should go forth to notify the slaves of the rendezvous; as fast as they came in they would receive the weapons: and then woe to the slaveholders! It was such a vision as might have risen before the mind of an opium eater, or perhaps of a dime novelist; but only John Brown would have attempted actually to take it out of the region of insane notions, and clothe it with flesh and blood.

Brown's recruits came in slowly; and by the time a dozen or more had arrived, the old man felt that he must strike. With his sons, his army numbered eighteen all told. But that, in one sense, was already more than enough; for the neighbors, though Brown had avoided all association with them as much as possible—and he was not a man easy to approach at any time—were beginning to show curiosity as to why eighteen farmers who never did any farming were living in a small cottage out there in the wilds of the hills. They must show what they were there for before they were asked, or it would be too late.

Therefore, on the evening of Sunday, October 16, 1859, John Brown took his gun and ordered his men to fall in. Down to the village by the river they tramped, the eighteen men who were to put an end to slavery. On the way they met a negro, one of the race they were going to save; and Brown bade him fall in, and enjoy the distinction of being the first recruit of his color in the emancipating army. The negro was no doubt a fool; but he may have had brains enough to make a rapid calculation of the odds between this army and the power of the United States; and he decided, on the instant, that the right thing for him to do was to run away. But here he showed his folly; he had not calculated on John Brown. The negro was a slave, and Brown was ready to die for him; but meanwhile he shot him down to prevent him from hindering his emancipation. It was the first blood shed in this war; and it indicated that Brown was determined to rescue the victims of slavery even if, in order to do it, he was obliged to kill not only their tyrants, but themselves. He was what the English would call "thorough."

Sunday evening villagers, who have never seen a shot fired in anger, are not likely to put up much of a fight on so brief warning; and Brown and his army succeeded in getting into the arsenal without loss, except of the one recusant recruit above-mentioned, who was free, indeed, however abruptly. He was the only slave whom Brown succeeded in freeing with his own hands.

But the first step in the great campaign was a success; and Brown fortified himself in his narrow quarters, and was ready for a siege; meanwhile he posted guards on the railway bridge, and, not to be unprovided with all supplies which an army should have, he captured a couple of prisoners. When the train came along, he stopped it; but presently allowed it to continue on its way to the North, possibly imagining that it would come back filled with armed abolitionists. No other evidence is needed to prove that he had no conception whatever of the position he occupied in the eyes of the entire law-abiding population of the United States. The North was just as anxious to put a stop to him as the South was; even Wendell Phillips and Lloyd Garrison did not start for Harper's Ferry. The inhabitants of that village, in addition to keeping up a desultory firing on the arsenal, had dispatched telegrams up and down the line, whose tenor indicated that a vast slave rebellion had broken out, and that everybody was going to be massacred out of hand; and by morning of the 17th of October, soldiers were on their way to the seat of war, not knowing how many hundred thousand desperate revolutionists they would have to encounter. The mayor of Harper's Ferry, and a few other citizens, had been killed or wounded by the fire from the arsenal before the soldiers arrived. It was not until after dark that night that a soldier who had seen war, Colonel Robert E. Lee, with a detachment of marines, appeared on the scene, and upon learning that the entire revolution, so far as was yet known, was cooped up in that little arsenal, felt like the leader of a fire-brigade which rushes to extinguish the conflagration of a city, and finds only a burning match-box. Artillery was not needed, he thought, to reduce this fortification; a scaling ladder applied as a battering-ram would suffice. It was desirable to take this army prisoners; and besides, there were citizens of Harper's Ferry inside there, whose lives must not be endangered. So the marines, under his directions, advanced with the heavy ladder, and pounded in the door; and there knelt John Brown, a ghastly spectacle, with six or seven wounds on his body, two of his sons dead on the floor beside him, and eight other men beside them. The war of emancipation was at an end; now were to follow the consequences.

Brown and the other prisoners were jailed, and they were tried and hanged with inspiring promptness. One can imagine what a red-handed ogre of iniquity Brown must have appeared to the South. But in fact, the letting of blood, and the refusal of a single slave to join his banner, had cleared the brain of the old man, and he realized his mistake. Possibly, too, he realized that his defeat and death would win for his cause more than he himself could have hoped to gain. He did not assume the airs of a martyr; sensational to the last degree though his exploit was, he was not in the least capable of conscious scenic display. He sat, with his wounds, amid his enemies, quiet and unrepining, ready for the end, reasonable and gentle enough, but if he had any regrets, they were not that he had wished and tried to free the slaves, but that he had lacked the means to do it. He loved the negroes with the strange, impersonal love of the fanatic; and the little negro pickanniny that he kissed on his way to the scaffold was to him a symbol of the race—no more. He maintained his rude dignity and stoic courage to the end; and the authorities, as they choked the life out of him, doubtless wished, like Othello, that the wretch had twenty thousand lives: one was too poor, too weak for their revenge. But it turned out, later, that the execution of a single John Brown was quite as much as this nation could afford. His body mouldered in its grave, but his soul, militant still, marched from battlefield to battlefield, and witnessed the sacrifice of hundreds of thousands of human lives, poured out to defend or to defeat the cause for the sake of which he had put his head in the halter. The excuse of the Civil War was indeed secession; but its reason was slavery. And after all had been said as to Brown's insanity, and folly, and treason, and unconstitutionality, and bloodthirstiness, and wickedness, our people saw only the figure of a man who had laid down his life for an idea, and a noble and unselfish one. It was a revelation, for it was not a tendency, nor a purpose, but an accomplished fact. A man had been found, not to talk about this thing, but to actually do it. And he was not a pale priest or a metaphysical ascetic, but a plain ordinary American such as you may meet in the village grocery on Saturday afternoons. He had done and suffered terrible things, but so may any plain American with strong thoughts in his mind, and little education; and with a heart that could be both fierce and tender. The North understood him, felt with him, pitied him and gloried in him; and his name and story were better known to this nation than those of any other man of that age. There was nothing factitious in the feeling he aroused; it grew slowly, but it gathered strength surely; and the final verdict of history, now that passion is no more, is kinder and more respectful than ever to Old Brown.

The South was in a tremor for some time after this episode, for it seemed incredible that Brown had not been the cat's-paw of some gigantic conspiracy in the North, which would be revealed later. But when investigation showed that he had been utterly alone in his enterprise, he was called a murderous madman, and everybody felt relieved; but all the same, measures were taken by the South to get in a defensive position. If one such madman could come from the North, there might be others. In Congress, defiances were exchanged between Democrats and Republicans. There were a good many outspoken remarks on slavery, pro and con, which would not have been uttered before John Brown died. The North, of course, would not in any way justify his deed; but it felt less inclined than before to maintain a conciliating attitude toward the South. Brown had not been conciliating: why should they?

In June of this year, Buchanan vetoed the Homestead bill, on the ground that Congress had no power to give away the public domain; but the true reason was lest the lands should pass into the hands of free labor; for Southerners were not able to take advantage of such a law for themselves. Soon after Covode of Pennsylvania carried a motion to investigate the acts of the administration; and in spite of the President's protests, the inquisitors unearthed a large mass of testimony indicative of corruption, favoritism, bribery, violence and treachery; for, indeed, it was notorious that every kind of political iniquity had flourished under his rule. The committee made no attempt to impeach Buchanan; they were satisfied to let the matter rest with the exposure; and Buchanan could only say that if wrong had been done, it was inadvertently, in the dispatch of routine business. The inquisition was certainly partisan; it was of no benefit to the country, however much it may have hurt Buchanan; and its chief use was to show, what had been already suspected, that Congress is a place where a great deal of evil may be done. By way of diverting attention, the President tried once more to intrigue the country with Mexico, with a view to further annexation; and there were rich jobs afoot in relation to transit routes across the Isthmus; but no change of policy could be effected. The country was becoming too much absorbed in its own affairs to take interest in anything else.

The Democratic Convention met at Charleston in the spring of 1860. The platform committee reported that Congress and territorial legislatures had no right to prevent the holding of slaves in any territory; the Douglas men could not accept this except on condition that the Supreme Court first pass upon it; the Convention adopted the Douglas side of the argument, and the other delegates thereupon withdrew. They met in a convention of their own, and nominated Breckinridge for President. Douglas was nominated by the others a month later, with Fitzpatrick of Alabama for Vice-President. In Baltimore assembled a sort of respectable coalition convention, which named Bell and Everett for their candidates, on the platform of "no political principle other than the Constitution of the country, the Union of the states, and the enforcement of the laws." The Republican Convention met in Chicago, which thus first takes its place in national political history; it already had the indomitable spirit of which we see some of the results today. There was danger of the Republicans, in their search for a candidate, going astray among the cranks and hypocrites of whom their ranks afforded many specimens; but Seward, Chase and Lincoln were finally brought to the front as the best men from whom to select a winner. Seward's long and clear record of ability and service entitled him to first consideration; but along with many friends he had made many enemies, not all of them outside of his own party; and it was necessary to pick a man who would win. Abraham Lincoln had many friends, and he had kept out of public life to a degree that left him to a great extent unhampered. His speeches during his contest with Douglas two years before were remembered favorably; and things seemed to be coming his way. Chase was also strong, but was thought not to have so good a chance. Other candidates were Bates and Cameron.

The hall in which this Convention met had been made for them, and was gayly decorated; there was space for an enormous audience in addition to the Convention members themselves; and the most lively interest was shown. Seward led in the first ballot; but Lincoln, greeted with a great shouting, was second. The next ballot gave Lincoln all Cameron's votes, and brought him within three of Seward, amid great excitement; then Ohio and Massachusetts fell into line, and gave him a majority; still other states followed these, until, with a whirlwind of commotion, and the thundering of cannon, Lincoln was made the Republican nominee by 354 votes out of 466. The result was undoubtedly a popular one; but of course no one knew of what vital importance it really was. The election was not to be the triumph of orators or famous names, but of fundamental principles; and as a matter of fact it was to the exposition of these that the candidates devoted themselves. Morality was the watchword of the Republicans; they had tried the effect of compromising with wrong, and had been defeated. Concession was the cry of the Democrats, whose split put them at a disadvantage. All except Breckinridge were for the Constitution; and he was also, with the proviso that the equality of states be maintained. Lincoln, who kept quiet and made a good impression on all who saw him, gained strength and influence daily; Seward generously took the stump for him, and Cameron brought Pennsylvania to his support. Carl Schurz, who had lately become a citizen, harangued the Germans with good results, and Henry Ward Beecher and George William Curtis lent their aid; but Wendell Phillips seemed to scent some suspicion of negro slavery in Lincoln's garments, and with his usual patriotism and sagacity denounced him as "the slave-hound of Illinois." On the popular and demonstrative side, this campaign somewhat recalled that of "Tippecanoe"; there were vast meetings and torchlight processions and emblematic standards; and Lincoln having once earned a living splitting rails, rails were prominent among the insignia; and the shout of thousands of lusty lungs in unison—"Abraham—Lincoln—Rail—SplittAR!"—will never be forgotten by those who heard it. He was a John Brown with all Brown's virtues and none of his faults; a man of the people, a great man, and a good man. And he was indefinitely more than John Brown could ever have been; the depth of his mind, the breadth of his sympathies, have never been sounded or measured. His humor was a national treasure, and all the simple and manly facts of his early life, as they became known, endeared him more and more to his countrymen. His stature has only within these last few years been appreciated by the generality; but wherever an American goes in this world, he will find no better passport to take with him than that of being Lincoln's fellow-countryman. The love and reverence with which his name is regarded in many out-of-the-way corners of the old world would be hardly credited by those who have not witnessed it. Goodness, and faithful labor for others, go far, and the memory of them dieth not.

Buchanan gave his support to Breckinridge, though he announced that Democrats might take their choice of either him or Douglas, no regular nomination having been made. Douglas, though he was left to fight for his own hand, was the more formidable candidate of the two. He took the stump in his own behalf, and no man could have done it more effectively. Breckinridge was the disunion candidate, though he would not admit it; and the force of sentiment behind him was as strong at least as that behind Lincoln; but it lacked numbers. The South were fighting for their reputation, and for their existence as members of the old Union; for it would be a mistake to think that the majority of Southerners at this time wished to secede. They only thought that if their principles suffered defeat at the polls, not only would they be discredited before the world, but they would be obliged to set up housekeeping by themselves thereafter. If some of them anticipated war, they fancied it would be short—a mere matter of form. But the prevalent idea was that the secession would be accomplished peaceably, as Calhoun had dreamed long ago.

The October elections favored the Republicans, and showed which way the popular verdict would fall. The polls for the Presidential election closed just after sunset on the 6th of November, and by midnight it was known that Lincoln was President of the United States. Breckinridge got the vote of eleven out of the fifteen slave states; Douglas did better with the popular than with the electoral votes; Bell carried Virginia, Tennessee and Kentucky. There was to be no more slave domination in the Union. Even the prospects of expanding in other directions than northward were dispelled. It seemed to the South that they had stood by the Constitution, while the North had played fast and loose with it in order to win. But the result at the polls was undeniable; there was no question of fraud; and it was the duty of the South to accept the result. Instead of that, the threats of secession began to be heard immediately; and South Carolina took the lead. A convention was summoned on the 17th of December, two weeks after the meeting of Congress, and on the 20th passed an ordinance of secession. Among their grievances they named abolitionism at the North, abuse of slavery as sinful, the passage of the acts to prevent the recapture of fugitive slaves, and Lincoln's declaration that the house divided against itself could not stand. The North, they affirmed, taxed the South for its own benefit. But if the slaveholding states would stand together, their cotton and tobacco would make all the world court them, and their territory, larger than Europe, would become the richest and happiest in the world. The other states showed themselves well disposed to follow their sanguine sister.

Three commissioners were now sent to Washington to arrange for the division of public property in South Carolina, and for the surrender of the Charleston forts. All the Southern States, of course, had within their boundaries a great deal of government property, paid for by Northern as well as Southern taxpayers, and to this property they had no more right than they had to the Tower of London or the Porcelain Pagoda in China. At this time there were in Charleston Harbor three forts—Castle Pinckney, Fort Moultrie and Fort Sumter; Moultrie was occupied by a garrison of sixty men— more than ten times too small for it; Sumter was not in fighting order; but it was more defensible, being on an island in the center of the harbor, and to it Major Anderson moved his men on the night of the 26th of December, after the adjournment of the Convention, and the announcement of secession. Anderson was a faithful officer, and saw that it might be necessary to stand on his defense. The next morning there was great to-do in Charleston; and acting upon the principle that might makes right, the local authorities baldly appropriated Pinckney and Moultrie and hoisted over them the Palmetto flag of the state. Anderson had taken the precaution to spike Moultrie's guns before leaving; but the arsenal was taken a few days later, with half a million dollars' worth of national arms in it. This picking of the national pocket by the seceding states was an awkward accompaniment of secession; but there seemed no way of avoiding it. It would have been more dignified had it been preceded by a definite act of war. It is amusing to note that, with the breathless American haste to be up with the events which they themselves were creating, the South Carolinian newspapers headed their dispatches from the Northern states, "Foreign News." The three commissioners carried out the game; they demanded to be recognized as representatives of an independent country; while poor Buchanan was still master of the White House, and for aught any one could say, the President-elect might never live to hold the reins. They ordered Buchanan—for the tone they took was that of masters rather than of ambassadors —much less of traitors who merited hanging—to move Anderson out of Fort Sumter at once, otherwise their outraged country would put him out by force of arms (stolen from the United States for that purpose). Buchanan deserves no sympathy for this insult; for he had unfaithfully refused to adopt Winfield Scott's advice, given long before, to put these forts in a proper posture of defense, in view of precisely the contingency which had now happened. All he could do now was to submit the correspondence to Congress. His Cabinet was by this time dissolving; he accepted Howell Cobb's resignation as Secretary of the Treasury, though it was known that his conduct of the office had been grossly imprudent if not much worse; the molluscous Cass next left him; and Floyd, Secretary of War, who had taken advantage of his position to prevent the re-enforcement of Southern forts, followed. The President took it all very meekly. The country gained by his appointment of an unknown lawyer of Ohio, Edwin M. Stanton, as Attorney-general. Stanton was destined to see Secession out as War Secretary under Lincoln; and proved himself to be the right man in the right place. An order to send the cruiser "Brooklyn" with re-enforcements to Anderson was delayed; and finally the "Star of the West," with two hundred and fifty men, but no armament, was dispatched; upon her arrival at the harbor, she was fired on by the Charleston batteries, January 9th, 1861, and she immediately put about and returned. Two other members of the Cabinet, Thomas and Thompson, both disloyal, and dishonest into the bargain, now resigned; and again the nation profited; for John A. Dix was called to Thomas's place (Secretary of the Treasury), and it was he who soon after ordered his officers, "If any man attempts to haul down the American flag, shoot him on the spot." During the few remaining weeks of Buchanan's term, a sort of armistice with the South was agreed upon, according to which the forts were to remain without re-enforcements, and were not to be captured by the South.

Meanwhile delegates from six seceding states met at Montgomery, Alabama, and made a constitution for the provisional government of the Confederate States of America. It made slavery its *piece de resistance;* and matters relating to public property and debts were to be adjusted between them and the United States on just and equitable terms. The proposal was for peaceable secession. Jefferson Davis was elected President of this new Confederacy, though no appeal had been made to the people, even in choosing the delegates that elected him. The government was an oligarchy. Alexander Stephens was made Vice-President; his views were more conservative and moderate than those of the others, and he was willing to accommodate the quarrel even yet, if the North would repeal its "personal liberty" bills, preventing return of fugitive slaves. He was of opinion that the best men at the North would always be ready to agree with the South as to national measures; and remarked, not without truth, that "the South has controlled the government in its every important action from the beginning." Nor did he consider that Lincoln's election was fair cause for secession. Lincoln wrote to him under date of December 22, 1860, that the Republican administration would not interfere with slaves; but that the point of divergence was that "you think slavery is right and ought to be extended; while we think it is wrong, and ought to be abolished." Stephens's response to this was that the pride of the South was touched at being made the object of moral diatribes. This seems childish, but after all, it is pride of this kind that influences men and nations more strongly than almost any other cause, and has led to more wars than any other. It was pride that made England fight the war of the Revolution, and pride that prompted Mexico to undertake the struggle that lost her California and Texas. Such pride is costly; but it is worth its cost; since without it a nation is neither respected nor respects itself.

At the same time that the Confederacy between the six states (South Carolina, Alabama, Georgia, Louisiana, Florida, and Mississippi) was formed, a peace convention met in Washington, at the instance of Virginia. The scheme was got up by John Tyler, the ex-president, and the meeting contained representatives of twenty states, North and South, the North being in the majority. It seems probable that Tyler had treasonable designs in this affair; he asked for a truce while it was deliberating, and thus kept the North from making needful preparations; and when the sittings had issued in no result, he returned to Richmond and declared that the Union could not be saved and that the sooner Virginia joined the seceding states the better.

Lincoln left his home on February 11th and traveling by Pittsburgh, Buffalo and New York, reached Washington on the 23d, having journeyed from Philadelphia incognito, guarded by the detective Allan Pinkerton; for it was believed that a plot was afoot in Baltimore to kidnap or kill him while crossing the city.

At the Capital there was great anxiety and uncertainty as to what would happen. Absurd propositions were advanced from various quarters to ward off the danger, or at least to retain the wavering border states in the Union. Lincoln took Seward and Chase into his Cabinet at once, indicating that his policy would not be one of compromise. Seward had made a conciliating speech some six weeks before, in which he urged fidelity to the Union, but added, it could not be saved by compromises; he warned the South that secession would involve civil war; and he opposed the attitude of some in the North, who would let the South go and try her experiment, and return when she had found it unsuccessful. But in truth it was now too late for argument or reconciliation. The pulse of war had begun to beat in the veins of the people on both sides, and they wanted no further parley. The Southern members withdrew from the Capitol; the bill admitting Kansas as a free state was passed, and received the President's signature; Colorado, Nevada and Dakota were made new free territories. Nothing now remained but for the orderly lapse of events to get rid of the pusillanimous and half-treasonable Buchanan, and to bring in the new leader on whom the hopes of the nation were fixed. The politicians were slower to believe that war was inevitable than were the mass of the people, who trust more to intuitions. The conflict was truly irrepressible. Upon the whole, it was as fair a quarrel as was ever fought. Both sides firmly believed they were in the right; and neither doubted of victory. The South was used to war, and was warlike; the North were peaceful traders, and had forgotten the art of the sword and musket which their forefathers knew. They had forgotten; but now they began to remember; voices seemed to call to them from the past, bidding them do honor to their ancestry. The anger of the North rose slowly, but it rose at last, and it burned with an increasing flame until the end. The South had the splendid courage of the cavaliers who fought for Charles; and the desperate earnestness of men who defend their homes and their political existence. And both South and North were Americans.

CHAPTER THIRTY-THIRD

BULL RUN

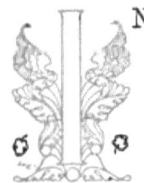N respect of numbers engaged and losses suffered, the war which was now about to begin was the greatest ever fought. It also seemed to be the most deplorable; for it was a war of like against like: of brothers against one another. After nearly two and a half centuries, the sons of the pioneers who had settled Virginia and Massachusetts, and of those who followed them, were marshaled against each other, with deadly enmity in their hearts. From a few score—a few hundreds—they had increased to full thirty million of as enlightened and enterprising a people as were in the world; and they were about to plunge into the hideous work of mutual destruction. Together they had resisted Europe, and their blood had mingled on a hundred battlefields, where freedom was the stake; they had together built up a great civilization, and had presented to the world the spectacle of a vast democracy living in freedom, with no ruler but themselves; they had upset the predictions of failure which the wisest of the old nations had made; and the populace of the old monarchies and despotisms had heard of their liberty, and millions of them had crossed the ocean to share it. Already America was the hope of mankind. And yet, at the height of their seeming success, they had quarreled with themselves—these sons of the new day—and were gathering their mighty energies to annihilate the work which their great fathers had made. It

was a grievous sight to see, and an ominous failure to confess; for if America failed, there was no rational hope that the cause of civil and religious freedom could ever succeed. Never again could the experiment be tried under conditions so favorable; and even could another continent be found, and another people with the spirit of the Puritans and Pilgrims to colonize it, the precedent of the American collapse would discourage and handicap them. We had believed that God led us to the Wilderness, and had protected us there. But if, after all, we were to go down in ruin, undermined by our own hands, would it not be a sign that God had no part in our attempt? Except the Lord build the city, they labor in vain who build it. It had all been a vast mistake and delusion from the beginning. Let us call back our kings and czars, and surrender our liberty and equality. Man is not able to govern himself. Let Moses lead the Israelites back to Pharaoh, and cast the tablets of the Divine Law into the depths of the Red Sea. The Pillar of Cloud by day, of Fire by night, was but a mirage and a mockery; and a few selfish tyrants shall have dominion over many helpless slaves.

But the conflict was irrepressible. During forty years every means of composing it had been tried, and had miscarried. The Frankenstein monster of slavery which had been forced by alien and then by geographical agency upon the South, was a growing monster, and must be fed and given room to stretch his shackled but formidable limbs. Above all must he be left undisturbed where he was, or his sinister force, which now was given to giving his masters wealth, would be turned against their throats. The Southern slaveholder could never feel fully safe. Those black figures bending and toiling in his fields were obedient only to force, and the force was absurdly inadequate—it was the mere intellectual domination of a superior race. But should a Toussaint arise to tell them of their strength, and lead them to put it forth, what would become of the planter?

ADMIRAL DAVID G. FARRAGUT, U.S.N.

MAJ.-GEN. GEORGE B. MCCLELLAN, U.S.A.

ABRAHAM LINCOLN

What had become of the French in San Domingo? Or, failing a leader of their own color, should another John Brown, or an army of them, appear—as from indications at the North might well happen—the days of the South would be numbered. Their only security, then, lay either in spreading the slave system over the entire Union, so that all alike should be concerned to maintain it: or in retiring from the Union, so that the peril of the Abolitionists might be removed. "Peaceably if we may—forcibly if we must!" said the South, taking the words from the mouth of Josiah Quincy of Massachusetts sixty years before. New England had no right to protest; she herself had knotted the lash which was now laid across her shoulders. The Boston Federalists had sown the wind, and the whirlwind was now to be reaped. The pretext was different, but the argument was the same.

But the North could not yield, in spite of the tu-quoque taunt, and in spite of pusillanimous mutterings from a fainthearted minority, of whom Buchanan was the type:—the Copperheads, as they came to be called. They were willing to let the slaves stay where they were, and promise never to meddle with them; but they could not corrupt free labor by suffering slave labor to compete with it on its own soil; nor could they allow the Southern minority to pre-empt the untrodden regions which yet lay to the north and west. Well, the South would agree, so far; but what objection had the North to letting her peaceably secede? Let the land of staple-producers separate from the land of traders and manufacturers. There was no real union of interests between them; why should a forced political union be maintained? Let each go its own road, parting with mutual good wishes, and be happy and prosperous in its own way. There was space and to spare on the American continent for two mighty empires at least.

To this proposition, what should the North reply? It seemed far more reasonable than the other. The Consti-

THE NEW YORK
PUBLIC LIBRARY

ASTOR, LENOX AND
TILDEN FOUNDATIONS.

GEN. ROBERT E. LEE, C.S.A.

tution seemed to admit it, for though the doctrine of state rights was denied by the North, it was supported by powerful reasoners, and might at least be considered open to argument. And was it not more politic to be separated from a friendly community than to tie an unwilling one to one's self? Moreover, so long as South and North made one country, there would always be danger of contamination from slavery either covert or overt; but if they were politically foreign to each other, no such contingency would exist. Why, then, not let the South go? Independent of us, she could do us as much good as before, and would do us much less harm.

There was a good deal of talk of this kind at the North during the first months of 1861, and it sounded plausible and prudent. Yet the weight of feeling in the North was against it. Against policy, against profit and utility, the decision was that the South must be compelled to remain in the Union. Was this the result of a determination to back one interpretation of the Constitution against another? Was it sullen pride, or obstinacy, or stupidity? Was it fear that a severance of the bonds of Union would weaken us to the attacks of Europe? Was it apprehension that if the principle of secession were once recognized, the practice would spread, until the great American Republic became a cluster of helpless and snarling principalities, such as already vexed the tropical regions of the continent?

Considerations such as these may have entered into the thoughts of the North upon the subject; but they were not the controlling ones. The answer given was usually in the words, "The Union must be preserved." Literally, this would imply only a reluctance to relinquish a material bond; but there is no doubt that it was the expression of a spiritual conviction of a remarkable kind; a recognition of the truth that God had placed us here to make one nation, and that we were bound to fulfill His purpose. There were generations of historical consciousness in that resolve; an unseen influence transmitted from father to son, becoming incorporate with our growth, an organic part of us, not to be rooted out. The United States was one, and one it should forever remain. Our ancestors had not suffered from hunger and Indians, from royal oppression, from insolent war, to have the work of their blood and brains and hearts destroyed by the shallow and infidel impatience of a hot-headed and arrogant minority. These planters were not the nation, for they were willing to destroy the nation; their attitude was not buttressed by the august and deep-laid foundations of history, for they cast history aside, and acted from the selfish and immediate impulse of personal comfort and prosperity. What was the true motive that actuated them?—the maintenance of slavery! For the sake of this sin—for sin it was, no matter what expediency might say—they would destroy the edifice of ages, in which were involved the purest hopes of mankind. It should not be permitted. The higher law forbade it. We had a trust to guard, and we would guard it. War was a terrible evil, and we had put it aside as long as we could—until concession could no further go —until honor and submission were no longer compatible. Now, therefore, let war come, if it must; and let us rather die to uphold a truth than live to profit by a sin. Such were the inner sentiments contained in the words, "The Union must be preserved!" and they constituted an irresistible power. The North, indeed, had physical resources not possessed by the South; but these could not have been called forth, nor kept in action, had not a profound spiritual conviction of right and duty animated them as soul animates body. By no lesser force could the local patriotism and fiery ardor of the South have been overcome. The South fought for their homes, and for slavery; the North fought for the America of the future; and it was a cause worth all the blood and treasure it cost. But the North, too, had sins of commission and omission to answer for; she too, in the past, had been selfish and impatient for ends of her own;

and the punishment which the war inflicted upon her was not undeserved. She came out of it purified and strengthened, and having learned a lesson of the fruit of tampering with evil which could never be quite forgotten; but a full generation must pass away, and deep wounds be healed, before South and North could forgive each other, and enter with sincerity into new bonds of brotherhood.

Though the ultimate strength of the South was less than her opponent's, her immediate resources were greater, so far as material and preparation went. Floyd, while drawing his salary as a sworn officer of the government, had been busily engaged in crippling in all ways the national power; he had dispersed the army in places where the Union could least avail itself of its services; he had sent arms and ammunition where the South could get hold of them, and had left the forts which guarded the coast below Norfolk without garrisons or supplies; and he had done this with Buchanan's connivance, and in defiance of the repeated protests and advice of Scott. Washington, Baltimore, and places yet further north, were full of disloyalty; and movements made toward suppressing the rebellion were immediately telegraphed to southern points. So long as Buchanan remained in office, the South would not be interfered with; and she used the opportunity to hasten her arrangements, while the North was obliged to look on without being able to lift her hand.

Yet the North was not wholly idle; the people were deeply interested in the progress of affairs, and every Northern town had its company drilling every evening on the common; old guns and old uniforms were routed out of the local armories, or from private hoards, and one beheld queer and motley assemblages marching and countermarching at the word of command, before the winter snows had left the ground clear. The younger folk entered into this work with a certain pleasurable excitement, the instinctive pleasure which the idea of battle supplies; the old people looked on gravely, and often shook their heads as they turned away. After Lincoln had taken his oath as President, and his early orders had proved that he was not going to accept the Southern acts supinely, the excitement rose, and the clash of opinions became sharper between those who still wished to temporize, and those who desired to go right ahead and fight, leaving talk till after the fighting was done. Then were repeated the painful scenes which had been enacted more than fourscore years before, when American tories and patriots had taken sides against one another; men hitherto of weight and repute in the local community suddenly found themselves looked at askance, or ostracized, because they expressed opinions which were out of accord with the general feeling. There was a great deal of intolerance, and hard names were bandied about; as for argument, there was little, but only plentiful contradicting one of another. Feeling had taken the place of argument, and all breath expended in arguing was breath wasted. North and South were going to fight; and nothing was now worth talking about except how to get to fighting as quickly and as effectively as possible.

At ten minutes before five o'clock on the morning of April 13, 1861, a mortar in Charleston Harbor discharged a shell, which burst in the air above Fort Sumter, arousing Major Robert Anderson and his threescore men to realization of the fact that war between North and South had actually begun, and that the South had fired the first shot. It hurt nobody, nor did any of the many hundreds which were discharged on both sides during the remainder of the day and night, and on the following morning; Major Anderson keeping his garrison behind the bomb-proofs, and letting the guns on the parapet, which were the biggest in the fort, be knocked off their places rather than risk lives for the sake of firing them off. The reluctance to kill people was observable in the early days of the war, more on the Northern than on the Southern side. The enemies were polite and "chivalrous" to one another, and seemed desirous to convey the idea that though they were fighting, their mutual regard for one another was in no way impaired. But this sort of flummery presently wore thin and disappeared; and we came to think no more of sacrificing a thousand men to capture a battery, than we did of the solitary unfortunate who was killed in Sumter, not in the battle, but by the accidental discharge of a gun fired in salute after the surrender. It is not that armies become more bloodthirsty as their experience ripens; but they learn to regard killing as a mere business, to be pursued, like any other, on business principles.

When Sumter had been pounded from the shore batteries in the harbor for a day and a half, its fire slackened, and a certain hasty General Wigfall unexpectedly appeared upon the esplanade outside its gates, demanding to see Anderson at once to arrange terms of surrender. After some parley he was admitted, for indeed he was in acute peril of being killed by the bombardment of his own side if he were not; and he offered Anderson the honors of war and permission to go home if he would give up. Anderson was a brave and faithful officer enough, and lived to raise again over Sumter the flag he now pulled down; but he was a Kentuckian and a slaveholder, and he had not yet got accustomed to the idea of fighting his kindred; and he knew, besides, that the fort could not hold out much longer, and could not inflict any loss upon the enemy if it did. So he accepted Wigfall's terms, and hoisted the white flag; and only discovered afterward that Wigfall had been acting entirely on his private responsibility, and that the terms he had accepted were liable to be disallowed. However, at that stage of the war, such technicalities were not insisted on; and Anderson was allowed to depart without further molestation. That night it was known all over the Union that the war had begun indeed; and every one North and South stiffened himself for the fight. The Southerners needed no further stimulus or signal; the North waited for the word from Washington.

What would that long-legged, humorous, peaceable-looking Illinois President say or do?—The waiting was not long. The proclamation calling for seventy-five thousand volunteers appeared on Monday morning, April 15th. The response was almost as quick as the call. Massachusetts was in the lead; her Sixth Regiment passed through Baltimore on the 19th of April—a day remembered in Massachusetts, and now to be signalized again. For Baltimore was full of secession, which was only kept from declaring itself as in the other Southern cities by the fact that Baltimore lay, geographically, between two fires, Philadelphia being loyal, and Washington at least partially so. But when the mob in Baltimore saw Northern troops passing through their city on the avowed errand of killing their fellows in the field, their wrath overcame all considerations of prudence, and they first cursed and then attacked them. One of the cars in which they were crossing the town broke down, and the soldiers began to suffer from the missiles and revolver-practice which made them their target. One does not like to hear of troops firing upon citizens in the streets of their own city, and Massachusetts men had not forgotten the Boston Massacre. But these Northern soldiers were certainly not looking for trouble in Baltimore; they had expected no such reception, and were merely doing what had to be done—pass through that fiery city on their way to Washington. Accordingly, not they but the citizens are to be blamed for the fusillade with which they finally replied to the attack upon them. Several of the soldiers were killed, and their bodies left upon the streets; more were wounded; it cannot be known what casualties happened to the Baltimore men. But the first blood of the war, on both sides, may be said to have been spilled here; and the increase of mutual animosity which it caused was extraordinary. The best campaign song of the war was drawn out by this episode; a local journalist in his early twenties, of scholarly proclivities and enthusiastic temperament, being moved to call upon "Maryland, my Maryland," to avenge the patriotic gore which had flecked the streets of Baltimore on this occasion. Maryland did not respond to the poet's summons; and, on the other hand, the North, failing to produce as good a song for her side, unblushingly purloined Mr. James Ryder Randall's production, which, with the change of a few words, was found to serve just as well to fire the Northern as the Southern heart. And yet, after all, the "John Brown's body" hymn, as thundered forth by the marching myriads of the North, was a better campaign document than its graceful and spirited rival.

During the ensuing weeks there were many tender partings of sons from parents and sweethearts; though the terms of enlistment were commonly short, and it was still believed on both sides that the war would be a matter of not more than "a hundred days" or so. If either party had foreseen four or five years of continuous and terrific fighting, between armies aggregating two million men, and with losses altogether of near seven hundred thousand, the emotions of those partings would have been more poignant still. But in these first weeks there was displayed a kind of sentiment which could only belong to the early stages of the war. There had as yet been no gaps made in the family circles of the nation; there were no wrongs to avenge, no sufferings to requite; the harsher aspect of the struggle had not yet come. There was only the exaltation of fighting for one's country, the pathos of saying good-by, the hope of glory, the glow of facing untried dangers. The boys left their classes in Harvard and Yale, the farmers, mechanics and artisans left their work, the clerks laid down their bargains on the counter, the merchant raised a company or a regiment and put himself at its head. Gentlemen of elegant leisure found at last the opportunity for action which they had missed all their lives, without knowing what ailed them; ne'er-do-weels and black sheep started for the front with a determination to prove that there was stuff in them after all. They all went into camp green, ignorant, loose, awkward; the men were independent and free-and-easy; the officers, men of education and refinement, unused to the exigencies of military discipline, asked their rank and file (with many of whom perhaps they had been acquainted in the walks of peace) to "please step this way"; "kindly present arms," and so on. But such softness wore off before long; and when the first three-months-men came back to their native villages, they were hardly recognizable for the gawky citizens who had gone forth so lately; their figures were wiry and erect, their lean faces were tanned by the summer suns of Virginia, they walked in pairs or threes with the long, springy, measured step of war; they were now disciplined soldiers, who had shot and been shot at, had faced death, had obeyed orders, had made a part of battles. The difference was wonderful, and it never wore away. The familiar village was not the same village any more. Many who marched forth returned no more forever; those who came back were changed; there were empty places in almost every household, as the years went by; and the family group round the hearth, if it were still full, never looked the same as before; there was another spirit, another feeling in it. And everywhere you saw the badge of mourning; women, old and young, in black gowns, with crape veils; it was a sight so common that one ceased to notice it. And the talk was all of campaigns, battles, generals, captains, regiments, charges, retreats, victories, defeats. The war-correspondents of that day were few, but the newspapers were absorbing reading nevertheless; and they had news to tell. There were the black headlines; the columns of terse narrative; the list of dead and wounded—but these soon had to be given up, save for the names of leading officers; what should a newspaper do with the losses of forty and fifty thousand which some of the great battles brought? Short or long, those lists of dead, wounded and missing were as trying to the women's hearts at home as was the charge that caused them to the soldiers who faced the guns. Yes, far more trying; for the charge was made in hot blood and fierce excitement, with glory to win and only one's own death to face; but the lists were read at home; cold and trembling fingers held the paper; the eyes were painfully strained, the lips were parted, the cheeks pale; and the heart stood still or leaped by turns. There was no excitement to sustain the wife or mother; no glory to gain; and the death, if it came, came not to her, but to him she loved best. No adequate history could ever be written of the women of the Civil War; but it is strange indeed that no great sculptor or architect has been commissioned to erect some mighty monument, to commemorate forever in enduring marble and bronze her heroism, her sacrifices, and her achievements.

The Union army must concentrate at Washington, and thence proceed to the defense of the line along the Potomac and the Ohio which marked the boundary between South and North. For the capture of Sumter had added to the Southern array the states of Virginia, North Carolina, Arkansas and Tennessee. The western, mountainous part of Virginia was finally saved to the North, after several sharp battles had been fought there; Kentucky also remained loyal, Missouri too, and the new free state of Kansas. The Confederacy, therefore, was bounded on the north by the old Compromise line of 1820, and included Texas as its western frontier. The North held all the rest; but practically, the states involved in active war on the Northern side were less in area than those on the South. On the other hand, the North surpassed the South in wealth and population, and in means of sustaining a long conflict. The City of Washington, lying as it did on the borders of Virginia, was in danger of Southern attack, and its defense was the first problem of the war; coupled with that, was the attack on Richmond. The true theory of tactics for the North, however, was not to capture Richmond, for although that was the Capital of the Confederacy, its possession was not vital to their cause, as that of Washington might have been to the North. And since it would be impossible within our limits to follow this war in detail, it seems advisable here at the outset to give an outline of the entire contest. The story of the strategy of modern battles, however edifying to the expert, goes in at one ear and out of the other of the unmilitary reader; the latter can appreciate the description of a charge, the heroism of a siege, the sublimity of a forlorn hope; but the details of maneuvers in the field are more than he can digest. To comprehend the general plan of a whole war is less difficult, and to the student of history far more important.

The South hoped for victory on two grounds: first, because the North had no practice in war—for the trifling operations by land of the war of 1812 were hardly worth considering, besides that all who took part in them were already gone to their reward; the only considerable battle had been at New Orleans, and in that the South had borne the chief share. The Mexican war, again, had been fought mainly by Southern troops; and the South had ever since been engaged, unofficially, in border raids and filibustering expeditions, which had kept her familiar with the idea of war, and ready to take part in any fighting that came her way. She felt, therefore, the same sense of superiority over the North that a boxer does over a man, bigger perhaps than he, but uninstructed in the art of self-defense.

In the second place, the South trusted that no long time would pass after the outbreak of hostilities before Europe would intervene in her favor. For she supplied Europe with cotton and tobacco, and the old world would not long submit to be deprived of these necessities, as must happen were the war prolonged. The rest of the earth, in short, could get along without the aid of the northern states of the Union, but not without the Confederacy; and when England or France, or both, put their weight into the scale, the North must yield, even were she not beaten already.—All this was counting chickens before they were hatched, and, as it turned out, had the usual fate of such optimism; but it gave the

South a hardihood which she might else have lacked, which plunged her into the war so deep that there was no getting out except by the surrender which was inevitable upon her complete exhaustion.

As for the North, she believed that she would conquer by dint of her superior strength, wealth and lasting powers; she was far from estimating at its true value the resistance and vigor of the South, or the depth of feeling which attached her to her cause. She thought her fickle and easily discouraged, and she doubted not that when a few months had proved to her the futility of struggling against a resolute and stern adversary, she would be glad to come back, a repentant prodigal. So large a miscalculation on the part of both South and North goes to show how little the two sections knew of each other; lack of common interests had bred ignorance. They were far better strangers now than they were when the struggles with England came to an end. But they were in a fair way to remedy this deficiency.

The area of the Confederacy, geographically regarded, divides into three parts, like Cæsar's Gaul; the dividing lines being the Mississippi River, and the Alleghany Mountains. Of these three, that west of the Mississippi, comprising Louisiana, Arkansas and Texas, may be left out of consideration, for it was not the object of Northern strategy and its population was relatively small. This we may call the "right region," looking at it from the north. The "left region" is that between the Alleghanies or Appalachian range and the Atlantic, comprising Virginia, the Carolinas, and Georgia—all seacoast states, and able from their position to menace Washington. Along the whole coast line as far south as Pensacola (where the North, thanks to Captain Slemmer, still held Fort Pickens), the South, at the outbreak of the war, was mistress of every fortification. This gave her an advantage which it cost the North much fighting and many lives to counteract. The "middle region" is the great sloping plain between the Appalachian range and the

Mississippi, containing Tennessee, Alabama, Mississippi, and the western extremities of some of the eastern states. This was where most of the grand maneuvering of the war took place; it was the heart of the Confederacy, and was attacked and defended as such.

The town of Memphis, on the Mississippi, and Charleston, on the coast of South Carolina, were united by a line of railway; and at Chattanooga, at the east of Tennessee among the mountains, another road branched off in a northeast direction, and terminated in Richmond. Chattanooga, therefore, was a point of vital strategic importance; for this Memphis-Charleston-Richmond railroad was the only one connecting the west with the east of the Confederacy. If the North could seize and hold Chattanooga, the Confederacy would be cut in twain, to its serious detriment. Recognizing this, the North made the town the object of attack, and the South bent her energies to protecting it. This she did by defending a military line between one and two hundred miles to the north of the railway. One end of this line was at Columbus on the Mississippi, a little below the junction with it of the Ohio; the other or eastern end was at Bowling Green, in Warren County, Kentucky, some two hundred miles east of Columbus. This military line passed through Forts Henry and Donelson, midway on its route. A large river, the Tennessee, flows southward from the Ohio, until it reaches the Memphis-Charleston railway; it then turns to the east, following the railway line.

Now, Kentucky being a Northern state, the Union army, to attack the Columbus-Bowling Green line to the best advantage, would descend upon it by way of the Ohio, Mississippi and Tennessee rivers, capturing Forts Henry and Donelson; and after breaking the line, would march southeast through Tennessee to Chattanooga. Thereby not only would the Confederacy be divided, but the Mississippi would be opened. The Confederate armies in Virginia would be between two Union armies, one threatening them from

Chattanooga, the other by way of the North via Richmond. This strategy should be the key of the whole war, to which everything else would be subsidiary. The Confederate forces in the east could be attacked in detail, and Richmond would fall of itself. As the South had no navy, the Atlantic coast and the gulf could be blockaded, and with the Mississippi in Northern hands, she would inevitably be squeezed to death.—But it was some time before this general view of the situation was taken.

The first idea of the North was to capture Richmond: "On to Richmond," to the ordinary apprehension, seemed to be the cry that meant immediate victory. The attempt to reach Richmond, which would have been of minor value had it succeeded, was rendered impossible by the first great battle of the war, in which the two armies met at Bull Run in Virginia, with the result that the Northerners were stampeded, and thrown back in dire confusion upon Washington. The North was thereby admonished that this war was to be no hundred-days affair; and under McClellan as commander-in-chief an army of two hundred thousand men was carefully drilled during the fall and winter. By February they were ready to move, or at all events Stanton, the Secretary of War, thought they were, and General Grant performed the task of ascending the Tennessee River and capturing Forts Henry and Donelson. This exploit was accomplished on the 16th of February, 1862, and gave the North control of Kentucky and most of Tennessee, though the Mississippi was not yet clear. The South failed to recapture these points, being finally defeated in the attempt by the defeat at Murfreesboro on the last day of the year. But the war was still only at its beginning. The South suffered seriously this year from the blockade of her ports, which prevented her from selling her cotton, and thus obtaining the sinews of war. But neither McClellan, Pope nor Burnside was able to take Richmond. On the 22d of September Lincoln announced that from January 1st, 1863, all slaves in the seceded states would be declared free. Thus the second year of the war ended with no conclusive advantage on either side; but the South was straitened by the blockade and by Grant's successes, and had acted hitherto on the defensive.

The year 1863 gave the South several successes, though they were not so important as they appeared. General Lee, aided by storms, turned back Burnside in his attempt on Richmond, and almost annihilated Hooker's great army at Chancellorsville, in May. Galveston was retaken by the Confederates, while Banks failed at Port Hudson, Dupont in his naval attack on Charleston, and Southern cruisers did immense injury to Northern commerce. Lee, after destroying Hooker, advanced into Pennsylvania, and met Meade at Gettysburg. They fought for three days, the greatest battle of the war, and Lee was defeated and thrown back. The next day, July 4th, Grant received the surrender of Vicksburg, and the Mississippi, in the words of Lincoln, "ran unvexed to the sea."

After the surrender of Vicksburg, Grant won a battle at Chattanooga, which ended the conflict for that region; and in March of the year 1864 he was raised to the chief command of all the Union armies. Under his direction, the war was brought to a close with a series of masterly maneuvers worthy of the highest military genius. He left Sherman, whose worth he knew, to dispose of the Confederate force in Georgia; he devoted his own attention to the problem of overthrowing Lee in Virginia. Lee was his peer in the science of war, but the forces of which Grant was able to dispose were greater, and their steadiness was invincible. After a series of engagements lasting for more than a year, Grant at length planted the Stars and Stripes on the walls of Richmond, almost five years to a day after the first shot fired at Sumter. Sherman, coming up from his march through Georgia, had prevented Lee's junction with Johnston's army in North Carolina, and forced his surrender to

Grant at Appomattox Court House on the 9th of April. Johnston surrendered to Sherman two weeks later, and the final capitulations had taken place by the end of May. Such were the leading features of the Civil War; and though the agony and exhaustion inflicted upon the South were severe, she bravely and honorably accepted the issue of the hazard she had tempted. She might have maintained a harassing guerrilla warfare indefinitely; but the South were a civilized, not a barbarous, people; they had done their best and their utmost; there was no disgrace in their defeat; and they manfully faced its consequences. The leaders, however, were unwilling to give the guarantees which the North required against any future renewal of the war; and the result was the passage, two years after the war closed, of the Reconstruction Act, which divided ten Southern states into five military districts with Union army officers in command. These states could not resume their regular place in the Union until, in the words of the Act, a convention of delegates "elected by the male citizens of whatever race, color or previous condition" should frame a constitution, which being ratified by the people and approved by Congress, should go into operation; and the legislature thereupon elected should adopt the fourteenth amendment—which secured to freedmen the right of citizenship, declared the validity of the national debt, and regulated the basis of representation, and disqualification from office.

It is not surprising that some years passed before this ultimatum was accepted by all the states; the stumbling-block, of course, being the stipulation that the emancipated slaves should be entitled to vote. Indeed, the policy of this step is still open to question. White men, especially Southern white men, can never submit to negro domination; but if, as might easily happen, the negroes in a district outnumbered the whites, and chose to elect negroes to office, the whites must either submit or rebel. As a matter of fact it has usually happened that the negroes in the South have either been kept from the polls, or their votes have been cast under white direction; and the relations of the white and black races in the Southern states are in many respects unsatisfactory. Yet if the negro in the South is neither to be a citizen nor a slave, his position is anomalous, and open to another class of objections.

We will now proceed to fill in the above outline with some details. Missouri and Kentucky, as has been said, did not join the Confederacy; but their attitude led to some interesting complications. In Kentucky, the governor and civil officers were mainly Southern sympathizers; but inasmuch as the people were fairly divided, it was determined that the state should remain neutral during the war, affording succor to neither side, and operating against neither. This singular stand, which might be regarded as secession in another form, was maintained for nearly a year. But at the first opportunity, the Union party in the state contrived to elect a loyal legislature; and when, in September, 1861, General Polk, of the Confederates, moved his army into Kentucky, resolutions were passed declaring his act to be a violation of neutrality, and Kentucky declared herself a Union state. This put an end to the strange spectacle of enlistments for South and North going on in the same towns; and it was a severe loss to the Confederacy.

In Missouri the course of events was different. Here the Southern sympathizers predominated; but the Union class, the majority of whom were Germans, were the more alert and energetic; and they had the benefit of being led by two men—Frank P. Blair and Captain Nathaniel Lyon—who possessed phenomenal strength and ability. Blair attended to the political matters, while Lyon managed the military maneuvers. Blair combined the Union men with the neutrals with such effect that the secessionists found it impossible to elect delegates to a convention which had been called to discuss the question of leaving the Union. But when Lincoln's call for seventy-five thousand men was made, the state governor, Jackson, refused to supply men for an "unholy crusade" whose objects were "inhuman and diabolical"; though he did not scruple at the same time to raise and drill men with a view to their joining the Confederate army. Blair, on the other hand, raised a force of "Home Guards"; and these two forces were drilling at the same time under the flag of the United States. Neither party, however, had arms; and both plotted to seize the arsenal. Jackson secretly sent to the Confederate government for cannon, which were promised him; but Lyon, meanwhile, obtained the appointment of commander of the arsenal, and immediately issued arms to the Home Guards. A few days later he happened to be on the levee when the cases containing the cannon arrived, labeled "marble." Their appearance was suspicious, and following them up to their destination in Jackson's camp, he discovered the truth. The next day he led his men against the camp, in spite of the misgivings of many of his party, and captured it without a struggle. As he was marching back with his prisoners he was attacked by the mob, and fired at; his men returned the fire and killed or wounded twenty. He followed up this exploit by seizing St. Louis, the governor and state officials taking flight; and all further efforts to carry the state out of the Union ceased. Lyon was a veteran of the Mexican war, and a man of iron decision; and his service in saving Missouri at this early and important stage was of incalculable value.

The month following the surrender of Fort Sumter passed by with no shots fired, but in active preparation on both sides. The Southern troops were collecting in northern Virginia around the village of Manassas, about thirty miles from Washington; they blocked the Potomac, threw up fortifications, and laid plans for a forward movement. Finding themselves unmolested, they advanced their lines so far that President Lincoln, looking from the windows of the White House with a glass, could see their flag waving across the river. Winfield Scott was in command at Washington, and there were upward of twelve thousand troops in Washington; but the old general hoped the "revolt" would presently subside, and was reluctant to invade Virginia while any hope of peace remained.

But when, on the 23d of May, it became known that General Lee was laying out works on Arlington Heights, commanding the city, Scott ordered his troops across the river. The advance was in three divisions, the third being led by Ellsworth's Zouaves, which seized the town of Alexandria, the population of which was secessionist. A secession flag was flying from the roof of the hotel. Taking one or two men with him, Ellsworth entered the hotel, intending to lower the flag; on the second landing he was confronted by a man with a shotgun loaded with buckshot, who fired at him at close range, not only sending the charge through his heart, but forcing with it Ellsworth's gold badge inscribed "Non nobis sed pro patria." Ellsworth fell dead; one of his companions shot his slayer through the head and bayoneted him. Ellsworth was one of the most conspicuous of the young leaders of the North; he was a magnificent athlete, and his Zouaves were all picked men. The incident made a deep impression on the country, and both Ellsworth and the man who had killed him were regarded as martyrs by the opposing sections. The Union outposts seized Mount Vernon, the home of Washington, and Arlington House, the residence of Robert E. Lee; the site of the latter is now a military cemetery, in which repose the bones of sixteen thousand Union soldiers.

Meanwhile Fortress Monroe, at the end of the peninsula formed by York and James Rivers, was occupied by Union troops under General Butler; but the Confederates threw up earthworks to shut them in, using great numbers of slaves for the purpose. Some of these escaping into the fortress, their owners demanded them back, on the ground that rights of property were to be respected. But Butler informed the

Southern gentlemen that although property was to be respected, war material did not fall under that category; the negroes, having been employed in building fortifications, were war material, and as such "contraband of war." Therefore they would not be returned. This bit of reasoning caught the popular fancy, and the Southern negro was a "contraband" in the common speech thenceforth. The government also accepted Butler's ruling as good in law, and in future all negroes who came within the Union lines were declared free. They were in the same category with sandbags and picks, blunderbusses and mortars.

The peninsula afforded a direct road to Richmond, and in order to clear it Butler ordered an advance in two columns, from Hampton and Newport News, to surprise General Magruder at Great Bethel. Signals were devised by which the two columns should recognize each other when they formed their junction. But the officer commissioned to impart these signals to the Newport News column forgot to do so, and the consequence was that it was fired upon by that from Hampton. The mistake was soon discovered, but the firing had alarmed Magruder and put him on his guard, and the Union troops, weary with their night march, were repulsed from his works, losing fifty men, among them young Theodore Winthrop, a descendant of the famous Winthrops of Boston. For the second time in the short course of this war death had showed that he loved a shining mark.

The early actions of the war were little more than skirmishes, and showed only that the troops on both sides were brave, and that they were unfamiliar with the operations of war. The passes of the mountains of north and west Virginia were held by the Confederates, and as they afforded access to the interior of the state, McClellan determined to capture them. Detaching Rosecranz to march to the rear of the enemy's position on Rich Mountain, he prepared to engage in front; Rosecranz found General Pegram with two thousand men opposed to him; but after some irregular fighting he captured his positions, and compelled his **retreat;** and Garnett, finding his rear thus exposed, followed him, pursued by McClellan. Pegram was killed, and Garnett surrendered; and West Virginia was thenceforward **free** from Confederate armies. But the fear which McClellan had expressed, in his address to his troops, that they "would not find foemen worthy of their steel," was premature. McClellan was destined to hold another opinion of **South-ern** soldiers before long.

The evil of short terms of enlistment was now once **more** exemplified in our experience. Most of the seventy-five thousand men called out by Lincoln had enlisted for three **months,** and their term was nearly up, yet nothing had been done. Nothing, that is, that the people could recognize; **for it seems** to the uninstructed observer that troops drilling in camp are idle. The general officers were of course aware that drill is an indispensable preliminary to effective work **in the field;** and to the cry of "On to Richmond" they replied **that they** could not lead an undisciplined army on such an enterprise with any reasonable chance of success. But the clamor did not cease; and Lincoln and Scott were at length obliged to attempt something. And there was an operation which it seemed not too rash to undertake.

The railroad from Richmond and that from the Shenandoah Valley to the west, met at Manassas Junction in Virginia, five-and-thirty miles south of the Potomac. It was the key to the railway system of the state, and was held by the Confederates under General Beauregard, with an advance line along the brook known as Bull Run. The Confederates at this point numbered twenty-five thousand; but in the Shenandoah Valley was Johnston, with ten thousand more. He, however, was confronted at Harper's Ferry **by** Patterson, with double his number; so the chance of his being able to re-enforce Beauregard seemed remote. **Mac-dowell** was ordered to attack Beauregard with thirty thousand men. There was considerable delay in getting together the war material and supplies, and Confederate spies kept the Southern generals apprised of what was doing. Of this information they made excellent use.

Patterson was a soldier of 1812, and not proficient in the later developments of warlike science; but he had for some time been urging Scott to let him attack Johnston, and Scott finally gave him permission. He advanced accordingly, expecting a fierce resistance; but to his astonishment found the works empty and the guns spiked. Suspecting a ruse, he became exceeding cautious; and when Macdowell was ready to make his movement on Manassas Junction, and Scott wrote to Patterson to engage Johnston in order to prevent his re-enforcing Beauregard, Patterson delayed, and finally retreated, intending another maneuver. But Johnston was far more than his match in strategy; and was on his way to join Beauregard while Patterson was imagining that he had him in a trap.

On the 15th of July Macdowell, with his enormous train of impedimenta, was ready to move; and Beauregard, through a spy, was informed of the number of men who were to be led against him, and of the precise hour at which they would set out. They left Washington, in fact, on the night of the 16th, and advanced as if going to a picnic; it was impossible to keep order in the ranks; the scouts did not know their duty, and the officers had little control. They reached Fairfax Court House by noon of the 17th, and spent the night there in a frolic, looting several of the abandoned houses; some of them paraded the streets in women's clothes. At nine the next morning they were at Centreville, where a battle was expected. The Confederates had their base at Manassas Junction, and their advance line on Bull Run; the stream is sluggish, the country rolling and lightly timbered. Twenty thousand Confederates were posted along the winding course of the stream behind earthworks, extending eight miles. There were seven fords and one bridge to be defended. The obvious course for Macdowell to adopt was to outflank his enemy, and this he prepared to do on the south. His position at Centreville, on the north, was intended to hide his purpose. But his engineers reported that the southern or right flank could not be turned, and the plan had to be altered to turn the left flank. Meanwhile General Tyler, sent forward to reconnoiter, but with orders not to bring on a general engagement, disobeyed his instructions so far as to start up a lively and quite useless little battle at Blackburne's ford; after losing sixty men he retired, leaving the Confederates with the elation of victory. The night passed with nothing done; but Johnston was marching at full speed to re-enforce Beauregard, Macdowell flattering himself that he was safe in Patterson's grasp. It was not until Saturday, July 20th, that the engineers reported the ford passable; in the interval a regiment and a battery whose term had expired turned their backs on the enemy, and, in spite of the entreaties of Macdowell, marched back to Washington. Such are the incredible poltrooneries occasionally to be seen in war.

Macdowell's plan was now made—an attack on the right flank at Blackburne's ford; a feint at the center, and the main attack, under Macdowell, was to proceed by night to Sudley's ford on the left flank, and crumple up the enemy's line. This latter movement was accomplished, though the troops, unused to marching, spent two or three hours longer than had been calculated on the route, and were exhausted by their efforts. But the attack on the center had not been strong enough to deceive Evans, who commanded the Confederates at that point, and when he was apprised of the movement against the flank, he left the ford and faced it, holding the Federals until he was re-enforced. But by this time the engagement had become general, and there was a good deal of confusion on both sides among soldiers unaccustomed to battle; the Union men, upon the whole, slowly forcing back the Confederates. Presently the retreat became a rout, and men who had fought bravely and steadily an hour before were running in something like panic, too bewildered to respond to the frantic efforts of their officers to rally them. Everywhere was smoke, and the roaring and rattling of guns, and great bodies of men in motion. The day seemed lost to the Confederates.

But a brigade of troops, five regiments and a couple of batteries, had just arrived from the Shenandoah Valley, and were drawn up in line across the turnpike along which General Bee's brigade was retreating in confusion. In front of the line stood its commander. "They are beating us back!" cried Bee, galloping up to him. "Very well, sir, we'll give them the bayonet," replied Jackson, composedly. "See!" yelled Bee to his men: "there stands Jackson like a stone wall!" It was a famous word, and gave the then almost unknown commander his title.

The flying men rallied on the colors; Beauregard and Johnston came up; the Federal advance was checked. There was an interval during which both armies remained in position; but the Confederates had now learned that the main attack was on their left, and they were concentrating there. In a wood covering the crest of a hill they formed in strength, and their batteries began to shell the Federals below. Macdowell had to face a body of troops now equal in numbers to his own, many of them fresh, and strongly intrenched. He sent Rickett's and Griffin's batteries to open fire, but they were insufficiently supported, and the enemy's fire was masked by the woods. They would have maintained their positions, however, had they not at that juncture been attacked by a regiment coming up on their right, which were mistaken for Federals until they discharged their muskets pointblank into Griffin's battery. This regiment, under Kirby Smith, had just arrived from the Shenandoah, and their action settled the fortunes of the battle. The men supporting the batteries became panic stricken and fled, the Zouaves among them. The deserted guns were seized by a Virginia regiment. But a regiment from Michigan recaptured them. Meanwhile the

MAJ.-GEN. PHILIP H. SHERIDAN, U.S.A.

effort to carry the hill still continues and more than once almost succeeded; but at the critical moment the attackers are driven back; and they are weakening while the others are constantly gaining strength. For four or five hours the assault was kept up; then, gradually, the Union army began to crumble to pieces. The want of discipline again made itself felt, and now disastrously. Regimental organizations were lost; squads and individuals stopped fighting and walked off to the rear. Officers lost their men, and men their officers. There was no panic or stampede, but the Union army was steadily melting away. The Confederates did not know they had won a victory, and for a time the Federals did not think themselves beaten; but that impression finally gained upon them, and then they began to retreat in earnest. They were not pursued; they had not been defeated; but they ran, with ever-increasing good will. As evening drew on, a scene was witnessed such as had seldom before been seen in warfare. A great throng of sight-seeing non-combatants had come out from Washington in the rear of the army, to witness the defeat of the "rebels." These turned tail at the first alarm, and streamed headlong northward. All things that could retard flight were thrown aside, and the ground was encumbered with the most grotesque heterogeny of articles imaginable, from champagne bottles and note-books to cannon and brass horns. This headlong horde, pursued only by itself, converged toward a narrow suspension bridge over the stream called Cub Run, and there a terrible jam occurred; and to make it worse, a shell from a Confederate battery, which had been posted to command this bridge, exploded on an artillery wagon which had reached the middle of the bridge, and wrecked it there, blocking the way for all who followed. Here, accordingly, was a vast assortment of plunder for the surprised Confederates to pick up the next day. Onward poured the endless mob in a dismal flood; it had been very sultry during the day, and the yellow dust kicked up by the marching thou-

THE NEW YORK
PUBLIC LIBRARY

ASTOR, LENOX AND
TILDEN FOUNDATIONS.

THE NEW YORK
PUBLIC LIBRARY

ASTOR, LENOX AND
TILDEN FOUNDATIONS.

MAJ.-GEN. JOHN C. FREMONT, U.S.A.

LIEUT.-GEN. WINFIELD SCOTT, U.S.A.

THE NEW YORK
PUBLIC LIBRARY

ASTOR, LENOX AND
TILDEN FOUNDATIONS.

MAJ.-GEN. JOHN A. LOGAN, U.S.A.

sands hung in the air, and was mixed with the smoke of powder and the grime of the powder itself in the skins of the unhappy ones. A drizzling rain which set in on the Sunday night achieved what had seemed impossible in making the general misery greater. Such a draggle-tailed, wretched, shame-faced, exhausted, sleepy, disorganized and demoralized multitude of tramps as poured into Washington all the next day was never seen before. The dismay caused by their appearance (except among the numerous sympathizers with the South who dwelt in the city and ill concealed their triumph) was profound. It seemed as if the Union had gone to pieces, and the Confederates would presently come whooping down Pennsylvania Avenue. It was not quite so bad as that, however. Macdowell had succeeded in partly checking the rout at Centreville, and the brigades of Richardson and Blenker, which had been in reserve as a rear guard, formed in good order behind the fugitives and kept off the half-hearted pursuit of the enemy's cavalry. Indeed, it would have put the fugitives in much better conceit with themselves had a real pursuit taken place; they could not have run faster, and it would have helped them to explain to curious inquirers the reasons of their flight.

But all things have an end, and the retreat of the Union army was over at last. Jefferson Davis, on the battlefield, was declaring that "we have won a glorious but dear-bought victory." In truth it was neither dear-bought nor glorious; for the total losses on the Confederate side were but three hundred and eighty killed and a little over a thousand wounded, out of thirty thousand troops engaged; and the Federals had lost little more, except the fourteen hundred prisoners captured. The victory, moreover, turned out to be rather to the advantage of the Union than of the Confederacy; since the latter jumped to the conclusion that one Southerner was a match for five Northerners; while the Northerners perceived that they had no summer picnic before them, but a real war with men who could fight, and made their preparations accordingly. A new call for men was issued, and Congress voted five hundred million dollars to continue the war. The South, on the contrary, thinking the war over, lost thousands of men who returned to their homes from the front; and the Southern cities began disputing as to which of them should be the seat of the government, which was now believed to be finally established.

Walt Whitman, in a description of the retreat, written in prose which was intended to be such, but which has much poetic spirit in it, says of Lincoln that "if there were nothing else of Abraham Lincoln for history to stamp him with, it is enough to send him with his wreath to the memory of all future time, that he endured that hour, that day, bitterer than gall, indeed a crucifixion day; that it did not conquer him; that he unflinchingly stemmed it, and resolved to lift himself and the Union out of it." The President indeed rallied more quickly than did the army; while Macdowell was still at Centreville, trying to get something like order into the struggling mass, he received a telegram from Washington saying, "We are not discouraged." There was certainly no need for discouragement; what was wanted was longer terms of service, and its corollary, discipline. There were men enough to do the fighting, and of as good material as any in the world; but they must be molded into soldiers —between whom and persons who are not soldiers there are vital differences. Half a million men were summoned to defend the Union, and they came. But they had to be transformed into an army; and the work of transforming them was intrusted to George Brinton McClellan, who had already been fortunate in the little battle of Rich Mountain. McClellan suffered much criticism for his dilatory tactics later on, and was even thought by the censorious to be not so ardent in the Union cause as he should have been; but he did what was far better than setting mobs in motion toward Richmond: he spent eight months in drilling "the

Army of the Potomac," consisting of about two hundred thousand men. These men were enlisted for three years, and long before that period had elapsed they were the equals of any soldiers who ever fought. The country owes a lasting debt of thanks to the "Little Napoleon" for this, for the good effects of it were felt throughout the war. McClellan was a very young officer at this time, and very scientific, and he had the cocksureness of the cadet still about him; he was set in his opinions, and his opinions often betrayed a sore lack of wisdom and insight; but he was a good soldier in many essentials, and might, with sufficient experience in a subordinate position, have grown to be a great one. But to put such a man into the position of supreme command was to spoil him, and cut short his career. He was not ready for it; and what was more serious for him, he thought he was. He was very popular with his soldiers, and this increased his misapprehension of himself. But the trouble was, in those late summer days of 1861, that the North needed a leader, and had to take him who seemed likeliest without too much investigation. One after another must be tested—and a severer test was never applied to generals—and either discarded or adopted as the case might be. They must be tested in the field, for there was no military board to examine them; they must be judged by their performance, though often a judgment formed on this basis would be unjust or mistaken; for the men in Washington—Stanton and Lincoln—who had to make the appointments and pass the censures were wholly ignorant of war when they began, and had to learn, like the privates in the field, as they went along. Something must also be allowed to professional rivalries and jealousies, as tending to darken counsel. Many of these officers had been in West Point together; they had known one another there, and "had their opinion" as to one another's ability—and as to their own. All West Pointers alike, moreover, were disposed to look down upon the Volunteer officers with pitying contempt, though the record of these, when the war was ended, was far more than creditable. Taking all things together, the difficulties with which the Union government had to contend at the beginning of the war can hardly be exaggerated. It is not surprising that they did not do better; it is astonishing that they did so well. It was a stern school for all concerned, and they graduated from it with honors.

CHAPTER THIRTY-FOURTH

THE MISSISSIPPI AND THE POTOMAC

HILE the Army of the Potomac, under McClellan, was receiving its lessons in drill, a lively little war was going on in Missouri, which was about equally divided between secessionists and Union men; the division often extending to families, and separating father from son, or brother from brother. A motley army of Rebels, with no uniforms, and with equipments to a great extent improvised, was collected in the southwest corner of the state, and another crossed the Mississippi to New Madrid. The first army was commanded by Price and Macbride, the other by Pillow. Their united strength was about ten or twelve thousand men. They planned to effect a junction and move on St. Louis, driving the Federals out of the state; to oppose them was only Lyon at Springfield, half way between the two Confederate armies and to the north of them. He was joined by General Sigel, and they mustered about five thousand troops. The Confederates attacked after an exhausting march; but Lyon had sent Sigel round to attack their rear, and at first the day seemed going against them; but Sigel's men were surprised by a body of men under the Union flag, who, upon coming to close quarters, discovered themselves as Confederates, and drove the Federals in a panic. This left Lyon to continue the fight alone, which he did with great valor; but he was killed while leading his column at the enemy, having already been twice wounded. In that charge the enemy were temporarily repulsed, and the Union men seized the opportunity to retreat; they were not pursued: "we were glad to see them go," said a Confederate officer. The total losses on either side were not greatly over a thousand; but the death of Lyon, who had showed the finest soldierly qualities, outweighed that of many ordinary men. The battle was lost largely because raw troops cannot be trusted to carry out maneuvers under fire; but the Confederates were as raw as the Federals. It was numbers that won the day; in personal courage the two sides were alike.

Another defeat which was not a disgrace was sustained by the Union forces under Colonel Mulligan, a valiant fighter, as his name implies. He had with him three thousand men, and he intrenched himself on a hill to withstand the attack of Price with fourteen thousand. He was short of provisions and ammunition, and the conflict was hopeless; the army of Price, with plenty of artillery, completely surrounded his position, and might have carried it at once by assault; but being still too green to know their own strength, they proceeded by bombardment. At the end of the day Mulligan still held his position, though he had suffered loss and was in straits for water, and his ammunition was running low. The next day the attack was resumed; bales of hemp were used as movable breastworks by the enemy to approach the works. Mulligan set them afire with hot shot; they were extinguished and again pushed forward; suddenly the firing ceased, for, unknown to the gallant Irishman, a lieutenant of his command had displayed the white flag. He ordered it hauled down, and that the fighting go on.

But his officers protested that this was butchery, and he reluctantly called a council of war, which was unanimous for surrender. "We gave up the place, but I don't know nor care upon what conditions," said Mulligan afterward. His valiant resistance was a stimulus to Northern spirits, and his Irish Brigade carried the word "Lexington" on its banner ever after.

It was now November, and Fremont, who had been in the northeast part of the state, advanced with a considerable force toward the southwest, driving the enemy before him; and at Springfield a Polish officer of his bodyguard charged with one hundred and fifty cavalry upon fifteen hundred Confederates, put them to flight, raised the Union flag over the court house, captured the enemy's flag, and rode back. But Fremont apprehended that Price, whom he was pushing back, might be re-enforced by an army of ten thousand men under Polk, at Columbus, Kentucky; and he ordered a young subordinate of his, Ulysses S. Grant by name, to make a demonstration on the Mississippi to keep them in check.

Grant had resigned his commission in the regular army after serving through the Mexican war, but had re-enlisted at the outbreak of the Rebellion, and after some incidental disappointments, now found himself heading in the right direction. He set out by river for Cairo with five regiments, some cavalry, and a couple of guns, on the 6th of November. The enemy were in full force at Columbus; but at Belmont, above, there was a detachment which he landed to attack, sending down his gunboats meanwhile to amuse the ten thousand in Columbus. Polk was at first puzzled by Grant's movements, for he believed that a movement on Columbus must be intended, and was at a loss to understand why Belmont, on the other side of the river, should be attacked. Comprehending at length that the fighting was to be at the latter place, he began to move troops across the river to take part in it. Grant meanwhile was moving steadily through the woods on the Rebel camp; the fighting was stubborn, and he had his horse killed; but the Rebels gave way at last, and plunged down the steep bank to the river, where they might all have been captured had the Federals acted in a rational manner; but they turned to plundering the camp, and could not be rallied till Polk was upon them, between them and their transports. This was where a little discipline would have been worth many thousand men. They were panic-stricken, and could not obey orders; but "We cut our way in here, and we can cut our way out again," said Grant; and at length he reformed them and they succeeded in forcing a way to their boats. When they were ready to leave, Grant went back to look after his rear guard; but the rear guard had deserted its post and was already aboard. Grant himself only escaped by riding his horse down the almost perpendicular clay bank of the river. A plank was thrown out to the shore, and he rode on board the transport. The enemy fired on the boats from the banks; but the boats returned the fire with shell, inflicting some loss. A bullet went through a sofa in the cabin of the transport, on which Grant had a moment before been lying. Each army in this engagement lost about six hundred men. It was only another skirmish; but how near the North came to losing the man who was chiefly instrumental in leading her armies to victory! What is the meaning of these "narrow escapes"? The ways of God are unsearchable. Washington, Grant, almost all great commanders, have felt death brush against them as he passed. So does the common private in the ranks; and it is often the lives that seem most precious that are lost. But human history is evolved, and that which is to be is accomplished.

The so-called battle of Ball's Bluff was an affair hardly comprehensible. The banks of the Potomac thirty miles above Washington are steep and high, and are wooded to their edge, but at the bluff called after the name of the farmer who lived near it, there is a clearing about seven acres in area. Here, of all places in the world, a force of Federals numbering seven hundred, who had been sent over to reconnoiter, sat down to rest on the 21st of October. On the Maryland shore opposite was Colonel Baker with another force. Hearing firing, and finding that there were not boats adequate to bring the seven hundred back while an enemy was firing at them, Baker, a brave man but no tactician, reasoned that it was incumbent on him to go over to them; since they might hold the enemy in check till he arrived, when the combined forces would be sufficient for victory. The Confederates let him and his men come across, and then developed their attack. Three more Confederate regiments joined the others and fire was opened from the woods. Baker, walking up and down before his men to encourage them, was suddenly assailed by a single warrior, who came out in front of his comrades and killed him with his revolver at five paces' distance. The second in command ordered a retreat, and the Federals began to hurry down the steep slope to the river; the Confederates stood above and shot down the huddled masses at their leisure, and many were drowned in attempting to swim the swift stream. Between seven and eight hundred survivors were captured. If the Federals had arranged this battle especially with a view to insuring their own slaughter, they could not have managed it better.

All operations of this kind, from the battle of Bull Run to the time when Grant began to hammer at the line of defense extending between Bowling Green and Columbus, were in the nature of what boxers would call sparring for an opening, and to learn each other's style and resources. No comprehensive scheme of a general campaign had been worked out on either side. Indeed the Confederates, though they were successful in most of the engagements, were in a defensive attitude; they made no attempt to invade Northern territory. They evidently misunderstood the Northern situation and purposes, and fancied the war was practically over; and this seduced them into neglecting preparations, military and financial, which would have served them well later on. They were confident that they could protect themselves in their own chosen country, and did not think it worth their while to become aggressive. Their commissariat was inefficient, and they wasted power in incoherent activities. They gradually retreated before our advance in western Virginia, which was resolutely loyal; for the mountaineers had never had slaves, and owned no sympathy for those who did. Operations by sea during this first year of the war were favorable at the North; Pamlico Sound, within Cape Hatteras, was lost to the South by the capture of the two forts at Hatteras Inlet by Commodore Stringham, and their occupation by General Butler. Later, on the 29th of October, the forts at Port Royal were assaulted by Commodore Dupont of the Federal navy and garrisoned by a force under General Thomas W. Sherman. The efforts of the South were confined to blockade-running and to privateering, in both of which they were fairly successful: the privateer "Savannah" ran the blockade at Charleston in June; but her career was stopped by the United States brig "Perry," after she had captured one prize. The "Petrel," another privateer, was captured through the mistake she made in attacking the United States frigate "St. Lawrence," under the delusion that she was a merchantman. Suddenly the black sides of the warship grinned horribly with tiers of guns, and the "Petrel" was sunk before she could get out of range. Captain Semmes, however, of the privateer "Sumter," from New Orleans, achieved fame and made several valuable captures; but he was finally bottled up by the United States "Tuscarora" in the Bay of Gibraltar, and could escape only by selling his vessel.

The most stirring sea affair of the year was the holding up of the British ship "Trent" by Captain Wilkes of the United States steamer "San Jacinto," and the taking from her of the Confederate commissioners Slidell and Mason. These gentlemen were on their way to Europe to try to negotiate an alliance with England or France; being encouraged thereto by the recognition of belligerency which these countries had almost immediately accorded to the Confederacy. The seizure of them by Wilkes, while under the protection of a neutral flag, was contrary to international usages; and England, who was very sensitive to infringements of these usages when committed by any other nation than herself, made preparations for war. Her attitude toward the North throughout the war was covertly hostile; she favored the South for two reasons: first, because she perceived that the prosecution of the war would weaken both South and North, and, if it were decided by the victory of the South, would render America no longer formidable; and secondly, because the blockade of Southern ports was inconvenient to England. Northern feeling was much aroused; it was thought that England was taking advantage of our embarrassment to injure us; and there was a large party who advocated accepting her offer of battle. But Lincoln was not a man to risk the ruin of his country on a point of pique; England was technically in the right, and this country could not afford to fight in defense of a wrong, even were she otherwise in a condition to face so powerful a nation as England on the sea. The act of Captain Wilkes was therefore disavowed, and Slidell and Mason were returned. But there was a latent purpose in the North to "take it out" of England when opportunity hereafter served. Fortunately for the peace of the world, the prolongation of the war, and the complexion of affairs afterward, prevented this; but the incident kept alive a feeling of hostility to England which can hardly be said to have disappeared entirely even yet.

At the close of the year, then, the record showed that while the South had won the most considerable battles, the North had secured West Virginia, Kentucky and Missouri;

had established a tolerably effective blockade of the whole Southern coast, and had got possession of Fort Monroe, Fort Pickens, Hatteras Inlet and Port Royal. She had besides been successful in various small battles or skirmishes. In the ability of the general officers, both sides seemed on an equality; and the courage of the men on the field of battle was also equal. In this connection it may be observed that raw soldiers had been found to be almost as trustworthy as regulars for charges in the face of the enemy, or for holding positions against attack; what they lacked was steadiness in the face of either success or reverse; if they found themselves flanked, or were for any reason bewildered and thrown into confusion, they were apt to run. Only discipline and experience could correct these faults; and the armies on either side were sure of getting abundance of both. Operations in the field were now conducted on a scale, and with numbers, hitherto unequaled in warfare; and of course the chances of losing one's bearings were correspondingly increased.

By the time the year 1862 had set in, the Northern plan of campaign was mainly settled; there was to be no more sparring, but fighting in earnest. Half a million men were ready to serve on the Union side, and perhaps a hundred and fifty thousand less on the side of the South. Operations were carried on over a vast area, but the vital movement was that against the Confederate defense on the Tennessee and Mississippi rivers, for the command of the east and west railway. In this, co-operated Thomas on the east, and Buell and Grant, assisted by the gunboats of Commodore Foote, on the rivers. The defense was conducted by Beauregard and A. S. Johnston. The chief and decisive engagements were the capture by Grant and Foote of Forts Henry and Donelson, which compelled the evacuation by the Confederates of Columbus and Bowling Green; the great battle of Shiloh, which opened Corinth to the Federals; the three weeks' siege and capture of Island No. 10, in the Mississippi below Columbus, by Foote and Pope; and the surrender of Memphis. At this juncture Bragg, of the Confederates, who was stationed at Chattanooga, marched on Louisville, his course taking him across the states of Tennessee and Kentucky, with the object of cutting off the Union communications. Buell, who was moving southward, fell back to Nashville, and then, divining Bragg's plan, he raced against him for the Ohio, where he arrived first and received large re-enforcements. This obliged Bragg to fall back to Perryville, forty miles south by west of Louisville; here he turned on Buell and a severe battle was fought, Bragg getting away that night; and Buell, who had suffered him to escape, was superseded by Rosecranz. Grant, meanwhile, whose force had been weakened by the re-enforcements sent to Buell, was threatened by Price and Van Dorn, with a view to the recapture of Corinth. Grant maneuvered, with the aid of Rosecranz, to defeat them separately; but owing to a misunderstanding, Price escaped Rosecranz, and uniting with Van Dorn, the two besieged Rosecranz in Corinth, but were defeated, and pursued with loss. Assuming command of Buell's army at Nashville, Rosecranz set out to encounter Bragg at Murfreesboro', twenty-five miles southeast. Each general attacked the other's right. Bragg was at first successful, falling on his enemy as the latter's left was crossing a small river. Sheridan, however, supported Rosecranz's weak right until his left could get into action; upon which the Confederates charged in vain. Renewing the attack two days later, and being again repulsed, Bragg retreated; but the losses on both sides had been enormous— a fourth part of the number engaged. Chattanooga was thus laid open to the Federals.

A simultaneous attempt by Grant in co-operation with Sherman to capture Vicksburg, further down the Mississippi, was defeated by a brilliant cavalry raid by Van Dorn, destroying Grant's supplies at Holly Springs. Grant had meant to descend the river with Porter from Memphis, while Sherman was to make his attack at Chickasaw Bayou, north of Vicksburg. Sherman, knowing nothing of the event which kept Grant from moving, made his attack accordingly, but was repulsed. Farragut had already captured New Orleans; Burnside had got possession of Roanoke Island, controlling the coast of upper North Carolina. Successes in Florida and Georgia put every city on the coast except Savannah, Charleston and Wilmington into Federal hands; to counterbalance these victories, the iron-clad "Merrimac" entered Hampton Roads and sunk the "Cumberland" and destroyed the "Congress"; but on her return to finish her work on the rest of the fleet next day, she was challenged by the "Monitor," and obliged to retreat. This duel may be said to have saved the Union cause; for had the "Merrimac" not been opposed, she and other vessels of her sort could have destroyed the Union fleet, Fort Monroe, and the other coast defenses in Union possession; checked the Peninsular campaign, which was then in progress; given free egress for Southern Cotton, and won the support of Europe for the Confederacy.—Let us now examine some of these operations from a closer point of view.

At the beginning of the combined movements to break the Columbus-Bowling Green line, Buell was at Louisville. Zollicoffer, a Confederate, was at Mill Spring on the Cumberland River, some hundred miles to the south. Against him Buell sent General Thomas, who, after a march in the mud, made ready to attack; but the Confederates decided that they themselves would attack, and they moved by night on Thomas's camp at Logan's Cross-Roads, ten miles away. Thomas was too experienced a soldier to be caught off his guard; but the impact of the Confederates against his left was not to be resisted; Zollicoffer himself, in a rubber coat which hid his uniform, directed the attack. In the misty drizzle of the January dawn things were of ambiguous aspect, and Colonel Frye, a Federal officer, found himself rubbing elbows with the officer in the rubber coat; each mistook the other for one of his side. "Are you fighting your friends?" asked the Confederate, as Frye was ordering his men to fire on a Mississippi regiment.—"Certainly not!" returned Frye, staring: and at that moment Zollicoffer's aid recognized Frye's uniform and emptied his pistol at it. Frye could take a hint, even on a January morning; he drew his revolver, fired a bullet through Zollicoffer's breast, and was off, himself untouched. Zollicoffer's death took the heart out of his men; the Ninth Ohio drove through their center with a bayonet charge; they turned, and in a few minutes were utterly routed. Thomas pursued them back to Mill Spring, and made arrangements to cut off their escape; but a steamer stole up in the night and had ferried almost all the troops across the river before dawn. When she was discovered, a shot from the battery at the river bank sunk her; the stable door was once more shut after the horse had escaped. But abundant munitions of war remained to console the victors. The battle demolished Confederate resistance in the east, and Grant, Buell and Foote could conduct their operations with an undivided mind.

The Tennessee and Cumberland rivers, running nearly parallel for the last hundred miles of their course, empty into the Ohio within about ten miles of each other, and forty miles east of the Ohio's junction with the Mississippi, at Cairo. Roads were almost non-existent in this region, and indeed in most parts of the United States, at this time, and the only means of extended travel were by waterway or railway. The Tennessee and Cumberland, therefore, must be guarded to prevent the Federals from penetrating the Confederate line. This was done by the erection of Forts Henry and Donelson, about eighty or a hundred miles south of the mouths. Had it not been for the opposition of McClellan, this defense would have been attacked by the Union troops earlier in the war. But McClellan, just then, could think of nothing but drill, and Richmond. On the 2d of February, however, Grant got permission to attack Fort Henry on the Tennessee (the western of the two rivers), and was off from Cairo with seventeen thousand men. The flotilla, protected by iron-clad gunboats, took the army up the river in two installments; some torpedoes obstructing the channel were removed, and on the morning of the 6th the troops and gunboats advanced to the assault. The Confederates, who had but four thousand men, were additionally handicapped by the fact that a freshet in the river had inundated their fort, so that they were fighting mid-leg deep in water. On the other hand, the roads were almost impassable, and delayed Grant's march till the fight, conducted between the fort and gunboats, was over. It was a lively artillery duel, and the flagship was disabled; but the gunboats and the river combined finally prevailed, and Tilghman, having got most of his garrison safely off on the road to Fort Donelson on the Cumberland, twelve miles away, hauled down his flag, and the victors actually sailed into his works.

While Grant was preparing to follow on to Fort Donelson, he sent the gunboats up the river into Alabama to destroy whatever military works they could find. He reconnoitered Fort Donelson, and found it mounted on a high hill at the bend of the Cumberland—a position almost impregnable compared with that of Fort Henry. The approach up the river was commanded by two water batteries; it was skirted by log redoubts and earthworks with abattis extending for three miles up and down stream. The guns were heavy, and the garrison numbered twenty thousand men; for Johnston, who commanded in this district, had concentrated all his best troops here. Unfortunately he had intrusted the command to General Floyd, formerly Secretary of War under Buchanan, a man destitute of honor and courage. Grant knew Floyd's character, and planned his attack accordingly.

The delay caused to his advance by the rains enabled heavy re-enforcements to reach him by order of Halleck, and before the critical moment arrived, his fifteen thousand men had been increased to near thirty. On the morning of February 12th, a warm, spring-like day, he marched in two divisions along parallel roads. McClernand and Smith led the divisions till, toward sunset, they startled the enemy's pickets. In the morning a line was formed covering the land side of the enemy's works. While this was being done, sharpshooters were thrown forward to harass the enemy. Finding his line too thin, Grant sent back to Fort Henry for Lew Wallace, who had been left in charge there with the rear guard. He was stringing out his men over eight miles of country; and if the twenty thousand men in the fort made a sally at any point, it must be successful. But Grant thought that Floyd would not make a sally, and therefore he took chances. In his plan of battle, he had intended to use his troops only to hem in the enemy, letting the gunboats reduce the water batteries and guard the approaches up and down stream. But matters turned out differently. In the first place, McClernand, much annoyed by a battery on the Confederate left, ordered it taken, though it was a very strong position, and was defended by five regiments against the three which were to attack. The assault was gallantly delivered and long sustained, but it failed, and the loss was heavy. Night fell and with it came a frost, which added to the discomfort of the soldiers. But in the morning Wallace arrived with his command, and was stationed on the Union left. If Floyd had made a sally that night, he would have been successful; but now his chance was gone. The following afternoon the gunboats arrived, and opened their bombardment, receiving a vigorous reply. They inflicted serious damage on the works, but two of them were disabled, and at evening all dropped down stream out of range. The honors were with the fort; but Floyd had become alarmed, and wished to retreat. During the night ten thousand of his troops were massed on the left of the fort, whence a road goes southward to Charlotte. In the morning the sally began, the brunt of it falling on McClernand. His division was forced back, Lew Wallace hesitated to support him without orders from Grant, who had gone down the river to confer with Foote, and it was not until late in the day that he threw his command across the path of the advancing Confederates and checked them. At that moment Grant rode up.

He had not anticipated any sortie from Floyd, and had to make his dispositions at a moment's warning. Happening to hear from one of the soldiers that the Confederates were carrying three days' rations, he at once perceived that their purpose had been not to attack, but to fight their way out. He ordered Wallace to retake the position won that morning from McClernand, and then, riding to the Federal left, he directed General Smith to carry the formidable works on the Confederate right.

Wallace intrusted the assault of the position held by the Confederate Pillow to Colonel Morgan Smith with a Missouri and an Illinois regiment. They met a killing fire, but continued to go forward; Colonel Smith's cigar was cut from his mouth by a bullet; a soldier handed him another, which he lit, and went on. A few minutes later the Union men were in the works, and the line of escape which Pillow had opened, but had delayed to take advantage of, was closed again. Meanwhile, at the other end of the line, General Smith, on horseback, his gray hair blowing out behind him, was leading an even more perilous assault. The enemy's fire was very terrible; the hill was steep; concealed rifle-pits and breastworks commanded every part of it; a formidable abattis delayed the assailants at the most difficult moment; as they went forward, the ground behind them was strewn with bodies dead or wounded. General Smith was the most conspicuous figure there, but his bearing put a new heart in every man who followed him. The setting sun flung the shadows of the Federals before them as at last they reached the crest of the hill and poured into the works. The Confederates fled, nor could the valiant Buckner rally them. It was a great day for the Smiths. It was an ill day for Floyd and Pillow; and to make it worse, the latter, after his success in the morning, had telegraphed to Johnston that he had won a great victory, and the news appeared in all the Southern journals the next morning, at the very time that Fort Donelson was being unconditionally surrendered, and Pillow and Floyd, abandoning their trust, had saved themselves by flight, followed by the hisses of their own men. For Floyd, fearing to fall into Federal hands with his record in the War Department, had devolved his command upon Pillow, and Pillow had shifted it to Buckner; who, after their departure, sent word to Grant to ask him what terms he would accord him. All the world has heard Grant's reply: "No terms except an immediate and unconditional surrender can be accepted. I propose to move immediately upon your works."

On the Sunday morning, February 17th, the Federal troops marched into the fort with flags flying and bands playing, while gunboats fired salutes along the river front, and thousands of spectators cheered. "Had I been in command, general, you wouldn't have got Donelson so easily," remarked Buckner to Grant, afterward. "I shouldn't have tried it in the way I did," was Grant's reply. For in war, as in everything else that men do, the personal equation tells.

This victory took Kentucky and Tennessee from the South, caused the evacuation of Columbus and Bowling Green and Nashville, and depressed Southern stock in Europe. And all over the North gossips were saying to one another, "This fellow Grant seems to be a good man—who is he? U. S. Grant:—Unconditional Surrender Grant, I suppose!"

But Grant had enemies other than those openly opposed

against him; and some of these, induced by what dishonorable jealousy we need not inquire, sought to crush him in the bloom of his fame. An anonymous letter of abuse was sent to Halleck at Washington; his replies to inquiries from Halleck were kept back in the telegraph office; and he was suddenly suspended from command. Before the slanders were refuted, and he was reinstated, valuable time had been lost. He had already planned a movement on Corinth, and now commenced it; but Johnston, one of the best generals of the Confederacy, had foreseen that this railroad center would be attacked, and had been preparing its defense. Beauregard, Polk, Van Dorn, the brave braggart, and Braxton Bragg assembled there from all quarters with all the men they could muster, till the total reached fifty thousand. Grant had to work against different material from that which he had encountered at Fort Donelson.

Grant had about thirty thousand men at Donelson, and Buell, at Nashville, had thirty-seven thousand. These must be united, and the Confederates would be outnumbered. Grant got his army down to Pittsburg Landing on the Tennessee, twenty miles north of Corinth, and his camp extended to Shiloh church. He was waiting for Buell; but he neglected to fortify his position, and meanwhile rode off to look for news of Buell at the Landing. The Confederates knew that Buell was expected, and that if they wished to have the advantage in the battle, they must not wait to be attacked. A council of war decided to surprise the Federal camp at daybreak on the 5th of April. Whether it was a surprise, or whether it had been anticipated, may never be determined; the Southerners think it was a surprise; Sherman and Grant appear to be of another opinion. At all events the preparations to withstand it were not effective. The pickets were driven in early in the morning of the 6th, and though a line was formed after a fashion by Prentiss's regiments, it did not stand before the rush of General Hardee's troops. Had Hardee pressed on he might have carried the commands of Sherman and McClernand; but his men stopped to plunder Prentiss's camp, and they found the second Federal line more stubborn. As the battle continued over the uneven ground, it became divided into a number of separate engagements. Sherman was pressed hard by Hardee, supported by Bragg, and began to be outflanked. He was separated from Prentiss, but was joined by McClernand, and held his own. The nature of the ground and the confusion made it impossible for Grant to control the entire movements, and he applied himself to keeping the various divisions up to their work, being solicitous chiefly to defend his position at Pittsburg Landing during the day; for on the morrow Buell would arrive. But the Federals were being worsted, and numbers of them had given up the fight and were struggling for places of safety along the river bank. At two in the afternoon Sherman and McClernand, on the right, were being slowly forced back, until they had lost a mile; Prentiss and Wallace, hastily intrenched on a low hill, were holding the key of the Federal battle, and the day depended upon their resistance. Bragg attacked it again and again, and was repulsed with terrible slaughter. This was the "Hornet's Nest" which sent forth so many fatal stings to its assailants. Further on the left was the brigade of Hurlbut, intrenched on a similar hill, and making a like defense. General Johnston, seeing that his men were faltering, rode along the line and told them that he would lead them. He did lead them up the hill and over the first line, when he was struck in the leg by a ball, but maintained his seat for a time, not to dishearten his men. An artery had been severed, however, and he soon bled to death. It was an untoward moment for him to die, the best man in the Confederate armies; had he lived out that day, he might have defeated Grant and saved the Confederacy. His troops were put under the command of Beauregard, and for a while were kept in ignorance of their loss. Bragg now attacked Prentiss's and Wallace's position in the flank, and carried it, Prentiss being surrounded and captured and Wallace mortally wounded; but they had resisted for four hours, and, as it turned out, that was enough. Yet the battle was now practically won for the Confederates; for the Federals were shut in by their line on one side, and by the Tennessee and Snake Creek on the others. Bragg was about to head the final charge.

But an aid of Beauregard's rode to his side and delivered an order stopping the pursuit, lest the men be exposed to the gunboat fire: the "victory was sufficiently complete." The same order had been given to Polk, and he was drawing back. "Is a victory ever sufficiently complete!" exclaimed Bragg. But he obeyed, and the firing ceased. It was near evening, and the armies lay down where they were. Before daylight Nelson's, McCook's and Cullenden's divisions of Buell's army had arrived; and also Lew Wallace's force of seven thousand men. The latter had been on the march since the previous day, but had taken a road which would have brought him to the rear of the Confederate's attack, and might have changed the fortune of the day; but Grant, who had been looking for him by the river road, and was uneasy at his non-appearance, had sent messengers who found him and caused him to countermarch. The things that might have been and were not, in war, are past reckoning. Wallace and his seven thousand were welcome on any terms.

With twenty-five thousand fresh troops, it was Grant who attacked the next morning. The Confederates were no longer in the conquering humor of the day before; the death of Johnston was known, and the re-enforcement of the Federals; and they felt that Beauregard's incomprehensible blunder had taken victory out of their very teeth. They fought, but with the assurance that they would be defeated; and that assurance, in battle, is seldom mistaken. They gave back, point after point, like a reluctant tide; until toward evening Beauregard admitted his defeat.

and turned for Corinth. The night march along the narrow and difficult road, beaten upon by a rain which changed into a cutting hail, was terrible; there was little provision for the wounded, and three hunderd men died of exhaustion by the way. They had lost altogether nearly eleven thousand, and had inflicted a still greater loss on their enemy. But few defeats are so hard to bear as that which should have been a victory.

The battle had been a strange, anomalous, perplexed affair, full of heroic courage, of mistakes, of accidents; fought by troops as yet little accustomed to war, and showing the lack of military experience. But in such a school, lessons are quickly learned, and the soldiers who survived those two tremendous days might well claim the title of veterans. War had few horrors that could find them unprepared.

The capture of Roanoke Island, in Pamlico Sound, where the Confederates had fortified themselves after being driven from Hatteras Inlet, had been accomplished by General Burnside in January; and he followed it up by taking Beaufort and Fort Macon at the Southern extremity of the Sound. The Federals were greatly superior in numbers to their enemy in these encounters, and met with few difficulties and small losses. The true center of interest was still in the west. Polk, after being forced from his strong position at Columbus by the fall of Donelson, had betaken himself to the tenth island below Cairo in the Mississippi, placed at the bend of a sharp horseshoe curve, and easily fortified. The little town of New Madrid, further down the stream, but, owing to the upward bend of the river after passing Island No. 10, further north also, was likewise occupied. Pope soon captured the latter place, but Island No. 10 detained him several weeks, and he finally caused its evacuation by digging a canal twelve miles long across the neck of land made by the bend of the horseshoe, which gave him control of the lower river without running the gantlet of the Confederate batteries on the Island. Foote's gunboats had bombarded these works in vain for three weeks; but the garrison now prepared to escape, and ran right into the arms of a Federal force which Pope had placed along their route. Seven thousand prisoners, with guns and other material, were the reward of this operation; and Foote, descending the river, met and defeated a Confederate fleet above Fort Pillow, and that stronghold was abandoned. Still pushing southward, the Union gunboats engaged a second fleet off Memphis and destroyed it, compelling the surrender of the town. This action was on the 5th of June. It had been rendered possible by the battle of Shiloh, which broke the Confederate power in that region. The Union line now extended from Memphis, through Corinth, nearly to Chattanooga, and was confronted by the Confederates at Holly Springs, Iuka and Chattanooga, commanded by Van Dorn, Price and Bragg respectively. While the Federals were considering whether to make an attack or to await one, Bragg suddenly passed by their left flank and set off northward. Buell, fearing that his purpose might be to get in his rear, fell back on Nashville, where an intercepted dispatch indicated that Louisville, three hundred miles away, was Bragg's destination. There was no one there to oppose him, and unless Buell could outmarch him, Nashville was lost, and other valuable things also. At Frankfort, Bragg was joined by Kirby Smith from Knoxville, and his advance was continued, Buell racing him on a line constantly approaching his own. The two armies would have arrived simultaneously, had not a burned bridge at Bardstown delayed Bragg, which gave Buell the advantage by a day. He was re-enforced at this point till he mustered a hundred thousand men, quite enough to crush Bragg; but the Union general had taken a leaf from McClellan's book, and tarried to organize, while Bragg worked his will to the south of him. By the time Buell was ready to attack,

Brag was on his way back, with a baggage train forty miles long full of plunder. The battle of Perryville, fought on October 8th, was sharply debated, the success at first being with the Confederates, and half of the Union army not being engaged at all. At the end of the day, owing in large measure to Sheridan's efficiency and courage, there was little advantage on either side, the Federals having lost about four thousand, and the Confederates rather less. But Bragg perceived that he could not hope to win against Buell's numbers, green though most of the troops were; and during the night he slipped away. He had tried to dragoon Kentucky into the Confederacy; but though their hearts might be willing, their property kept them back, and they would not respond to his summons. But the supplies he took back with him were of great use to the meagerly furnished Southern army. Retreating by way of Cumberland Gap, he was not pursued by Buell, who retired to Nashville, and was superseded by Rosecranz; for to the minds of the government at Washington, an ounce of energy and dash, at this juncture, was worth a pound of caution.

After the minor engagements with Van Dorn and Price, Rosecranz moved south to intercept Bragg, who was bound on another foraging tour. Both generals had in the neighborhood of fifty thousand troops. On the night of December 30th they lay within striking distance, the lines running north and south, the country level fields with clumps of cedar, and the stream of Stone River flowing parallel with the army lines. Knowing that Crittenden's division faced the weakest point of the Confederate line, while McCook confronted the strongest, Rosecranz decided to pivot on the latter, and wheel Crittenden forward, driving the enemy before him. Bragg, on the other hand, had arranged to beat back McCook, and pivoting on Breckinridge, sweep the Federals to the northward. Had both attacks been made simultaneously, the two armies would have revolved round a central point; but the Confederates were the first to move,

FARRAGUT'S FLEET ENGAGING THE BATTERIES AT PORT HUDSON, MARCH, 1863
Copyright, 1896, by L. Prang & Co.

THE NEW YORK
PUBLIC LIBRARY

ASTOR, LENOX AND
TILDEN FOUNDATIONS.

and the Union right was outflanked and fell back. The struggle was desperate, and there was hand to hand fighting with the bayonet. But in less than an hour the Confederates had won the ground at this point, and McCook's division was cut to pieces. Three miles away, meanwhile, Rosecranz was directing Crittenden, not knowing what had befallen. The information he presently received did not convince him of the full extent of the reverse, and he sent insufficient reenforcements, and orders for McCook to hold his ground. But even Sheridan was now in full retreat. Rousseau, with his reserve, stayed the backward movement for a time, and then Rosecranz rode up, through the thick of the fire. He formed his new line at right angles to the first one, answering to the wheel of the Confederates. His best men and best generals were there, and his own example was an inspiration. Against this line the Confederates dashed themselves all day in vain. At nightfall, Rosecranz held his position, and the two armies rested for the night. Bragg had expected the Federals to retreat under cover of darkness, but finding them standing fast in the morning, he resolved to attack. Breckinridge was sent to take an enfilading Union force on a hill and drive them on to the river; the hill was taken after a bloody fight, but in pursuing them to the river the Confederates ran into a trap, and were cut to pieces by ambushed infantry, and a battery of artillery under Crittenden. Bragg did not renew his attack, but prepared to fly; and before midnight he was gone, leaving twenty-five hundred wounded in Murfreesboro'. In no battle of the war had there been fiercer fighting than in this; and it was Rosecranz's invincible determination not to be beaten that saved it. "Bragg is a good dog," he had remarked, with a touch of grim humor, during the engagement, "but Holdfast is a better." Van Dorn, earlier in the year, had been finally defeated by Curtis in a desperate battle at Pea Ridge in northwestern Arkansas; and the tug of war was transferred to other regions.

The northern part of the Mississippi had been cleared, but the part below Vicksburg and including it was still in Confederate hands; and when Stanton, in conversation with Butler at Washington, had suddenly exclaimed, "Why can't New Orleans be taken?"—the Massachusetts lawyer-general had sententiously replied, "It can." In the spring a fleet of forty-seven vessels under Captain Farragut, carrying several thousand troops commanded by Butler, appeared off Forts Jackson and St. Philip, defending the river approach, and began to bombard them. Green boughs covered them, so as to render them indistinguishable from the wooded banks where they lay. The firing continued for six days, breaking distant windows by the concussion, and stunning fish in the water, but not seriously injuring the forts. Farragut became impatient, and taking counsel of his daring, resolved to run the batteries. He protected his boats with chain cables and sand bags, cut the cable which had been stretched across the river above, and began the ascent, delivering and receiving a tremendous fire. Having passed the batteries, he had next to dispose of the fleet of thirteen ships which was in wait for him; he destroyed all but one, and kept on. On rounding the bend where New Orleans came in sight, the cotton bales along the levees were set on fire, with the shipping, and the smoke and flame roared up and down the water front for a distance of five miles, while drifting fire-rafts set his own vessels ablaze. Butler, attacking the forts in their rear, forced their surrender and occupied New Orleans, while Farragut continued up stream to Baton Rouge and Natchez, and still pushing upward, passed the batteries of Vicksburg, and joined the fleet above. Butler was made military governor of New Orleans, and his administration of it was one of the picturesque features of the war. The inhabitants did not love him; but he was an able and successful administrator.

On the 8th of March of this eventful year a naval battle took place in Hampton Roads which put an end to all the

FARRAGUT'S FLEET ENGAGING THE ENEMY NEAR NEW ORLEANS, APRIL 26, 1864

THE NEW YORK
PUBLIC LIBRARY

ASTOR, LENOX AND
TILDEN FOUNDATIONS.

navies of the past, and laid the basis of those of the future. The experiment of protecting ships with railroad iron and cables had already been tried several times during the war, with good results, such armor being generally applied for the occasion only; but the Confederates were the first to construct an armored defense for a vessel upon anything like scientific principles. When the Norfolk Navy Yard had been abandoned, the steam frigate "Merrimac" had been scuttled and sunk; but later, Norfolk again coming into their possession, they raised her, and covered her with a superstructure of iron plates, strong enough to resist ordinary cannon-shot, and sloping like the roof of a house. An iron beak was added in front, to enable her if necessary to ram an enemy. The whole was covered with grease, so that missiles might more readily slip aside from her metal scales. This ugly and formidable contrivance was brought into the Roads on Saturday morning, and after demanding the surrender of the United States sloop-of-war "Cumberland," Captain Morris, and meeting with refusal, she opened fire. Her broadside crashed through the "Cumberland" at close range, but the answering fire of the "Cumberland" rebounded from her armament like "hail from a roof of slate," as Longfellow describes it in his famous poem. The "Merrimac," not to be detained longer, rammed her antagonist, and the "Cumberland" sank, with a final broadside as she went under, and her flag still flying from the mast-head.

The United States frigate "Congress" was the next victim of this monster; her captain ran her ashore, but the "Merrimac" swung across her stern and sent shot into her till she surrendered, unable, like the "Cumberland," to make any impression on that iron hide. The "Minnesota," another steam frigate, dropped down to help her consort, but ran aground, and was exposed till sunset to the attacks of the gunboats which had accompanied the "Merrimac," and to an occasional shot from the latter. At the approach of night the Confederate champion steamed back to Norfolk, intending to resume her meal the next morning. The battle had been watched by a crowd from on shore; the day had been clear, and the features of the affair could be plainly seen; but a strong current of air setting along the coast prevented any sound being heard from the heavy guns; though in the other direction they were audible for over fifty miles.

The prospect for the North, at the end of this day, was dark. An engine of war which could visit any part of the coast and bombard any town with absolute impunity to itself was a new thing in war, and might alter the entire aspect thereof. But a man of genius had been at work in the North for several months past, and the result of his labors appeared in the very nick of time. The "Monitor" had been launched at New York, and had been making a troublous voyage thence to Hampton Roads ever since; she was commanded by Lieutenant Worden, one of those brave men whose bravery is not overcome by unprecedented conditions. The vessel, to all appearance, was a flat raft of steel, rising but a few inches above water; her decks projected over the lines of her hull like a sort of horizontal eaves, and were heavily plated with metal. In the center of her deck uprose a round turret, like a pill-box, which revolved by steam-power, and carried two eleven-inch guns, which could thus be directed toward any point of the compass. The vessel was small, and as the men had to live below the water-line, in their iron box, their discomfort, especially in a sea-way, was intense. But the "Monitor" was not designed to fight on the high seas, but for the defense of harbors; nor was she built for a pleasure-yacht, but for solid fighting. She was, at that time, the only machine in the world capable of resisting the "Merrimac." She was built by John Ericsson, a Swede, who had lived in England from his twenty-third to his thirty-sixth year, and in America since then; he had already gained distinction by applying the principle of the screw to steam navigation, and by the invention of the caloric engine; and he afterward invented the solar engine and the torpedo-boat destroyer. But for his timely aid, the Civil War might have had another termination. Worden was happily selected to command the new creation in action.

The "Monitor" took her station near the stranded "Minnesota"; and when, on the beautiful Sunday morning of March 9th, the "Merrimac" steamed back to her work, this little thing came forth to meet her. She did not look formidable, with only two guns and no visible hull; but it soon appeared that her two guns were as good as twenty, and her sunken hull made it impossible to hit her effectively. The turret was a difficult object to strike, and as it was plated with eight inches of iron, the balls of the "Merrimac" produced no impression on it when they struck. She was much quicker in maneuvering than was her unwieldy foe; and though in point of size and seeming power the Confederate vessel was beyond comparison superior, in actual effect the "Monitor" was the more formidable of the two. Her heavy balls pounded the "Merrimac" until the latter found even her armament insufficient; she prevented her from attacking the "Minnesota"; and the attempts of the "Merrimac" to ram her were wholly ineffective, for the great iron beak slid harmlessly over her steel deck. At length, therefore, the defeated monster turned tail and steamed away, sending back a parting shot which struck the pilot house or conning-tower in which Worden was directing his fight, and rendered him insensible and partly blinded him; this being the only casualty on board. The battle was never renewed. The "Merrimac" was afterward blown up in Norfolk harbor; and the "Monitor" foundered in a heavy sea off Cape Hatteras, while on her way to Beaufort. Sixty vessels of her type were built during the war; and the modern armored battleship comprises some of her essential features, with modifications which experience suggested.

While the contest for the possession of the Mississippi and the western states had been going on with the advantage on the Union side, there was in progress a stubborn struggle in Virginia, in which the Federals aimed at Richmond, and the Confederates, while defending their capital, occasionally menaced Washington. Indeed, Washington was a much more vulnerable point for the North than was Richmond for the South; the capture of the former would have opened the way for an invasion of the North; whereas the South could best be attacked along the Mississippi. Having in view the relative strength and resources of the South and North, it might have proved better strategy for the former to abandon any attempt to push operations in the latter's territory, and confine her whole strength to repelling the fatal blows which Grant and the generals with him were delivering at her vitals. But the fact remains that the best leaders of the South, and her finest armies, were concentrated in Virginia during the entire war; and it was there that her chief successes were gained. These successes however did her no good, save in so far as they occasioned the slaughter of tens of thousands of Union soldiers. But they also cost the lives of an almost equal number of Southern men; and the South could repair such losses far less easily than could her antagonist. The battles fought by the Confederacy in Virginia were brilliant, and the strategy shown by her generals was consummate, and superior in most cases to that of the Northern leaders. But while Stonewall Jackson, Robert E. Lee, and the rest, were victorious in this or that particular battle, the very life was gradually being hammered out of the South; her money and her men were being exhausted. She was like a skillful boxer who is slowly worn down by the mere exertion of fighting a gladiator of inferior activity and skill, but of indomitable strength and endurance. The advantage on "points" was hers; but she must finally succumb nevertheless.

Richmond might be approached in two ways; by marching overland directly south from Washington; or by sending troops by water to the Peninsula between the York and James Rivers, and forcing the way up the Peninsula in a northwesterly direction; the latter being the shorter and apparently the easier route of the two. It was this route which McClellan chose; but it left the other route to be protected against Confederate attack, and it involved (as McClellan found to his cost) many difficulties of its own. Lee and Jackson outgeneraled the Union leaders again and again, and Lincoln tried one after another with the same result of failure. It was not until Grant had captured Vicksburg and assumed the commandership in chief of all the Union armies, that the tide turned. Grant himself came to Virginia, and there, in a series of mighty battles, fought Lee to a standstill. With Lee's surrender, the war was practically at an end. But it was not until the South had shown that, with men and money in sufficient quantity, she would have been unconquerable.

The army of the Potomac was moved down the river from Washington on transports and landed at Fortress Monroe on the 4th of April, 1862, to the number of about one hundred thousand. Yorktown was their first objective point, on the southern bank of York River; it was occupied by Magruder with twelve thousand men, five thousand of whom were thrown out as an external defense; and such was the ability with which a line over twelve miles long was defended, that McClellan was kept at bay a month. He sent to Washington for heavy siege guns, but before he could open fire with them, Magruder, having accomplished his purpose, withdrew upon Richmond. It was at this time that Norfolk was abandoned, and the "Merrimac" blown up. General Joseph E. Johnston was at that epoch in command of the Confederate armies in Virginia, and, in order to guard his baggage train, he had left a strong force at Williamsburg, about the center of the Peninsula, which became engaged with the Federal advance. General Joseph Hooker, to whom the nickname of "Fighting Joe" was applied, led the Union forces, and a savage battle took place which lasted nine hours. McClellan was still behind at Yorktown, not suspecting that an engagement would occur. There was no connected handling of the Union soldiers, but they fought as they thought best. Hooker distributed his skirmishers among the trees and kept up a fire which temporarily silenced Fort Magruder; he was charged, but held his ground. While he was fighting, another body of Union soldiers under Smith was standing idle not far off, thirty thousand strong; and it was not till evening that they became engaged on their own account. Hooker, however, was not to be entirely abandoned; for General Kearney came up from below, at the sound of firing, and was just in time to support Hooker as he was beginning to fall back. Kearney charged with the bayonet and drove the enemy back; but night came on before the advantage could be followed up. At the same time Hancock, then a young officer, found and occupied some deserted redoubts on the right, and had a sharp brush with the enemy; McClellan arrived as the fighting ceased, ordered the positions to be held, and prepared for an attack the next day; but by the time he was ready, it was found that the enemy had escaped. McClellan did not pursue, but rested in Williamsburg. When he finally resumed his march, he found no obstructions but muddy roads, and kept on until Richmond was but eight miles distant. It seemed ready to fall into his hands; but there were years of time and hundreds of thousands of lives between him and his quarry.

Nevertheless, Richmond was in a panic, and every one, from Jefferson Davis down, feared their time was come; for they did not yet know McClellan. In spite of urgings from Washington, he would not move without re-enforcements; and these could not be sent, because Stonewall Jackson was threatening a descent on Washington the moment Macdowell should stir. "Either attack, or give up the job," Lincoln telegraphed; but McClellan would do neither. Meanwhile rains had so swollen the little rivers amid which his army lay that it was divided into two parts. Johnston was quick to appreciate this weakness, and sallied forth with thirty thousand against Casey with eighteen. The charge was overwhelming, and the Federals slowly withdrew, though Kearney delayed the retreat for a while. But after fighting from noon till five o'clock, with constant losses and reverses, the day was saved at the last moment by General Sumner, who came across a log bridge over the Chickahominy with a battery of guns. The Confederate general Johnston was wounded by a shell at the head of a charging column, and his followers fled. All the night the rain poured down, as it pours nowhere but on the Peninsula, and the Virginia mud was knee-deep. In the morning the Federals renewed the battle and drove the Confederates before them; thus winning the battle of Fair Oaks after it had been lost. Such changes of fortune were not uncommon in the war.

For a whole month after this fight—when he might have marched into Richmond without resistance—McClellan lay supine in the mud, planning, but doing nothing. The interval was improved by the Confederates to raise a large army and devise a plan of campaign. The result was to bewilder McClellan and create a panic in Washington to offset that which had lately been felt in Richmond.

Stuart made a cavalry raid in McClellan's rear, between him and Washington, destroying supplies and threatening his communications by rail. Macdowell, with thirty thousand men, who was marching to join McClellan, was also hindered by this move. To further delay their junction, Johnston ordered Jackson to threaten Washington by way of the Shenandoah Valley. Jackson, re-enforced by Ewell, chased Banks across the Potomac. With his fifteen thousand men he paralyzed sixty thousand and created a commotion that was unprecedented; never did the North so fear actual invasion as at that juncture. The union of Macdowell and McClellan was prevented, and Richmond saved for the time being. McClellan conceived the idea of changing his base from the York to the James River, thus obviating the peril to which Jackson's operations had exposed him. The same day that he had fixed upon to make this move, Lee, who had taken charge of the active campaign, attacked the Federal right at Mechanicsville. He was repulsed, but the Federals fell back to Gaines Mill, and held the bridge across the Chickahominy till night. By this time Lee had fathomed McClellan's purpose, and attempted to take advantage of it. Magruder went round by a road that cut his line of retreat, and struck him in the rear. But the Federals showed the benefit of their long drilling, and held their own steadily till night, when the retreat was resumed. As the columns passed Frayser's Farm they were once more assailed by Hill and Longstreet, but without effect. At length they assembled on Malvern Hill, and here was fought the last of the "Seven-Days' battles," on the 1st of July.

Malvern Hill is a high plateau, with the James River to the south of it; it is of oblong shape, about a mile and a half in length, and has in front a concave form, with terraces rising one above another; the summit is bare of timber. It slopes down from its height of less than a hunderd feet to low meadows and wooded marshes, with streams traversing them; a road ascended it on the north. Weary with their six days' tramp through woods and swamps, with the enemy ever hanging fiercely on flank and rear, hither came the troops of McClellan's Grand Army of the Potomac. They planted sixty cannon on the slopes, and behind them were ten thousand rifles. It was a position nearly impregnable; but Lee, believing that he had McClellan on the run, made one of his few tactical mistakes, and determined to force him to surrender. He did not reflect that a retreat conducted with such order and steadiness showed that the morale of the army was not broken, and that the men would fight when they were allowed to do so.

McClellan was not present on Malvern Hill; he was ensconced in one of the gunboats on the river; but Fitz John

Porter commanded the troops. He had not imagined that Lee would venture to storm the hill, but from its summit he saw the regiments forming and deploying. Here were the Union troops to take revenge for all that they had suffered since the movement began.

The conditions of the battle were of elemental simplicity. The Confederates had to advance across half a mile of swampy meadows, and ascend the hill. From the moment they came in sight, they would be exposed to a withering fire, which would more and more converge upon them as they drew near; until, if they ever gained the slope, it was almost impossible that any man would live to mount it. That it could be captured, so long as the fire continued, was an impossibility. Officers and men knew that they were being sent to certain death; but Lee and Jackson scrupled not to send them. "My men will be annihilated: nothing in the world can live there," said a colonel who received from Jackson the order to advance. "I take care of my wounded and bury my dead," was Jackson's reply—the least manly utterance of his ever reported. Charge after charge was hurled back without effort; the Confederates never got near enough to cause a moment's anxiety. They fell by thousands. At dark only they gave up the effort, utterly beaten and disheartened.

Nothing now intervened between McClellan and Richmond but the shattered remnants of a defeated, exhausted and demoralized army. Lee had brought his whole strength into this contest, and had none left now that it was over. He was helpless, and he and all with him knew it. All through that July day, in swampy ground, making terrific exertions, his men had fought and died; and for more than a week previous they had struggled through sweltering woods, in dust, in water, breathlessly pursuing a constantly disappearing foe. The Confederacy, in that hour, was on its knees; McClellan had but to advance, and in two days he could dictate terms of peace from Richmond.

"To have left our position would have endangered our communications, and have removed us from the protection of our gunboats," said the Little Napoleon; and he issued orders to retreat. The whole army protested. Phil Kearney expressed the general sentiment when he said, "I, Philip Kearney, an old soldier, enter my solemn protest against this retreat. In full view of the responsibilities of such a declaration, I say to you that such an order can be prompted only by cowardice—or treason!" History is unable to reverse his verdict. The Peninsular campaign ended there, and with it the reputation of McClellan. The problem of this man's character and conduct has never been solved. No officer in either army was more accomplished in the science of war; he had not his equal as a disciplinarian; he seemed to have high ambition, and self-possession. His six days' retreat has been pronounced the finest work of its kind ever done. But there was some strange deficiency in him. It is hardly conceivable that he was a coward; none who have known him can think so. It is extravagant to suppose that he was a traitor; such treason as that would imply, would be unique. But his excuses for inaction all through the Peninsular campaign were preposterous; and this final one was an insult to human intelligence. The passionate words of Phil Kearney remain in the memory, and it is to be feared that they may sum up the verdict of posterity on McClellan.

Copyright, 1896, by L. Prang & Co.
ENGAGEMENT OF THE "MONITOR" AND "MERRIMAC," MARCH 9, 1862

CHAPTER THIRTY-FIFTH

THROUGH THE VALLEY OF DEATH

WHAT remains of the story of the war will be told briefly. The description of battles is not the History of the United States. The annals of courage in the field are fascinating, and yet there is a certain monotony in them. The conditions vary, there are changing combinations, the character of generals is revealed, and traits of individual prowess are developed; but after all, the sum is that men fight, and face death, they die, they are defeated, they are victorious. Allowing for the difference of weapons, the battles of the Greeks and Persians, of the Romans and Carthaginians, of the Saxons and Normans, contain features which constantly remind us of the fights of to-day. It makes little essential difference that the range of the rifle is some miles, while that of the broadsword is the length of the arm. Men are killed in both cases.

The most deadly fighting, and many of the most striking achievements and episodes of the war, were still to come. Great reputations were to fall, and others yet greater were to be made and confirmed. Owing chiefly to the genius and marvelous vigilance of two men—Lee and Jackson—the South was to enjoy a period of apparent success; for a short time they were to carry the war into their enemy's country; but the success was technical and illusory, and the inevitable reverse was the more bitter. So many hundred thousand men must perish, and then must come the end. A civil war is not like other wars; the armies are fighting in their own country, and yield at last, not because they have lost one battle or another, but because the country is exhausted.

After the fight at Malvern Hill, McClellan remained where he was, feeding his army from ample stores, and leaving the Confederates to recuperate their strength and collect other men to supply the place of the 20,000 they had lost in those seven days. The only way to conquer such an army as Lee's was to keep pounding at it without a moment's cessation, as Grant afterward did. But McClellan, under one pretext or another, allowed his foe every chance to recover, and to forestall him; whenever, by accident or design, he had him at advantage, he turned away, and permitted him to rise again. At the present juncture, his army greatly outnumbered any that Lee could muster; but he waited until Lee was ready to march on Washington, as if the matter were no concern of his. The depression throughout the North was great; and the South, despite its terrible losses, was correspondingly elated.

Lincoln brought together the commands of McDowell, Banks and Fremont, which had been unsuccessfully opposing Jackson in the Shenandoah, and called Pope from the west to command them. Fremont resigned from jealousy, thus giving the measure and quality of his patriotism. Pope assumed control with a want of tact that set one's teeth on edge. "We have always seen our enemies' backs in the West: I come from an army which sought its enemy and beat him when found; whose policy has been not defense but attack." This was not the way to win the affection of his new soldiers. It made him enemies among his fellow officers; and there seems to be little doubt that McClellan deliberately denied him re-enforcements which he was in honor bound to supply, in order that he might be defeated and unseated from his command. That thousands of brave soldiers should die in order to gratify McClellan's spleen, seems not to have disturbed the latter.

"Let Pope get himself out of his scrape," he wrote to Lincoln. One marvels that Lincoln should have trusted him yet again after such a revelation.

Pope's force was now called the Army of Virginia, to distinguish it from the Army of the Potomac. McClellan being deposed from the chief command, Lincoln appointed Halleck, who had been in control over the Mississippi department, to succeed him. He could hardly have made a worse selection; Halleck had uniformly exerted his authority to spoil the plans of better men. He now ordered the Peninsula abandoned, counting all the money and lives spent in it as worse than wasted. The army must attack Richmond from the north. McClellan wished to cross James River and invest Richmond on the south, thereby stopping Lee's re-enforcements, and the supplies of the city. This was the plan which Grant carried out two years afterward. But Halleck had Jackson on his nerves, and the Army of the Potomac accordingly made ready to embark in the great fleet of transports waiting at Fortress Monroe.

Lee was only waiting to know whether it was to the re-enforcement of Pope or to McClellan that the army was to be assigned; for his plan was to strike either before the re-enforcements could reach them. From John Mosby, who had been a prisoner in the Federal lines, and who was afterward famous as a cavalry ranger, he learned that Pope was the man to whom the advance on Richmond with the consolidated army was to be intrusted. He at once made ready to throw his whole army into Gordonsville, where Jackson was already confronting Pope. The railroad south to Richmond and Charlottesville starts hence. He advised Jackson in advance. Cedar Mountain is in the vicinity, with a deep ravine on its northern side. Jackson stationed himself on this hill, overlooking Banks' camp below. Banks had sent to Sigel for re-enforcements, but Sigel had sent to ask the way, and before an answer could be returned, the battle had been fought and lost. Banks had 7,500 troops, Jackson thrice as many. The latter's force was concealed by the woods; he slowly advanced under cover of artillery, to which Banks vigorously replied. Banks, ignorant of Jackson's strength, at last resolved to attack him; and such was the courage of his soldiers, that the attempt came near resulting in a victory. Crawford outflanked them on the left, and rolled their wing back on the center in confusion. Meanwhile the Union center and left struck the enemy heavily, and were also successful. Early alone withstood them; but unless he was speedily supported, the battle was lost.

Jackson came to the rescue. At first, he too was forced back; but when he rode to the front and led the men himself, they recovered, and drove the Federals in their turn. But the latter made so strong a stand at the ravine that Jackson paused, and night put an end to the battle. Jackson thought he must have Pope's whole army before him, and he retreated to the Rapidan. The Federals had lost nearly half of their whole number; but they had fought the most brilliant battle against odds of the war thus far. Jackson, hampered by the very position which had seemed to give him the advantage, had been able to bring but a part of his huge force into action. The Federals suffered a technical defeat in being driven from the field which they had won; but such defeats are as good as most victories.

But the Confederates were soon to win more useful successes. A raid to the rear of the Federals by Stuart resulted in the capture of Pope's official papers, and very nearly of the general himself; and the papers showed the precise situation and plans of the Union army. Lee, in order to make the crossing of the Rappahannock possible for his army, sent Jackson by a detour to the Federal rear. Jackson set off with thirty-five regiments down the Shenandoah Valley; but Pope, though informed of this, did not imagine that he was going to perform the reckless maneuver which had been planned. Bearing to the right, Jackson kept rapidly on, reached the village of Salem, passed through Thoroughfare Gap, where Pope might easily have stopped his whole army with a few regiments, and descended on Manassas Junction, where were the stores for sixty thousand men. For an hour or so Jackson allowed his hungry, thirsty and ragged soldiers to help themselves to what they wanted, except to the whisky, which was poured on the ground. Then the march was resumed, and the remainder of the stores burned.

But Jackson was in a most perilous position, and Pope was soon awake to the facts. He made every preparation except the one that he should have made—he did not send a force to hold Thoroughfare Gap against Longstreet, who was following in Jackson's footsteps. Longstreet marched through without check; meanwhile Jackson chose the field of Bull Run, on which he had won his nickname, as the best adapted for the coming conflict. A part of Pope's command came in contact with a vastly superior force of the enemy concealed in Groveton Woods, and fought them till dark, killing General Ewell. At night the Federals continued their march in search of the very enemy with the bulk of which they had been contending. Jackson was waiting for Longstreet, and getting into the best position for the fray. A more absurd situation than that of Pope could not be imagined. He was by this time in force; but so wooded and uneven was the country that he could not lay his hands on his enemy, who was close at hand. And he knew that unless he could find him before he was re-enforced, the victory would be at least doubtful. He did find him at last, and the battle that was fought was one of the most desperate of the war.

Jackson had the embankment of an unfinished railroad in front of him. General Grover's division, on the Federal right, charged this, sustained a terrible fire, came into hand to hand conflict with the enemy, giving and taking the bayonet, drove them back, received the fire of the second line, drove that also back, and would have shattered the army had they been supported; but fresh troops came down upon them, and they in turn retreated. Kearney meanwhile was engaged at the other end of the line. He made charge upon charge, and forced back the enemy, which was reenforced, and held its ground. Again he charged, with the aid of Hatch; but now part of Longstreet's men, who had arrived, came to the support of the Confederates, and the Federals must retire. This ended the fighting for the day. Pope fancied he had won, and so telegraphed to Washington. He was, in fact, already defeated; and the losses on both sides were seven thousand men. The next morning Jackson's and Longstreet's forces were united like the two sides of a triangle; Pope, with blind confidence, attacked Jackson. He imagined that warrior was retreating. The charges of yesterday were repeated with even more determination. In one place the antagonists fought within ten yards of each other for an hour, and when they had exhausted their ammunition, continued the fight with stones. But when the whole Federal force was concentrating its attention on Jackson, who was getting beaten and calling for help, Longstreet opened on the flank with his batteries. Three times he shattered the Federal ranks, and thrice they re-formed under fire; but then comes Longstreet's infantry charge, and a whole fresh army throws itself against the exhausted battalions. Pope was all but surrounded. He threw a regiment of regulars on the hill where stood the Henry House; and the Confederates could not dislodge them. Night had fallen, with drizzly rain. Under cover of the regulars the rest of the army retreated in good order, having lost fourteen thousand men; the Confederates, ten thousand. The second battle of Bull Run, as it is sometimes called, had been as different as possible in its character from the first; but the result in both cases had been the same. Greater courage could not be shown than that which marked the men in the ranks on both sides; there were no green troops, no panics, here. But Pope lost, partly because he was no match for his great antagonists—Lee had come with Longstreet, and helped direct the battle—and partly through the accidents of war. He afterward tried to lay the blame of his defeat on Fitz John Porter, who was to have attacked on his left, but who confined himself to maneuvering. Porter was convicted by court-martial, but finally cleared himself. He had been ordered to engage unless opposed by Longstreet. Pope had not been aware that Longstreet had arrived; but Porter saw him, and his maneuvering was with a view of keeping him in check so as not to interfere with Pope's attack. In this he had succeeded till the end of the day, when Longstreet attacked from another position.

A few days later General Phil Kearney, during a heavy skirmish at Chantilly on September 1st, rode into a squad of the enemy, mistaking them for his own men, and was shot before he could get away. His body was returned by Jackson with a military escort; for he was one of the most gallant soldiers of the war.

Washington was now in a dangerous position. Lee crossed the Potomac and advanced into Maryland, which he hoped to win over to the Confederacy. McClellan, on the failure of Pope, whom he should have supported, had been tried once more with the supreme command. He reorganized the army and followed Lee. The latter had sent Jackson on a raid to Harper's Ferry, where Colonel Miles with eleven thousand men was stationed. Jackson stormed the heights and forced Miles to surrender; but McClellan had learned of his action, and that Lee's army had been depleted by Jackson's twenty-five thousand men, and he hastened on to strike Lee before Jackson could get back. He overtook his rear at South Mountain, and, after a short engagement, drove it before him and entered the valley beyond. Lee fell back to the other side of Antietam Creek. Had McClellan attacked at once he would have been victorious without difficulty; but he delayed for a day, for no other reason, so far as one can conjecture, than to allow Jackson time to get up. Jackson came, accordingly; but even with him, Lee had but forty thousand men—half the number under McClellan. There was a bridge across the creek; McClellan ordered Burnside, on his left, to cross this bridge and attack the enemy's left, as soon as Hooker's charge on the enemy's right should have been successful. But Hooker's attack on Jackson had the effect of nearly exterminating both parties; they were repeatedly re-enforced, and the slaughter continued with no result. Burnside crossed the bridge at one o'clock, but was repulsed by Hill. The next day McClellan did nothing; and suffered Lee to escape under cover of the following night. The battle was indecisive, with the honors on the Confederate side; but it stopped Lee's invasion, and he was compelled to recross the Potomac. It was not until six weeks after the battle that the army of the Potomac followed Lee; and then McClellan's pursuit was so deliberate that Lincoln and Stanton were finally disillusioned, and gave him his well-deserved dismissal. A sterner sentence would not have been unjust, in such circumstances.

Burnside was chosen to supersede McClellan; but the army he was called upon to command was now one hundred and fifty thousand strong, and he declared himself incompetent for the task. But Lincoln insisted, and he acquiesced. He had none of the faults of McClellan; he was only too brave and rash. He made his plan, and did his best to carry it out; and in the single battle of Fredericksburg he lost twelve thousand men, half of whom fell in the attempt to take a single position, where the Confederates were ensconced behind a solid stone wall four feet in height. Seldom has such a massacre been seen in war.

McClellan had taken his dismissal stoically, and Lee, with a certain humorous appreciation. His saying was, that he regretted the parting with the general, "because we understood each other so well. I fear if they keep on changing generals, I may get one that I don't understand." He proved that he understood Burnside well enough; and when Grant came, he probably understood him also; but Grant could beat him.

Burnside's plan was simply to cross the Rappahannock, with a feint at Gordonsville, and advance on Richmond. Pontoons were sent to take the army across. The Confederates were strongly intrenched on the heights on the south bank of the river. There was difficulty in laying the pontoons, owing to sharpshooters' fire from the houses in Fredericksburg; but volunteers went over in boats and drove the enemy out. The bridge being then completed, the army crossed, and was gathered about the town. Below, General Franklin had gone over with fifty thousand men. The total intrenched force of the Confederates was eighty thousand. It was the 13th of December, and a thick fog lay over the valley.

Jackson commanded the right wing of the enemy, and Hunter was ordered to attack him with his whole force. Instead of doing this, he sent only Meade's corps, which charged up the hill, and broke through the line, but, being unsupported, was forced to give way, and thus the only chance of winning the battle was lost; for had this flank been turned in force, it would have enabled the front and left attack to prevail. But the battle raged furiously on the slopes of Marye's Heights, where the stone wall crowned the hill. Upon the ascent was directed, by the defenders, a converging fire, somewhat like that which had mowed down the Confederates at Malvern Hill. The Union men advanced against it with the same bravery, and were slaughtered in the same way, only in much greater numbers. As then, too, the slaughter was wholly useless: there was no chance of taking the position. French and Hancock's corps were the first to be sent up the hill, and Meagher's Irish brigade distinguished itself where all were heroes. Hooker, against his protestations, was ordered to renew the struggle, and he sent General Humphrey's division to destruction. Seventeen hundred men fell in fifteen minutes. Burnside, obstinate even then, arranged to send in his own corps the next morning; but General Sumner persuaded him against it. At night the Union troops retired across the river, and another attempt on Richmond had disastrously failed. The armies went into winter quarters, and all was quiet on the Potomac.

In September of this year, Lincoln had, as a war measure, issued a proclamation declaring that on and after January 1st, 1863, all slaves in seceded states would be declared forever free. It was a measure which had long been in contemplation, but had been delayed owing to doubt as to its effect. Many thought it would create or confirm a party in the North opposed to the war, and that it would inflame and render implacable the resistance of the South. Lincoln had hesitated long, for the responsibility was his. He had made the first draft of the document in July, but had thought it prudent to wait till a decided Union victory was won; but there had followed a series of reverses. Finally came the battle of Antietam. "I had made a solemn vow to God," said Lincoln, "that if Lee was driven back from Maryland, I would crown the result by the declaration of freedom to the slaves." The Proclamation did not affect slaves in those slave states which had not seceded, such as Missouri and Kentucky. It proved to be as wise a measure as it was a bold one; it led to no murderous slave insurrections, as had been apprehended; and as the Confederates were already doing their best, it added nothing to the force of their resistance. But two hundred thousand negroes enlisted in consequence of it.

Burnside was succeeded by Hooker, to whom Lincoln sent a warning letter of rebuke and advice. But no movements were made till May; and meanwhile, events had been happening in the West. Grant renewed his attack on Vicksburg, his aim being to get his army and gunboats below the town. There was a bend of the river opposite Vicksburg, and the suggestion was made to dig a canal across the neck of the curve, as at Island No. 10, and turn the river into a new channel. Other ways of flanking the great river were proposed, and some of them were attempted; but none of them answered. Finally, Grant resolved to march down the west bank, in spite of the many topographical difficulties, letting the gunboats run the batteries, extending eight miles; which they successfully did about the middle of April. Meanwhile a corduroy road had been made through the swampy land, and the army, meeting the fleet below, was ferried over to Bruinsburg on the eastern shore. Grant now had two hundred miles to march, northward, overcoming whatever resistance he might meet by the way. It took him a little over two weeks to do this, and on the road he fought and won four battles. The first was with the advance guard of Pemberton's army at Port Gibson; then he threw himself between Pemberton and Joe Johnston, who was coming to Pemberton's assistance; defeated Johnston on May 14th, and beat Pemberton in two more battles at Champion Hills and at Black River. Thus he compelled him to take refuge in Vicksburg, where he designed to capture him along with the rest of the garrison.

After the failure of Sherman's Yazoo River expedition to aid Grant in the earlier movement against Vicksburg, he had been superseded by McClernand. But when Grant was given control of the western army, he gave Sherman a corps, and they made the campaign together. On the 18th of May he had a conference with Sherman, in whom he always reposed great confidence, and they arranged their plans for investing Vicksburg.

Johnston had advised Pemberton not to stand a siege in Vicksburg, inasmuch as he would ultimately be forced to surrender; and told him his best plan would be to evacuate while it was still possible, and take his men north. But Pemberton replied that he considered Vicksburg the most important point in the Confederacy, and would hold it at all hazards.

Grant believed that the garrison was demoralized by the beating he had given Pemberton in the field, and could be captured by assault. The bridge had been destroyed, but he built others, and Sherman sent a body of regulars under Colonel Washington to take a battery. The men reached the battery, but Washington was killed, and they retreated. But Johnston was in Grant's rear, and it was necessary to make another effort. On the 22d, accordingly, supported by the fire of gunboats and batteries, another assault in force was delivered, and the flag was planted on the bastion; but it was found impossible to hold the position. All along the line of attack there were the same gallant charges, and the same results. McClernand sent a report saying he was successful, which caused Grant to order another general assault; but the report turned out to have been erroneous, and at the end of the day the repulse was complete. Vicksburg could not be taken by assault. It must be reduced by regular siege.

The siege continued for nearly seven weeks; but Grant's restless energy would not allow of his waiting for starvation to do its work; he laid out elaborate approaches and diagonals; and a continual fusillade of the enemy's ramparts was maintained. The practice of the Union sharpshooters became almost miraculous. No one could put his head above the walls with safety. Mines were dug under the works, and countermines were made by the garrison. In a word, every device which American ingenuity could suggest was employed on both sides. At evening there would sometimes be an informal truce, when the antagonists would chat and jest together, and exchange tobacco for hard-tack. As time went on, starvation began within the walls. Rats were sold in the butcher-shops. Bombs falling continually in the streets caused constant deaths and terror; and the inhabitants burrowed underground for safety. Finally the sol-

MAJ.-GEN. T. J. JACKSON, C.S.A.

THE BATTLE OF ANTIETAM, SEPTEMBER 16 and 17, 1862

THE NEW YORK
PUBLIC LIBRARY

ASTOR, LENOX AND
TILDEN FOUNDATIONS.

Copyright, 1886, by L. Prang & Co.

THE BATTLE OF SHILOH, APRIL 7, 1862

FARRAGUT'S FLEET ENGAGING FORTS JACKSON AND ST. PHILIP, APRIL 24, 1862

THE NEW YORK
PUBLIC LIBRARY

ASTOR, LENOX AND
TILDEN FOUNDATIONS.

THE NEW YORK
PUBLIC LIBRARY

ASTOR, LENOX AND
TILDEN FOUNDATIONS.

ULYSSES S. GRANT

GENERAL W. T. SHERMAN

THE NEW YORK
PUBLIC LIBRARY

ASTOR, LENOX AND
TILDEN FOUNDATIONS.

THE NEW YORK
PUBLIC LIBRARY

ASTOR, LENOX AND
TILDEN FOUNDATIONS.

UNION ATTACK ON FREDRICSBURG, VA., NOVEMBER 12, 1862

BATTLE OF CHATTANOOGA—THE UNION ADVANCE, NOVEMBER 25, 1863

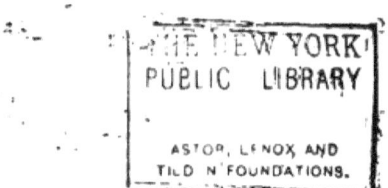

BATTLE OF GETTYSBURG, JULY 1, 2, and 3, 1863

diers told Pemberton that unless they were fed they would mutiny. Pemberton consulted his council as to the chances of cutting their way out, and was told that the condition of the men made it impossible. He then resolved to surrender; and on the 3d of July a white flag appeared above the works. Pemberton and Grant met, and Grant announced that his terms were unconditional surrender; and Pemberton, after a show of resistance, submitted. The surrender was on the 4th of July. It was the most important victory of the war until the battle of Gettysburg; forty-six thousand prisoners went with it, sixty thousand stand of arms, and two hundred and sixty cannon. The total Federal loss was under ten thousand men. When Banks, who was besieging Port Hudson, heard the news, he caused a salute to be fired; and the garrison, upon learning the reason of it, surrendered likewise. The Mississippi was now open, and Grant was recognized as the great soldier of the army.

Rosecranz began in June a series of maneuvers which resulted in driving Bragg into Chattanooga, where he meant to shut him up as Grant had shut up Pemberton; but Bragg was not to be so caught, and got out; Rosecranz pursued him, and his line became so extended that Bragg, being reenforced, turned to strike it. It was rapidly drawn together, and at Chickamauga another great battle was fought.

It lasted two days, the leading feature being the tremendous and sustained attack which Bragg directed against the Union left under Thomas. Rosecranz kept the latter supported, but on the second day, removing a brigade too hastily, Bragg saw the opening and pushed in on the right, breaking up the Union formation, and driving the right and center back on Chattanooga, whence Rosecranz telegraphed his defeat. But Thomas stood like a rock and was not dislodged by the assaults of Bragg's whole army. The attack on him was given up at sunset, and he returned to Chattanooga during the night, bringing five hundred prisoners with him. The Federals intrenched themselves; Rosecranz was superseded by Thomas; and Grant made preparations to relieve him.

The boot now began to get on the other leg. Grant, who had gone down to New Orleans, came up in haste; Hooker was detached from the army on the Potomac, and Sherman forced his way through from the Mississippi. Altogether there were eighty thousand men on the ground, besides the twenty-five thousand with Thomas already inside the Chattanooga line. Davis, utterly misapprehending Bragg's danger, had ordered fifteen thousand of his men sent away to engage Burnside at Knoxville two weeks before.

Chattanooga is surrounded with hills. On the 23d of November Thomas's troops came out as if on review, and charged straight for an elevation called Orchard Knob, facing the Confederate position, captured it after a brief struggle, and occupied the batteries upon it. The Confederates lay in a line twelve miles long between Missionary Ridge and Lookout Mountain, the latter an abrupt height rising two thousand feet. Earthworks ranged along the intervening valley. Grant's strategy assigned to Hooker the task of attacking Lookout Mountain, and to Sherman the Ridge; Bragg would deplete his center to strengthen these points, upon which Grant would direct his main strength upon it. Under cover of the early morning mist of the 23d, Sherman began his attack upon the Ridge, and gained a footing on its northern end. Hooker not only assaulted the mountain, but, warming to his work, performed the almost incredible feat of fighting his way to the dizzy summit, where he unfurled the Stars and Stripes, and his camp fires were seen sparkling in the sky. In this exploit, as in other episodes of the battle, the men in the ranks took matters into their own hands, and outdid the orders and expectations of their commanders. The air of the hills seemed to inspire them, and they achieved things which seemed impossible.

Sherman, after establishing himself on the northern end

BATTLE OF MOBILE BAY—FARRAGUT'S FLEET ENGAGING FORT MORGAN, AUGUST 5, 1864.

Copyright, 1886, by L. Prang & Co.

THE NEW YORK
PUBLIC LIBRARY

ASTOR, LENOX AND
TILDEN FOUNDATIONS.

of the ridge, waited for the morrow to renew his attack. But his progress the next day was unsatisfactory, and it became evident that he would need help. Grant had sent Hooker to threaten Bragg's rear, but a swollen river and a broken bridge embarrassed him, so that the desired diversion was not accomplished. Grant, standing on Orchard Knob, ordered twenty thousand men to take a line of earthworks along the base of the ridge. Not only was the order carried out, but the men kept on up the ridge, at first leading their own officers. The latter, however, speedily leaped to the front; and at the same time Grant, perceiving that at last the time was come, directed that a charge be made along the entire line of battle. No finer spectacle could be imagined; the setting sun flung the shadow of Lookout Mountain far across the plain, but sparkled on the arms of the advancing soldiers; they were met by a fierce fire to which they did not reply, but continued to ascend the rugged steep, each man climbing as best he might, following the standards, which waved beyond; they rolled up the crest like a long wave of the sea, and overtopped it. Down sank the sun, and with it the hopes of the Confederate army; they retreated, and their own guns turned upon them made havoc in their crowding multitudes. The great battle of Chattanooga put eastern Tennessee in the power of the Federals, and removed the defenses of the eastern states, Georgia, Alabama, and the Carolinas. Bragg had lost the confidence of his soldiers, and resigned. Burnside, who had been transferred from the Potomac to the Ohio, had been checked in his southward march by Longstreet's ragged but heroic corps; but now Sherman, set free by the victory at Chattanooga, raised the siege of Knoxville. Sherman's troops had, since the 27th of September, marched five hundred and twenty miles and fought at Chattanooga; they were in training for their historic march through Georgia to the sea.

But before that decisive event, Lee and Jackson were once more to win, against all probabilities, in their conflict with the Army of the Potomac under its new leader, Hooker. Hooker had assumed the command at a time when the spirit of the army seemed broken, and desertions were numerous. He reorganized it, and made it, as he thought, the finest in the world. Possibly it was; but it had not yet got its fitting leader. Hooker's plan was good: he would feint at Fredericksburg with Sedgwick, while he himself, with the bulk of the army, crossed above Chancellorsville and attacked the Confederates' rear. He had one hundred and twenty thousand men, and the withdrawal of two divisions under Longstreet to the James had diminished Lee's strength to about fifty thousand.

Hooker reached his strategical position without mishap, and fancied he had Lee at his mercy. He was in communication with Sedgwick by way of Bank's Ford; and had he advanced it is difficult to see how he could have failed. But at the critical moment he fell back from the open plains into the Wilderness—a thick and tangled jungle, unsuitable for the movements of either cavalry or artillery. Lee had meanwhile turned his army so as to face Hooker, and then, detaching Jackson to make a fifteen-mile detour with twenty thousand men to fall on Hooker's rear, he attacked in front. The first part of Jackson's movement was toward the south, and Sickles, seeing one of the flanking regiments, jumped to the conclusion that the whole Confederate army was in retreat to Richmond; he captured the regiment, but Jackson kept on, swung to the right; passed behind the Federals, and, rushing suddenly through the thickets, surprised them at supper. There was a wild stampede, only checked by Keenan's devoted charge, which allowed Pleasanton time to get his artillery in position. It was while Jackson was rallying his men from the backward movement to which Pleasanton had forced them, that he was hit by his own men, who mistook his reconnoitering party for the enemy. He died a week later; and those last words of his—"Let us cross over the river, and rest under the shade of the trees"—

are peculiarly happy, as showing that amid all the shocks of war, in which he had ever borne a leading part, the heart of the great soldier was at peace. His loss was irreparable to the Southern cause, and was an omen of the end.

Hill, succeeding Jackson, was also wounded, and the command devolved upon the picturesque cavalier, Stuart; Hooker altered his formation during the night; his headquarters were at Chancellorsville, and his two flanks on the river, his line thus forming a sharp curve. Stuart seized Hazel Grove, a small hill opposite the center, and Sickles and Slocum had to meet the whole force of the Confederate attack; five charges were repulsed; but Hooker was stunned by a cannon ball which struck the pillar of the house against which he leaned; Lee effected his junction with Stuart, and the day was lost for Hooker's invincible army.

But while this was going on, Sedgwick had been successful in his attack on Fredericksburg and was marching against Lee from behind. Lee turned like a panther, drove Sedgwick back across the Rappahannock, and was back before Hooker had realized his opportunity. During the night the latter moved his army back to its former position on the Washington side of the Rappahannock; and seventeen thousand men had been lost with no gain to show for it—except the death of Jackson and thirteen thousand men; but these were not due to Hooker's strategy. He had been a mere bewildered monster in Lee's hands, and the losses he had inflicted were due chiefly to his blind kickings and strugglings to escape. Strange was the destiny of the Army of the Potomac; but its hour came at last.

Lee, who had been so brilliant in defense, was now to prove, for the second and last time, what he could do in attack. His advance into Pennsylvania was well planned, but he missed the help of Jackson, who, at Cemetery Ridge, might have turned the fortunes of the invasion by one of his inimitable maneuvers. On the 3d of June Lee marched up the Valley of the Shenandoah toward Chambersburg, the

Union army following in the same direction, but on the other or eastern side of the Blue Ridge. Stuart's cavalry held the passes, and prevented the Federals from knowing what was going on on the western side. Lee's army was the best yet collected by the Confederacy; he lived upon the country as he went forward, but forbore to plunder property. Hooker having resigned, Meade succeeded him. After crossing the Potomac, the two armies began to feel each other; Lee, facing east, was coming from the west of the town of Gettysburg, and Meade was taking his position on Cemetery Ridge, at the south. Lee was not then looking for a general engagement, but wished to distract Meade from threatening his communications. Neither did Meade contemplate a decisive battle; but his cavalry under Buford, put forward to veil his march to Pipe Creek, where he proposed to fight, came in contact with Lee's advance guard on the 1st of July. The valiant General Reynolds was killed here while making a reconnaissance; the Federals were forced back and suffered losses in the town; but night came on, and during the dark hours the armies on both sides came up, and were marshaled by moonlight. There were, on each side, about eighty thousand men.

The real battle began on the afternoon of July 2d. Sickles, too far in advance of the main body, was outflanked and compelled to retire to Cemetery Ridge, where he stood. The range of hills of which Cemetery Ridge is a part has the general form of a hook; the shaft of the hook runs north and south; it bends over toward the east; Cemetery Ridge is at the bend; Culp's Hill at the barb; Little Round Top and Round Top are at the southern end of the shaft. The entire chain is south of Gettysburg town. After forcing back Sickles, Longstreet, who had driven him, was opposed by Warren with Vincent and Weed, and prevented from following up his advantage; and the position of Sickles, though he had retreated, was stronger than at first; while **Ewell of the Confederates,** who had in the meanwhile captured Culp's Hill, was compelled to evacuate it the next morning. The day had gone against the Federals, but they were now for the first time in a favorable position to fight.

At one o'clock on July 3d Lee began, and for two hours maintained, a cannonade of unprecedented fury on Cemetery Ridge. Everything was torn to pieces; the Union guns could not reply effectively, and their fire ceased. At three o'clock eighteen thousand Confederates, in a double line two miles in length, preceded by skirmishers, emerged from the woods and charged. At a distance of four hundred yards the Union artillery got to work upon it; but they only quickened their advance. Now they were within range of the infantry fire; even this they braved, and with Pickett leading them they rushed up the slope. They carried the first Union line, and placed their flag upon it; but behind it was another and a stronger line. From this opened a terrific fire, striking the Confederates full in the face. It was irresistible. Not a tenth, not a quarter, nor a half of the Confederates were cut down; but three-fourths of the attacking columns were destroyed. It was the end of the charge, the end of the battle, and for practical purposes the end of the war. The invasion was over. Lee had lost thirty-six thousand men. Altogether, his two attempts to invade the North had diminished the force of the South by ninety thousand of the best troops in the world. Each had lasted about two weeks. The game might have been worth the candle, but there was not candle enough for the game. A campaign, at that rate, would cost two million men a year. Meade had lost twenty-three thousand men; but they had saved the Union.

Meade allowed Lee to retreat slowly across the Potomac. Two or three months afterward, Lee made a rapid dash across the Rapidan in the hope of getting round Meade's right flank; but Meade eluded him, and Lee too rashly pursuing his retreat, was suddenly attacked by Warren, losing nearly all of Early's command. At the end of November

Meade in turn crossed the river, intending to catch Lee's army in separate parts; but Lee brought it together and fortified it so strongly that Meade gave up his purpose, and the campaign of 1863 was over. 1864 was to be the year of Grant, and the beginning of the end.

There had, however, been one incident of the campaign which deserves mention for more than one reason. A number of monitors had been building since the famous fight in Hampton Roads, and a fleet of them were now placed under the command of Admiral Dupont and taken to the harbor of Charleston. Undue confidence was felt in the ability of the armor to withstand any punishment; but it was presently apparent that it had its limits. Obstructions had been placed in the channel by the Confederates, in such a position that, while the fleet was detained by them, the concentrated fire of three hundred guns could be poured upon them. The aim of the gunners was good, and the vessels were pelted as by a hailstorm of iron; the "Keokuk," struck nearly a hundred times, was sunk, and the rest of the fleet more or less maimed. Three months later, Gillmore renewed the attack by land. Fort Wagner had been erected on the north end of a sandy spit called Morris's Island. It had resisted one assault; but on the night of July 18th a force of several thousand men under General Strong attempted it again. With these troops was the Fifty-fourth regiment, composed of negroes. Shaw was its colonel, and among its officers was young Lieutenant Higginson—the former known to be affiliated with the abolition party, and the more hated by the Southerners. This was perhaps the only battle of the war in which the animosity felt against the Northern forces by the Southern soldiers was inflamed by a sort of personal venom. That they should be called on to fight against their own former slaves, arrayed against them by their white enemies, was regarded as a wanton insult. On the other hand, the North was in great doubt as to whether these negroes, brought up to regard themselves as inferior beings, could be relied on in battle. The result was to prove that a man may be a dauntless soldier, though black, and with a lifetime of slavery behind him. Gallantly led, these men, with the others, crossed the half mile of open sand which was swept by the Confederate fire, and mounted the walls of the fort. The advantage could not be held; Shaw was killed; in a few minutes Lieutenant Higginson found himself the ranking officer of the remnant of the regiment. Twelve hundred Federals were killed or wounded; among the latter a youth named Robley Evans, long afterward famous as "Fighting Bob." The Confederate loss was less than a twelfth that of their assailants. The result was in a measure satisfactory to both sides; the Federals, though utterly defeated, had proved the worth of the negro; the South had wreaked its vengeance on the latter, but was forced to concede his bravery. An ungenerous resentment marred the conduct of the victors; in burying the negroes, they flung into the same common pit the body of their gallant leader. The enmity which pursues its object beyond death is unworthy of a civilized people. The survivors of the Fifty-fourth were led back by Higginson. A siege was begun and the fort was bombarded till it was untenable, and the garrison escaped a last assault only by evacuating the place during the night. Sumter was hammered into ruins, but an assault upon it failed. The "Swamp Angel," an eight-inch Parrot gun, threw huge shells into the city of Charleston; but all efforts to capture the city failed.

Both nations were already feeling the terrible strain of the war; conscription at the North had reached men of forty-five years of age, and in the South it finally included the entire male population. Lincoln's emancipation of the slaves, and employment of them against their masters, was severely criticised at the North as well as denounced at the South. Draft riots broke out in New York, and a thousand of the mob were slain before order was re-established. But beneath all surface disturbances the deep purpose to urge the conflict to the end remained. Lincoln rose to the full stature of his greatness, and took his place beside Washington as the champion of his country under conditions even more appalling than those which Washington had met. On the 19th of November he made the speech at Gettysburg, on the occasion of the dedication of the cemetery there, which still remains the most memorable utterance of the war, and embodies the highest thought that any war undertaken for righteous causes can inspire. "We cannot consecrate this hallowed ground," said he. "The brave men, living and dead, who struggled here, have consecrated it far above our power to add or detract. The world will but little note, nor long remember, what we say here; but it can never forget what they did here. It is for us, the living, rather to dedicate ourselves to the unfinished work which they so nobly advanced; to consecrate ourselves to the great task remaining, and to gather from the graves of these honored dead increased devotion to that cause for which they gave their lives. Here let us resolve that they shall not have died in vain; that this nation shall, under God, have a new birth of freedom; and that government of the people, by the people, and for the people shall not perish forever from the earth." Only a mind and heart of the very highest quality could have given this idea an expression so without flaw. The words take their place by an inevitable law of nature, like sea and sky and mountains. Lincoln had always been a man of great elements; but he was now arrived at almost the loftiest stage of human development. The sublimity of patriotism cannot further go; and the leader of a people in battle cannot, while the battle continues, mount above patriotism. In a calmer hour Lincoln might have spoken of the heroes who had fought against the North on that day, whose merit was no whit less than theirs; and we know that his vast magnanimity would have cordially included them. But mortal man lives in time, and according to the time must he act and speak. It is rather marvelous that

Lincoln, speaking as he did at a moment when the feeling on both sides of the struggle was at its bitterest, let fall no word which should still further inflame it. The rude boatman and rail-splitter of Illinois had risen to the compass of the mightiest whom God has made.

Passing over minor episodes, including the harrowing annals of Libby Prison, we come to the military chieftainship of Grant in 1864. Sherman and Johnston, two masters of strategy, maneuvered against each other in Tennessee and Georgia. Sherman had the larger number of troops, but Johnston fairly matched him until Davis, failing to comprehend his merits, superseded him with Hood. He thrice attacked Sherman on his way to Atlanta, but was each time repulsed; Sherman moved his army to the rear of Atlanta, where Hood was intrenched, and when the latter sent Hardee to protect his communications Sherman threw his men between him and the city; Hardee retreated, and Hood evacuated, escaping capture. But Atlanta and Georgia were severed from the rest of the Confederacy. In the four months' campaign the two armies had lost seventy thousand men. Finally Hood collected his force and threatened Sherman's line of supplies from Nashville. Sherman, after chasing him into northern Alabama, left Thomas to meet his advance in Nashville, and turned to march seaward through Georgia with sixty thousand men. Kilpatrick's cavalry guarded against surprise; the army destroyed the lines of railway between which it journeyed on its long tramp of three hundred miles. It subsisted on the country, having entirely cast loose from its base. Leaving a wake of desolation sixty miles wide behind it, it headed for Savannah, having by a feint toward Augusta induced the force of old men and boys, who alone remained to defend the state, to gather there. For a month the North had no news of the army, and the South added to the uneasiness by circulating reports of its destruction. But by the middle of December Sherman sent news of his safe arrival at Savannah, whose garrison evacuated the town without a contest. With a loss of but five hundred men, Sherman had destroyed a hundred million dollars' worth of property and suodivided the Confederacy. This, with Savannah and twenty-five thousand bales of cotton, was his Christmas present to the North.

Meanwhile Thomas, at Nashville, was attacked by Hood, whose courage only needed some discretion to be perfect. He pushed back Schofield and Stanley, sent out to delay him, but at the cost of a loss nearly twice as great as theirs. After some delay Thomas sallied forth to attack him. He feinted at his right and drove back his left on the 15th of December; the next morning he charged along the whole line, and Hood's army, after a fierce resistance, broke into hopeless flight. Forrest with his cavalry gave some protection to the retreat; but the pursuit was not slackened, and under its effects Hood's entire army disappeared and was never again assembled. Such an event had never before occurred.

Grant's campaign before Richmond, which now began, was a record of slaughter which one is averse from needlessly recapitulating. It was based upon Grant's determination to conquer this last of the Southern armies by exterminating it. The war thus far had showed that whichever of the antagonists was in an intrenched position generally defeated the attacking party, even when superior in numbers. Exceptions there had been, but such was the usual result. Lee had fewer troops than Grant, but in defending Richmond he was uniformly behind fortifications, which long practice had enabled his soldiers to construct in a marvelously short time. These Grant was forced to assail; his losses were fearful and often much greater than his enemy's; but so many thousand Southern soldiers fell on each occasion, and their places could not be filled. In marching to

ENGAGEMENT OF THE "HARTFORD" AND "TENNESSEE," AUGUST 5, 1864

turn Lee's flank Grant had to go the longer distances; Lee, moving on the inside, and divining or being informed of his intention, was always beforehand, prepared for an assault. At point after point of a great circle round Richmond Grant resolutely pushed against the defense; from the north to the south he moved, and was finally besieging Petersburg. The earlier battles were fought in the Wilderness, which had already been fatal to the Union armies; it was blind fighting, in which death came from unseen sources; the tangled woods dripped with blood and were choked with corpses; they caught fire, and the wounded were roasted to death; the trees were cut down by the flying bullets; scenes were enacted surpassing in sustained horror anything known in war. Staggering from the fearful punishment, but still fighting coolly and fiercely, Lee faced his terrible opponent in these last rounds of the mighty struggle, and did all that man could, and almost more than man could be believed capable of, to destroy him as he was being destroyed. The losses were now numbered by the tens of thousands; human life seemed to have lost its value. Only an invincible soul could have endured to continue, as Grant did, so awful a conflict. "I shall fight it out on this line if it takes all summer," said he; but he fought it out on many lines, and still the heroism of the defenders kept him from his object. The silent power of this man, conscious that the refinements of strategy were here but of small avail, and able to steadily inflict wholesale slaughter on his own men in order to wear down his enemy, is one of the most impressive spectacles ever seen. He had thought it out during the earlier years of the war; he had made up his mind what to do, and now that the time was come, and the men, he unfalteringly did it. The maneuvers were for the most part of the simplest sort; Richmond was the goal; Grant edged round further and further, Lee following him on the shorter line; now and then there would be a swift countermarch, a cavalry dash, a turning back on Washington to deliver and parry an attack;

In order to oversee and direct the battle, he took his station in the shrouds of his vessel, the "Hartford." He had both wooden and iron-clad ships; but his leading monitor, "Tecumseh," was destroyed by a sunken torpedo. The fleet ran past the forts, receiving and delivering a tremendous cannonade; within the bay were the Confederate ram "Tennessee" and other war vessels. Farragut had rigged false bows of iron on his wooden ships, and they attacked the "Tennessee," trying to sink her both by shot and ramming. The shot could not pierce her armor, except in one point where a shutter of a port had been destroyed; and so accurate was the Federal fire that this small aperture was penetrated by a shell, and Admiral Buchanan was wounded by it. The ram became the center of attention from the whole Federal fleet, and finally surrendered. The forts likewise capitulated; but though the port was thus closed, the city itself, until the war had ended, remained in Confederate hands.

There was still one uncaptured port in the Confederacy—Wilmington, N. C., defended by Fort Fisher. Grant sent Commodore Porter, with a fleet, and General Weitzel, with an army, against it; but General Butler usurped the command over Weitzel, gave the fort a short pounding, decided that it was too strong for him, re-embarked his troops, and went back to Fortress Monroe. Porter, remaining with his ships, asked leave to make another attempt. He forced the garrison behind their bomb-proofs by his fire, ran approaches close to the walls, and with his sailors and marines, and a somewhat larger army than before, under General Terry, made a combined assault on two sides of the fort on the afternoon of January 14, 1865. For resolute hand-to-hand fighting, both the attack and defense equaled anything seen in the war. The sailors were repulsed, but the soldiers forced their way, the garrison was driven from point to point, to the water's edge, and by midnight was compelled to surrender. "Conquered and conquerors looked upon each other with pride." In February General Schofield occupied Wilmington. Had it not been for cruisers built in England for the Confederacy, to take the place of their destroyed privateers, the South would have been driven from the sea; but these cruisers, manned by English crews, practically ruined Federal commerce. Semmes, in the "Alabama," captured sixty prizes, but was finally challenged and sunk by the Federal "Kearsarge." The impossibility of getting supplies into the South by sea caused great dearth and enormous prices; fifty dollars in paper brought but one in specie; coffee was fifty dollars a pound, and other things in proportion. Even such soldiers as those of the Confederacy cannot fight without food and clothing, though they came as near as possible to doing so. The interior railways had been torn up, and even such food as was obtainable could not be carried to the troops at the front. The men began to desert; yet the leaders would not admit defeat, and braced themselves for the final struggle before Richmond.

Besides Lee's army at Richmond, the only other Confederate force worth considering at the beginning of 1865 was that under Johnston in the south. But against him, Sherman was arrayed; and he left his winter quarters, if such they could be called in that mild climate, in the early part of February, and headed northward; Johnston retiring before his advance. It was the season of rains, and Sherman's march was difficult, preceded as they were by Confederate cavalry, which threw every obstacle in their path; but they were veterans and it was impossible to stop them. When they crossed the boundaries of South Carolina—that state to whose initiative the secession of the southern states was due —they began a system of destruction. No consideration was shown; the country was laid waste; over it hung a canopy of smoke from burning towns and desolated farms; this was vengeance rather than war. The state capital, Columbia, was burned; Hardee evacuated Charleston, which for the better part of two years had withstood every effort of the Federals to capture it, and before the latter could occupy it, a great magazine of powder had been accidentally exploded, and hundreds of the inhabitants were killed and the city was afire. The Union troops helped to put the fire out; but Charleston, ruined by its long resistance, was hardly worth saving. Passing on into North Carolina, Sherman was confronted by an amalgamation of Johnston's army with the troops which had garrisoned the principal towns of the region; but no opposition that could seriously retard him was made. Schofield and Terry joined Sherman at Goldsboro, and this great army of one hundred thousand men was massed along the Neuse, on which Goldsboro stands. It was now possible to consider in what way Sherman should co-operate with Grant in relation to the possible attempt of Lee to escape from Richmond.

Lee's army was by this time, owing to various causes, not more than fifty thousand strong, though three times that number appeared on the rolls. He had against him what might be called a nation in arms, and never so well supplied as now with material and training for war. Lee's only hope was to make a dash through almost impossible obstructions and unite with Johnston; yet, even could he have done this, the ultimate destruction of the Confederate forces would have been none the less inevitable. Had he surrendered then, he would have lost nothing, and would have saved the lives of thousands. But though all else in war was easy to this general, surrender seems to have been almost impossible to him. When a leader's only fault is dauntless courage, he may be forgiven. He would fight to the end.

His first attempt to break out was begun by a fierce attack on Fort Steadman, toward the east; but this was only to mask a real movement in force toward the south. Grant however did not move his left; the fort was carried, but only to the loss of those who took it, for it was commanded by other batteries, which opened fire and compelled the surrender of the assaulting division; upon which Meade advanced and took up a position nearer the city. Grant now marched two corps of infantry from his right, behind his own lines, to the extreme left, where they were joined by Sheridan with nine thousand cavalry, and proceeded toward the railway which gave egress in that direction. Sheridan had occupied Dinwiddie Court House, and was about to start on a raid, when, on the 30th of March, Grant apprised him that all was ready for the final blow; but Lee, anticipating Sheridan's attack, took the offensive himself, and fell with all his strength upon Sheridan at Five Forks, directly south of Richmond. Pushed back some distance by the impetuosity of Lee's attack, Sheridan re-formed his troops at Dinwiddie, and the Fifth Corps under Warren got in the Confederate rear. Lee was now merely a fighting fugitive. On the night of April 1st a great bombardment opened on Petersburg, and the whole Union line left its intrenchments on April 2d and swept the enemy before them. The heroic defense of the garrison of Fort Gregg, two hundred and fifty strong, of which only thirty were left, deserves to be remembered. Lee, forced back within his last lines, informed the inhabitants of Richmond that they must surrender. Jefferson Davis fled, and the city became a scene of terror, horror and lawlessness. Lee, meanwhile, with the remains of his faithful troops, set out for Burkeville on the west. Grant instantly pursued him with an overwhelming force. Delayed by the necessity of collecting food for his men, Lee found himself checked by Sheridan at Jetersville. Turning aside, he tried to reach Lynchburg, but Grant had foreseen every contingency, and hemmed him in on the right, the left, and the rear. Davies attacked his wagon train; Custer struck and shattered his retreating column and forced the surrender of six thousand. Lee still pressed on, and fancied he might yet escape; he was fighting front and rear, and the march was a race with death. Sheridan, tireless as a bloodhound, at length flung himself across his path; Fitz Hugh Lee charged with his cavalry; but as the Union troopers retreated, their movement revealed a solid mass of infantry, in vast numbers, drawn up beyond. The war was over.

Lee and Grant met at Appomatox Court House, and with the simple forms of brave Americans at a supreme moment, drew up and signed the terms of Lee's surrender. "We have fought through the war together; I have done the best I could for you," were the words in which the great Virginian took leave of his troops. It was a war which had cost in killed and wounded nearly a million men; it had destroyed slavery; and it had determined that this country should become one again. The wounds it made took long to heal, but we may confidently believe that they will never again be opened.

Four years had passed from the date of the firing of the first gun against Sumter, when the Confederate army of Virginia laid down its arms. Two days later Johnston surrendered to Sherman. Smith's army on the further side of the Mississippi capitulated a month after. Jefferson Davis was captured in Georgia, while trying to escape in disguise. He had been overestimated in the South, and in the North there were many who demanded his trial and execution for treason; but neither the execution nor even the trial took place, though he was indicted. The country felt, upon second thought, that it would be an unwise and undignified act to punish in such a manner the mistaken ideas of patriotism and duty which had ruined this man. He was not suited for the position to which he had been called. He was too narrow, too rigid, too personally proud and ambitious, to be the leader of the South; he was not truly representative of what was best and noblest in them. He had neither the heroism, the tenderness, the manhood, nor the true dignity of Robert Edward Lee.

The Civil War was the result of the collision between the centrifugal and the centripetal forces which constitute the weakness and the strength of our political constitution.

They had heretofore not been truly adjusted, so that first one and then the other was in excess, and threatened destruction. The war effected this adjustment; for it proved that secession was against the will of the nation, and at the same time showed the dangers of overcentralization. Justly balanced—the states against the State—our system is the strongest and healthiest yet devised; it is elastic, yet it can be neither crushed nor disrupted. It was slavery which led to the effort to disrupt it; that was expunged from our escutcheon by the blood of those who fell on either side, and thus, it may be hoped, the sin which we stood accountant for as a nation was washed away.

CHAPTER THIRTY-SIXTH

PAST AND FUTURE

ON the 9th of April, 1865, Lee surrendered; on the 12th, his soldiers stacked their arms and were paroled; meanwhile, Lincoln visited Richmond, and walked about its scarred and smoke-blackened streets; in the afternoon he held a reception in what had been the Confederate executive mansion; on the evening of April 14th he was due to attend a play in Ford's Theater in Washington; he felt ill, and would have stayed at home, but for an unwillingness to disappoint the people, whose joy at the conclusion of the war had sharpened their desire to see and greet the President who had piloted them through the greatest storm that ever fell upon the Republic. Six months before, they had avouched their confidence in him by reelecting him to his office, McClellan, the representative of faint-heartedness and discouragement, being his opponent.

Andrew Johnson, another man of the people, a tailor by trade, had been chosen Vice-President.

During the heat of battle the South had doubtless hated Lincoln; for he had freed their slaves; and by the Thirteenth Amendment of the Constitution, ratified in December following his death, the corollary of his Emancipation Proclamation was accomplished; it declared slavery forever at an end in all parts of the United States. But the South was magnanimous, as are all brave peoples, and it was capable of realizing that this quaint, uncouth great man was no enemy of theirs, but loved them as a part of the nation he was appointed to govern, and had only opposed them with the whole strength at his command so long as they mistakenly fought against what he knew to be their own ultimate good. Faithful are the wounds of a friend; and the South was on the way to see and confess the friendship of Abraham Lincoln.

For his part, his mind, in these first moments of light after the long darkness, was occupied with plans for the reinstatement of the seceding states in the privileges assured by the Constitution; and the terms of peace offered by Sherman to the army of Johnston may be taken as a sketch in the rough of what Lincoln hoped to confirm by regular legislative process. These terms spoke of recognition of state governments in the South, of restoring to them the franchise and political rights, and of a general amnesty. The terms were sent to Congress for consideration, and had not of course been passed upon on the 14th of April. But Lincoln believed that the way to win back the heart of the South was to be generous to them, and trust to their honor loyally to submit to what the test of war, so valiantly invoked, had decided. They were ruined, in power and fortune; but they were our brothers, and it was to the interest as much of the North as of theirs to take every means to heal their wounds and support their faltering footsteps, until their strength and health returned to them.

But there was in the South a small and obscure knot of irreconcilables who desired revenge, and who regarded Lincoln as their arch-foe. By what process of reasoning they persuaded themselves that his death could profit the South, we cannot conceive; and it is possible that their governing thought was to inflict sorrow on the people which they had failed to overcome in battle. But it would seem that the most elementary perception of the motives which govern human action should have apprised them that an act of deadly violence against the Chief Magistrate, at a time when the war was done, could result only in hardening the heart of the North against them, and causing the terms granted to them to be more severe than otherwise they would be. Be that as it may, a conspiracy was hatched by the extreme wing of this small group of malcontents, and eight persons were afterward known as having been actively concerned in it. The protagonist of the conspiracy, its boldest and most urgent member, was a hare-brained and dare-devil actor, John Wilkes Booth, representing the narrowest and most fanatical spirit of the South; a young man, handsome, vain, high-flown, and reckless of life. His profession, or rather his conception of it, had inflamed and confirmed the cheap, sensational, histrionic views of mortal obligations which were native to him; and he stood forward as the instrument by whom the chief crime contemplated was to be done. His fellows were to strike down, at the same moment, other distinguished members of the Cabinet, and the Vice-President—for the rumor that Johnson was in any way or degree cognizant of the conspiracy never had foundation, and was on the face of it preposterous. We must suppose that it was hoped thus to paralyze the North, and terrify them into yielding the government to hands which might guide it in Southern interests. A more perverse and impossible notion could hardly have entered the brain of a madman.

We need not be concerned to recall the dark details of

the plot. Lincoln entered his stage-box at the theater, which was draped with the American flag, which had been rent, and was now whole again. Several persons were with him. The box was but little elevated above the stage, so that an active man might easily leap thence to the stage without injury. The performance had not been long in progress, when the door of the box was opened, and a young man entered. It is said that he locked the door behind him with his left hand. In his right hand was a revolver. No one knew who he was; and the suddenness of his entrance prevented his being questioned. Probably he might have been mistaken for some person employed in the front of the house, or perhaps for a messenger with dispatches from the State Department. The time was counted by seconds. He took a step forward, leveled his weapon at the back of the unconscious President's head, and sent the bullet through his brain. Then, pushing forward at once to the front of the box, he vaulted over the railing to the stage below. It is said that in so doing the spur on his heel caught in the folds of the flag, causing him to strike the stage in such a way as to snap the bone of the leg above the ankle. The audience had heard the sound of the shot, but for an instant fancied it to be in some way connected with the performance. But the spectacle of a man leaping from the President's box upon the stage was too extraordinary to be accounted for; and when he was seen to throw up the arm which held the weapon, and to exclaim "Sic semper Tyrannis," immediately passing across the stage and out by the rear, the theater was in an uproar.

The shot had stricken Lincoln senseless, and his body inclined forward as he sat. The wound was mortal, and he never spoke or had a conscious thought from the first; he survived several hours, and died the next day, the 15th. The other conspirators were unsuccessful, though Payne forced his way into Seward's chamber and attacked him with a knife. The other intended victims, including General Grant, were not approached. Booth had been the only one whose success was complete.

Had this assassination been perpetrated in 1863, when the South was winning victories, and when many in the North thought the cause of the Union was lost, it might have had a profound effect upon the complexion of affairs. But now it could have no effect, except to curdle the milk of human kindness which was beginning to flow in the breast of the North for their conquered brethren. At first it was surmised that the crime might have been conceived in high quarters; but a little reflection showed that it was impossible that Southern gentlemen could have lent themselves to an act so dastardly. Booth was pursued and shot in a barn where he had taken refuge, which had been set on fire; no man of the attacking party having the courage to go up and take him prisoner. A story was told to the effect that the man thus killed was not Booth; that the latter had made good his escape, and died many years later in the West Indies. Such legends are apt to spring up in the surroundings of a great crime; they amuse the popular imagination; but they never sustain the test of serious examination. The other conspirators were arrested and executed, Mrs. Surratt, at whose house the conspirators met, included. But beyond this, no attempt at retaliation was made by the North. Jefferson Davis, after his arrest, was imprisoned for a couple of years in Fortress Monroe, and then unconditionally released. Meanwhile the era of Reconstruction had begun, and Johnson and Congress were at odds upon the questions involved. It was now that the harmonizing influence of Lincoln was missed, and the South was brought to a practical realization of how wise and charitable a friend they had lost in him.

Johnson, on assuming office, saw the army of the North quietly disbanded; for a day the procession of two hundred thousand men, in weather-worn uniforms, with tattered flags and polished guns, defiled before the President; the men who had made history, the preservers of the Union, the citizens who had taken up arms and transformed themselves into the best soldiers in the world, who were now to lay down their arms and be reabsorbed at once into the body of the population from which they had come forth. Both to the eye, and to the mind and heart, it was a spectacle of unexampled grandeur and impressiveness. These men could have marched, as they were, to the conquest of the world; but their thoughts were not of ambition, or of the seizure of power, but of home, and of the quiet and industrious productive life which is proper to the citizens of a republic. Yet a profound difference had been wrought in them by the war, and in the main it was a beneficial one; their military discipline had taught them the meaning and uses of discipline and the sway of just authority in the life of peace: a lesson of peculiar value to a great democracy, whose foible it is to lapse into loose ways of action and thought. It had taught them the worth of patriotism, and steadfast courage in meeting the stress of battle in the matters of daily routine, which are often not less trying than is the shock of arms in open war. By revealing to them their own strength, it rendered them gentle and charitable, and less sensitive to the criticism of others. Incidentally, it had given them an acquaintance with their own country which might otherwise have been postponed for generations; and a sympathy with and respect for the men against whom they fought, which might else perhaps never have been attained at all.

So far all was well; but the politicians who had remained at home now once more became prominent, and sowed the seeds of legislative trouble. Johnson's theory was that the states had never in fact seceded, because the result of the war had proved secession to be ineffective; therefore, as soon as certain formalities had been observed, they should be readmitted to the rights of citizenship, voting, and representation in Congress. Upon this basis he acted, during the period while Congress was not in session; but on their reassembling

BOMBARDMENT OF FORT FISHER, N. C., BY ADMIRAL PORTER'S FLEET, DECEMBER, 1864

they adopted a stricter view of the situation, and disallowed some of the President's acts. Strife ensued between the executive and legislative branches; Johnson vetoed the bills of Congress, and the latter, having a two-thirds Republican majority, passed the bills over his veto. The law of appointments to and dismissal from office was a bone of contention, and the quarrel came to a head over Johnson's dismissal from the office of Secretary of War of Stanton, who had acted efficiently under Lincoln, but whose brutality on several occasions had raised him up many enemies. In the stress of emotion and anxiety caused by the fortunes and doubts of the war, much should be forgiven to men of honest purpose and sterling patriotism, like Stanton, who temporarily lost temper and judgment, and so committed acts of injustice. The determination of Congress to continue him in office in spite of the President, led to an attempt to impeach the latter, in which much time and breath were wasted, and no good result whatever attained; for neither was the motion successful, nor was the conduct of public business promoted; on the contrary, feelings of mutual enmity were aroused which were injurious to all concerned, and most of all to the public, which had elected these men to attend to the affairs of the nation. The Reconstruction measure which Congress carried over the veto was to the effect that the states had in fact seceded and were unassimilated as yet to the Union, and could become so only through act of Congress. Citizenship was given to negroes by a Fourteenth Amendment, and representation was reduced according to the number of citizens admitted to citizenship. No person who had violated his oath by joining in the act of secession should be allowed to hold office under the United States, and compensation for freed slaves should not be accorded. These laws were not wisely framed; their effect was to exclude from responsible positions the men of the South who were best qualified for holding them, and to put in power the tribe of irresponsible adventurers, known as "carpet-baggers," who for real or assumed party services had been let loose on the Southern states. Hard feeling and disturbances ensued, as might have been expected; and the military governors who ruled the seceded states by martial law did not throw oil upon the troubled waters. Johnson's policy was the wiser of the two, though it also might have been wiser. In matters of this kind, action should not be taken according to the strict dictation of logic. It was bootless to ask whether or not the states had seceded; the thing to do was to trust so far as possible to their common-sense and good faith, and to remove instead of placing obstacles in the way of bringing a proud people once more into the fold from which they had broken forth. Military laws and alien interlopers should not have been permitted; Americans should not have to be told that, for any community not actually barbarous, home-rule is the only rule admissible. Disturbances might of course have occurred under such liberal terms, but they would have been discountenanced by the weight of public opinion, and could readily have been checked by more stringent means if necessary. As it was, the states subscribed to the new regulations slowly and reluctantly, and the acerbities of the war were kept alive. The Republican Party, which had gloriously brought the country through the war, here began already to abuse its pow.r; and though its predominance was to be prolonged for ma ;.y years, and was still to be productive of much good, its decline had commenced, and from some of its mistakes we are still inconvenienced. But the Republican Party was, for the present, a Hobson's choice for the people; they could not again trust the Democrats, who had become in a measure identified with the principle of disloyalty. Centralization was a natural tendency, after the experience of the perils incident to the opposite point of view; and we should perhaps wonder that the Republicans, as chartered libertines, did not do more mischief, than that they did any mischief at all.

During Johnson's term occurred the culmination of the

Maximilian incident in Mexico. Napoleon III., aiming at foreign empire, had long been plotting to get hold of Mexico; and our Civil War gave him the opportunity he desired to set at naught the warning of our Monroe Doctrine. Persuading the English and the Spanish to act with him, he made with them an effort to collect damages for injuries sustained or alleged in the past; and to induce the anarchical populace to accept a permanent ruler. Spain and England soon retired from the combination, perceiving its true objects; and Napoleon then sent an armed expedition to Mexico City, which forced the Mexicans to accept a king in the person of Archduke Maximilian of Austria—who, for his part, agreed to ascend the throne upon the assurance (falsely given by France) that the entire Mexican people desired him to do so. That the popular desire had been for a republic he was not long in discovering; but with Austrian obstinacy, he would not recede; and a long course of intestine trouble might have been the result, had not the ending of our war admonished France that her support of the king must cease. Lacking Napoleon's support, Maximilian was unable to make head against the leader of the republican element, Juarez; he was court-martialed and shot. Except in Brazil and Canada, there were now no traces of empires in the western hemisphere; and the former was soon to throw off her royal yoke, though it had been an easy one.

In 1866 Cyrus W. Field, after twelve years' labor and three experiments, accomplished the laying of the Atlantic cable by means of the steamship "Great Eastern"; it was one of the renowned victories of peace. Not less important in another way was the purchase from Russia, for about seven million dollars, of the vast territory of Alaska, which was supposed to be valuable only as a fur country, but which has since, in a single year, yielded gold enough to repay its cost many times over. Nevada had been made a state in Lincoln's time; Nebraska was admitted in 1867. The general prosperity of the country was great, in spite of the destitution of a large part of the South; the public debt, which had risen to over two and a half billion dollars during 1865, underwent a steady reduction from this time forth, beginning with a sum of over seventy millions in the very first year of peace. The revenue from duties, taxes and stamps, at the same period, was more than three hundred and twenty million dollars.

When the national conventions assembled, that of the Republicans unanimously voted for Grant as the next President; the Democrats nominated Horatio Seymour, who was defeated at the polls by one hundred and forty electoral votes, but only by about three hundred thousand votes cast by the people. Grant was the third soldier to assume the office of Executive since Washington; and though he had not the political ability of Jackson, nor even, it may be, of Taylor, he was so strong, straightforward and firm that his administrations were a success. The chief industrial feature of his first administration was the completion of the Atlantic-Pacific railway, which gave an immense momentum to the prosperity of the country; and its chief disaster was the great fires, which almost destroyed Chicago, laid a large part of Boston in ruins, and devastated Wisconsin, Minnesota and Michigan. Threat of war with England was averted by the payment by her of damages for injuries to commerce sustained from the cruiser "Alabama," built and manned by England; and by the rectification of the northwest boundary in our favor; both being the result of arbitration. Grant was in favor of accepting the tender of annexation made by the Republic of San Domingo; but Congress rejected it, whether or not wisely is still matter of dispute. Grant was made his own successor, the coalition candidate of liberal Republicans and Democrats, Horace Greeley, the journalist, being defeated, much to his own surprise. A war with the Modocs, who had left their reservation, and murdered commissioners sent to treat with them, was one of the first incidents of Grant's second term; and a similar difficulty with the Sioux occurred in 1876, and was marked by the death of Custer and his men, who attacked an Indian village with inferior numbers, and were surrounded and killed before re-enforcements could arrive. The first Centennial Exhibition was given at Philadelphia in 1876, three years after the disastrous panic caused by the failure of the bankers, Jay Cooke & Co., who had dabbled overmuch in railway stocks. The American people are fond of anniversaries, and uniformly observe them with heartiness and elaboration. The centennial of the Republic was a specially glorified Fourth of July, and it was delightful to the patriotic American to compare what we were in 1876 with what we had been a hundred years before. The material progress was certainly surprising; but it might have been edifying to inquire how far we rose above the moral and self-abnegating virtues which had characterized us in Washington's time. The behavior of a people varies with its conditions of life; but prosperity, sudden and excessive, is of all conditions the most hostile to the development of civic integrity and faithfulness. Looking upon our increase in population, power and wealth, we were easily forgetful of the principles which had laid the foundation for such an unprecedented advance, and we tended to give undue credit to that kind of ability which wins material success and accumulates money. That the true greatness of a country does not lie in this direction has of late been recognized by a part of our people, and it may be expected that a change in the object of our energies may gradually be made.

Grant went out of office with the affection and respect of his countrymen, which his services both in the field and in the White House had well deserved. After his retirement he made a tour of the world, which he had intended to be a private affair, but which became the most famous "progress" of modern times; he was everywhere received by the governments of the countries he visited with honor, as the most distinguished living American; and nothing that he said or did during his journey failed to confirm the good repute which had preceded him. His simplicity and his greatness were at all times and in all places equally apparent, and greatly elevated the foreign estimate of his country. The mind dwells upon every act of his career, public and private, with satisfaction; and a few years before his death he made the unusual reply to a question on the subject, that had he his life to live over again, he would choose to live it as before. His last years were saddened by a financial misfortune, for which he was not to blame; and they were ennobled by the constancy with which, while dying from a painful disease, he continued to write his "Memoirs," in order to secure for his family support after his death. He lived just long enough to finish the book, the sale of which justified his hopes. It is an important contribution to the history of the war; and the modesty of its tone, and the strength and simplicity of its style, recall and reflect the qualities of the man who wrote it.

Besides the Democrats and the Republicans, there was a third party in the Presidential contest for 1876—the Greenback Party, whose platform called for the issue of greenbacks based on the credit of the country, with which bonds should be bought up. Peter Cooper, a venerable and rustic old gentleman, of great wealth and philanthropic disposition, was nominated by this party; Samuel Tilden was the Democratic choice; and the Republicans put up Rutherford B. Hayes, a person of correct private life and limited caliber, who had been a respectable volunteer officer in the war, but who was destitute of any personal qualifications or deserts for the office. The processes of the election were unusually fraudulent; the whole power of the Republicans being exerted for their candidate, while Tilden was the undoubted preference of the majority of the nation. In spite of all that bribery and intimidation could do, the count was so close that danger was feared should Hayes be declared elected; and a commission was therefore appointed to pass upon the returns. It was made up of fifteen members, appointed in consequence of the recommendation of a Congressional committee:—five Senators, five Representatives, and five associate justices of the Supreme Court. The commission decided each case brought before it in favor of the Republicans, by a constant vote of eight against seven, and Hayes was accordingly declared President. Preparations were secretly made to suppress with an iron hand the revolt that was apprehended; but the Democrats, though convinced that the election had been stolen, acquiesced with admirable loyalty, and Mr. Hayes assumed his functions.

His colorless administration, streaked with pallid efforts at "reform," requires little notice. Evarts, a distinguished New York lawyer, was his Secretary of State, and Carl Schurz was his Secretary of the Interior. Hayes withdrew from South Carolina and Louisiana the United States troops which had been sent there by Grant to maintain order; and those states in consequence came at once under the normal Democratic control. In 1877 the industrial situation was threatened by large and violent strikes and riots at Pittsburg, Chicago, Reading and Baltimore; property was burned and destroyed, the troops were called out, and many persons were killed; the strikers gained nothing. There was a severe yellow fever epidemic in the South. Hayes in vain vetoed the Bland Silver Bill which authorized the coining of a $412\frac{1}{2}$-grain silver dollar at the rate of between two and four million dollars annually, and made it legal tender; and recommended, but without result, the fixing of a ratio between gold and silver by international agreement. The sum of five and a half million dollars was awarded by a commission to England as compensation for alleged interference with English fisheries rights Gold reached par in 1878, from a maximum advance of 285 in 1864. Specie payments were resumed a few days later. The census of 1880 showed the population to have increased over eleven millions during the past decade, numbering upward of fifty millions. The most curious minor incident of Hayes's administration was the crusade against wines and liquor undertaken by Mrs. Hayes; the only result being that, by her orders, wine was not served at White House dinners. Mrs. Hayes was the wife of a public servant to whom had been temporarily intrusted the stewardship of government property; and her conduct illustrates her conception of her rights in the premises.

Parties were still further multiplied in the canvass of 1880; the Prohibitionists and the Anti-Masonic parties being added to the former three. General Grant also stood for a third term. Garfield and Arthur were the regular Republican nominees; General Hancock was selected by the Democrats; General Weaver by the Greenbackers; Neal Dow by the Prohibitionists, and John W. Phelps by the Anti-Masons. Here were five generals against two civilians. Arthur, however, was but a quartermaster-general; and Garfield can hardly be said to have reached mediocrity as a volunteer general. But he was a clever politician, and a useful man to his party. He was successful over Hancock by a moderate margin; Neal Dow had some ten thousand supporters in the United States, and the Greenbackers could muster but three hundred thousand.

Garfield's Secretary of State was James G. Blaine. The Republican Party was divided into two hostile camps at this time; the dispute between them being as to who should control the division of the spoils. Roscoe Conkling, the leader of the "half-breeds," as the opponents of the "stalwart" administration were called, resigned his seat in the Senate on account of an appointment by Garfield which displeased him. The wrangling which ensued caused some excitement, which turned the brain of a wretched office-hunter named Guiteau; and he shot Garfield in the back at a Washington railroad station on July 2d, 1881. Garfield's youth and vigorous constitution kept him alive till the 19th of September; meanwhile great sympathy was expressed for him. Upon his death, Arthur succeeded him. Garfield had been a poor farmer's boy; had married a farmer's daughter, and owed such education as he had to his own efforts. Arthur was a rich man and an "exquisite," a genial fine gentleman of popular manners. Only two matters of importance are associated with his administration: the Chinese exclusion bill, and the tariff reform bill. The former was passed, with many dissentients; the latter is still a bone of contention between parties; and the attempts which have been made to solve the problem which it involves have cost us much money and more ill-feeling. Statesmanship, politics and finance become mixed in an inextricable snarl, and the multitude of advisers do but darken counsel. Upon the whole, fortune was kind to Arthur in giving him nothing of moment to do; and he retired from office with the commendation and good will of all.

In the ensuing election the frivolity of the time was shown in the still further increase of so-called parties; not to mention others, there was the woman's rights party with Belva A. Lockwood for President and Mrs. Dr. Lozier for Vice-President. The Democrats were represented by Grover Cleveland and T. A. Hendricks, the Republicans by James G. Blaine and John A. Logan. Cleveland and Hendricks were elected. Cleveland was another poor boy; but he had early got into politics; he had sent a substitute to the war, and applied himself to making a political career. He rose through various civic grades till he was elected governor of New York by a majority unusually large, which put him in the presidential race. He was bold and firm, and honest as politicians go; confident in the soundness of his own views, and apt to be independent in his attitude. He caught the fancy of his countrymen, and was in many ways a favorite of fortune. He had an advantage in being the first Democratic President for many years, and his ambition to make a record was no doubt genuine and honorable.

The epoch was necessarily one of small things. There

were no foreign complications, except the chronic petty squabbles with England about the fisheries, which led, this term, to the dismissal of Lord Sackville, the British minister to Washington, on account of a foolish letter he had been betrayed into writing on the subject. The Indians, on whose behalf much pretentious legislation, with a view to their education, had been passed or mooted, gave trouble again after a period of quiet, owing to invasion of their rights in Oklahoma. Senator Blair got a bill through Congress forbidding the importation of aliens under contract to perform labor in this country; upon which a notoriety-loving member of the St. Andrew's Society brought an action to restrain the sermons of an English clergyman who had been asked to officiate in an American friend's pulpit during the latter's absence. A New England Senator, anxious to be doing something for his constituents, conceived the idea of a presidential succession bill, which specified the order in which the office should pass from one Secretary to another, in the event of their all dying one after the other. Some tinkering was done with army and navy bills, with no results perceptible outside of Washington. Against any improvement or strengthening of our army or navy the threadbare and thrifty argument was used that we were at war with nobody, meant to attack none, and would be attacked by nobody; therefore, why should we accumulate means of offense and defense? They cost money, and could be of no use. It was a policy of shopkeepers, humanitarians, Trusts and bankers; people who form a not inconsiderable class of the community, and whose operations give them exaggerated prominence, but who in no degree represent the spirit of the nation. The nation, however, attending, each individual of it, to his own affairs, takes little note of proceedings in Washington, unless what occurs there happens to touch the popular imagination. Politicians, and those whose secret or open subsidies constitute the springs of their activity, are allowed to have things their own way, until some scandal or turpitude of

THE FIGHT AT SPOTTSYLVANIA COURT HOUSE, VA., MAY 10, 1864

unusual baseness takes place, making the people growl menacingly for a while, and sending the offenders scuttling to cover. But soon the many-headed monster turns to its affairs again, and the noxious creatures creep out once more. In general, little vital mischief is done; the country is strong enough to support vast quantities of parasites without feeling a drain. But the money annually paid out by Uncle Sam to persons who, to put it in the most delicate way, have done nothing honestly entitling them to it, would maintain an army and navy as large and efficient as those of any European power, and would place a belt of steel round our entire coasts. It is vain to suppose that other nations will respect us because we are big and rich, if we turn out to be, at the same time, strengthless and pusillanimous. On the contrary they will regard us as a goose to be fattened, and, at the proper time, to be killed and eaten. An object lesson of the fate of a great nation which has no civic unity and power of co-operation, is afforded by the recent history of China. With a population of hundreds of millions, and immense resources of treasure, this nation was defeated in war by a few thousand foreign soldiers and sailors. The nation had become, during centuries, self-centered; the mass of the people, overawed by combinations of the rich and ambitious, had lost all sense of nationality and patriotism, and were sunk into a kind of industrious barbarism, each atom working for itself or for its immediate master. At last there was no longer a nation, but only countless hordes of disconnected individuals, more or less in subjection to arbitrary tyrants. It would be inaccurate to say that China went to war with Japan, or was beaten by her. Only a minute fraction of the Chinese inhabitants of the country were ever aware that any war had taken place. But they were and are helpless to repel aggression, and we now see their country being divided up among the alien invaders, whose only consideration is not for the Chinese but for one another. No one who understands history will say that it was exclusiveness which brought China to this pass; it was selfishness, in the whole and in all its parts; the policy of each one for himself, with its inevitable corollaries of gradual subordination of the many to the few, the spread of ignorance, and disintegration. If the industrial affairs of America should continue to be managed by trusts, insensibly increasing in strength and independence; if its financial interests are left to combinations of bankers; if its government is abandoned to politicians; the fate of China must ultimately be ours. Like causes produce like results in the end, though that end may seem so distant as to be non-existent. —But, in truth, the conditions which have suggested such a peril are transient, and do but warn us to keep to our duty.

Civil Service Reform, and the Tariff, were the chief objects of attention during Cleveland's term. Some steps were taken toward making tenure of civil office dependent upon fitness for it, instead of upon party services; and there was a show of competitive examinations, and assurances that there should be no removals except for cause, one of which was specified as "pernicious activity." But the broad principle first enunciated by William Marcy and enforced by Andrew Jackson, that to the victors belong the spoils, still holds practical sway in our government; with the consequence that a large part of the President's time is occupied in the mere clerk's drudgery of removing and appointing incumbents of consulships, post-offices, and the like petty offices. The men who apply for these posts are usually, of course, men who have failed to make a living by ordinary trades or professions, and who, knowing that their tenure is limited to four years, try to make as much as possible out of their brief opportunities, and give small thought to the welfare of the interests confided to them. But were office-holders to be kept in their positions year after year and term after term, during good behavior, the government would be deprived of the vast patronage which their constant rotation supplies; and patronage means the votes and political support of subordinates, and money extorted from them under various pretexts, most of which goes into the pockets of their superiors. Our government is a government of the people by and for the people; and until the majority of our people shows itself explicitly and persistently opposed to this rotation system, it will continue. Public spirit, civic virtue, not sporadic and spasmodic, but general and continuous, are needed. The American people is capable of them, when poignant need arises; but they do not as yet show themselves willing to take time and attention from private affairs, year after year and decade after decade, in order to enforce measures and principles which all admit to be right. It is only after public abuses have begun obviously to interfere with the prosperity of private business, that we can expect a genuine movement of reform. The supporters of corruption fight hard, because they fight for life; their opponents are at the disadvantage of fighting them against their own personal convenience and inclination. Corruption has a strong and highly organized system, patiently fortified against every attack, prepared to bow before a passing storm, and to rise again after it has passed, often seeming to enlist under its opponents' banner, in order the more thoroughly to defeat and discredit them. The considerable body of political reformers and independents known in our nickname language as Mugwumps, has numbered in its ranks many men of sterling character and ability; but they have not won hearty popular sympathy. They seem, as a whole, to have been lacking in sympathy with average human nature, in political sagacity, and in knowledge of the world; they have put forward excellent moral propositions, and have been perplexed at their own failure. But in order to win the confidence of the average American, who is slightly cynical and full of common-sense, though capable, upon occasion, of fighting and dying for an abstract idea, these Mugwumps must give us something which they have not given as yet. They have their value as showing a growing tendency or the part of the community to achieve better conditions; but the magnetic word that shall unite all in accomplishing such conditions has not yet been spoken; the leader whom all cannot choose but follow has not yet arisen. We recognize that the political and industrial bosses are men who do what the average citizen might do if he had the chance and the ability; and therefore there is a half-heartedness about our condemnation of them. Mere ability, the faculty of managing, receives great admiration in this country, without too much regard to the methods by which results are attained. This is but natural in a republic where every man must fight for himself or go down. The boss relieves the average citizen of a great deal of trouble, and thereby sets him free to look after his personal interests. The trusts crush the small dealers, but they are a convenience for the consumer, and the increased price which the latter may be obliged to pay is set off against the facility of making purchases. Wage earners are wronged, but low wages cheapen products. Many doctors of political economy have arisen, with medicines for the cure of these ills; but it will probably be necessary for us to wait for experience to prove to us that the welfare of each depends in the long run on the welfare of the whole, and to live accordingly.

The tariff developed the existence of two opposite opinions in the country, one holding that foreign goods should be taxed in order to protect the manufacturers of the same lines of goods here; the other, that such protection is really of little help to the manufacturer, while it injures the consumer. Free trade and protection are irreconcilable enemies, and their quarrel, too, must be settled by experience. Under Cleveland, Roger Q. Mills introduced a bill favoring free trade, which passed the House but was halted in the Senate. Cleveland's first administration had about it a good deal of personal flavor, but the people liked it partly for that reason, inasmuch as Cleveland was held to be honest, uncorrupt, and to mean right. His intellect was not great, but he was a man who learned as he went along. There was a massiveness about him which was comforting. Nor, as an element in his popularity, should we neglect to notice his marriage to a beautiful and intelligent woman. Sentiment catches many votes in this hard-headed people.

In 1888, the two chief candidates were Cleveland and Benjamin Harrison, the grandson of the former President Harrison, of Tippecanoe. Benjamin Harrison was in every way a worthy gentleman, who had always done work given him to do with faithfulness and energy, and who continued that practice in the White House. He had been a good soldier in the war, liked by his men, and attentive to their welfare and discipline; and his commands to them in battle uniformly began with "Come"—not "Go." He was a lawyer by profession, and had served in the Senate; his opinions, as drawn out during the canvass, were such as might be expected from a man of integrity and respectability, who was a Republican. He favored Civil Service reform, but turned out and put in as many civil servants as had any of his predecessors. He appointed Corporal Tanner Commissioner of Pensions. The pension payments had risen from thirty-four millions in 1884 to nearly fifty-three millions in 1887; and within a few months Tanner had raised this sum to over eighty millions, and was still going on. The national surplus was being wiped out, and Tanner was compelled by public opinion to resign. By the agency of Blaine, the Secretary of State, negotiations were opened looking to reciprocity with South American states—import duties to be mutually lowered or abolished. The revenue of the country, internal and customs, was larger than ever before. Idaho and Wyoming were admitted as states. William McKinley introduced a tariff bill, raising some duties and lowering others; it was relied upon by the Republicans to confirm their hold on power; but its first effect was to change the majority in Congress from Republican to Democratic, and in connection with other things, it defeated the Republicans at the polls for the next Presidential election. The continued free coinage of silver was beginning to unsettle financial matters, and much opposition to it was developed. An international copyright bill was passed, giving, under certain restrictions, American ownership of their work to authors foreign to America, and conferring similar privileges on our authors in foreign countries. In 1891, the Italian secret assassination society, called the Mafia, murdered a police officer in New Orleans; the culprits were tried and acquitted; but the mob broke open the jail and killed them. The Italian minister at Washington protested, and our government paid twenty-five thousand dollars damages. The following year, members of the crew of the American man-of-war "Baltimore" were killed or hurt in a popular emeute in Valparaiso, Chile; and at first the Chile government made unsatisfactory replies to our demands for satisfaction; but subsequently apologized, and paid seventy-five thousand dollars indemnity.—Such are the ripples that varied the general calm of Harrison's administration.

After a tame campaign, in which the party differences concerned chiefly protection, and Federal supervision of elections, which Republicans favored and Democrats opposed, Grover Cleveland, renominated by the Democrats, was successful against Harrison. Cleveland returned to power to the sound of the guns which celebrated the four hundredth anniversary of the discovery of America. Business depression and financial troubles were great and numerous; but in the meanwhile the preparations for the Columbian Exposition, held in Chicago to commemorate Columbus's discovery, and to illustrate the industrial condition of the world, were actively making. The exhibition was held during six months, ending November, 1893, and was in all respects a success; the instruction it gave to the country was of permanent value, and it also, incidentally, enabled the people of all sections to see and become acquainted with one another. But while this splendid picture of material progress and wealth was being displayed, the condition of the country, owing to artificial causes, became worse. One of the President's first acts was to recall from the Senate the Hawaiian annexation bill. The Wilson bill, reducing tariff on imports, was passed, though strongly opposed; but such was the agitation in the country, traceable to no well-ascertained cause, that failures became constant. No one was sure what was the matter; but the people, in these cases, are apt to lay the blame on the existing administration, though often the latter may be wholly innocent, and but suffers from the evil legacy of its predecessor. The Democratic majority in Congress was reversed. The tariff did not pay the expenses of government, and the income tax, which had been much disliked, was finally declared unconstitutional by the Supreme Court. The discussion of financial problems at this period was unprecedented, but little light was thrown upon them. The repeal of the Sherman silver bill was demanded, and it began to be evident that the next election would turn on financial questions; the Republicans demanding the adoption of a gold standard, in harmony with Europe, and the Democrats, led by their nominee, William Jennings Bryan, urging the free and unlimited coinage of silver and the establishment of a ratio between silver and gold of sixteen to one. Meanwhile there was another threat of war with England; not, this time, on account of cod fisheries or seal fisheries; but because England refused to accept our proposal to arbitrate her dispute with Venezuela as to the true boundary between that country and British Guiana. Solicitude for our Monroe Doctrine urged us to take a hand in the matter; and Cleveland sent a message to Congress recommending an ex parte commission to inquire into the merits of the case. This menaced war with England; stocks and United States bonds fell; the price of money rose from two per cent to eight. But the danger was finally averted through moderation on England's part. A rebellion which had broken out in Cuba against Spanish official tyranny and outrage attracted some attention at this time, though its ultimate consequences were not foreseen; attempts to secure recognition of a Cuban Republic by this country failed. There had been a previous, unsuccessful rebellion twenty years before; and it was evident that the conditions in the island were become intolerable.

The campaign of 1896 was in some respects remarkable. Bryan was a very young man for a presidential aspirant; he was gifted with eloquence, and he had the utmost sincerity of conviction that the principles he enunciated were true, and would pull the country out of its financial hole. More money was wanted, so that the poor might be enabled to live; he believed that by coining silver freely, its value as one-sixteenth that of gold might be maintained; he thought other countries would follow our lead in fixing this ratio, and meanwhile he declared that America did not have to go to Europe to find out what was good for her. These opinions, cogently expressed during a tour which covered almost every state in the Union, took great hold upon the minds of the poorer classes, and enlisted also the support of many who were not poor; and vast multitudes in the middle and western states, and in some parts of the south, came together to listen to Bryan, and seemed to regard him as a sort of savior divinely appointed to rescue them from their troubles. The Republicans rallied the support of the wealthy and conservative element, the men of property and vested interests, the bankers and trust proprietors, and the employers in general of labor. The campaign was as bitter as the previous one had been apathetic; and the result was in doubt till the last. Then it appeared that McKinley, the Republican candidate, was elected by a small majority, so far as the popular vote was concerned.

The country now looked forward, too optimistically, to an immediate reappearance of prosperity. We have learned to live our personal lives so rapidly, and so many striking events crowd upon one another in this age of electricity and turmoil of governments, that we have become prone to imagine that effects in national affairs follow causes more quickly than they used to do. But erroneous methods, or partial solutions of economic problems, are not followed by good results any more than they formerly were, nor are the processes of evolution to be hurried because we are breathless and impatient. The people that does not know its true way does not get forward, no matter what its strength and activity. Our attention has been turned of late years almost exclusively to the expedition of business, and we are able, individually, to conduct our business with as much promptitude and efficiency as the conditions allow. But there are great secrets in the chemistry of finance, labor and government which have not yet been guessed; hitherto we have got on well enough without fully guessing them; but now the adjustments of life are finer than they were, we are confronted by hitherto untried situations, and we are consequently arrested in a fog of perplexities and wanton experiments. This nation has come to the end of one period of its growth, and is arrived at the threshold of another. Fifty or a hundred years from now we shall be able to look back and understand the position we occupy at this moment; and we shall probably see, then, that not one new thing, but many, awaited us. The next century may be expected to be not only different, but very different from the last.

To speak in the broadest terms, what is needed seems to be more of the spiritual quality in our affairs. There was a spirit dominating us in the Seventeenth Century, which drove us hither and anchored us in the wilderness; there was a spirit in 1776 which defended against oppression what we had won; and there was a spirit in 1861 which labored fiercely to rid our broad shoulders of the burden which stealthy ages had bound upon them; and which succeeded, though the knife with which we severed the bonds entered deep into our own living flesh. But now, during the succeeding decades, a great body of trade and industry has grown up, which is as yet without an inner soul: it has no ruling and guiding spirit within it. It is a vast, inorganic mass, which only seeks to grow bigger, instead of taking on intelligent form and proportions, and discovering its own meaning and its right to be. It is engendered of ambition and competition; it aims at possession and enjoyment of life—the good things of life: and this is no aim at all, nor can it ever be so; the real good of life comes only while we seek better things and, finding us with our eyes and hearts set elsewhere, suddenly is revealed humbly moving at our side. The utmost that commerce, agriculture, finance, government, science can give us, is in itself not worth stooping to pick up; the garment without the body is nothing, the body without the soul is nothing, the soul without immortality is nothing. We must learn the ultimate use and value of this vast accumulation of things which we are gathering together, like slaves, imagining ourselves masters of the world when we are its helpless drudges and lackeys. We must develop a soul to animate withal this huge corporeal mass of impedimenta, of conveniences, luxuries, curiosities, redundancies. We must lift it and organize it and rationalize it out of its present abject and selfish sprawl, and cause it to occupy its proper office and place in our human economy. Much of it will then disappear as worthless or obstructive; much more will be regarded as incidental merely to the attainment of better things. Material prosperity will become an instrument of life, not its object. As we value it less, it will become less irregular, more evenly distributed; not congested arbitrarily here and there, with spaces of want and misery between, but spread over the surface of the community like a comely skin or fitting garment. Our present careers are prone to insanities, collisions and the cruelties of neglect and preoccupation; we need to consult each the interest of his neighbor, as of his larger and completer self, and therefore the self which merits most consideration and service. We cannot solve from below the problems which now perplex us; we must rise to a height where they become indifferent to us, and then we shall look down upon them and understand them.

How shall this elevation be accomplished?—Not, if the testimony of history be valid, by spinning theories or enunciating moralities, however lofty and ingenious. Not by our own ambition or initiative; but by an inward inspiration from the Creator, to which it shall behoove us to give heed. Work will be given us to do; and according as we respond to the stimulus and duty, will our future be. The faithful and zealous prosecution of that work, be it what it may, will open to us the larger and purer horizons for which we ignorantly languish. America has performed the first task laid upon her—she has wrought herself into a great nation. Another task awaits her: what is it?—None can tell; but we may surmise that it may be, to bear our part, a leading one, in doing by others as we have done by ourselves. To make an America of the world would be a worthy work, and one which would collect our energies from their present waste and dispersion, and apply them to the grandest issues. Did God collect this people here, in order that they might live to themselves alone, and leave their fellow creatures to welter in darkness? Beware of that fatal policy of seclusion! There are many plausible and soothing arguments in its favor, but there is nothing Christian or immortal in it. What we have, in measure as it is good, becomes not ours exclusively, but somewhat held in stewardship for the race. If we try to monopolize it, it will breed in us fever and corruption; if we dispense it, it will be a blessing universal. Let us not forget that our forefathers said—"We hold these truths to be self-evident—that all men are created equal; that they are endowed by their Creator with certain inalienable rights; that among these are life, liberty, and the pursuit of happiness." Were these words meant to apply only to the three or four million human beings who at that time constituted the civilized population of this continent? "All men" was the word; and having secured the rights specified for ourselves, is it not incumbent upon us to seek in all ways open to us to secure them for others? Nor need we go out of our way to find opportunities; they will be offered to us. There is oppression and suffering on all sides of us, from where the sun rises to where it sets. Only let us not stop our ears to its voice, nor avert our eyes from the spectacle of its misery. Let us rather stop our ears to those who tell us it is none of our business, and avert our eyes from those who would unroll before us alluring pictures of ease and luxury kept within the boundaries of this mighty land, which God gave us in trust, therein to raise a race of men whose destiny it shall be to give freedom, light and happiness to the world.

SIEGE OF VICKSBURG.—CHARGING THE CONFEDERATE WORKS, MAY 19, 1863

THE NEW YORK
PUBLIC LIBRARY

ASTOR, LENOX AND
TILDEN FOUNDATIONS.

BATTLE OF SPOTTSYLVANIA, MAY 12, 1864

CONFEDERATE COMMANDERS

1. COL. J. A. MOSBY.   2. GEN. J. E. JOHNSTON.   3. GEN. JAMES LONGSTREET.
4. GEN. J. E. B. STUART.   5. GEN. A. P. HILL.

THE NEW YORK
PUBLIC LIBRARY

ASTOR, LENOX AND
TILDEN FOUNDATIONS.

"SHERIDAN'S RIDE"—CEDAR CREEK, NEAR WINCHESTER, VA., OCTOBER 19, 1864

CAPTURE OF FORT FISHER, N. C.—THE ASSAULT, JANUARY, 1865

THE NEW YORK
PUBLIC LIBRARY

ASTOR, LENOX AND
TILDEN FOUNDATIONS.

THE NEW YORK
PUBLIC LIBRARY

ASTOR, LENOX AND
TILDEN FOUNDATIONS.

UNION GENERALS

DESTRUCTION OF THE "MAINE," FEBRUARY 15, 1898

ROOSEVELT'S "ROUGH RIDERS" IN ACTION, NEAR SANTIAGO,
CUBA, JUNE, 1898

SUPPLEMENT

WAR WITH SPAIN

LLUSIONS to Spain have not been rare in the preceding pages; for that nation is connected with the earliest annals of our country. They have been uniformly critical, because whatever Spain has done in America has, from the first, been evil. Her influence has always been exerted on the side of oppression and against enlightenment and liberty; it has been marked by cruelty and selfishness. She has gained much wealth from her American possessions, but it has not been honestly acquired, and it has been expended for ill ends. Spain, in spite of her opportunities, is now a bankrupt nation and a by-word of reproach in Europe. She is not, in the modern sense, a civilized nation, but is still in many respects barbaric. In no European nation is ignorance so prevalent as in Spain. None is more brutal in its customs, or more narrow and perverse in its aims. At the end of the Nineteenth Century, the hour for her chastisement was ripe; and destiny intrusted the duty of administering it to the United States.

These facts are summarily stated; for we are not now concerned to prove them by citing the leading events of Spanish history. The geographical position of Spain, almost as isolated by the Pyrenees as if it had been an island, is in part responsible for her character and annals. She was naturally maritime, owing to the extent of her coasts; and prevented from sharing the civilized advance of Europe, owing to her seclusion. But her coasts also laid her open to Moorish conquest; and from her conquerors she derived many of her worst as well as most of her good traits. From the Moors she learned courage and strength in war, and finally used it to drive them from her confines; from them she drew the imaginative quality which, for a time, made her famous in literature. From them, also, she inherited the fantastic cruelty, the love of blood, the animal lusts which from the first have stained her records. But the Spaniard shows the Moor degraded; he is less noble than his dark-skinned master, less generous, less highly organized. Socially and politically he has always been corrupt. It is not too much to say that, since their history begins, there has been no female chastity in Spain, except by accident or under compulsion; nor any masculine honor, save that grotesque parody of honor which Spaniards are quick to assert, and which, with their "pride," renders them the solemn laughing-stock of modern ages. Spanish rulers and the entire governing class, have always been types of inhumanity, tyranny, and greed. Religion has been to Spain but a means of oppression and the infliction of misery on others. She was Catholic with the rest of Europe; but her priests perceived in the Church only an instrument of acquiring material aggrandizement and power through spiritual terror and imposition; and with the establishment of the Inquisition she drove the last nail into the coffin of her own future. For the true significance and offices of Christianity, Spain has never betrayed the faintest comprehension or inclination. In the name of Christ she has exterminated populations, and shed more blood than runs in the veins of all living Spaniards to-day. Spain and Turkey, at opposite ends of Europe, are alike anachronisms; and it has been only the mutual jealousies of the rest of Europe that has permitted them to survive so long. Europe has her duty by the Moslem still to do; but we found the burden of Spain laid upon our shoulders; and during the last few months, at a cost to ourselves that seems miracu-

SHORTENING SAIL ON THE U. S. CRUISER "LANCASTER," THE OLDEST VESSEL IN THE SPANISH-AMERICAN WAR

lously small, we have been dealing with it in a manner which leaves little yet to do.

The true story of Cuba has yet to be written in its inner details; one does not envy the historian his task. It is a monotonous tale of baseness, robbery, and inhumanity. First, and promptly, the native population was exterminated; then a new race began to exist, compounded of Spaniards and negroes, with an admixture of other strains in minor degrees. This race, in the course of some centuries, begot characteristics of its own; but it was always oppressed by the Spanish governing class sent over from the Peninsula. We have seen how England attempted to tyrannize over her American colonies, and how selfish and short-sighted were the laws she tried to impose upon us. But the worst that we suffered was mildness compared with the normal situation in Cuba; and the Cubans lacked the Anglo-Saxon passion for liberty and independence which marked the men of New England and Virginia. Individual industry and enterprise were discouraged or paralyzed, because the governors from Spain left the native producers barely enough for the needs of existence. Cuba, potentially rich as any region of equal extent in the world, and richer by far than all save a few, has never yielded a hundredth part of the returns which could have been realized by an enlightened administration. Nevertheless, she and the other island colonies of Spain, east and west, have been of vital use to her in arresting the downward course which she has so long been pursuing; Spain's life, such as it was, depended on them; and now that they are to be withdrawn, sentence of death upon their former owner has been passed. Even were her domestic politics favorable—and they are at the furthest remove from that—she has no internal resources to adequately meet her expenses, to say nothing of her indebtedness to others; and she seems likely to become the mendicant of Europe for generations to come, and finally to vanish from the roster of distinct nations, more completely than

Hungary or Poland. It is a terrible punishment; but it has been well merited.

The Cubans endured much; but at length even their limits were overpassed, and they rebelled. They had before them the example of free America; and even the quasi-liberty of the so-called republics of Spanish-America was an object of envy to them. The topography and climate of their island made it difficult to subdue them, though, on the other hand, they were powerless to drive out the Spaniards; and the consequence was a long-drawn-out and inconclusive struggle of ten years, exhausting to both parties. It ended in a compromise, by which Cuba was to receive certain concessions, including representation in the Spanish Cortes; but no real advantage accrued from Spanish promises, and the abuses and cruelties became more virulent than ever. The United States was restive under this chronic sore, festering close under her eyes; and during the past half century various schemes and suggestions have been mooted having in view the taking or purchasing Cuba from Spain. . But the feeling was strong in this country against saddling ourselves with a possession which, rich though it was, was encumbered by many objectionable features; and Spain herself evinced the strongest disinclination to relinquishing the victim whose blood she had sucked so long. The rebellion ended in 1878. Several American agencies were operating in the island, and drawing large profits from their investments; and there were not a few American holders of Spanish securities guaranteed by Cuban duties. These persons were naturally content that Spain should retain control of Cuba, since in the event of the island being taken from her, the value of their securities would be extinguished. Great European financiers, like the Rothschilds, were interested in Spanish supremacy for the same reason; and because they were in the habit of assisting our banking and capitalistic class with loans and accommodations for their enterprises, they were able to exert great influence upon the attitude of the latter; so that it was certain that war with Spain would always find resolute opponents in our moneyed men. Another apologist or champion of Spain was the Roman See; because, when Spain, in the fore part of the century, confiscated church property in her colonies, compensation was made by the issue of interest bearing bonds to the amount of some hundreds of millions of dollars, which were held by the Church. If Spain, through war, were to become utterly bankrupt, these bonds would be worthless, and the Church in that amount a loser. Finally, Austria and France were both anxious to protect Spain; France because she was a large holder of Spanish 4's, and Austria because the Queen Regent of Spain was a member of the Austrian Royal House. The Queen's son, Alphonso, was ostensibly, of course, the son of Christina and the late king; though strong doubts have been cast on the purity of his descent, on the paternal side.

Spain, therefore, like other nations and persons before her, depended for her maintenance upon the consequences of her own misdeeds, and inability to govern herself. And doubtless no other European nation, or combination, would have thought it worth while to interfere with her. But in the United States there is a vast body of persons who detest outrage and injustice for their own sakes, and when they are thrust too impudently into their field of vision, will demand that the nuisance be abated. These persons have no regard for international etiquette, or for compromises, or for Spanish pride; but they hate to see inoffensive and helpless people starved and murdered, with accompaniments of the most revolting brutality. Consequently when, for the second time, the Cubans broke out in revolt, there was heard a voice in this country, speaking from every part of it, demanding that the iniquity of Spanish misrule cease, and insisting that we bring about its cessation, peaceably if we could, forcibly if we must. This voice had nothing to say about the acquisition of Cuba by the United States; no such burden was desired; but Spain must concede freedom to her colony, and abstain henceforward and forever from torturing and robbing it.

So long as this voice was not official, Spain paid no heed to it; not being aware that the real official voice in the United States is the voice of the American people, which first speaks for itself, and afterward, if its hints are not attended to, utters itself through the mouth of its official representatives. But Spain was again failing to put down the rebellion, which, instead of being confined, as in the former one, to the eastern part of the island, had spread to the west, and left to the Spaniards only those towns in which Spanish soldiers were stationed. Immense numbers of soldiers—two hundred thousand, if accounts are to be credited—had been sent to Cuba; but they did no fighting worthy of the name, and were not intended to do any; they were mainly to serve as a means for the enrichment of their officers, who appropriated all the money sent out to pay them, or otherwise available for that purpose, except just so much as might serve to keep the soldiers alive. It was the policy of the Spanish officials not to fight the war out, but to prolong it; and gradually to exterminate the Cuban population. The Captain-general first in command, Martinez Campos, was recalled after a year of unsuccess, and in his place was installed General Weyler, the catalogue of whose crimes and bestialities perhaps surpasses that of any living being, and who has never been outdone even by his own countrymen in the past. He is the man who caused Cuban ladies to be haled naked to his room, who there witnessed their rape by his soldiery, and who answered their appeals for mercy by kicking and stamping upon them, and tearing their flesh with his spurred heels. These women and maids had done nothing to offend him, except to be the wives and daughters of Cubans who were suspected of disaffection to Spain, or who had failed to deliver to the general the amount of money which he had chosen to think they possessed. We need not further detail Weyler's crimes; they were given full rein during his lease of power; he was the idol and model of his followers, and he and they became rich to the extent of many millions by the theft of money not only from the Cubans, but from embezzlement of the sums sent from Spain for the prosecution of the war. From first to last, no one has been found to relate of this monster one single redeeming trait.

With a view to hastening the extermination of the Cuban race, Weyler conceived and put in execution an idea which could occur only to one whose thoughts found their inspiration in the source of all evil. It was on the 21st of October that he issued the famous order of reconcentration.—"I order and command that all the inhabitants of the country now outside of the line of fortification of the towns, shall, within the period of eight days, concentrate themselves in the town so occupied by the troops. Any individual who after the expiration of this period is found in the uninhabited parts will be considered a rebel and tried as such."

There were then living in the regions neighboring to the towns in question persons whose number has been variously estimated at from four hundred to six hundred thousand. Most of them were women and children. They were of all social grades, from the peasant to the independent proprietor. Weyler's order caused them to abandon their homes and crowd into a barren space around the towns, where they must remain without other shelter than what they could erect with their own hands, without furniture or any of the appurtenances of civilization, without food, or any means of obtaining any save by beggary. Beggary from the soldiers of Weyler was not a lucrative occupation. Such of the women or virgins as had the ill-fortune to be passably good-looking were subjected to the lust of the soldiery in the open camp. The homes which these people had been compelled to leave were destroyed by the Spanish guerrillas, and the lands laid waste. If any inhabitants were found still hiding

in the outer country, which was constantly scoured by the
guerrillas, they were hacked to death with the machete,
shot, or subjected to lingering tortures. Many were murdered for amusement even while obeying the reconcentration order. But the great majority were permitted slowly
to starve to death on the bare ground outside the towns.
The process lasted days or weeks according to circumstances, and was attended with every circumstance of insult and mental anguish. They perished in heaps and rows,
and their bones—for flesh there was little or none left—were
tossed into pits, or left to be devoured by vultures. Half a
million reconcentrados had been removed in this manner
at the time that war was declared between Spain and the
United States; and there can be no doubt that the remainder long since ceased to exist. The story was told again
and again by the press, but the very horror of it restrained
belief. The reports of our consuls were suppressed. Weyler's campaign, as he facetiously termed it, seemed likely to
continue unchecked, within six hours of the highest and
most humane civilization of the world. Why was the effort
made to keep our people in ignorance of the truth, and to
delay action? Because, should the facts appear, the holders of Spanish securities in this country, and their friends
abroad, would lose their money. This fact should not be
forgotten by Americans, when the time shall come to bring
before the court of public opinion, for reward or punishment,
the persons and parties by whom the war with Spain was
advocated or opposed. It is also historically significant as
showing the extent and weight of the influence which
money is able to exert, for a time, upon the conduct of
this Republic.

Before the end of his Presidential term, Cleveland had
said, in one of his messages, referring to the Cuban situation, that higher obligations than those of neutrality might
be imposed on us by the manner in which Spain was prosecuting her war in Cuba. The time chosen for this utterance

was shortly before the Presidential canvass which was to determine whether or not Mr. Cleveland was to be his own successor. Since he retired to private life, he has expressed himself as strongly opposed to our war against Spain for the liberation of Cuba. Any man may honestly change his opinion, and the time to pass judgment on the men concerned directly or indirectly with this war has not yet arrived; but it was unfortunate for Mr. Cleveland, and the many whose record in this respect resembles his, that he and they are affiliated with persons whose financial interest it was that Spain should be left undisturbed. It is natural and even commendable for a man to be solicitous to save his property, and to aid his friends to save theirs; but there are limits to be observed even here; and it is generally conceded that money bought at the expense of condoning such crimes as those of Weyler, is expensive. Moreover, if a man decide to oppose a given line of action, such as our Cuban war, in order to secure his holdings of stock and bonds, it is expedient that he declare frankly his true reasons; it is unwise for him to attempt to disguise them by putting forward humanitarian pleas, as that war is an evil, a barbarism which should be out of date; and that the United States should meddle with no affairs not directly her political concern, on pain of violating the Constitution, and the maxims of Washington, Jefferson and Monroe. A miser may be respectable; but a miser who hides his greed under the guise of philanthropy and loyalty to high political or other principles, falls into an error which time will surely reveal to him and to others.— We must not, however, neglect to notice the existence among us, and in all communities, of that timorous but strictly honest conservative instinct which clings to the methods and traditions of the past, and dreads any departure toward new ways and ideas. Of such we number many in our most respectable societies; and they swelled the number of the Peace-at-any-Price men who joined in the outcry against the war with Spain on behalf of Cuba.

When McKinley was elected President, the platform on which he stood referred to the existing war with Cuba in terms which favored the supposition that, should the horrors alleged prove to be true, this country would interfere in the cause of humanity. For some time, however, the insistence of matters of domestic concern, and other reasons, produced a certain sluggishness or apathy in regard to Cuban affairs. But stories of Spanish brutality still continued to appear in the press; and there was one story in particular of a young Cuban girl of beauty and social position, Evangelina de Cisneros by name, who had been captured under painful circumstances, and whose ruin had been attempted by a Spanish officer and friend of Weyler's. Because this girl had resisted violation, she was imprisoned in the common jail in Havana with the dregs of the population, and had been condemned to a Spanish penal colony, where her fate would be death, preceded by a fate far worse than death itself. This tale struck the imagination of our people, and diplomatic efforts were made to induce Weyler to surrender her—of course without effect. At that juncture she was rescued from her jail by a young journalist named Karl Decker, representing a New York paper; and the boldness and dash of his exploit strongly enlisted American sympathies, and led to closer scrutiny of Spanish doings in Cuba. Finally, a number of members of Congress undertook a trip to Cuba to investigate for themselves; and their report, when delivered, fully corroborated the worst stories printed for a year past in the newspapers.

Meanwhile, Weyler had retired from the Captain-generalcy of Cuba, and had been succeeded by General Blanco, who ostensibly proceeded to put forward a policy of mercy and autonomy. Cubans were to be permitted to govern themselves, under Spanish supervision; the reconcentrados still surviving should be at liberty to return to their homes. This concession on Spain's part was due to the representations of the holders of Spanish securities, who convinced the Spanish government that the American people could not much longer be held in check, and that if war were to be avoided, some appearance at least of conforming to the dictates of humanity must be made. But the hollowness of the concession was almost immediately apparent. The Cubans themselves, taught by bitter experience, repudiated the autonomy pretense, and pointed out that the conditions under which Spain claimed rights of supervision were amply sufficient to insure a continuance of every abuse of which they now complained. As for the relaxation of the rules governing the reconcentrados, it soon transpired that it concealed a sinister motive. Most of these unfortunates were too far gone in starvation and despair to avail themselves of the permission to return to their homes; those who did return found them burned to the ground; and while they were debating what next to do, they were set upon by the bands of guerrillas and slaughtered in cold blood. In a word, Weyler's policy was in no degree revoked; it was only prosecuted under a hypocritical disguise by his successor. All hope for Cubans, except by direct intervention of the United States, was at an end.

Before this time, indeed, the mass of our people had come to the conclusion that war could be avoided only by the retirement of Spain from Cuba definitely and forever. It was impossible for us to stand by and see these horrors accomplished without raising a hand to prevent it. While there was still a doubt as to the truth of the reports, we might hesitate; but that doubt was dissipated, and action must follow—or the disgrace of having refrained from action under such circumstances—a disgrace to which Americans refused to submit. We were, however, willing to let the war initiative come from Spain; we insisted only on relieving the reconcentrados at once, with supplies which we furnished. About the same time, our fleet began to gather together at Key West, and in other places neighboring to Cuba and the West Indies; and a number of our ships, under Dewey, was known to be off the Chinese coast, within a few days' sail of the Spanish colony of the Philippines, which had also been in revolt, for causes similar to those which animated the Cubans. In January, one of our warships, the "Maine," was sent to the harbor of Havana, nominally on a friendly visit, on the same basis as that on which the "Vizcaya" was even then preparing to visit New York Harbor. But it was understood in this country that the "Maine" was intended to inspire the Spaniards in Cuba with respect for the Americans living there at the time; and to secure safety for the agents who were conveying our consignments of food to the reconcentrados. For it would have been manifestly futile to intrust to Spanish hands the distribution of these supplies; and on the other hand the lives of Americans were not safe in Havana and the neighboring towns; even the consuls, Consul-general Fitz Hugh Lee not excepted, were more or less in peril. But after the arrival of the "Maine," a distinct improvement in the Spanish bearing toward Americans was noticeable; and Miss Clara Barton, who had come to oversee and direct the relief of the starving people, was treated with courtesy and permitted to carry out, in some degree, her measures of mercy. At the same time, beneath this surface courtesy, was readily observable an undercurrent of hatred and covert menace; and the presence of the "Maine" was evidently most irksome to the population of Havana. A word let fall by the Spanish consul in Key West at this time —that it needed but a turn of the hand to send the "Maine" to hell, with all on board—was remembered afterward.

Let us now consider the physical position of the "Maine" in Havana Harbor. This harbor—though the fact was not known, however keenly suspected, previous to the 15th of February, 1898—was sown with mines, as they are technically called: a kind of bombs filled with gun-cotton, dynamite, or other explosives, connected with the shore by wires, and exploded at any desired moment by turning on an electrical current through the wire. An Englishman named

Gibbons testified to having supplied a number of mines to the Spanish government for use in Havana Harbor; and an American, Crandall, admitted having laid mines in that harbor in 1896, at the order of General Weyler. In July of the next year, at Weyler's special direction, he laid a large mine close to buoy number 4, in the center of the harbor. This mine, if touched by the keel of a vessel lying over it, would reveal the fact automatically at the keyboard on shore; and a person on the watch there would then only have to touch a button, in order to discharge the mine and destroy the vessel. Access to the keyboard could be had only by officers in the confidence of the Spanish authorities. All this, of course, was entirely legitimate as a measure of harbor defense; but it is to be remarked that the Cubans had no navy, and that the planting of mines in Havana Harbor could therefore have had no reference to them. On the other hand, there was no nation except the American from which the Spaniards had any reason to anticipate hostile action.

Such was the setting of the scene when the "Maine" entered Havana Harbor. Captain Sigsbee was proceeding to choose his own anchorage, when he was directed by the harbor-master, acting under the directions of the Captain-general, to station his ship at buoy No. 4. He of course complied, and the "Maine" remained attached to that buoy until the moment when the mine placed there was exploded, and blew her up. This event occurred on the night of the 15th of February, about nine o'clock, when the major part of the crew was below in their hammocks; and two hundred and sixty-six officers and men were killed, and the ship herself utterly destroyed.

The survivors on the ship, and all disinterested persons who were cognizant of the conditions, were at once convinced that the catastrophe was not the result of chance. The mining of the harbor was known, although it had uniformly been denied by the Spaniards; and it had been a topic of common gossip among the men of the "Maine," that there was a mine under her bottom. Threats to blow her up had several times been heard from Spaniards in Havana; and when the deed had been done, there was slight attempt to disguise the feeling of joy which it caused in the city. Spanish officers, meeting in the cafes, toasted one another on the success of the *coup*. The hand of some Spanish officer, connected with the Weyler interest, had probably done the deed; but, of course, there was an immediate official disavowal of it. Meanwhile, the American flag was hoisted over the remains of our ship, and an investigation was begun, to determine by direct and scientific evidence the cause of the explosion. The court of investigation consisted of United States officers, who went to Havana for the purpose; divers were sent down to examine the shattered hull; great secrecy was observed as to the results of the examination, and the sittings of the board were prolonged for no less than forty days. Less than a fourth as many would have amply sufficed; but there were reasons for the delay: first, in order to give time for the Pope and the other creditors of Spain to try to influence Congress against war; and secondly, to afford us time to get ready for possible hostilities. The story of the negotiations behind the scenes may yield interesting reading at some future epoch; for the present, their tenor can only be conjectured. The Peace-at-any-Price party put forth their most desperate efforts; and Mr. McKinley's attitude was ambiguous. If he desired to be assured of the true attitude of the country before acting, he was not left in doubt. The sense of outrage was marked on all sides, and it became daily more obvious that no tampering with the situation would be permitted. The Peace party protested that it was impossible to believe, or to prove, that the act had been committed deliberately by Spain, because, first, Spain denied it; secondly, such a thing in time of peace was unheard of; and again, because the chances were that Spain was right in her contention that the explosion was occasioned by the negligence of the men and officers on the American ship, and was due to touching off one of the magazines on board. But the great mass of the American people, whose opinions were not controlled by considerations of politics or finance, and who were aware that the destruction of the "Maine" in the manner charged was anything but inconsistent with Spain's conduct at all periods in her history, was convinced of the truth from the first; and "Remember the 'Maine'" became a watchword everywhere. American Roman Catholics, from all sides, evinced the heartiest patriotism; and Archbishop Ireland's request to the President that opportunity be given for the Vatican to plead with Spain to evacuate Cuba, was honorable and Christian; it is the duty of the Church to oppose war—though, as the sequel has shown, the loss of life in this war falls vastly below the mortality which the delay enabled Blanco and his men to inflict upon the surviving reconcentrados. But this, of course, was hidden from the Archbishop.

When, at length, the report of the Court was allowed to appear, it bore out to the full the worst anticipations. Every part and fragment of the wreck had been scrutinized by experts, and they all indicated a force applied externally, and from below upward. The Spanish authorities afterward made a perfunctory examination, lasting a few days, and announced, in the face of the evidence, that the explosion was from within; but the manifest falsity of this conclusion only went to show, not only that a mine destroyed the "Maine," but that the firing of the mine was deliberate on Spain's part. Her profession of a willingness to submit the matter to arbitration was regarded as an insult; and her pointblank refusal to make restitution made an appeal to arms inevitable, quite aside from the question of the reconcentrados. Yet there were Peace men still found to declare that the Court of Inquiry had proved nothing against Spain, and that no justifiable grounds for war existed. Prominent among these persons, in New England, was Mr. Charles Eliot Norton, a professor of Harvard College, who declared in a speech to the students that war would be an infamy. But the patriotism of Harvard had been proved in the Civil War, and was not likely to be wanting now.

The President sent the report to Congress, with comments thereon, which by many were thought unduly conservative; and in the message which he issued April 11th, asking authority to use the military and naval forces of the United States to compel Spain to evacuate Cuba, he based his request on Spanish inhumanity to Cubans, and on her inability to conquer them; and not upon the destruction of the "Maine." This was no doubt due to lack of technical proof that it was by Spanish officers, acting in connivance with the Havana authorities, that the explosion was produced. The certainty was a moral one; but it was desirable to eliminate every ground of criticism from our proceedings. It was in the name of humanity, therefore, that this country finally declared war.

After a few days of animated debate, a joint resolution of the two Houses of Congress was promulgated, which, after calling attention to conditions which had for three years existed in Cuba, characterizing them as a disgrace to civilization, and remarking that they had culminated "in the destruction of a United States battleship, with 266 of its officers and crew, while on a friendly visit to the harbor of Havana," goes on to declare that the Cubans are and of right ought to be free and independent; that it was our duty to demand that Spain at once relinquish authority in the island and withdraw its forces therefrom; that the President be empowered to use the entire land and naval power of the United States, and to call out the militia, to effect these ends; and that the United States "hereby disclaims any disposition or intention to exercise sovereignty, jurisdiction or control over said island, except for the pacification thereof, and asserts its determination when that is accomplished to leave the government and control of the island to its people." Not for conquest, profit, or aggrandizement did we undertake this war, but purely for the sake of averting murder and robbery, and in order to give a brave people civil liberty. A more disinterested and honorable war was never undertaken; and it was strictly in harmony with the traditions and mission of America. The date of the above resolutions was April 19th —a day already famous in our annals.

Already measures having a warlike tendency had been taken both by Spain and by the United States. A Spanish fleet was being gathered at the Cape Verde Islands, which belong to Portugal, as early as the 2d of April; numbers of Spaniards in Havana had enlisted in the volunteers; the President had replied to representatives of six European powers (expressing a hope that peace might be preserved), that the war of Spain on the Cubans must cease; Consul-general Lee was recalled from Havana, together with other Americans living in Cuba; the Spanish Cabinet, on April 13th, voted an extraordinary war-credit; orders to concentrate our fleets were issued, and several war vessels were purchased in Europe. On the 15th of April England declared coal contraband of war; on the 19th, troops were moved from various garrisons to Chickamauga Park, whence lines of railway radiate to the southern Atlantic coast, and to ports on the Gulf of Mexico; on the 20th our ultimatum was cabled to Spain, and on the 21st, before Woodford, our minister at Madrid, had delivered it to the Spanish government, he was given his passports and escorted out of the country. On the same day, the fleet under Sampson was ordered to proceed to blockade Havana, and the foreign governments were duly notified. Dewey was directed to proceed to Manila, in the Philippines; and on April 26th, McKinley issued a call for one hundred and twenty-five thousand volunteers, apportioning to each state its quota. Three days before this Sampson's squadron had captured a Spanish prize steamer, the "Buen Ventura," which was entering Key West in ignorance that the war had begun. The shot which caused her to bring to was fired by Patrick Walton, on board the United States ship "Nashville," about half-past five in the morning.

At this time, neither nation was fully prepared for war, though Spain had been urging preparations ever since January; but she had perhaps doubted whether we really meant to fight, being misled by the vociferousness of the Peace party. The European powers were divided in their sympathies, France and Austria favoring Spain, as did also a part of the German press; while Italy was disposed to adopt a friendly attitude toward us, and Russia intimated that she had nothing to object to in our course. England, however (although, in common with the rest, declaring a strict neutrality), took occasion in various ways to express a cordial friendship for the United States, and entire approval of our course. It was semi-officially intimated that an alliance would not be unwelcome to England, in the event of any other power siding with Spain against us; and a great deal was said about the bonds of kinship binding together the two great English-speaking peoples. Americans, as a whole, met these advances in a spirit of cheerful recognition, though permitting the inference that friendship rather than a regular alliance would meet our view of the greatest expediency. We thought ourselves well able to take care of Spain without assistance; and it was generally felt that, in the long run, England might profit more by an alliance with us than we should. But all this was premature; and the sickening sentimentality of poets on both sides, who instantly broke into a piping chorus of mutual congratulation at the prospect of the great Anglo-Saxon bond, probably was of service in making sensible persons shy of committing themselves too far. But the future of Europe is dark, if not ominous, and this war might easily cause us to take a far more intimate share in coming events on the other side of the oceans than we had lately believed possible. In that case, it seems reasonable that England and America would be found standing side by side.

The navies of Spain and of the United States were considered by experts to be about equal, with a slight preponderance in favor of Spain. Of trained soldiers under arms Spain undoubtedly had by far the greater number; and the remark was already being made that she would have a powerful ally against us in Cuba, in the shape of the yellow fever, which would be due about the time fighting in the island began. It was conceded that after the first months of the war, America would begin to gain, owing to her enormous superiority in resources of men and money; but it was thought that, meanwhile, Spain might be able to inflict staggering losses on us by sending a swift fleet to bombard our great seacoast cities, and collecting ransom. Indeed, there was something approaching a panic in some of these exposed places, and regrets were freely expressed that, in time of peace, we had not prepared for war. As it turned out, there was never any danger from the Spanish fleet, which was presently to prove itself incapable of either enterprise or fighting ability. But had we been opposed by the navy of any other power, we might no doubt have been forced to pay a fearful price for our neglect.

But if the Spanish fleet could not fight or attack, it could puzzle us sorely as to its whereabout and intentions. After collecting at St. Vincent, Cape Verde Islands, it remained there as long as the dilatory tactics of Portugal, which was the last of the nations to declare neutrality, would permit. It finally set sail in a westerly direction; but it might be aiming at any point of our coast; and reports of "phantom fleets" seen or heard of at the most diverse points began to come in. Now mysterious ships were seen off Nova Scotia; now they were approaching New York, now Boston, or Charleston; or they were descending in force on Havana, or they were sailing to cut off our battleship "Oregon," which had started from San Francisco, and was now coming up the coast of South America. Until we could know which of these several points to protect, we could form no definite plan of campaign; and thus Spain kept us guessing for what seemed a long time. Suddenly the report was sent with every sign of authority that the fleet had returned to Cadiz, Spain, and had given up the idea of crossing the Atlantic. But shortly after, it was heard of from Martinique, and its destination was surmised to be Cienfuegos, on the south coast of Cuba. If we could intercept it, a naval battle might be expected off the coast of Porto Rico. Schley, who had been on guard at Hampton Roads, was sent to the west end of Cuba, on the chance of the fleet's appearing there; while Sampson, after testing the defenses of San Juan, Porto Rico, by a short bombardment of its forts on May 12th, repaired to the Windward Passage, east of Cuba, in the hope of catching the Spanish fleet on its way north or west. Study of the map made it seem impossible that Cervera's ships could escape; but the feat was not so difficult in the actual waters of the Caribbean; and on May 19th the report was disseminated that the Spaniards were safe in the landlocked harbor of Santiago de Cuba.

Long previous to this date, however, several skirmishes by land and sea had taken place on the Cuban coast, and one great and memorable naval battle had been fought and won in the bay of remote Manila. The skirmishes are interesting chiefly as having bestowed their baptism of fire upon our soldiers and sailors; the losses were trifling, and the results unimportant. On the 27th of April the earthworks at Matanzas, about sixty miles east of Havana, were bombarded for fifteen minutes by the "New York," "Puritan" and "Cincinnati," of Sampson's squadron. The first gun was fired from the waist of the "New York" by Ensign Boone, one of the cadets who had been sent to the front from Annapolis before the regular time of graduation. The earthworks were destroyed, and it was supposed that the enemy suffered some losses; no one was injured on the American ships. On April

29th, a force of Spanish cavalry near Port Cabanas was dispersed by the "New York." On May 11th, while Sampson was on the Porto Rican coast, there occurred at Cardenas an engagement which was notable as being the first in the war in which Americans were killed by the enemy. There were concerned in this affair two gunboats, the "Machias" and the "Wilmington," under Commanders Merry and Todd; the converted revenue cutter "Hudson," Lieutenant Newcomb, and the torpedo boat "Winslow," under Lieutenant Bernadou. It had been discovered that there were in Cardenas Harbor three Spanish gunboats; but the waters were so shallow that not all of the American vessels could maneuver within, and a partially successful attempt was made, on the 8th of May, to draw the Spaniards out. On the 11th the "Hudson" and the "Winslow" undertook to run into the harbor and engage the gunboats where they lay off the wharf of Cardenas town. The harbor had been buoyed in places in order to fix the range, and as the "Winslow," which was in front, passed amid these buoys, she was hit by guns from the shore, and Bernadou was wounded in the leg. He bandaged his wound, and continued to direct his ship; but meanwhile another shot had broken the steering-gear of the "Winslow," and others passed through the boiler and disabled one of the engines. By the aid of the other engine, moving the vessel alternately backward and forward, it was found possible to get out of the region of the buoys; and Ensign Worth Bagley was stationed amidships to pass orders to the engineer below. The "Winslow" had all this while been firing her one-pounders continuously. The "Hudson," a slower ship, had meanwhile arrived within hailing distance, and Bernadou asked her to tow his ship out of the harbor. Up to this moment, no one except Bernadou had been hit, though ten shells had struck his boat. But while the "Hudson" was trying to pass a line, a shell struck in the midst of a group of men standing near Bagley. Three were killed at once, including Bagley; two more died soon after, and five were wounded; thus putting nearly half of the whole crew hors de combat. The "Hudson" succeeded in passing a line, but it broke, or was shot in two; and the same mishap happened to the second. The "Hudson" then went alongside the "Winslow," made fast to her, and in this manner took her out of range; while the "Wilmington," from outside, destroyed the Spanish gunboat lying by the wharf, and silenced all the shore batteries. It is a singular fact that more American seamen were killed in this little incidental skirmish than in all the other naval engagements of the war combined. The behavior of all the men in action was daring and cool throughout, and sufficed to show, without Dewey's superb demonstration, that the spirit of the American navy was all that it had ever been.

On the very next day there was a sharp little affair at Cabanas Harbor, on the other side of Havana, which was notable as being the first occasion on which troops were landed and engaged with the Spaniards. Two companies, E and G, of the First United States Infantry, were ordered on board the transport "Gussie" to carry three Cuban scouts, Major Donato Soto and two others, to some point on the Cuban coast, to communicate with the insurgent armies in the interior. A week was spent in running up and down the north shore, looking for a good landing-place; but the Spaniards were found everywhere actively on the lookout; a place near Cabanas was finally decided upon, though here also there were signs of the enemy, and in fact two thousand Spanish troops were posted at the town; but, at the time of the landing, most of these were engaged in repelling an attack from an insurgent force on the other side. Company G was left on board the transport; to Company E was accorded the honor of landing in the face of the enemy's fire, the operation being covered by Company G firing from behind a breastwork of bales of hay on the transport, assisted by the gunboats "Wasp" and "Manning," accompanying the expedition. Captain O'Connell was in command of the landing force.

At the moment of getting the men into the landing boats, a heavy tropical rain began to fall, and continued its deluge until after the landing was accomplished, accompanied by gusts of wind which threw up a choppy sea. Midway to the shore the men had to jump out on a reef and lift the boats across it, while exposed to the Spanish fire, which was copious, but did no damage. Reaching, at length, a thickly wooded point, the men were formed in skirmish line, with twenty paces between each of them. At a bridge, a little distance inland, the enemy was encountered, and retreated after exchanging a volley. The engagement then extended along the entire front of the advance, but, as usual, the enemy could not be seen. The Americans held the line until the Cuban scouts, in the rear, had saddled and mounted their horses, and passed round the flank into the interior country; whence they returned a month later, having obtained and communicated valuable information. While the line was held, or for about half an hour, the two gunboats and the transport were unable to give any assistance, lest their fire might fall among our own men, who, like the Spaniards, were invisible; but after the scouts had escaped, the line was withdrawn toward the shore, and placed behind a hasty intrenchment; and then the boats opened fire and put the enemy to flight. No Americans were killed, but many Spanish dead were found after the engagement. The men were safely re-embarked before the regiments in Cabanas fort had arrived at the scene of action. They seem to have looked over the ground after we had left it, and to have reported to General Blanco, in Havana, a great Spanish victory.

But it is more than time that we cross the Continent, and the Pacific, and follow the doings of Admiral Dewey at the

The American squadron left Mirs Bay at two P.M. on Wednesday, April 27th, and reached Bolinao Bay, on the Philippine coast, early on the morning of Saturday, April 30th: the run having been made slowly, to economize coal. The "Concord" and "Boston" were then sent ahead to look for the enemy in Subig Bay, and the "Baltimore" afterward followed to support them; the rest of the ships arriving there in the afternoon. No enemy was in sight, and the conclusion was, that Montojo must have chosen to do battle under the Manila batteries. The entrance to the harbor was forty miles further on, and orders were given to steam thither at six knots an hour, in order to pass the batteries there about midnight. The nerves of the men were tested by this slow approach to unknown dangers. The entrance to the bay is five miles wide, but in its mouth are three islands: Corregidor, the largest, a mass of volcanic rock, well-fortified, and mounted with Krupp cannon; Caballo, four hundred feet high, near it on the south, and El Fraile, a small rock mounted with a battery, a little off the southern main. The northern channel is narrow, and was said to be mined; the southern channel is three miles wide, but is exposed to a cross-fire from the three islands. Dewey decided to pass in by the latter, and hoped to get by, under cover of the darkness, without being seen.

Contemporary history cannot be accurately written; there has been no opportunity to collate evidence and cancel out the incompatible features. We do not know when the American ships were first seen by the Spaniards, or to what cause their discovery was due. Their arrival at Bolinao Bay might have been telegraphed thence to Montojo. But if so, it would seem that he should have prepared some surprise for them on their arrival. He did nothing, but remained to the last self-immured in the little harbor within Cavite. Some accounts state that our approach was heralded by rockets from the Spanish forts at the mouth of the harbor before we had fairly entered it; others say that we were all

Philippines. He was at that moment a commodore; but after the 1st of May he suddenly received an admiral's rank; and the cause of it was as follows.—On the 26th of April he received a cablegram order from the President, directing him to "capture or destroy" the Spanish fleet in Pacific waters. On the 27th he sailed from Mirs Bay, on the Chinese coast, prepared to carry out the order. Dewey, it appears, had long ago foreseen that there would be opportunity for work on the Pacific station, and had applied for the assignment; and ever since he had been carefully studying the situation. His squadron consisted of two transports, "Zafiro" and "Nanshan," laden with coal, and stores enough for six months; four cruisers, one of which, the "Boston," was partially protected, while the three others, the "Olympia," the "Raleigh" and the "Baltimore," were protected; two gunboats, the "Concord" and the "Petrel," and a revenue cutter, the "McCulloch." Thus there were seven fighting ships in all, though the "McCulloch," being very lightly armed, and unprotected, did not take part in the engagement. The armament was fifty-seven big guns, including ten 8 inch and seventy-four rapid-fire and machine guns.

The Spanish force against which this squadron was to fight numbered one wooden and six steel protected and iron cruisers, five gunboats and two torpedo boats; the largest of their guns were not above 6.2-inch, and none of their ships was so large as the "Olympia" or the "Baltimore"—which measured, respectively, 5,870 and 4,600 tons. On the other hand, the Spaniards had the advantage in numbers, and a great advantage in the guns mounted in Cavite and the shore batteries, many of which were 10-inch, and of the best modern make. The harbor was also sown with minefields and torpedoes; but only one or two of these were exploded during the engagement, and they did us no harm. Their moral effect, however, should not be left out of the account. Admiral Montojo commanded the Spanish fleet; and he had 1,950 men against our 1,808.

but through, when a shower of sparks from the funnel of the "McCulloch," in the rear of the column, betrayed our presence, and that it was then that the rockets were sent up. All that can be declared with certainty is, that as our ships passed under those tall, silent walls, over the smooth surface that might conceal sudden destruction, a signal from the unknown was heard or seen, and then a flash from the direction of El Fraile showed that the enemy was awake. But nothing could be seen of our ships except gliding gray shadows, and the lanterns hung over the stern of each to guide its follower; and that shower of sparks from the "McCulloch." The Spaniards, therefore, had no good mark to shoot at; and, as we have constantly seen since, they can hit nothing save by accident, be the conditions never so favorable. The several shots they fired, therefore, plunged harmlessly into the water to right and left; and they were replied to only by some half dozen shots from the "Concord," "Boston" and "McCulloch," the effect of which was undetermined. Dewey's orders were not to engage, and in a few minutes silence resumed its reign in the mysterious darkness. But the incident had somewhat relieved the nervous strain of the men, and they breathed freer for those few explosions.

From Corregidor to Manila city is about thirty miles, and it was the commodore's purpose not to begin fighting before daylight; consequently there was more than enough time to cover the distance. Dawn in the tropics comes suddenly. The speed of the ships was still further reduced, until it equaled the pace of a man walking. The air was still and hot; the water smooth; silence was kept on all the vessels, except for the whispered orders. Perhaps the enemy's fleet might creep upon them and suddenly open fire; or perhaps a mine might yet tear its way through the vitals of a ship. At such times a man inevitably holds his breath, and hears his heart beat. One of the officers, a man of unquestionable bravery, was found reading his Bible. Characteristic acts were performed unconsciously. The omnipresent darkness seemed to mold itself into strange shapes. None had been in those waters before; they were sailing by a Spanish chart, which, like all else Spanish, might lie. We may believe that the hours between midnight and five o'clock on Sunday morning were long ones. The only thing certain was, that a great battle was imminent; and unless the Americans won it, their total destruction was sure; for they were eight thousand miles from home, and the laws of neutrality would prevent them from getting succor short of San Francisco. They must win, or never again would they pass Corregidor. Commodore Dewey had thought of these things, but with the rare union of daring with sagacity which marked his character, he had determined what to do, and would do it without faltering.

It had been a cloudy night, and the dawn was gray: the first objects seen by the men on lookout were the embattled promontory of Cavite, jutting out from the line of the shore, and beyond it, the low houses of flat Manila. Shots came from both directions, but fell short; the Spanish fleet was then discerned under the lee of Cavite, from the citadel of which hung heavily the flag of Spain, stained with every crime and baseness known to humanity. The ships had been cleared for action long since; the men were ready. They stood to their guns with a smile. As the fleet turned to pass before the enemy, the transports and the "McCulloch" were left in the center of the bay, not out of range, but out of action.

The Commodore's plan was to pass back and forth before the ships of Spain and the forts, delivering port and starboard broadsides alternately; thus giving each of his vessels its equal chance, and at the same time offering the difficulty of a moving target to the enemy. Montojo had apparently made no preparations for battle, except to ensconce himself in as safe a place as possible; it does not appear that he even had steam in his boilers. Did he imagine that his foe was going to anchor in front of him, ship for ship, and hammer it out to the end? So far as events can indicate, Montojo knew no more about naval tactics than little King Alphonso in Madrid; and for all the benefit his presence bestowed upon his fleet, he might as well have been in Madrid with the little king. Before the action was over, he doubtless wished he had been.

Dewey's ideas were bolder and less medieval. He knew that his men could shoot straight, and that they would do their duty without the spur of a revolver at their backs, or a jug of rum in their bellies. The accuracy of aim of American gunners has been one of the deciding features of this war. It indicates true, as distinguished from impulsive, courage. Spaniards have no staying power, but only the audacity of excitement, which is transient: it lasts as long as the man can forget himself; and if during that time it prevails, all goes well. Resisted, it relaxes, and then the cowardice which is beneath it comes uppermost. Moreover, the Spanish soldier or sailor knows that if he flinches his officers will kill him; and he has been taught to believe that if the Americans capture him they will massacre him without mercy. The officers themselves know that if they surrender, or fail to conquer, court-martial and probable execution await them at home. It would be no wonder if men fought frantically under such stimulus; it is remarkable, rather, that they have invariably been so badly and often disgracefully defeated. Except when the advantage has been enormously on their side they have made no appreciable resistance to us; and no amount of odds has been sufficient to give them the victory. Neither in intelligence, discipline, physique or bravery are they fit antagonists for us; the bubble of Spanish valor, being pricked, collapses utterly; so far as one may judge, they are the worst fighting men in the world.

As the American squadron advanced to the attack, the scene was beautiful and peaceful; as fair a May-day morning as was ever seen. As the sun rose, its level rays streamed over the pallid bay, painting it with increasing azure. All round that great amphitheater of inland sea, distant mountains rose; the stretches of nearer landscape were densely shawled with the variegated greens of tropical vegetation, fading into aerial perspectives of purple and blue. An impalpable veil of lovely color shimmered everywhere; delicate films of haze lingered in unsunned tracts; soft mists gave a warm pallor to the horizon; but the vault of sky above was untroubled sapphire. To the left, as the ships moved round for their first advance, lay the irregular expanse of white Manila; a white beach bordered the bay like a silver line. The waters were placid, with here and there a darkening flush of ultramarine, where little breezes scudded across the surface; and dancing images of the massive gray vessels were reflected in the glossy undulations, as they moved on. On the shore, between Manila and Cavite, was seen a constantly augmenting throng of people, dressed mostly in white; they were coming to witness the annihilation of the Yankee fleet. But nothing could be less suggestive of annihilation than this quiet and lovely scene. It was a perfect Sabbath and May-day; but the posies with which Dewey was going a-Maying were steel shot and shell.

At this juncture, a string of party-colored flags fluttered from the "Olympia," the Commodore's flagship; which was no sooner seen, than a deep burst of sound, again and again renewed, broke from the hitherto silent vessels—the cheering of the Yankee tars. The signal had been displayed with good judgment and knowledge of human nature; in the language of naval emblems it communicated a thought that filled every heart in the squadron with desire for battle. To the Spaniards it meant nothing, and they replied to the cheering with a further dropping fire of ineffective shells; but to the Americans it brought up a picture of a dastardly deed done six weeks before and eleven thousand miles away, whereby near three hundred gallant lives had been extinguished in a moment with no chance to defend themselves.

The warlike passion to avenge these murdered brethren of theirs was awakened in every man of Dewey's fleet. "Remember the 'Maine'!" It was a word to aim every gun on board those grim, gray champions, now almost within fighting distance of the enemy. Let every Spanish ship be sunk and every Spaniard die, if it might be—yet the balance would not be even between us and them.

Though no additional reminder was needed, about this time there leaped heavily up from the level surface of the bay a huge pyramid of foaming water darkened with mud and sand, accompanied with a dull and muffled roar. A mine-field had been fired; but so much out of distance as hardly to be remarked. A new signal now showed from the "Olympia"—"Hold your fire until close to the enemy." And that might have recalled another, more distant day, when the embattled farmers on Bunker Hill kept finger to trigger till the red-coated ranks of invaders toiling up the hot slope were so near that one could see the whites of their eyes. Americans waited then, and would wait to-day, with results even more terrible.

But the time was at hand. The captains on their bridges kept their eyes on the Commodore, who stood quietly observing the diminishing distance between his ship and the Spanish line. When within five thousand yards he turned and spoke to Captain Gridley: it was eighteen minutes to six. Gridley gave an order; the naked, sweating men in the turrets, who had waited so long, made their quick, sharp movements: and all at once there broke from the "Olympia" such a volley of sound as that quiet bay had never known before. The great cruiser herself reeled backward from the shock of her own mighty voice; the bridge on which stood the Commodore seemed about to burst upward from its fastenings; men standing on the decks staggered as from a giant blow. Forth from the gun-muzzles streamed a horizontal flash of death, with white volumes of smoke that hid the ship; an instant later, she spoke again, and destruction sped across the expanse, which shuddered and swung aside beneath. In less time than one draws a breath those huge bolts of steel had crossed the space to the "Reina Cristina," on whose bridge the Spanish admiral stood. Before the effect could be seen, the "Baltimore" had taken up the refrain with a bellowing as great; and after her the "Raleigh," "Petrel," "Concord" and "Boston"; and all were hidden in palpitating clouds—the pungent breath of the prismatic brown powder. Meanwhile from the entire Spanish fleet, and from the batteries, and Cavite, came a roar and tempest of detonations and deep explosions, mingling together in one stupendous diapason: the high vault of sky seemed too narrow to contain the sound, and the air shook, riven asunder by blows beyond the force of titans. Human senses were outdone and numbed; the naked men worked like demons in the smutty reek and heat; the joy of fighting flamed in their souls. Far below, in stifling iron chambers, engineers and firemen labored to work the ships and feed their incandescent maws; buried beyond hope in blind hells of heated metal, but deserving no less the crown of heroism. "Down with Spain! Hurrah for Old Glory! Remember the 'Maine'!" went as heartily with the hurling of coal into the furnaces, as from the gunners' deck, or the captain's bridge, or the fighting-tops aloft.

What things are men! What agonies, triumphs, despairs, miracles, do they achieve and suffer and create! What infinity in such an hour as this—in these tremendous moments! In every human soul may be awakened Heaven, or kindled Hell.

The second round passed without special incident, the fire on both sides being kept up without interruption. On the third turn, a rip of the tide carried the "Raleigh" close to the Spanish fleet, but so flurried were the Spanish gunners that none could hit her, though she poured in destruction. Then Montojo, perhaps fancying that he should respond to such a challenge, moved out to attack the "Olympia." He posed, for a moment, as the champion of Spain. But his ardor soon subsided; he was met by the concentrated fire of half our fleet, and half-way out he stopped, turned, and began to scuttle homeward. As the stern of the "Reina Cristina" swung into view a shot from one of the "Olympia's" 8-inch guns struck it fairly, with an effect as if the unhappy vessel had been kicked violently from behind. The gigantic impact started her forward, and the shell, passing through all obstructions, exploded in her boiler, killing half her crew and tearing her almost to pieces. Montojo abandoned his ship forthwith, and got on board the "Isla de Cuba"; but this too was riddled and shattered by our fire, and made for the shore, where it sank. At this juncture, however, occurred an episode which partly redeemed the Spanish admiral's timidity. The two torpedo boats which had been lying hidden behind the larger ships, came forth to destroy the "Olympia." They offered but a small mark for the big guns, and kept on until a range of eight hundred yards brought them within the scope of the rapid-fire weapons. Then, in a moment, the first of the two was hit in the boiler, and exploded and sank; the second turned tail and hastened in a sinking condition to the shore. A little longer lease of courage might have achieved a notable exploit for Spain; but in this, as in all else, they failed. Anglo-Saxon tenacity is not to be looked for in the degenerate Latins of the Peninsula.

After the fifth round, the "Olympia" turned and steamed out of range, to the dismay, at first, of some of our fleet, and to the delight of the Spaniards, who seemed to fancy that they must in some way have gained a victory. But it was only that Dewey had made up his mind that his men needed a chance to cool off and to get some breakfast. The ships drew together some miles out, while the forts continued to pour tons of shot into the bay, with the same blind unreason that had marked their shooting throughout. A conference of the American officers elicited the astonishing fact that not a man in the fleet had been killed, and but a handful were wounded throughout. The "Baltimore" was penetrated by a shell, which did not interfere with her fighting capacity; and the other ships were more lightly marked. Spanish gunners, like women, seem to turn away their heads and shut their eyes when firing. But even so it is perplexing that with such a rain of steel they should hit nothing. Our ships passed slowly, broadside on; and some of the lighter-draught boats ran close in to the batteries; but nothing touched them effectively. This led one of our gunners to remark that God was behind our guns, and the devil behind those of Spain. But it is also to be remembered that the Spaniards were "rattled" and inexpert, whereas our men were practiced and cool.

After a three hours' intermission, Dewey returned to the attack. But the first battle had practically disposed of the Spanish fleet; the "Reina Cristina" and the "Castilla" were burning, and all the others were more or less incapacitated. Therefore, the plan of the second battle was different from the first; the ships advanced one by one, or in pairs or threes, took up a chosen position, and poured their fire, carefully aimed, at the Spanish forts on Cavite and elsewhere. The "Baltimore" was the first to advance; then the "Olympia," shooting heedfully, for her ammunition was running low. For a time the forts replied rapidly, though as ineffectively as ever; but at last only three guns on Cavite were in action, and one shot from the "Boston" disabled all of them. Attention was then given to the remainder of the Spanish ships, and one after the other they were destroyed or sent to the bottom. The "De Ulloa" had the distinction of going down with her flag flying. Much of the finishing work was done by the little "Petrel," which fearlessly entered the Cavite harbor; and it was a shot from her that changed the flag flying over the navy yard from yellow to white. It was just past one o'clock when the surrender of Cavite took place—about eight hours from the opening of the engagement, including the three hours' intermission. Higher praise cannot be given to the marksmanship of the Americans than to say that it was as good as that of the Spanish was contemptible. Never was less ammunition wasted in battle than by them in this fight. The number of Spanish dead is not exactly known, but it was about a third of those engaged, and the wounded were correspondingly numerous. Not one of their fourteen ships survived; and the guns of all the forts were silenced. Such a victory made the American navy, man for man and ship for ship, the most formidable in the world, and more formidable absolutely than any except the greatest two or three. As an object lesson for foreign nations the result was most salutary; and on Americans it had the excellent effect of reviving a desire to command the seas, and foreshadowing a future for the nation which has long been the dream of a few, but had been constantly postponed by the greedy and unpatriotic selfishness of a dishonorable moneyed clique.

Admiral Dewey, as we may now call him, might have bombarded Manila and caused its surrender; but as he had not men enough to garrison it, this would have thrown the inhabitants into the power of the Filipinos, who would probably have massacred them and looted the city. He contented himself, accordingly, with sending home news of the engagement, and a demand for troops to complete the conquest of the islands. Manila is a town of three hundred thousand inhabitants, a few thousand of them foreigners; it stands on Luzon, the largest of the twelve hundred islands and islets of which the Philippine group consists. Pending further operations, Dewey occupied Cavite and the forts at the entrance of the harbor, and put Aguinaldo, a rebel leader who had accompanied him from Hong Kong, in command of the insurgents—Aguinaldo agreeing to co-operate with the Americans. As the operations in Manila were distinct from those in the West Indies, we may conveniently review the leading events there up to the close of the war.

To General Wesley Merritt, an officer of experience, was intrusted the task of dispatching troops to the islands; and after some delay, partly due to the incompetence of contractors, which had been disagreeably conspicuous in all matters throughout the war in which they have been concerned; and partly to the refusal of Merritt to undertake his duties unless a much larger force of regulars than was at first given him was placed at his disposal, a series of little armies was sent forward from San Francisco. The first of these expeditions, convoyed by the "Charleston," Captain Glass, stopped at the Ladrones group of islands, beyond the Sandwich Islands, and executive officer Braunersreuter was sent ashore with a few men to receive their surrender from the Spanish commandant. The latter asserted that he had not heard of the declaration of war; but he and his men were taken prisoners, and the Ladrones became American soil. They will be of great convenience as an intermediate coaling station. Continuing her voyage, the "Charleston" brought her transports to Manila on June 30th. Another expedition was by that time part way across the Pacific; and General Merritt himself, with the third convoy, had left San Francisco the day before. He arrived out about the first of August, a fourth expedition having left the California coast by that date; and the land investment of Manila was at once begun. There were in the garrison about eight thousand Spanish soldiers, under Captain-general Augustin; and smaller Spanish forces held positions in other parts of the islands. A large number of insurgents were speedily collected by Aguinaldo as general-in-chief, and they beleaguered the town and the neighboring strongholds, capturing most of the latter with small resistance; for many of the defenders were Filipinos forced to serve by the Spaniards, and ready to desert at the first opportunity. But the final attack upon the city itself was postponed until the American troops should be ready; for it was apprehended that the insurgents, should they obtain control of Manila, would massacre and rob the inhabitants, in revenge for the outrages which they had endured for many generations at Spanish hands.

A singular state of things insensibly resulted. The Americans found themselves in opposition to both the Spaniards and to the insurgents, though of course on different grounds. We had to conquer the Spaniards, but at the same time to protect them against the barbarism of the natives. Thus while we were acting with the insurgents on general principles, we were yet acting with the Spaniards against them from a special point of view. The situation was complicated by the behavior of Aguinaldo, who had at first been a protege of ours, and professedly our firm ally. The successes which he met with, and the urgency of the desires of his followers, led him gradually to adopt an ambiguous if not semi-hostile attitude toward us; and though the expulsion of Spain from the islands would be wholly due to us, we were given to infer that our presence and control were considered undesirable by the insurgents. It was a possible issue, therefore, that, after disposing of Spain, we might be constrained to fight the natives also. This raised a question as to the motives which had brought about our invasion of the Philippines. Had we originally contemplated their conquest and annexation? The answer must be a modified negative. We had attacked them because Spain held them, and would be crippled by our seizure of them. But having seized them, we must hold them; we could not surrender them to the Filipinos, because they were incapable of establishing a strong and orderly government; we could not give them back to Spain, because her rule was there, as everywhere, a stench in the nostrils of humanity and civilization; and we could not leave them to be divided up between European powers, because they had a commercial value, and it was our right to secure that for ourselves, as recompense for the losses of the war. The situation was forced upon us by the logic of events.

Meanwhile, the critical aspect of Europe's warring interests in the East made the securing of a foothold in the group desirable to them, or some of them; and the tactics of the German squadron at Manila rendered it probable that Germany, more than the other powers, was anxious to possess herself of a station there at least. England, on the other hand, seemed to favor our retention of the whole group, and Japan, so far as her feeling could be surmised, would not oppose our doing so. But the officers on the German ships openly fraternized with the Spaniards; and Aguinaldo was believed to have made promises of concessions to the Germans, in return for moral or physical support from them against us. There was, altogether, a curious and delicate complication, which might easily have been inflamed into serious trouble by an indiscreet or feeble representative on our side. Fortunately we were represented by a man of exceptional executive and diplomatic ability, as well as of great courage and resources. The war has produced no figure comparable to Admiral Dewey; and there is obviously no position in the gift of his country which he is not fully competent to fill, whether in war or in peace. He firmly and sternly checked the German admiral when the latter presumed to push his arrogance beyond the bounds of technical right conduct; he kept his temper and his wits on all occasions; he fathomed the character and position of Aguinaldo, and knew how to hold him in hand. He perceived that with every day that passed our own stand, both moral and physical, would become more unassailable. He understood the evil of political interference in military affairs, and kept the cable connecting him with Washington unrepaired: he had cut it the day after the battle of Manila, and all communications to or from him must go by dispatch boats plying between Manila and Hong Kong. Thus he retained control, and was free to use his own discretion as to what should be done or left undone; and his native intelligence, his experience, and the advantages he enjoyed in being on the spot, enabled him to do all well.

We may surmise that Dewey perceived the necessity of our ownership of the Philippines, and took his measures with that end in view. Of the twelve hundred islands included in the group, only four hundred are inhabited; and but half a dozen of these are of considerable size. They are occupied by two races, in addition to the Spaniards, the half-breeds, and the representatives of other European nations than Spain. The aboriginees are a race of savages called Negritos, of whom little is known, and who have never been conquered. With them, but quite distinct from them, are the Malays, with whom alone Spain has dealt during her three hundred years' occupation of the islands. The Spaniards have never penetrated into the interior parts of the islands; they hold only the coasts of some of them, with the towns which they have built there. Little or nothing is known, therefore, of the inland topography of the group, or of its mineral and other resources. The total population has been roughly estimated at about ten millions; the principal commercial products are tobacco, sugar and hemp. At a minimum valuation, the exports are given at about $50,000,000. But here, as in other Spanish colonies, a very large proportion of the revenues goes into the pockets of the official thieves whom Spain sends out to rule her possessions. The taxes are innumerable, iniquitous, and preposterously high. Under a more liberal and just system of government, the receipts from the islands would undoubtedly be enormously increased. A great part of the real estate is held by the Church, which has aided to impose a superficial civilization upon the bulk of the Malays, the effect of which however is of very questionable benefit. There is also a large number of the natives who profess the Mahometan faith. It is evident that such a population is incapable of self-government; and the power of a general like Aguinaldo is insecure and limited. On the other hand, we shall doubtless find grave difficulties in introducing order and subordination in the islands; but the task is not beyond the abilities of Americans, and there will be many collateral advantages, in addition to commercial profits. There is a great deal of both latent energy and of capital in this country, which could nowhere find such suitable employment as in ruling and developing colonial possessions.

During July, the successive bodies of American troops were landed on the shores of Manila Bay, and got in readiness for the assault on the Manila fortifications. By the end of the month there were about fifteen thousand troops under General Merritt, of whom a third or more were regulars. The number of soldiers wearing the Spanish uniform was about eight thousand, the majority of them regulars. They were well intrenched, and the advantage was apparently on their side; but in truth there was no misgiving as to the American superiority. The Spanish troops were poor in physique, and still poorer in spirit, from Augustin down; the latter, as his dispatches to Spain indicated, would have surrendered long before, but for the dread of court-martial. He also dreaded the numerous insurgent troops who now surrounded the city on every side; and he appeared to be trying to secure a promise from us to hold Aguinaldo in check in case of surrender, and on the other hand intriguing with the rebel chief to join against us with him. It is not in this temper, or under such conditions, that victories are won. The arrival, toward the end of July, of the powerful monitor "Monterey" greatly strengthened our position, both as regarded the contending parties, and the Germans, whose naval force was now so inferior to ours as to make an overt demonstration on their part impossible. It was, nevertheless, full time for us to act; since the rainy season was beginning, and the health of our army would be impaired by long inactivity in the trenches. Dewey would of course have taken and occupied Manila long before, had the troops been available; but with his own men he could not have policed the city, or taken charge of the prisoners and prevented disorders and massacres. But his diplomatic resources proved equal to maintaining the status quo until the right juncture should arrive.

Aguinaldo was between two fires, or possibly three. He feared to support the Americans, lest his followers charge him with intending to transfer them from one master to another; he could not trust the Spaniards, knowing their faithlessness of old; and yet, if the Germans took part with the Spaniards, he would be in peril should he refuse the latter's overtures. In this predicament, he issued a statement not devoid of acuteness, though it was amusingly transparent. "Why should the Americans expect me to fight blindly for their interests when they will not be frank with me?" he asked. "Am I fighting for annexation, protection, or independence? I can take Manila, but to what use?—If America takes it, I save my men and arms for what the future has in store for me. I am not both a fool and a rogue, but the interests of my people are as sacred as yours." Evidently Aguinaldo had taken his first lessons in Oriental diplomacy. As has been pointed out, annexation, with a strong and just government, is all that could be promised to the Filipinos; the period when they could develop the ability to govern themselves was so remote as not to be considered. The manifesto was therefore significant, for practical purposes, only as showing that the insurgents could not be depended upon as allies, and that it might be necessary to guard against them as enemies. Orders were given to enter into no negotiations with them. A few days later, Aguinaldo proposed to General Merritt that, in the event of the surrender of Manila, he should be permitted to lead his troops through the city in a triumphal march; and that hereafter American officers should be put in command of native troops. This indicated a moderation of his attitude toward us; there were arguments for and against such a suggestion; but Merritt and Dewey decided that all questions must be postponed till Manila had fallen, when the answer would be controlled by circumstances and prospects.

As the decisive moment drew near, it seemed likely that Augustin might surrender without a conflict: the hopelessness of contending against our army and fleet simultaneously being apparent. This, also, would be the best way to secure the city against being looted by the insurgents, in the confusion of the first hours of our entry into it. But on the other side were to be considered the punctilios of Spanish "honor," which demanded some show of a battle; or, in other words, if Augustin surrendered without a fight, or the pretense of one, he would be shot on returning to Spain. Dewey and Merritt were desirous to avoid bloodshed, and useless destruction of property, but they could not enter into intricacies of this kind, and announced that unless the city was surrendered, it would be attacked from land and sea, with results the responsibility for which must rest on Spanish shoulders.

At this juncture, our troops were assembled in Camp Dewey, some miles south of Manila, but near the Spanish intrenched lines on that side. Immediately in front of them were insurgent troops under Aguinaldo, in breastworks constructed by him. Before the 30th of July, a section of the insurgents moved out of that part of their breastworks which adjoined the shore of the bay, and were replaced by our troops, who thus lay with their left wing on the shore, and their right adjoining the left wing of the insurgents. The distance between them and the Spanish lines was about one thousand yards. The town here held by the Spaniards was not Manila, but a southern suburb called Malate, several miles below it, and connected with it by a road passing through the suburban village of Paco. The number of Spanish troops at this point was about thirty-five hundred, all regulars. The number of our men in the trenches was about nine hundred on the night of July 31st; and they were nearly all volunteers, lately arrived, who had never been under fire. The fleet was at Cavite, opposite Manila, some miles to the north.

As evening fell, a violent typhoon set in, with pitchy darkness, and torrents of rain. Either for the alleged reason that the following day was a holiday, or owing to a secret understanding with the Spaniards, Aguinaldo withdrew his troops from their position this evening, thereby leaving our right flank exposed. At eleven o'clock, in the midst of the storm, our pickets were fired on, and retreated slowly within our lines, the enemy following in force, with artillery. Our troops were called to arms and responded promptly, and amid the fury of the tropical downpour a severe battle began. The first of our troops to sustain the onset of the enemy was a battery of the Tenth Regiment of Pennsylvania volunteers, who held the Spaniards in check with a well-directed fire until some companies of the First California Volunteers and the Utah Battery, under Captain Young, could move forward to their support. By the time the relief came, the Pennsylvania men had but four rounds of ammunition left. A partial penetration of their right had been made, when the regulars of the Third Artillery charged as infantry, and drove the enemy back in confusion, the volunteers assisting. The Astor Battery, which was on the ground, was unable to do any execution, owing to the boats in which they landed having capsized in the storm, ruining their ammunition. After the repulse of the first attack, there was a lull for two or three hours, and then the enemy advanced once more, and maintained his attack for half an hour, with the same result as at first. They had moved some artillery to our right, and directed a harassing fire from that direction; but again fell back. The storm continued with unabated vigor, and the only indication for our men of the whereabout of the enemy had been the flash of their guns, so that the fighting was of a blindfold character; but toward four o'clock the Spaniards came on a third time, though now in a half-hearted manner. Our men, on the contrary, were now in a better position, and their fire was more effective than at first; the Spaniards were repulsed with loss, and were pursued for some distance toward Malate. This ended the battle for the night, and such further fighting as took place on the morrow was between artillery forces on either side. The defeat of the enemy was complete.

Their attack had been well planned, and ought to have been successful. Our men had been engaged in digging new intrenchments in advance of the main line, and were flanked and nearly cut off before they could resume their former position. The roads leading from our camp, in the rear, to the intrenchments, along which our supporting troops must move, were under a heavy flanking fire throughout, which would not have been possible had not the insurgents abandoned their positions at the outset of the engagement. Considering the bewildering circumstances of the battle, and the rawness and inferior numbers of our troops, they deserve great credit for holding their ground; but it has always been a desperate enterprise to attack Americans in intrenchments. The losses of the Spaniards in killed and wounded have been variously estimated at from one thousand to five hundred; our own loss was again miraculously small—nine killed and forty-five wounded. The Spaniards used Mauser rifles, and had they known how to aim them, they might have exterminated our entire force.

The fact that their first attack was directed precisely at the junction point of our line with that of the insurgents, combined with Aguinaldo's ambiguous conduct during several days previous to the battle, made it seem more than probable that he had had information of the attack, and had withdrawn in order to facilitate it. Had our men been driven from their trenches, the camp would have been open to the enemy, and even without the active help of the insurgents, they could have driven our troops into the sea. Several transports full of American soldiers were lying off shore, waiting for the storm to cease before disembarking. But the moral effect of a defeat would have been a strong encouragement to the Spaniards, and disastrous to us, and might have indefinitely prolonged the war in this quarter. It transpired after the battle that the Spaniards had confidently expected victory, and were both astonished and discouraged by their repulse. The usual stories had been circulated as to the incapacity and cowardice of the Americans; and the report was rife that we had been defeated in the West Indies and our chief coast towns bombarded. The credulity of the Spaniard seems to be surpassed only by his ability as a fabricator.

The sally from Malate was the overture to the American attack upon Manila and its defenses, which took place on Saturday, August 13th. By that time all the American troops and guns had been disembarked, and were in position, and the fleet was ready to co-operate. Many of the Spanish troops, being natives, were untrustworthy; many more were in hospital; their morale was gone, and their guns were inferior to ours. They had just learned of the failure of Camara's fleet to come to their assistance, and this completed their disheartenment. Finally, the insurgents, admonished by the result of the Malate battle, had ranged themselves emphatically on our side, to the number of at least ten thousand men. Under these circumstances, it was not to be expected that the Spaniards would make a serious resistance. Their intrenchments were ten miles in length, and could not be adequately manned.

Dewey had given notice on Friday that he would bombard the town on the following day unless it were surrendered in the meantime. Saturday mornnig the demand for surrender was made, and declined. At a little before ten o'clock the "Olympia," lying off Malate, fired the first gun at the defenses of that town. The rest of the American fleet was ranged along the coast between Malate and the Pasig River, which flows through the center of Manila. The ships of the French and Germans lay to the north of this point, while the English and Japanese were near the Malate end of the line.

For an hour and a half the American fleet kept up the bombardment, directing their fire at fortified places only. Most of the non-combatants had before this taken refuge in vessels in the harbor. At half past eleven the American troops, led by the First Colorado Regiment, charged the Malate defenses. The Spaniards retreated to their second line of intrenchments, where for a while they made a stand; but the Americans were re-enforced, and drove them into the town itself. At half past one, the white flag was hoisted, and Manila was ours. That evening, Augustin accepted the offer of a German warship, the "Kaiserin Augusta," to carry him to Hong Kong; he was smuggled aboard at ten o'clock, leaving his subordinate, General Jaudenes, to hand over the city to Dewey and Merritt. It was given out that he had deputed Jaudenes for this service ten days before; and that Admiral Dewey had given him permission to take his departure on the German war-vessel.

This, the last battle of the war, was fought a day after peace had been agreed upon and the protocol signed at Washington and Madrid; but, as in the case of the battle of New Orleans, three-quarters of a century before, the news did not reach the contending parties in season to avert the engagement. In other respects, the two battles had little in common with each other. The shooting at Manila was careful and slow, and was not meant to be deadly; the object of the fleet was to destroy the Spanish works rather than to slaughter their defenders. The latter did little except keep out of the way, and, after a proper interval, move out of the works and hoist the flag of surrender. There were no casualties on the fleet; only the "Olympia," "Raleigh," "Petrel" and "Callao" took part in the active operations; the others were not needed. After all was over, Merritt, with Lieutenant Brumby, went up the Pasig River and landed in Manila; and after some searching found the modest Jaudenes "in a church, crowded with women and children." The insurgents were not allowed to enter the town; the position taken by our Government being that we could not tolerate, in the same jurisdiction, an army of another nation which does not place itself under the command of the American commander-in-chief. Measures were taken to keep back the insurgents by force if necessary Our loss in the battle was estimated at seven killed and about forty wounded; the Spanish losses were not ascertained.

Thus the first and the last important engagements of the war were fought by Dewey, in a place nearly twelve thousand miles distant from the normal seat of hostilities. They were perfect victories, marred by no errors, and followed by acts of humanity and charity. They showed that American men-of-war were models of discipline, order and efficiency; and so far as the land troops had opportunity to partake in them, the duty to be done was accomplished valiantly and cleanly. The political future of the Philippines still remains to be settled; and we can express no better aspiration than that our statesmen may acquit themselves, in the premises, as well as our soldiers and sailors have done.

We must now return to the situation in the west, and to the month of May, with Sampson and Schley guarding the east and west ends of Cuba, in the hope of intercepting the Spanish fleet under Cervera. When it became certain that Cervera was in fact hidden in the narrow-necked harbor of Santiago, Schley placed himself on guard opposite the entrance, and was soon joined there by Sampson; for it would not have been impossible for the Spanish ships to escape under cover of some dark and stormy night, and it was a matter of vital importance either to keep Cervera where he was, or, if he came out, to fight and destroy him. There was the third alternative of entering the harbor and fighting him there; since Dewey had done a similar thing at Manila, why might not Schley do it at Santiago. But the two cases were very different. For Dewey, there had been no alternative, nor could he afford to delay. He had braved a great peril, but he had been justified in doing so because there was nothing else to be done. But to enter the harbor of Santiago was not justifiable, until all other methods had been tried.

The channel, instead of being three miles wide, was but little over four hundred feet. It was filled with torpedoes, and was commanded lengthwise and crosswise by guns of heavy caliber, from some of which a plunging fire could be directed on the unprotected decks of our vessels. There was hardly a chance that the first of our ships to enter that channel would not be blown up or sunk; and her hull would then obstruct the passage for the rest. Our loss was certain to be intolerably large, and the odds were great that it would also be entirely futile. On the other hand, if we let Cervera alone, his capture and that of Santiago were only a question of time. Troops could be landed east and west of the bay, and completely invest the town on the landward sides; so that even without a battle the garrison and crews would finally be starved out. Meanwhile our fleet could bombard Morro and the other outer defenses at leisure, and perhaps, when they were reduced, either throw shells into the town, over the intervening hills, from the mouth of the channel, or devise some means of exploding the torpedoes in the channel, preparatory to entering in force. The only objection to deliberate operations was that, until Cervera was disposed of, nothing else could safely be attempted. We had not ships enough at our disposal both to keep him where he was, and to carry the war in other directions. Besides, the rainy season was coming on, and the health of our troops was sure to be impaired if they were forced to remain for an indefinite time in trenches.

On May 31st, the day before Sampson's squadron joined Schley's in front of Santiago, the latter bombarded Morro and the other fortifications with the ships "Massachusetts" and "Iowa," and the cruiser "New Orleans." The Spanish "Cristobal Colon" came out near the mouth of the harbor, and added her guns to those of Morro, and four land batteries, in defense. Morro was severely pounded but was not reduced; three of the land batteries were silenced, and it was thought that the "Colon" was hit. On June 1st, Sampson arrived and took command of the entire fleet of sixteen warships. Among other attendant vessels was a collier, the "Merrimac"; and on June 3d, with this collier as the instrument, a deed was done which immediately took its place as the most daring and brilliant of the war, and one of the most heroic ever planned and executed in naval history.

The protagonist of this exploit was Richmond Pearson Hobson, a young graduate of Annapolis, and a naval constructor of eminence. He was born in the South in 1872, and graduated at the head of his class in 1889. For some years he pursued special studies in France and England. His official duties would ordinarily keep him in the home office; but Hobson asked and received permission to go to sea; and he sailed on board the "New York," as a member of the commodore's staff, with the rank of lieutenant. On the way to Santiago he perfected and communicated to Sampson his plan for preventing all further apprehension from Cervera. In its principle, it was simplicity itself:—to sink a vessel in the narrowest part of the channel, so as to obstruct the egress of the Spanish fleet. It was the details that were interesting. Who was to navigate the ship to the proper place in the channel, and sink her there at the right moment? And how was the sinking to be done?

Hobson had his answers all ready. He would take in the "Merrimac" himself, with a crew of six men only, who of course must be volunteers. He would have anchors at bow and stern, the former to be dropped when the proper point was reached, and the other when the tide had swung the ship athwart channel. Torpedoes would be arranged along the sides, which could be exploded at the right moment by electricity, and the ship thus sunk immediately—the rather as she would have on board a load of two thousand tons of coal. That, broadly stated, was Hobson's plan. He had thought it out carefully, and could see no valid objections to it; it did but involve the loss of a collier—and the probable sacrifice of his own life and those of his volunteers. In view of the result to be obtained, Hobson thought the expense was not worth considering. Commodore Sampson took the matter into consideration, and finally told Hobson that if he wanted to do the thing, he was at liberty to try. Between two brave and patriotic men there need be little palaver. Hobson set to work to prepare the "Merrimac" at once.

In fine weather, in broad daylight, in time of peace, the project presented no extraordinary difficulties. A firm and true hand at the tiller, a prompt and disciplined crew, ordinary good luck with currents, and all would be well. But the conditions under which Hobson must carry out his exploit were very different from these. He must go into the jaws of death under cover of darkness, because otherwise he would be sunk by the guns of Morro and the batteries before he could reach his objective point. At the best, before he could be ready, he would have risked death a thousand times. When he attained the desired point in the channel—if he ever did attain it—he must risk death at his own hands by blowing up and sinking his vessel. And after that was done, how was he to escape? He had prepared a catamaran, or raft, on which he hoped to be able to paddle to safety; but it was a forlorn hope. A fellow officer, young cadet Powell, was to cruise off the mouth of the harbor for a time, on the chance of picking him up; but what a desperate chance it was! No: the odds against his accomplishing his object were almost beyond computation; but the odds against his coming out alive were entirely so. No one understood all this better than Hobson, but it did not for a moment dash his cheerfulness or diminish his earnestness. His eye was single to business; he would do the best he could; let the rest take care of itself.

The attempt was to have been made on June 2d. The matter of getting volunteers caused some embarrassment, because all the sailors of the fleet wished to go. Out of upward of a thousand likely men, six were selected; but a seventh managed to smuggle himself on board, for the mere pleasure of the adventure. All was ready on the night of

June 2d, but there had been delays, and after the collier had started, it was so near daylight that Sampson recalled her, lest she be uselessly destroyed. The men had been keyed up to a high pitch, and this recall was very trying; and Hobson himself, grimy with sweat, oil and coal-dust, mounted to the commodore's quarter-deck and told him, with a certain fierceness, that "there must be no more recalls!" And the next night he was allowed to go.

It was dark when they set out; the clouds covered the sky, there was no moon, and a brisk breeze threw up a choppy sea. The "Merrimac" did not steer straight for the entrance of the harbor, but made a detour, in order to avoid rocks. Being at length on her right course, she was driven ahead at full speed. The men were ordered to lie on the deck, and not to stir until ordered to do so; they were to pay no attention to the fire poured upon them, and if hit, were not to move. These trying instructions every man faithfully observed. Before the big collier had entered the channel, she was discovered, and the rain of shot began. The tall walls of rock on either hand made the darkness more intense than ever, but Hobson steered a true course amid the darkness and the roar of shot and shell and the difficult twistings of the channel. The Spaniards thought they had to deal with a battleship, and turned loose everything they had upon her; though they might have wondered why she made no reply to their furious attack. She kept on her course in silence; but ere she could reach the appointed spot, a shot disabled her steering gear. She was already sinking, without aid of her own torpedoes; but she forged ahead a little, and then began to swing round with the rush of the tide. At this moment, every element of terror at sea was present, except that the ship was not on fire. But her crew had not the relief of fighting back against their enemies; they must keep quiet and lie still, while they sank. They were alone; and nature and man were conspiring to crush them. But they knew that they were doing a mighty service to their country; and there was not a man of them who would have changed places with any other man alive. Let us remember that they were not exceptional men; they were Americans such as you may meet daily in the street. They were six volunteers chosen out of a thousand like them. Those who were not chosen, envied them. The spirit of a man is a marvelous thing.

The "Merrimac" gave a final plunge, and sank; and a whirlpool formed over the spot where she went down. Hobson and his men found themselves in the water: how, they did not exactly know. With all their strength they swam away from the whirlpool, lest it suck them under. In a few minutes, the suction ceased to drag on them; and then they turned to climb on the catamaran, which had been fastened to the roof of the midship house. But before they could reach it, boats containing Spaniards armed with rifles appeared round the point of rock up the channel. To have climbed upon the raft would have been certain death, for these Spaniards would shoot before asking questions. What should they do, then? The only thing to do was to take shelter underneath it; and this was rendered practicable by the accident that the rope which moored the raft to the deck-house of the sunken ship was a foot or more too short, so that the raft was submerged on one side, while the other stood up out of water. Under this providential roof they swam, and remained huddled together, with only their noses above water, while the Spaniards searched everywhere for traces of the crew which brought this mysterious craft into their harbor, and found none. They barely ventured to breathe, or to converse even in whispers. Hour after hour passed by, and still the curious Spaniards hovered about the spot, ejaculating, conjecturing, and inquisitive. The water, which had at first felt warm, got cold, and their teeth began to chatter till they feared the noise would betray them. One man started to swim ashore, but was ordered back, almost revealing the whole party. At last morning dawned, and then appeared a launch, with officers on board. Hobson hailed them, and clambered out on the raft; after a few minutes' hesitation, the launch allowed him to swim toward them and surrender himself. Admiral Cervera himself pulled him aboard, heard his story, recognized the officer's belt which he wore over his underclothing, and accepted the capitulation of himself and his shivering comrades. General Linares, to whom they were handed over, confined them in a blind' dungeon in Morro, and threatened them with the question by torture; but to the inquiry, "What was the object of your act?"—a superfluous inquiry, one would think— one of them made the answer, "In the United States Navy it is not the custom for seamen to know or to ask to know the object of the superior officer." Had their fate depended on Linares, they would doubtless have been shot; but Cervera would not permit it; it was he who sent word of their safety to Sampson, and obtained better quarters for them, after they had been subjected to a day's shelling in Morro.

It all seems like a chapter of romance by Stevenson or Cooper. The rush into the black channel, the frenzied cannonade, the explosion and the sinking, the eight heroes, unscathed every one, breathless under the raft, holding on by slipping their fingers between the crevices of the boards; the coming of the admiral, and his grotesque meeting with Hobson, whose rank he recognized, we may be sure, not so much by the belt he wore as by the eye and aspect which all the smut and filth of the night's work could not disguise; the day in the dungeon, with the shells of his own fleet screaming and splintering around him; and at last his removal to Santiago town, where he and his companions witnessed with thrilling hearts the charges of American soldiers on the Spanish breastworks;—was ever fairy-tale more wonderful? The matter-of-fact, prosaic Nineteenth Century vanishes as we read, and the great days of classic heroism are present with us once more. But, indeed, they are never absent, so long as human souls are brave and devoted.

One might almost say that this exploit marked the crisis of the war. For though the "Merrimac" was found not to lie exactly across the channel, she was enough of an obstruction to make it unsafe for Cervera to attempt escape at night; and if he came out in the day time, his fate was practically certain. His fleet was done for, all but the actual smashing; and Spain without a fleet either west or east was already a conquered nation. The conquest of Cuba and Porto Rico could be accomplished at our convenience, with no possibility of interruption; and we could prosecute the war in Spain itself by sending troops and ships to its coasts. It is true that Spain presently conjured up another phantom fleet, under Camara, and pretended to dispatch it to the Philippines to wipe out Dewey; but it never caused us a day's anxiety, and after being dragged through the Suez Canal, it could only be dragged back again, crippled not by battle, but simply by being handled by its own ignorant crews. In order to defeat a Spanish navy, it is necessary only to leave it in the unrestricted charge of its own officers and men; in a year or so, at most, its machinery will be hopelessly ruined, its bottoms foul with seaweed and barnacles, and a few smartly-managed American gunboats or converted pleasure-yachts can do the rest.

The American people is impatient of delay, and the government felt the pressure of public opinion, demanding that the war be prosecuted with vigor. Hitherto our troops had done nothing except congregate in camps and learn drill. No better material for an army was ever got together; but it must be admitted that there was shown, in the management, transportation and commissariat of an army, considerable incompetence. It must be remembered that more than a generation had passed since the outbreak of the Civil War, and that there existed few of the men who, at that epoch, had made themselves familiar with the work of handling and supplying large bodies of troops. Mistakes were inevitable, and in the case of contractors there may also have been negligence or recklessness. The problems of a campaign in a tropical country were likewise novel and of especial difficulty. The story of abuses was vehemently told, but no such evidence was adduced as to justify retailing it here; the time will come when a full accounting will be demanded, and equal justice dispensed. In the great picture of this conflict, as of others, there are dark shadows as well as brilliant lights; and men like Dewey and Hobson are set off by creeping scoundrels whose names soil the page of history. The worst as well as the best qualities of human nature come uppermost in wars. The ruin of Spain is largely due to the unrestrained and sinister luxuriance of noxious growths, the germs at least of which have appeared among ourselves. We may take her example as a warning to us, to stamp out the evil before it gains greater headway.

The first thing to be done, now that our navy had prepared the way, was to get our troops ashore; and some time was spent in selecting a place in which to land them. There was a harbor east of Santiago, and some forty miles distant from it, which answered our needs; but there was a force of Spaniards there which had to be taken into consideration. Admiral Sampson, supposing, as he had every reason to do, that transports must already be on their way with troops, put ashore at this harbor of Guantanamo a force of six hundred marines, under the charge of Commander McCalla. This officer's career had been interrupted a few years before by the sentence of a court-martial, convicting him of cruelty to his men; and he was anxious to redeem himself. The adventures of this little detachment of marines, commanded by Lieutenant-colonel R. W. Huntington, is a stirring episode by itself; but it cannot be treated in detail here. They were attacked by Spanish guerrillas, fighting in the bush and the tall grass, and concealing themselves with screens of leaves, on June 11th and following days; the enemy were numerous, and our men were in an exposed position. They began to suffer from the loss of sleep and continual nervous strain;

two officers and two men were killed. On June 12th they changed the place of their camp, and were again attacked, but drove the assailants off, losing two more men killed and several wounded. Meanwhile a force of Cubans had joined the Americans, and did good service in scouting and bush-fighting; and on the 14th of June, the soldiers of the two peoples fought for the first time side by side and pursued the Spaniards, inflicting an estimated loss of two hundred upon them. The following day, the warship "Marblehead," Commander McCalla, with the "Texas" and "Suwanee," shelled the fort at Caimanera, the port of Guantanamo; but all this while nothing had been seen of the promised transports with sixteen thousand troops under General Shafter. They should have arrived on the 10th; but as a matter of fact, they did not start from Tampa until the 15th of June. An additional force of marines had been meanwhile landed from the fleet, and the Spaniards had been repulsed in every engagement; but the number of the enemy far exceeded ours, and there seemed to be no reason why they might not receive important re-enforcements. For a time, therefore, some uneasiness was felt about our men. Intense indignation was also aroused by the report that the bodies of our men killed in the bush had been mutilated by the Spanish guerrillas. The statement was embodied in one of the official reports; but the defense was made that the apparent mutilations were in fact caused by the spreading of the bullets fired by the Spaniards, causing them to make lacerated wounds suggesting wanton disfigurement. Admiral Sampson, in a subsequent dispatch, accepted this interpretation of the matter, being naturally anxious to disbelieve that the enemy against which he fought was unworthy of civilized consideration. Unfortunately, however, the stories told were subsequently shown to be too true. An American officer who personally examined the bodies of our men found that they had been subjected to the same wanton and obscene outrages which had been inflicted upon the bodies of Japanese soldiers during the late war between China and Japan. The work was deliberate and unmistakable; no room was left for the plea of accident. We are, however, able to record that, so far as is known, no repetition of the mutilations occurred in the battles before Santiago; and it may fairly be inferred that the work at Guantanamo was done by Spanish irregular troops only, without the cognizance or authority of their officers. In most of the cases in which our troops have met those of the enemy, the Spaniards seem to have fought with reasonable courage and persistence; though there can be no comparison in this respect between their troops and the American ones. They always had the advantages of position and of superior artillery; and being armed with smokeless powder, they could not readily be located by our men; in spite of which they invariably abandoned their positions when attacked.

The delay in sending forward our re-enforcements from Tampa was due to the confusion incident to handling an unexpectedly large number of troops; and General Shafter undoubtedly was embarrassed by the task assigned to him. He was lacking in experience and, as it afterward appeared, in tact, as shown in his dealings with our allies, the Cuban troops and generals. It was fortunate for him and for our army that the war was so short-lived, and that the men against whom we fought were so lacking in spirit as well as in leaders.

Before the transports arrived, two Cuban leaders, Rabi and Garcia, had effected a lodgment at Acceraderos, a coast town west of Santiago, having a good wharf. June 20th the transports hove in sight, over thirty in number; next day Shafter and Sampson conferred with Garcia as to his co-operation with us; and on the 22d the landing took place at Baiquiri, a feint of landing being made at the same time at a point just west of Santiago, and the coast being shelled by the fleet along a stretch of many miles. No serious opposition was met with; the weather was fine, and in two or three days the sixteen thousand men were ashore.

The road from Baiquiri to Santiago runs first west and then north, passing through the towns of Demajayabo, Juragua, and Sevilla, and crossing streams which are rivulets in dry weather, but torrents in the rains. The country is rough and difficult to a degree incomprehensible to those who have not seen tropical forests; the roads are but bridle paths through dense and briery jungle, and in wet weather become terrible sloughs of slippery mud. It is impossible to see for any distance, the heat is intolerable; travel for a single person is difficult enough, but for an army, subjected to the fire of unseen foes, loaded with trappings and carrying supplies, it is appalling indeed.

Besides Baiquiri, we had secured a base at Siboney, between Baiquiri and Santiago. The Spaniards fell back from Demajayabo and Juragua to Sevilla; before reaching that point our advance met the enemy in a sharp skirmish. An ambush had been prepared for us in the hills of La Guasima: whether or not it was a surprise was a question; General Wheeler, an ex-Confederate soldier, says it was not, and his word may be trusted. At all events we suffered relatively severe losses. An unknown number of Spaniards, conjectured to be fifteen hundred, had constructed effective defenses and strung barbed wire at points of vantage; they used smokeless powder, and it was hard to locate them. The number of our troops at this point was about nine hundred, under Colonel Young: they comprised the 23d Regular Infantry and the 1st and 10th Cavalry, and a regiment of volunteer cavalry known as Roosevelt's Rough Riders. All were on foot. The chief loss fell on the Rough Riders, who maintained their ground with great courage and steadiness; among the first killed of this regiment was Sergeant Hamilton Fish, and at the same time with him fell Captain Capron, a gallant officer. Altogether, in the hour's fight, we lost sixteen killed and fifty-two wounded; but the enemy could not withstand our advance, the persistency of which amazed them, and they fled, leaving Sevilla open to our occupation.

The two armies now confronted each other along a line stretching from the coast town of Aguadores, a few miles east of Morro, to El Caney, northwest of Santiago. The country was better adapted for defense than for attack; the enemy's positions were strong and well chosen, and the earthworks and block houses were rendered more effective by barbed wire fences, so placed as to delay our troops at points where they would be under the direct fire of the enemy, who knew the range, and were themselves unseen. Three things were imperative for the attacking force: thorough knowledge of the ground; a leader who could control and co-ordinate all movements; and abundance of both heavy and light artillery, to prepare the way for the charges of the infantry. None of these conditions were present; the ground was almost entirely unknown; Shafter himself was stricken with fever and compelled to remain in the rear throughout the battle; and the heavy artillery was quite wanting, though some batteries of light artillery, which proved ineffective against the earthworks and block houses, were got into position. The burden of the battle was therefore thrown upon the infantry, and our victory was due to their extraordinary courage and intelligence, and to the heroic leadership of some of the regimental commanders. It was a battle of soldiers, captains and colonels, not of generals; and probably no soldiers in the world, under the conditions, could have acquitted themselves so brilliantly as did our regulars during those trying and exhausting days; and the volunteer regiments caught inspiration from them, and in the desperate charge up San Juan Hill men of the 71st New York kept side by side with the regulars and fully shared their glory. Nor were the Rough Riders ever found wanting; their dash and daring were worthy of their leaders, Wood and Roosevelt, who exposed themselves with perfect gallantry wherever danger was sorest. But it was a military error to send our men forward to carry positions which had not previously been shelled by heavy artillery;

and the losses of the battle—over fifteen hundred—might have been almost entirely avoided had a leader of greater experience and discretion directed affairs. It must be remembered, however, that the rainy season had begun, and that the roads, always rough and difficult, were rendered immeasurably worse by the deluge of water which was daily poured upon them, and by the constant passage of large bodies of men. In war, an initial mistake or misfortune is apt to produce others; and there is no doubt that the delay in getting the men off from Tampa was in a great degree responsible for the calamities that afterward occurred. Had we begun active preparations a week or two earlier, the capture of Santiago might have been effected at the date on which its siege actually began; and not only would the movement of siege trains have been easier, but the army might have been saved from the fever which overtook it before arrangements could be made to remove it from the island. Were the campaign to be made over again, the experience gained through our errors and oversights would cause it to be conducted in a very different manner.

The disposition of our army was as follows:—It was technically known as the Fifth Army Corps, consisting of infantry, cavalry (unmounted), and light and heavy artillery. The infantry was in two divisions; the cavalry in two brigades; and there were two brigades of light artillery and four of heavy artillery, which last could not be made effective in season for the attack. Of the infantry, the first division under General Kent occupied the center of our line; it comprised Hawkins's, Pearson's and Wikoff's brigades—eight regular regiments and one (the 71st New York) of volunteers. General Lawton commanded the second division on our right, made up of Chaffee's, Ludlow's and Colonel Miles's brigades—eight regular regiments and one (the 2d Massachusetts) volunteer. Our left, whose duty it was to attack Aguadores, was commanded by General

Duffield, and consisted of two Michigan volunteer regiments and two thousand Cubans. The cavalry was under the orders of the veteran General Wheeler, Sumner and Young being the brigade commanders, but Young was incapacitated by illness. Sumner's brigade was all regulars; Young's contained two regular and one volunteer regiments—the latter being Roosevelt's Rough Riders. The army, it will be seen, had twenty-one regular and five volunteer regiments—an unusual preponderance of the former arm of the service. As to the volunteers, it should be mentioned that the authorities had made the singular mistake of arming them with old-fashioned Springfield rifles, which carried scarce half as far as the enemy's Mausers, and burned ordinary black powder, which made a smoke that afforded an excellent indication of their position to the Spaniards. Thus they were not only in constant peril themselves, but to the regulars fighting beside them as well. More than once, owing to this cause, they were ordered to cease firing; and it was partly owing to this that the confusion occurred in the 71st Regiment to which further allusion will be made presently. In addition to other embarrassing circumstances attending our advance, was the fact that Spanish sharpshooters, with smokeless powder, were posted in tall and thick-foliaged trees all along our route, and even occasionally in our rear; these men did great execution, and fired constantly upon the wounded, and upon the litters in which they were being taken to the rear, and upon the surgeons and Red Cross officers engaged in tending them. The Spaniards, as has been said, proved themselves not altogether despicable as fighters; but from the blowing up of the "Maine" to the end of the war, the conduct of Spanish soldiers and sailors was consistently that of people beyond the pale of decent civilization.

In spite of all obstacles, errors and drawbacks, the Spaniards were forced to abandon all their positions, and withdraw to the immediate defenses of Santiago itself. It might almost be said that our men fought each man for himself; there was no united action, or comprehensive knowledge at one point of what was doing at another. Wherever our troops saw the enemy, they advanced to attack him, and sooner or later drove him back. At the end of the fighting, a general advance would have overwhelmed the dispirited enemy and given Santiago into our hands; but at this juncture, which a brave and competent general would have seized upon, Shafter so far misunderstood the situation that he would have ordered a retreat along the whole line, had he not been restrained by decisive orders from Washington. A vast calamity was thus averted; but one only less serious was invited by the failure of the war department to order an immediate advance. They directed him to demand the surrender of the city; this led to prolonged delays, during which our troops were compelled to remain in trenches, exposed to the horrors of the tropic rainy season, half starved, owing to the failure of the commissariat, and drinking water which was full of the germs of death. The inevitable consequence was the outbreak of an epidemic of yellow and typhoid fevers which killed hundreds and shattered the health of thousands. There was again delay in sending the sick and dying men home; and when transport was at last provided, the ships were so inadequate in furnishing and supplies that they became veritable pest ships, and caused the death of many who might otherwise have been saved. The responsibility for these blunders has not been fixed; but the blood of brave men needlessly destroyed cries out to the nation, and will not be silenced by evasions and prevarications.

Let us now consider the various reports of the battle, which are by no means all compatible one with another, but from which some facts may be elicited. The attack upon Aguadores, on our left, was, as has been mentioned, withdrawn, the positions being considered too strong; it had been designed to prepare the way for the attack and capture of Morro, which had been shelled by the fleet, though without the effect of entirely silencing the guns. The failure, which was afterward described as a feint, was, as it turned out, not of vital importance, inasmuch as the Spanish fleet was destroyed on the 3d of July, while attempting to escape from the harbor; and this led to the surrender of Santiago, with all the surrounding defenses. Meanwhile, the movement of our right and center was successful.

The battle began on July 1st, and continued three days. On the right, the objective point was the heights of El Caney, protected by earthworks and by a stone house or fort. Our artillery was on a ridge facing it; but the range was known to the Spaniards, and our guns were not heavy enough to drive them from their positions. In order to reach the position with infantry, it was necessary to cross a river under heavy fire, and ascend the opposite slope. With the exception of the stone fort, the enemy's batteries were invisible; but their fire, from cannon, machine guns, and rifles, was very heavy and destructive. During the shelling, the infantry slowly advanced from point to point, fighting their way on; the quantity of ammunition expended on both sides was great, but in this preliminary work the losses on our side were the heavier. From four in the morning till two in the afternoon the struggle continued; our extreme right was held by Chaffee with the 7th, 17th and 12th infantry; down in the low land to the south was Ludlow, with his ineffective light battery of four guns. It was evident that the Spanish could not be dislodged by shelling; and when a force of our men, under Clarke, had reached the foot of the hill on which the stone fort stood, with its surrounding concealed earthworks, Chaffee sent them the order to charge up the hill and capture the positions at the point of the bayonet. And these men, after ten continuous hours of the most exhausting kind of fighting, prepared promptly to obey the command. It was the turning point of the battle in this quarter; the last moment of earth for many who were to take part in it. With the taking of the stone fort, the left of the Spanish position would be turned, and its evacuation forced, including that of the village of El Caney, from the stone houses of which a fire had been all along maintained.

The charge was made in full view of both armies; its success seemed impossible. The grass was long and slippery; the ropy vines coiled round the limbs of our men; the thorny branches of the tropic vegetation caught their garments and tore their faces; the bullets and shells of the enemy beat upon them in a continuous stream. The ascent was steep and long. Glancing upward, as they struggled on, the men could see only death flashing down on them from the crest of the hill that was so far away. They were faint with heat, thirst, hunger, and the long day of exertion, but they went on. The Spaniards redoubled their fire, confident of sweeping them back; but no: they still advanced. They were so near now that their comrades in the rear with the batteries feared to continue their fire, lest they kill them. It seemed, to those who watched, that human endurance and courage could do no more; the charge would be repulsed. But even then, the men gathered themselves for a last effort; they forced their way on; they were at the fence of barbed wire that protected the outer trenches; they cut it and tore it down, and leaped into the trenches. The first man in was a war-correspondent, James Creelman; he found himself in a hideous pit of blood and death; corpses stared up at him with glassy eyes; wounded men crawled under his feet, and held up their faltering hands in token of surrender. The others had fled. In poured our panting, victorious troops; they swept over the breastworks that had defied them so long, and on to the stone block-house. There was none to oppose them now. In the fort were seven dead men in one room; the place was full of dead and wounded; the walls splashed with blood, the floor slippery with it; and there were four living men and an officer, who held up their hands in supplication, expecting to be butchered, as they would have butchered us had the situation been reversed.

Passing round to the rear of the fort, Creelman found the Spanish flag; it was received with cheers, as well it might be, for it had been hardly won. The 12th regulars, in particular, suffered severely. Following the charge, up came Chaffee with the rest of his command, and occupied El Caney. The Spaniards were flying headlong into Santiago; above the blood-bespattered town waved the Stars and Stripes, and our victorious troops looked down at last into the streets of the city, under the declining sun.

Meanwhile our center under General Kent had been engaged all day in the attack on San Juan Hill. Grimes's battery was in position on a height opposite San Juan before seven in the morning; and Hawkins's brigade was near the sugar-house at El Poso; he was moving forward with the First Brigade, when orders were received to allow the cavalry to precede; but the advance of the latter was seriously delayed, owing in part to the difficulty of fording the San Juan River, and to the necessity of the men's ridding themselves of their blanket rolls and other encumbrances. A large part of the command was subjected to the enemy's fire at this time, and their position was trying. Hawkins attempted to turn their right, but the fire proved too heavy. A balloon, sent up for observation purposes by Shafter's orders, was drawing the fire of the enemy upon the First Brigade; bullets seemed to come from all directions, even from the rear, where Spanish sharpshooters were posted in the tall trees. At this juncture the existence of a narrow trail leading across the river on the left was discovered, and into this trail the 71st Regiment of New York Volunteers was sent. The dense tropical jungle impeded their movement; the fire of the enemy upon their van was severe, and the conduct of some of the officers commanding them seems to have been questionable. Contradictory orders were given; the soldiers were thrown into confusion, some having been directed to retreat, others to conceal themselves in the jungle and cease the advance. The men were meanwhile dropping under the fire, and were in the agony of mind of brave men who desire only to be led against the enemy, but have none to lead them. While the men of the first battalion of the regiment were in this predicament, the second and third battalions came up, and moving in good order, went forward to the ford. Upon their heels came the Third Brigade, but their way became blocked by men of the first battalion of the 71st, who were still without leaders, and several of whom cried out for some one to take them forward. Additional confusion was caused by the long delay of the cavalry, already alluded to; since the orders were that the cavalry was to lead the movement. Kent finally decided to wait no longer; and Wikoff's brigade, consisting of the 9th, 13th and 24th regular infantry was sent forward across the stream, part of them passing over the battalion of the 71st, which had been ordered to lie down. A few minutes later, Wikoff was killed, and three officers of the brigade were wounded. Following these men came the Second Brigade, the 10th and 2d infantry following the path of Wikoff's men, while the 21st proceeded along the main road to support Hawkins.

But anything like an orderly advance was out of the question; the men could not see one another, and the different commands got mixed together. Through the confusion, however, the Third Brigade, in conjunction with Hawkins's troops on the right, and accompanied by a part of the 71st Volunteers, who attached themselves to other leaders rather than remain in the rear, massed together, and went forward through a terrible fire up San Juan Hill. It seemed as if no man could stand up in the face of that fire and live; but regulars and volunteers dashed forward side by side, without faltering, though constantly falling. The hill was steep and difficult, like most of the hills in this region; the position was strong by nature and science. It was defended by deep trenches and by a brick fort, loopholed, and with surrounding fences of barbed wire. Besides the men of the 71st Volunteers, this charge was made by the 6th, 9th, 13th,

16th and 24th regiments of regular infantry. Immediately after this charge, which took place at half past one in the afternoon, the Third Brigade captured the hill on the left, driving the enemy before them. This movement was led by Colonel Pearson. The enemy retreated to a line of rifle pits in the rear of their first position, while our men intrenched themselves on San Juan Hill, with the exception of the 13th regulars, who were detached to re-enforce Colonel Wood of the Rough Riders and General Sumner, who were being hard pressed on the right. To speak of individuals, the glory of the San Juan charge centers round Hawkins, who led his men up the hill, placing himself between the 6th and 16th Infantry. But every man who went up that hill was a hero, and deserves the thanks of his country.

The capture of El Caney and San Juan caused the evacuation of the positions at Aguadores, so that the success of the Americans was carried out along the whole line, and our army surrounded Santiago on all sides except the northwest. Fearing that a retreat through this opening might be attempted, the lines were extended in that direction, but were thereby so weakened that Shafter telegraphed for help, and six thousand troops were sent forward to him. Attempts by the Spaniards to retake the positions we had captured were repulsed with little difficulty. On July 3d the surrender of Santiago was demanded. It was refused by General Toral, who succeeded General Linares, who had been wounded, and made this a pretext for keeping in the background of the negotiations; but Toral was allowed till the next day to think better of it. By this time, the destruction of Cervera's fleet had been accomplished. Toral further delayed a decisive reply, and Shafter continued to humor him, while our troops imbibed the germs of the fevers which were soon to destroy so many of them. Finally, on the 11th of July, the fleet opened a bombardment on the town, firing over the hills; the land batteries took but small part in it, and little damage was done—the non-combatants having been previously permitted to pass through our lines and encamp in the rear. On the same day General Miles arrived at the front, not, as was explained, to supersede Shafter, but for purposes of observation, previous to undertaking the campaign against Porto Rico. Negotiations went on until the 14th of July, when Toral at length agreed to surrender, provided his men were treated with the honors of war, and were sent home to Spain at the expense of the United States. So many of our men had ere this been prostrated by yellow and malarial fevers, and by the starvation to which they had been subjected from the outset of the campaign, that any terms were welcome to us. The surrender professed to include that part of Cuba east of Santiago, though the right of Toral to do this was afterward called in question. Shafter, having recovered from his indisposition, now went to the front, and rode into Santiago, with Wheeler and the other generals, and an adequate force of American troops. The Cubans were not represented, and General Garcia charged that Shafter had entirely ignored him and them in the negotiations, and had neglected to invite him to witness the surrender. The courteous diplomacy of General Miles alone averted a serious disagreement.

Our losses during the three days' fight were given as fifteen hundred and ninety-five men; over eight hundred of whom fell in the attack on San Juan, and half as many in the capture of El Caney. But before the men had been moved to the north, nearly five thousand had succumbed to fever—an entirely unnecessary sacrifice. Not only, as has been stated, were the accommodations on the ships which brought them to Montauk Point, on Long Island, scandalously deficient, but even after they arrived there, within a hundred miles of New York, they were restricted—sick, wounded and well alike—to food unfit to eat, such as rotten canned beef, mouldy hardtack, and bad and insufficient water; and for some time they were obliged to lie without blankets or tents on the bare ground. Many who might have been saved died within sight of their homes from starvation, exposure and exhaustion, as well as from the result of sickness contracted in Cuba; and had it not been for the efforts of persons in New York, and in the towns of Long Island neighboring to Montauk, and to the liberality of a few wealthy benefactors like Miss Helen Gould, the mortality would have been far greater. The 71st Regiment of Volunteers were the greatest sufferers; and some of their own officers, who had already made themselves conspicuous by their absence during the fighting at San Juan, unblushingly "requisitioned," for their own use or profit, food and supplies sent to individual soldiers in the regiment by their own families.

Let us, however, return to the 3d of July, and listen to the story of a victory upon which rests no cloud of any kind; the story of a naval victory worthy to stand beside that of Manila.

At half-past nine on the morning of that day, the American fleet under the command of Admiral Sampson was stationed off the mouth of Santiago Harbor, where it had been for many a weary week. It consisted of the "New York," the flagship, with Sampson himself; the "Brooklyn," carrying Schley, the second in command; the "Oregon," Captain Clarke; the "Texas," Captain Philip; the "Iowa," Captain Robley Evans; the "Indiana," which, owing to her position at the beginning of the action, and her slow speed, was soon left behind in the running battle; and the "Gloucester," formerly the yacht "Corsair," property of the Wall Street operator J. P. Morgan, and sold by him for her full value to the government. This little boat was entirely unprotected, but had a good armament of rapid-fire guns which were effective at short range. Short ranges suited her commander, who had been executive officer on board the "Maine" at the time she was destroyed by the Spanish; and who was anxious for an opportunity to "remember" his lost battleship. One other vessel of the blockading fleet, the "Massachusetts," had chosen this of all days in the year to run down to Guantanamo to coal. The "New York" was unable to take active part in the fight for a similar reason—she had gone to Siboney to enable Admiral Sampson to confer with General Shafter. The only ships, therefore, that had the honor of personally assisting in the reception given to Admiral Cervera, were the "Brooklyn," "Oregon," "Iowa" and "Indiana," and the little "Gloucester," who in spite of her size and defenseless condition did some of the most useful work of the famous day. The "Vixen" was another small auxiliary boat similar to the "Gloucester"; but she, finding that her position when the Spanish fleet came forth, placed her between our fire and theirs, passed through our line to the south, and there remained during the engagement; but rendered important service, together with the torpedo boat "Ericsson," in rescuing Spanish seamen from their burning ships afterward. But the "Iowa" and the "Indiana" were speedily left behind in the race, so that upon the "Oregon," "Brooklyn," "Texas" and "Gloucester" rested the chief laurels of the battle; and against them were arrayed the Spanish ships "Infanta Maria Teresa," "Cristobal Colon," "Vizcaya," "Almirante Oquendo," and the destroyers "Pluton" and "Furor," who came out in the rear of the procession, and fell to the share of the "Gloucester" before many minutes had passed. It will be seen, therefore, that the odds were on the side of the Spaniards, and had they fought instead of running away, the story of the battle might have been modified.

The positions of our ships in the line was as judicious as possible. The "Brooklyn," one of the fastest of our ships, was at the extreme west; the "New York," also fast, was at the extreme right; the "Oregon," which proved to be one of the fastest of all, was near the center, ready to move either way. The "Texas" was next to the "Brooklyn," and the "Iowa" and the "Indiana" were on either side of the "Oregon." Whether, therefore, the Spanish fleet on emerging should steer east or west, or whether they should steam straight ahead, or disperse in different directions, we were equally ready for them. Our distance from shore was from 4,000 to 6,000 yards, and as a whole we were rather east of the mouth of the harbor than west of it. The sea was quiet. The day, as that of the Manila fight, was Sunday, and the men were at Sunday quarters when the lookouts reported that the Spanish fleet was coming forth.

It was, indeed, with the knowledge of this fact that Admiral Cervera had chosen that hour for his attempt. But what had induced him to make the attempt at all? His ships had been of great assistance in the defense of Santiago from the attack of the land forces on the two preceding days; and the doctrine of probabilities made him at least as safe in the battery-guarded and torpedo-intrenched harbor as he would be outside. Why did he hazard all upon this desperate sally?

The first reason he afterward gave was, as is invariable with Spaniards, a false one; he said he would rather be destroyed fighting gloriously than rust to pieces inside the harbor. The truth came out later—he acted in reluctant obedience to positive and repeated orders from Madrid. The Spanish government had no concern for the fate of the fleet, or of the army, in their conflict with the Americans; they did not hope to win; all they wished was to be defeated in such a manner as to save the throne to the son of the Queen Regent. There was imminent danger that the Carlists would revolt if opportunity were offered by management of the war such as to displease the bulk of the Spanish people, who were profoundly ignorant of the impotence of their country. Let the Spanish sailors and soldiers be killed, therefore, as convenience might dictate; and then a peace could be concluded which would leave Alphonso a chance to keep his seat.

Be that as it may, Cervera had no alternative, and he made what preparations he could. He got all the coal aboard his squadron that was available, and had steam up so as to be able to move at full speed at once after getting clear of the harbor. His ships were nominally faster than ours, so that if he got a fair start, he might hope to get away with some at least of them. Meantime he would direct his concentrated fire, on emerging, at the vessel in our fleet whose speed he most feared, the "Brooklyn"; if she and one more were disabled, or crippled enough to diminish their pace, all might be well. Of course he would expect to meet with some losses; but on the other hand he might fairly calculate on inflicting some; and as all he wished was to get away, while our object was to capture or destroy him, he had by far the easier part to play. There remained another difficulty to be solved: the crews of the Spanish fleet betrayed an almost invincible reluctance to go forth to battle. But fortunately there was a great stock of Spanish wines in Santiago; and by dint of serving out these to the men in unlimited quantities, until they were crazy drunk, and then keeping them to their work with loaded pistols, the forlorn admiral was enabled to undertake his enterprise.

At 9.31 the nose of the Spanish flagship, the "Maria Teresa," was seen round the point of the islet Cay Smith, within the mouth of the harbor. No doubt the fleet would have come out six or seven hours earlier, had not the sunken hull of the "Merrimac," Hobson's work, made the passage in the dark hours too dangerous. The ships were moving, when first seen, at the rate of about eight knots an hour. Our ships covered an arc some eight miles in length. The nearest to the Spanish fleet was the "Gloucester," and when she sighted the destroyers, she made straight for them. The "Vizcaya" was next to the "Maria Teresa," then came the "Colon," and then the "Oquendo." There was a space of about half a mile between each of them. The destroyers, "Pluton" and "Furor," were nearly three-quarters of a mile behind the "Oquendo." As the "Maria Teresa" cleared the headlands, she aimed her guns at the "Brooklyn," but the shots flew wide; the other ships, as they followed, imitated her example. The movements of our men, though taken by surprise, were so rapid that in eight minutes from the first alarm we were returning the Spanish fire; and our shots did not go wide, but reached their quarry. The sound of the guns had been heard by the "New York," several miles down the coast, and the admiral at once gave up the idea of a conversation with Shafter, turned his boat about, and started for his foe, flying the signal, quite unnecessarily of course, "Close in and attack." Schley's whole soul, and that of every captain under him, had been fixed from the first moment upon doing just that thing. Cervera had turned to the westward, and with his flying start had got well ahead. But the "Brooklyn" and "Texas" were hot upon his trail, and the "Oregon," starting at a tremendous speed, was rapidly overhauling them. The slower "Iowa" and "Indiana" gave the Spaniards their broadsides as they passed, and also sent some useful shots at the two destroyers, as they came out. But the "Gloucester" had taken the latter for her share, and closing in upon them with apparent recklessness, she poured into them from her rapid-fire batteries a deadly hail of steel. In twenty minutes she had finished both of them; the "Pluton" was sank in deep water, and the "Furor" reached the beach and sunk there. Then Commander Wainwright, having remembered the "Maine," remembered the calls of humanity, and gave all his energies to saving the lives of the crews of the wrecked vessels. The commander ought to have slept well that night, in the consciousness of duty well performed to God, humanity and his country.

Meanwhile the chase was streaming off toward the west, beneath the high green mountains of the coast; and probably no more exciting chase, both to pursuers and pursued, ever took place. The Spaniards were flying for life; the Amer-

ADMIRAL SAMPSON'S FLEET SALUTING AT GRANT'S TOMB, AUGUST 20, 1898

THE NEW YORK
PUBLIC LIBRARY

ASTOR, LENOX AND
TILDEN FOUNDATIONS.

icans must either overtake and destroy them, or not only suffer the disgrace of losing their prey after all these tedious weeks of anxiety and suspense, but subject our coasts to the possible attacks of the enemy. Both sides consequently strained every nerve, and one shudders to imagine what the condition of things in the engine-rooms must have been. And the blue water was churned white by the steel bows, and the smoke of the funnels streamed backward, a heavy black plume, spreading through the upper air; and the white smoke from the thundering guns eddied and billowed about the ships, and lay along the astonished sea. The sea was likewise bursting into columns of foam where shots which missed the ships plunged into the water; and all but a very small fraction of the Spanish shots met this fate. As the two lines of ships sped onward, the Americans gradually crowded the Spaniards toward the shore; and it also began to be noticeable that our leading vessels were slowly closing upon their adversaries. This may be ascribed to several causes. In the first place, the forced draught of the Spaniards was gradually getting exhausted, while our steam was gaining power; possibly, too, the Spanish stokers were stopping for another pull at the wine bottles. Again, the effect of our gunnery began to tell; it not only drove the Spanish gunners from their work, but it interfered with the running-power of the ships; and before the chase had lasted twenty minutes, several of them were on fire. In less than half an hour, the "Maria Teresa" and the "Oquendo" had received their coup de grace; they turned and ran for the beach, seven miles from Morro, and there burned and blew up. There were left only the "Vizcaya" and the "Colon," the latter being ahead; and they made a final desperate effort. The "Vizcaya" found herself subjected to the fire of the "Brooklyn," "Oregon," "Texas," and even of the "Iowa," which was still within range; it was not in human nature, nor in steel plates, to stand up against such an onset; and though Captain Eulate might kill forty of his despairing men in order to keep them at their guns, it was in vain. Just an hour after leaving the harbor, the "Vizcaya" struck, firing upon her ceased, and the work of life-saving began. In this the "Iowa" participated; for the "Colon," the only other Spanish ship, was by that time far away, pursued by the "Brooklyn" and "Oregon," both of whom were overhauling her, and the "Texas." But the "Iowa" had justified the fighting reputation of her illustrious commander. It was largely owing to her tremendous broadsides, delivered at ranges of from six thousand to twelve hundred yards, that the quick destruction of the "Maria Teresa" and "Oquendo" was due. Each of these had received the entire weight of steel from one or other of the "Iowa's" batteries, Evans's maneuvering of his vessel being a masterpiece of seamanship and strategy. He also contributed to the destruction of the destroyers. Nine times was he struck, twice seriously, but with no loss of life or casualty to his men.

While Evans was receiving on board the remains of the crew of the "Vizcaya," and afterward, from the "Gloucester," Admiral Cervera and his surviving officers, taken from the "Maria Teresa," the chase of the "Colon" continued. The "Oregon" now led the "Brooklyn," though the latter was close behind her; the "Texas" could not keep their pace; far behind her was coming the "New York," at a speed of over sixteen knots. It had been during the last moments of the "Vizcaya" that Philip uttered his famous saying, which will last as long as the memory of the fight, "Don't cheer, boys; those poor fellows are dying." And he it was too who, after the battle was over, stood on his deck and took off his cap, and said, "I want to make public acknowledgment here that I believe in God the Father Almighty. I want all you officers and men to lift your hats, and from your hearts offer silent thanks to God Almighty." It was a spontaneous and manly utterance, befitting the time, and characteristic of the spirit of our navy. The "Texas" had been struck in the fight, and a shell had swept the bridge a moment after Philip and his officers had stepped off it; but none of either officers or crew lost his life or was wounded.

The "Colon" was not maintaining her reputation for speed; her average during the hours of the chase was but little over thirteen knots, though her record had been more than one and twenty. This must be laid to the gross carelessness and ignorance of her officers and crew; and they now paid for it with the loss of her. Gradually the ship fell back, and the "Oregon," looming terribly in her rear, fired a 13-inch shell which passed her and flung up a warning column of foam before her bows. The "Brooklyn" also overshot her; and with this demonstration of his certain destruction, the "Colon's" captain, though he had not been struck by any disabling shots, decided that he had had enough. He turned in shore, eight and forty miles from "Morro," making signals of surrender, and ran upon the beach at full speed. His surrender had made the ship the property of the United States by the laws of maritime war; yet her captain treacherously ordered the sea-valves to be opened, and she sank. She would have gone down in deep water, irrecoverably, had not the "New York," coming up, set her stern against the great vessel, and pushed her forward into the shallows, where she lay on her beam ends. It was hoped that she could be raised, and as she was practically uninjured, she would be an important addition to our navy.

The "Brooklyn" and the "Oregon" had been in the thick of the fight throughout; the latter, with her great speed and big guns, had perhaps done the more execution; but the "Brooklyn" carried forty-one scars; and it was on her deck that the only man killed in the entire battle, on the American side, fell; his name was G. H. Ellis, and his function was that of chief yeoman. The total result of the thousands of shots fired by the sailors on the Spanish ships, and the gunners in Morro and the shore batteries, was this one man killed and one wounded, and some fifty dents in our ships' armor. In this respect, the battle was that of Manila over again. Drunken men behind the guns cannot be expected to shoot straight; but the fact that during four hours' continuous firing less than threescore shots should have hit anything but the sea, seems apocryphal. Our men, on the other hand, wasted very little; and Schley, in his report of July 4th, remarks that he "never before witnessed such deadly and fatally accurate firing as was done by the ships as they closed in on the Spanish squadron. I have never served with a braver, better or worthier crew than that of the 'Brooklyn' during the combat, lasting from 9.30 until 1.15 P.M., much of the time under fire; they never flagged for a moment, and were apparently undisturbed by the storm of projectiles passing ahead, astern and over the ship. I am glad," he adds, "that I had an opportunity to contribute in the least to a victory that seems big enough for all of us."

Two days after the nation had been made proud and glad by the news of this success, the Newlands resolution passed the Senate, and on the 7th of July it received the President's signature. After five years of diplomatic maneuvering, underhand plotting, and interminable speechmaking and expert literary efflux, Hawaii was annexed to America, and became to all future time bone of our bone and flesh of our flesh. The struggle over the question of its admission to the Union first became prominent five years ago, when President Cleveland was put in the position of countenancing an intrigue to re-establish the so-called Queen Liliuokalani on the throne, deposing the elected President of the Hawaiian Republic, Dole, an American, a man of integrity and ability. From then until now, there has always been a majority in this country favoring annexation; and Dole and his Republic itself have been steady advocates of it. But the minority against it was active and wealthy; aside from the political ambitions of the "Queen" and her party, the interests of the sugar trusts have been arrayed against annexation, because it was thought that the prosperity of the beet sugar industry here would be imperiled by the admission of free cane sugar from Hawaii. The point raised was one of temporary significance only, so far as national interests are concerned; but it meant a great deal to the monopolists of beet sugar, who had prevented action in Congress, and might have continued so to do indefinitely, had not the war with Spain occasioned Dewey's victory at Manila. Between Dewey and us stretched eight or nine thousand miles of sea; he needed reenforcements, and they must be sent at once. But by the neutrality laws, we could not coal or stop for any purpose at the independent Republic of Hawaii, and yet it would be wellnigh impossible to get to Manila with our transports without doing so. Of course, we could easily violate Hawaiian neutrality; but in that case, Hawaii and Spain would appeal to Europe, which would welcome any pretext for checking us; and the war might easily expand into a general conflict beyond even our strength to handle. From this predicament we were delivered by the prompt action of President Dole himself, who refused to be neutral, and on the contrary opened his port to us for any purposes we might desire. It was, of course, a shrewd diplomatic stroke on Dole's part; but he was not the less actuated by motives truly patriotic. The enormous value of the islands to us for strategic purposes was now too obvious to be denied, not to speak of other advantages; and the opponents of annexation had no longer any presentable leg to stand on. They maintained an obstructive fight for three weeks, being aided by Speaker Reed in the House, who, from whatever motives, had always been an enemy of the policy which most true patriots approved. But Democrats and Republicans alike joined in supporting the resolution; the Democratic leader in the House, Bailey of Texas, being deserted by his followers when he tried to gather them in caucus for the opposition. The stars in their courses were fighting to invest us with a colonial empire which already stretches round the world, and may in time rival that of England.

The result will be to bring about a change in our policy as radical as that which differentiates the functions of the mayor of a city from those of the ruler of a nation.

In a war of this kind there are many minor episodes which show the quality of the men engaged in them as clearly as do the great ones, which yet can hardly find place in a brief resume of the general conduct and features of the campaign. But for neatness and completeness nothing could surpass the affair at Manzanillo on the 18th of July, when seven vessels of our blockading fleet burned and destroyed three Spanish transports, blew up a store ship, burned a pontoon, and destroyed four gunboats, without suffering any casualties whatever. The harbor was shallow, so that our gunboats, the "Wilmington" and the "Helena," were the largest that could venture in; they were accompanied by the converted yachts "Scorpion," "Hist" and "Hornet," and the tugs "Wompatuck" and "Osceola." In order to avoid the fire of the shore batteries, the boats were kept at long range. The guns used were 5 and 4-inch, and six-pounders. The leader of the expedition was Commander Todd of the "Wilmington." His success shows to what perfection the art of naval war has been brought; this action reminds one of a piece of watch-work, it was so accurate and finished. It lasted two and a half hours, and when it was over, nothing in the shape of war material was left in the harbor, and at the same time, all injury to the town itself had been avoided. In apparent strength and advantage of position the odds were on the Spanish side; but it was once more made plain that, so far as power of offense is concerned, the Spanish, in this war, might almost as well have been without any arms at all. They are unable to use them.

It remains to review the campaign in Porto Rico, which affords an agreeable contrast with that at Santiago from the technical military point of view, and was also, happily, attended with no loss of life worth mentioning. Porto Rico is an island hardly one-tenth the size of Cuba, but with a larger population; the distribution of inhabitants being over two hundred to the square mile. It has very few large towns, and is remarkably prosperous for a colony of Spain, though, in common with the others, it is at odds with its Spanish rulers and welcomes emancipation from them. A range of hills, about two thousand feet high, traverses the oblong island from end to end, and the rest of the area consists of rich alluvial plains, plentifully watered by rivers, many of which are of surprising size, admitting navigation for several miles. There are some excellent roads in the island, which have been maintained in good condition; and a few miles of railway which are serviceable so far as they go. The country is divided up into plantations of sugar, tobacco and coffee, and is interspersed with small villages. The coast is indented with many good harbors, the chief of which is that of San Juan, the principal town on the island, and the only one effectively fortified. The people are not of an elevated type or character; but they are not likely to give any trouble to their American rulers. America has for some years been the largest consumer of Porto Rican produce; and under an intelligent administration the supplies from this source may be expected to be multiplied many fold.

Porto Rico has had no history to speak of since its conquest by Ponce de Leon in 1508, at or about which time the native population of Caribs, six hundred thousand in number, was enslaved and exterminated. Ponce's name is preserved in the town of Ponce, on the southern coast; and by the story of his search in Florida for the Fountain of Youth. He did not find the fountain, but an Indian arrow found him, and ended his adventures. The next conqueror of the island was our own General Miles; and instead of slaughtering over half a million people, like his eminent predecessor, he killed none but a handful of Spanish soldiers, and received from the inhabitants flowers, cigars, and a welcome which, whether or not inspired by genuine enthusiasm, was for practical purposes just as good.

Miles set out for Porto Rico on the 20th of July, and appeared off the little port of Guanico, fifteen miles west of Ponce, about a week later. It had been given out that his objective point was some place near San Juan, and such it may have been in the anticipation of the Board of Strategy at Washington; but Miles had ideas of his own, as Dewey had; and when he was once afloat and emancipated from telegraph offices, he undertook to carry them out. The general plan of his campaign seems to have been similar to that which he had designed to prosecute in Cuba; landing at the side of the island opposite to that of the city which he meant to attack, he would advance toward it, crossing the breadth of the island (about eighty miles), pushing the detached parties of the enemy before him, and accelerating their retreat by a flank movement on the right of his march. Outnumbering them at every point, and surrounding them where they did not fall back in time, he would either kill, capture, or drive them into San Juan, where his army and the fleet, in co-operation, would finish the work at their leisure. This arrangement also had the merit of causing the native population, who could be relied on to espouse the side of the stronger battalions, to aid him in his advance, and to receive such object lessons in the civilizing and beneficent intentions of Americans as to reassure their minds regarding the future. All that the Porto Ricans had to dread was the revengeful onslaughts upon them of the retreating Spaniards themselves.

On July 26th the expedition arrived from Guantanamo, Cuba, with four ships of war and eight troop-ships; and a boat was sent to Cape San Juan to apprise General Brooke, who was to make the campaign with Miles, of the alteration in the plan of the invasion. The "Gloucester," one of the convoying squadron, fresh from its exploits before Santiago, entered the harbor early in the morning to reconnoiter. Commander Wainwright saw a quiet sheet of water, bordered by cultivated fields, and backed at a distance by hills thickly covered with trees. Close to the beach was a little hamlet of a dozen or twenty houses. East of the village stood a block house, with the Spanish flag floating from it; and the first intimation the garrison had of the presence of the enemy came in the shape of a shot fired by the "Gloucester" as an intimation that the flag must come down. At the same time a launch was lowered, containing thirty men and a rapid-fire gun, and the crew, landing without opposition, replaced the Spanish flag with the Stars and Stripes.

Hardly had this been done when fire was opened on the Americans by a concealed force of Spaniards; the crew replied with their Colt, and the "Gloucester" herself joined in with her three and six-pounders. In half an hour the enemy retreated, leaving four dead behind them; no Americans were hit. The transports then entered the harbor, and disembarkation was begun; and Miles sent out orders that all vessels detailed for the invasion should rendezvous at Guanico. The troops thus concentrated would amount in the aggregate to little less than thirty thousand men.

After setting outposts a few miles out, in order to keep the enemy at a proper distance, Miles dispatched Commander Davis of the "Dixie" to demand the surrender of Ponce, which was expected to involve some fighting. Ponce is the second largest town in the island, with a population of 15,000. With the "Dixie" went the "Wasp" and the "Annapolis"; the "Wasp" was the first to enter the harbor. The wharfs were thronged with people; and there were the batteries, with guns jutting out from them. It looked like war; but Ensign Curtin and four men stepped into a boat, and rowed ashore. As they drew near, covered by the guns of the American ships, they saw that the aspect of the crowd was not hostile; on the contrary there were heard shouts of welcome, and, as they mounted the steps of the landing, the people pressed forward with fruit, cigars and flowers, instead of weapons, in their hands. Curtin announced that he was there to receive the surrender of the town; being referred to the military commander, he said that the latter must come to him. He added that he would give him half an hour to capitulate; and with that he gave way to Davis, senior officer of the squadron, who now landed, and stood watch in hand. The capitulation was made within the specified time, and the Spanish soldiers forthwith fled to the hills, leaving most of their arms and ammunition behind them. Lieutenant Haines hoisted the American flag on the custom house, the people cheered, and the American troops, landing, were given an ovation. Thus fell the ancient town of Ponce, bloodlessly. The occupying troops were the 6th Pennsylvania and the 2d and 3d Wisconsin.

While this was going on, the brigade of General Ernst, at Guanico, had been pushed forward to Yauco, a small town three miles inland, commanding the military road to San Juan; and the town of Guanico, which lies some miles north of the port, was taken by General Henry with regiments of Massachusetts and Illinois troops, led by General Garretson, with a loss of three men wounded; the Spanish loss was four killed and thirteen wounded. A junction between Ernst's and Henry's troops was then effected; and the southern part of Porto Rico was already in American possession. General Miles made his headquarters at the Ponce custom house. There was general holiday among the inhabitants, the women putting on their prettiest gowns, kissing their hands to the American soldiers, and leading the cries of "Viva los Americanos!" "Puerto Rico libre!" The alcalde was informed by Miles that no changes would be made for the present in the local government; and a proclamation was issued defining the purposes of the invasion, and calling upon the inhabitants to co-operate in their own emancipation. "This is not a war of devastation and dissolution," concluded our general, "but one to give all within the control of the military and naval forces the advantages and blessings of enlightened civilization." The effect of these assurances was shown by the response of the people. On July 31st Miles cabled to Washington that "four-fifths of the people are overjoyed at the arrival of the army. Two thousand from one place have volunteered to serve with it. They are bringing in transportation, beef, cattle, and other needed supplies. The custom house has already yielded $14,000." Business, instead of stagnating, enjoyed a boom, and the shopkeepers proved themselves shrewd hunters of American gold. A large number of American flags was run up on all sides, the Porto Ricans seeming to have laid in a supply for the occasion; and the campaign had the likeness of a love feast and triumphal procession rather than of a war. As for Spanish soldiers, it was impossible to find any of them. When a report came from the town of Juana Diaz, a little way in the interior, that the enemy were concentrated there, a part of the 16th Pennsylvania went forward to engage them; but they were met by a brass band and troops of cheering citizens, with the usual gifts and compliments, including kisses from the women. By the 1st of August, nine towns, all of which had had Spanish troops in them, sent their submission to the Americans; among them were Arroyo and Guayamo. At Guayamo the large garrison was driven out by the inhabitants before the Americans arrived, and the mayor made a speech declaring that the day of Porto Rico's deliverance had come; while the women "fell on their knees and worshiped our soldiers." It is needless to remark that all this enthusiasm must be taken with reservations; had the Spanish been strong enough to resist our advance, the emotions of the inhabitants would have been no less demonstrative in favor of the heroes of Castile. But for all practical purposes the protestations of the Porto Ricans were just as useful as if they had been sincere.

But in spite of all this cordiality and smoothness, there were Spaniards not far off, and they had all the will possible to do the Americans harm if they could. They were supposed to be from seven to nine thousand in number; but they were indisposed to risk a fight in the open, and were slowly falling back to Aibonito, a mountain town some thirty miles north of Ponce. It was here that the first battle of the campaign was likely to be fought. The road there twisted about through high mountain walls, and could be commanded by artillery from many points; and it was presently reported that the direct road had been extensively mined, with a view to blowing up the invading army as it approached. The American outpost having been fixed at Cuamo, a few miles south of Aibonito, an interval of time elapsed during which the rest of our troops disembarked, and dispositions were made to attack Aibonito from several points at once. A second fleet of transports brought some cavalry detachments, the Indiana and Missouri batteries, five or six infantry regiments, including one of regulars, and a month's rations for thirty thousand men. On the 2d of August, General Brooke, who had landed at Guayamo, east of Ponce, whence there was a good military road to Aibonito, marched with five thousand troops to positions in the rear of the Spanish intrenchments. The Spaniards, supposed to number five thousand at this point, were therefore between two fires, our main army being established on the main road between Aibonito and Ponce; and they must either surrender or, should they attempt to escape, run the risk of being cut to pieces. On August 3d another disembarkation of troops was effected, from the "St. Paul" and the "St. Louis," at Arroyo, a manufacturing town without defenses, east of Guayamo. The civil guards in the town retreated, and did not share in the surrender that was immediately made by the local authorities; and during the next day or two, there was some firing from ambush in the outskirts of the place, but no damage was done.

There is little doubt that a bold and alert enemy might have inflicted some loss upon us in the early days of the invasion, had they attacked our advanced posts and reconnoitering parties. But San Martin, the Spanish commander at Ponce, was panic-stricken from the first; and when, after his retreat, he was superseded by Otega, the latter sent him under arrest to San Juan, to be dealt with by court-martial. But Otega himself confined his operations to those of defense only; and though the position finally occupied by the Spaniards was intrinsically of great strength, it could not hold out against a siege which should isolate it from the rest of the country. But even were the road to San Juan left free to the Spaniards, no help could have been sent to Otega from that town, which had enough to do to take care of itself. By the 4th of August the American fleet had begun to arrive there; the "Montgomery," the "Amphitrite," the "Annapolis" and the "Puritan" were in the offing; and though Captain-general Macias kept up a bold front, and his daughter was said to have aided in drilling the gunners in the fort, he was aware that there could be but one issue to the struggle. He had, at the time of the invasion, rather less than ten thousand troops under his command; but others were on their way to the city from interior points, retreating before the American advance. The only chance the enemy had was before the Americans had obtained an adequate foothold in the island; failing to take advantage of that, their final defeat was inevitable.

On the 7th of August there was a general advance along all the American lines. The remainder of Ernst's brigade, constituting the center, and supported by two batteries, moved out of Ponce at six in the morning; and General Henry's division on the left was strengthened by a part of the 11th infantry. General Wilson established his headquarters at Juana Diaz; General Schwann moved through Yauco toward Mayaguez, and General Brooke with ten thousand men advanced northward from Guayamo. Meanwhile General Brooke's transportation column was being convoyed along the coast road through Salinas to Arroyo, and General

Roy Stone, assisted by five hundred natives, and supported by the 2d Wisconsin and a battalion of the 19th regular infantry, cleared the road from Adjuntas to Utuado. On the 8th of August there was a skirmish before Coamo, where a small force of Spaniards was intrenched, and three hundred and eighty of them were captured by the 16th Pennsylvania and the 2d and 3d Wisconsin, and twenty were killed, including the commandant Illeseas. Our loss was five wounded, all members of the 16th Pennsylvania. A part of the enemy escaped toward Aibonito; they were pursued as far as the Guyon River, where the Americans were checked by the blowing up of the bridge; and a Spanish battery on the other side threw some shells at them. The cavalrymen returned the fire and held their position. Meanwhile the advance from Guayamo met with a slight check. Two companies of the 4th Ohio Volunteers were ambushed by the enemy a few miles north of the town; they were under the command of Colonel Colt, and were reconnoitering to discover whether some bridges on the road to Cayey had been mined. They reached a point where the road made a sharp turn through the hills, when the Spaniards opened fire on them from a blockhouse on the hill at one side, and from earthworks on the other. The companies threw themselves into a ditch beside the road, where they returned the fire; but they would have been annihilated had not a battery of two dynamite guns come up, and sent a couple of gelatine shells among the Spaniards. The first exploded near the blockhouse, tearing up the ground for fifty feet; and the second shell caused the enemy to break and retreat. They were pursued over the top of the hill, but escaped through the gorges to the north and east.

On the 12th of August General Wilson's column was five miles beyond Coamo, in sight of the Spanish defenses of Aibonito, which were seen to be of great strength, including seven lines of intrenchments, and a battery of two guns. Wilson sent forward one Lancaster battery to shell this position. As our guns rounded a curve of the road, about two thousand yards from the enemy, the latter opened with a heavy infantry and artillery fire, in the face of which the Lancaster battery unlimbered and began firing, soon silencing one of the Spanish guns. One of our men was killed and two wounded, all by shrapnel, and two were wounded by Mauser bullets. A gun of our battery was now sent forward four hundred yards; but before it could reach its appointed position, the Spanish received a reenforcement of infantry, and poured a severe fire on our gun, compelling the battery to retire. Lieutenant Haines was shot in the body by a Mauser bullet just before this episode; and, so far as is known, he was the last American to be wounded in the war. For it was on this very day that news of the conclusion of the preliminary peace negotiations, which had been in progress for upward of a week, reached the front, and General Wilson at once sent forward a flag of truce, apprising the Spanish commander of the cessation of hostilities. A battle, which would probably have cost many lives and for which we were just prepared, was therefore avoided; and General Miles's campaign can be judged from its preliminary stage only. It seems to have been wisely and strongly planned, and its success, had it been carried out, cannot be doubted. Our army outnumbered the Spaniards, and outclassed them in other respects; and the chief problem that Miles had to solve was, how to do what was to be done with the least loss to his troops. But Spain had had enough, and the war was over. It turned out later that the Spanish in Aibonito were entirely dependent upon Cayey for their food supply; and that had General Brooke occupied that town before the armistice, they must at once have succumbed.

The terms of peace mentioned in the protocol as agreeable to us were moderate in the extreme: Cuba was to be free, under the government of the Cubans, and the Spaniards were to evacuate it. They were also to evacuate Porto Rico, which was to become our property; in short, the West Indies was to know Spain no more. Their flag was also to disappear from the Ladrones Group in the Pacific; but room was left for negotiation as regarded the Philippines. The presumption was that we were to retain the island of Luzon and probably some others permanently; but concerning the remainder of the little archipelago our government seemed unprepared to make a definite announcement. Certainly, they suggest questions which must be thoroughly ventilated, and about which there may be more than one honest opinion.

The longer the matter is contemplated, however, the more likely does it appear that we cannot evade the responsibility which the fortune of war has forced upon us. The islands were in revolt against Spain when our war with Spain began; and the causes of their revolt were such as to command the sympathy of all impartial observers. Spain had for centuries robbed the Filipinos without limit, and had cruelly murdered those who resisted her robbery. To give her back the islands would thus seem out of the question. But it seems not less impossible to allow the inhabitants to attempt the experiment of self-government. As has already been pointed out, the population is not homogeneous; the Negritos are mere savages; and the Malays have never ruled themselves, and their long subjection to Spain is the worst of preparations for such an enterprise. Morover, they were not fighting Spain for independence, but for reforms; and had Spain conceded to them what they were fighting for, they would have remained content. If then the Philippines are not to be given back to Spain, nor to be given to themselves, two alternatives remain:—we may dispose of them to some other nation or nations, or we may govern them as a colony ourselves. The proposition to dispose of them to other nations may be dismissed at once as almost impracticable; it could only lead to disputes and embroilments. We are brought therefore by the process of exclusion to the conclusion that we must keep the islands ourselves, with all which that implies. And it implies, among other things, the entrance of this country upon a new career; the bursting asunder of the limitations of the past; the leaving behind of a policy which in its generation was wise, but which would become foolish and finally suicidal if persisted in under changed conditions. The flag which we have planted in the Orient must be protected, and the beneficent influence which goes with it must be impressed upon other nations. We do not seek war or territory, but we must accept both if they come to us, and so conduct the one and administer the other as to deserve the respect and the gratitude of the world. The tropical countries which have been placed at our command afford rich fields for development and investment, and offer a career to our young men which many of them will be glad to adopt. The opportunities for agriculture and mining, along unfamiliar and stimulating lines, bid fair to be practically inexhaustible; and dealings with and management of strange peoples will create in us qualities of manhood and unselfishness, and the habit of handling large problems in a liberal and enlightened manner, which our present self-seeking way of life does not favor. The benefit to England of her colonial empire does not consist so much in the revenues derived from it—which, indeed, in the case of India, hardly pay expenses—as in the training it gives to a class of her people. Young men are intrusted with the control of provinces as large as some kingdoms; and after ten or thirty years of occupation with their duties, they build up in themselves a type of character which makes England the greatest and most influential of peoples. During those long, lonely years they work for others; they learn how to govern; they learn justice, firmness, and foresight; they gain an understanding of life attainable in no other way. Such a school is needed by the young men of this country; and the results of this war seem likely to give it to them. Another school only less valuable which will now be opened to us is that of diplomacy, which, in the new and close relations to be established between us and other nations, must become for a class among us a chosen and permanent career. Our consuls, ministers and ambassadors will be carefully selected, after having been carefully educated with a view to their duties; and instead of being superseded in office just as they are beginning to comprehend the nature and possibilities of the work intrusted to them, will continue during their lives the studies and negotiations which interpret one country to another, and multiply the benefits which they are able to confer on one another. Native genius will do much; but for sure results, it must be supplemented by training and experience; and then we may expect the arising of a body of broad-minded statesmen who will carry the science and art of government to heights as yet only imagined, never successfully realized. Of self-involved politicians we have already too many; but every citizen ought to be a statesman in his degree.

The maintenance of empire also involves the creation of an army adequate to police and protect it. There is an immense number of youths in America who were born with the soldier instinct, and only need drill and discipline to form the finest army in the world. And this drill and discipline are of incalculable value in a community of this kind, where the democratic tendencies and practices of the people predispose to carelessness and inaccuracy of thought, and to irregular and unpolished behavior. Reverence for just authority, and that respect for the rights of others which is born of self-respect, are much needed among us; and so are order, system and regularity in all our employments and conduct. The efficiency of the nation would be greatly increased by the existence of an army which should be large enough to keep the people aware of its existence, without, of course, being so large as to make any perceptible drain upon the producing class, or a noticeable burden on the tax-payers. We have been in the past at once too warlike and too little military.

With an army of three hundred thousand men on a peace footing, these conditions would be improved. The instinct that draws a man to warlike employments and studies would find a sufficient and permanent satisfaction; and the rest of the community, conscious that America would be prepared for battle whenever the necessity might arise, would cease to be sensitive to the real or imaginary provocations of other nations—who, for their part, would be more careful than hitherto to avoid giving grounds for a misunderstanding. An army of reasonable size, and, still more important, a navy able to stand comparison with any other in the world, seem to be among the probable developments of the near future, and likely to be even more beneficial as object lessons to the nation, than necessary as means of a defense which we should hardly ever be called upon to make.

The growth of commerce, and a great expansion of our merchant marine, are also inevitable in view of our new obligations and opportunities. America is already a cosmopolitan nation in virtue of its inhabitants, who come from all quarters of the globe; but in another sense it is almost provincial; its prejudices and peculiarities are too pronounced, and still more so are its indifferences and frivolities. Ordinary travel is not enough to counteract these faults, because travelers are usually members of the well-to-do class, which has little weight with the mass of the people; and also because many of these travelers go abroad chiefly to see one another, or to associate with the class in foreign countries which most nearly resembles their own at home. But the give and take of commerce brings about a kind of intimacy with the ways and traits of foreign peoples which is practically useful, and produces a recognizable effect on manners and customs. Men who have business dealings with one another must of necessity learn to know one another well; and they will be quick to discern what characteristics of one another are worth adopting or adapting. The light-minded and easy cynicism of which we see too much among us will be gradually discountenanced by a better appreciation of the relations of things and the resources and meaning of existence.

The future of Cuba is the problem of most immediate interest at present. The island has never known self-government; and, like Manila, it has been to the worst school in the world for learning it. The case was otherwise with us; we came to America with traditions of freedom in our history, and the aspiration for civil and religious liberty in our blood; and we came to a new world, wherein were no relics of past evil and oppression. We looked to God first, and then to ourselves; and by inevitable degrees and natural processes we proceeded from one position to another, until at last political independence was the final logical step. But it has been far otherwise with Cuba. The Cubans are not a pure race, and the admixture of negro blood with Spanish does not promise well for strength and constancy of character. Those who most intimately know the Cubans are not those who are most sanguine as to the outcome of their experiment. Yet their record for a generation past proves that they love freedom, and are willing to die for it; and it may not be impossible to teach them how to preserve it when it is theirs. The chief difficulty appears to be, the ignorance of the common people; for though there are particular Cubans who have shown the possession of high qualities and great intelligence, this does not insure a stable republican government as a necessary consequence. Rather might we expect that the Republic will be in fact a monarchy, without the permanence which a monarchy might possess. The United States has been successful because its citizens are individually intelligent and educated; and their governors and rulers are not superior to the fair average of the population. But in Cuba there would be no ratio between the rulers and the ruled, and the suffrage could not be exercised in such a manner as to make the vote of the people express their genuine and free opinion and desire. The better class having once obtained political power would not afterward willingly relinquish it; the people would either acquiesce in their authority, or would rebel against it in response to the selfish solicitations of demagogues, with such results of confusion and anarchy as we have seen in Central America. Moreover, the entire Cuban population of the island was never over a million and a half; and this war has reduced the number by one-third, most of whom were women and children. It may be said, therefore, that there is no next generation of Cubans; when the present generation dies, they will leave no successors, or so few as to make the formation of a self-sustaining community impossible. The United States could not of course allow the island to become a center for European intrigue; and the only alternative would be to undertake the government ourselves.

In this connection, it is useful to recall a letter written to President McKinley by President Masso of the Cuban republic, shortly before the surrender of Spain. He declares that the desire of the Cuban leaders is "to know what is desired of us, and what are the views entertained by the United States Government regarding us, with reference to the solution of the problem of the future of Cuba." He affirms that fully seven-eighths of the Cuban people are agriculturists, who have neither ambition nor ability to hold office, but wish only to be left to the enjoyment of their home life. The other eighth comprises the leaders, political and military, many of whom have been educated in the United States, where "they have imbibed the true spirit of liberty, and learned the meaning of a true republican form of government. Our first step, with the approval of the United States Government, will be to call a new assembly, which will represent as far as possible every section of territory and condition of people. This Assembly will elect a new Provisional Government that will possess more powers than the present one, which is of necessity a government of the revolution.

But the result of the new Assembly will be to form a government which will still be limited in power, and whose most important work will be the establishment of a permanent and complete government on the lines of the United States, and one which we hope and believe will be satisfactory both to the United States and to Cuba."

This programme is moderate in tone, and shows a desire to adopt an attitude favorable to the recognition of the United States as a friendly adviser and protector. When we entered upon this war, we pledged ourselves to give Cuba to the Cubans when we had ejected Spain; and this we must surely do. We must give the Cubans every chance to show that they can rule themselves, and afford them every honorable help in so doing. But it is to be feared that the experiment will fail, not only for the reasons already suggested, but because, inevitably, a large number of Americans will take up lands in Cuba, and develop its resources; these men cannot avoid exercising a great influence in Cuba, and some of them would probably appear sooner or later in the legislatures. The strong and the weak would be living side by side, and the strong could not help prevailing. So far as mortal foresight can discern, Cuba will as certainly become American as the sun will rise in the east. But so long as Cubans live, they will be safe from oppression; their incomparable island will be the scene of a prosperity and productiveness the like of which has never been seen in the world; and from the blood which Spain has shed will spring up a felicity which may compensate, at last, for the evil and misery which God, through our agency, has caused to pass forever away.

THE END.

www.ingramcontent.com/pod-product-compliance
Lightning Source LLC
Chambersburg PA
CBHW051234300426
44114CB00011B/729